Pontius Pilate on Screen

Visit the series website at:
https://edinburghuniversitypress.com/series-screening-antiquity.html

Pontius Pilate on Screen

Sinner, Soldier, Superstar

Christopher M. McDonough

EDINBURGH
University Press

Edinburgh University Press is one of the leading university presses in the UK. We publish academic books and journals in our selected subject areas across the humanities and social sciences, combining cutting-edge scholarship with high editorial and production values to produce academic works of lasting importance. For more information visit our website: edinburghuniversitypress.com

Edinburgh University Press Ltd
The Tun – Holyrood Road
12(2f) Jackson's Entry
Edinburgh EH8 8PJ

Typeset in 11/13 Sabon by
Cheshire Typesetting Ltd, Cuddington, Cheshire, and
printed and bound in Great Britain

A CIP record for this book is available from the British Library

ISBN 978 1 4744 4688 4 (hardback)
ISBN 978 1 4744 4690 7 (webready PDF)
ISBN 978 1 4744 4691 4 (epub)

Contents

Figures

Acknowledgements

Many thanks to Monica Cyrino for all her support, and to the editors and staff at Edinburgh University Press for their patience and professionalism. I am very grateful to those in the film industry for their time, the archivists who have been so obliging, my students and colleagues at the University of the South for their insights and generosity over the years (especially with regard to the Alderson-Tillinghast chair and fund), fellow members of the Antiquity in Media Studies who are a pleasure to work with, Zach Zimmerman for his steady help as an undergraduate, Rosemary Macedo for her hospitality, Thomas Lakeman for his brilliance, Dave Wharton and Lisa Stanley McIndoo for their encouragement, and George and Susan Core for their sharp editorial eyes. And of course, I am all gratitude to Joseph and Daniel, who have suffered under Pontius Pilate quite long enough, and above all to Kelly for her kindness, wit and judgement that have been an inspiration to me for decades in every scholarly endeavour.

Series Editors' Preface

Screening Antiquity is a series of cutting-edge academic monographs and edited volumes that present exciting and original research on the reception of the ancient world in film and television. It provides an important synergy of the latest international scholarly ideas about the onscreen conception of antiquity in popular culture and is the only book series to focus exclusively on screened representations of the ancient world.

The interactions between cinema, television, and historical representation are a growing field of scholarship and student engagement; many Classics and Ancient History departments in universities worldwide teach cinematic representations of the past as part of their programmes in Reception Studies. Scholars are now questioning how historical films and television series reflect the societies in which they were made and speculate on how attitudes towards the past have been moulded in the popular imagination by their depiction in the movies. Screening Antiquity explores how these constructions came about and offers scope to analyse how and why the ancient past is filtered through onscreen representations in specific ways. The series highlights exciting and original publications that explore the representation of antiquity onscreen, and that employ modern theoretical and cultural perspectives to examine screened antiquity, including stars and star text, directors and auteurs, cinematography, design and art direction, marketing, fans, and the online presence of the ancient world.

The series aims to present original research focused exclusively on the reception of the ancient world in film and television. In itself this is an exciting and original approach. There is no other book series that engages head-on with both big screen and small screen recreations of the past, yet their integral interactivity is clear to see: film popularity has a major impact on television productions and for its part, television regularly influences cinema (including film spin-offs of popular television series). This is the first academic series to identify and encourage the holistic interactivity of these two major media institutions, and the first to promote interdisciplinary research in all the fields of Cinema Studies, Media Studies, Classics, and Ancient History.

Screening Antiquity explores the various facets of onscreen creations of the past, exploring the theme from multiple angles. Some volumes will foreground a Classics 'reading' of the subject, analysing the nuances of film and television productions against a background of ancient literature, art, history, or culture; others will focus more on Media 'readings,' by privileging the onscreen creation of the past or positioning the film or television representation within the context of modern popular culture. A third 'reading' will allow for a more fluid interaction between both the Classics and Media approaches. All three methods are valuable, since Reception Studies demands a flexible approach whereby individual scholars, or groups of researchers, foster a reading of an onscreen 'text' particular to their angle of viewing.

Screening Antiquity represents a major turning point in that it signals a better appreciation and understanding of the rich and complex interaction between the past and contemporary culture, and also of the lasting significance of antiquity in today's world.

Monica S. Cyrino and Lloyd Llewellyn-Jones
Series Editors

The author with Barry Dennen (Pilate in *Jesus Christ Superstar*) sharing a meal in Hollywood, July 2016. For his warm encouragement of this project, this book is affectionately dedicated to Barry.

Prologue: 'Do You Enjoy Being a Symbol, Pontius?' The Trial of Pontius Pilate *and Governor Collins*

DRUSUS:
(LOOKING DOWN)
Are there always such crowds in the streets?

PILATE:
Oh, no – this is a special occasion. . . . Ordinarily, we see little of these miserable people. We live in Caesarea, where there is a Roman colony, such as it is. But I must be here on their feast days – to remind them of the symbol of Empire.
(HE SMILES AS HE HANDS DRUSUS A CUP OF WINE)

DRUSUS:
Do you enjoy being a symbol, Pontius?
                    – Robert Sherwood, *The Trial of Pontius Pilate*[1]

The prefect of Judaea, Pontius Pilate, was looking out at an angry mob below, and the governor of Florida, LeRoy Collins, was watching him do so that Easter Monday evening in 1957. He and Mrs Collins had just moved into the new gubernatorial mansion in the state capital, and that weekend they had hosted several hundred locals who had come to tour. The calendar for the next few days was sure to be exhausting as well, with a large midweek reception planned to which numerous state dignitaries had been invited. But that Monday night, thankfully, the governor had some time to relax and so, settling into his new living room, he decided to turn on the television set. Consulting the 'Entertainment Log' of the *Tallahassee Democrat*, he might have chosen to watch the sitcom *December Bride*, which was playing at 9:30 pm on either WMBR-TV Channel 4 from Jacksonville or Pensacola's WEAR-TV Channel 3. But WCTV Channel 6 was the local station with the best reception, and besides, the *Robert Montgomery Presents* programme that evening looked like it would be more appealing, an original Easter-themed drama by the award-winning playwright Robert Sherwood.[2] Governor Collins was glad that he had selected *The Trial of Pontius Pilate* to watch that night, as it would give him serious food for thought in the years to come – and, make no mistake, the years to come would be challenging ones, not just in Florida, but all over the American South. New ways of thinking would be demanded from the governor, as well as a good deal of courage, for by the spring of 1960 the streets of Tallahassee would be in a state of uproar over race relations such as they had never seen. A sit-in staged by black students at a segregated Woolworth's lunch counter in Greensboro, North Carolina, had set off two months of demonstrations all over the region, and some of these had turned violent. In Florida's capital city, the arrests of a large number of activists from Florida A&M University led to wide-scale protest marches, which law enforcement officers broke up with fire hoses and tear gas, means that had not been employed against whites involved in equally unruly rallies nearby. Public disorder grew in the city, and police dramatically increased their street presence in response to wild rumours about civil rights groups organising an armed resistance. Businesses in Tallahassee were crippled by the boycotts that had been underway for weeks, boycotts that scattered acts of vandalism and growing public fears had only exacerbated.

The capital was in the grips of a panic, simply put, and as governor, Collins felt he must make some public response. Elected to the gubernatorial office in 1955, Collins was an old-school Southern Democrat, although of a more centrist nature than the hardcore segregationists of his party. He had disagreed with the previous year's decision by the US Supreme Court in *Brown v Board of Education*, which he considered a usurpation of power on the part of the federal government. Nevertheless, he recognized that the court's decision was the law of the land; regardless of his personal opinion about how it had been reached, he was bound by the oath of his office to enforce it. His fellow politicians in the state by and large did not agree. An overwhelmingly Democratic Florida legislature passed a resolution in 1957 to counteract the *Brown* decision, declaring it not to be in effect in the state, a measure to which Collins was adamantly opposed. Not legally capable of vetoing their bill, the governor signed his name with a handwritten addendum decrying the resolution 'as an evil thing, whipped up by the demagogues and carried on the hot and erratic winds of passion, prejudice, and hysteria'.[3] His attempt to chart a moderate course had won him few friends, so when the situation in Tallahassee came to a head a few years later, Collins's advisers urged him to follow the pattern of other Southern politicians and avoid a public stance on the unrest. Thus it was that, as a man very much caught in the middle, Collins spoke to the people of Florida in a live television address on 20 March 1960.[4] As he took to the airwaves that spring evening, Collins was well aware that most white voters in the state were in favour of segregation. Knowing it would cost him politically, Collins nevertheless felt he owed it to the people to tell them in open and honest language his evolving opinion on the matters afflicting the state. Following a remark about unrest needing a moral rather than a legal solution, LeRoy Collins took his first tentative step away from the traditions of the Old South and into the new era of Civil Rights. Imagining someone who might respond to him saying that 'coloured people should stay in their place', the governor replied forcefully:

> Now, friends, that's not a Christian point of view.
> That's not a democratic point of view.
> That's not a realistic point of view.
> We can never stop Americans from struggling to be free.
> We can never stop Americans from hoping and praying that some day in some way the ideal imbedded in our Declaration of Independence, that all men are created equal, somehow will become a reality, and not just an illusory distant goal.

In making these remarks, LeRoy Collins was the first governor of a Southern state to publicly denounce segregation on moral grounds.

In his address that late March evening of 1960, Collins had spoken before the people of Florida in a heartfelt way that gave a measure of authenticity to his remarks. He talked sincerely about the disagreements over race that his own parents had, and how sometimes he differed even with his wife on the subject. Urging the people of Florida to show 'more reason and less emotion' and 'more love and less hate' in these matters, he then reminded them that it would soon be Easter. Collins then, in the midst of his address, turned to the example of the television programme he had watched one Easter Monday night just after moving into the new mansion in Tallahassee: 'About two years ago the distinguished playwright, Robert Sherwood, wrote a play for Robert Montgomery and it was presented on television. The title of it was "The Trial of Pontius Pilate"'.[5] To be sure, this was not the first time that Pontius Pilate's name had been invoked in the fight for civil rights. In an Easter sermon called 'A Walk Through the Holy

Land' delivered at Montgomery's Dexter Avenue Baptist Church only a year before, Martin Luther King Jr had recounted for his congregation seeing the very spot in Jerusalem where Jesus had once stood before the judge who knew his innocence but condemned him nevertheless. 'And one cannot leave that point without weeping for Pilate', said King. 'For here is a man who sacrificed truth on the altar of his self-interest. Here was a man who crucified justice on the cross of his egotism'.[6] In like fashion, the governor of Florida sought to clarify his political position on civil rights by discussing the choices that the governor of Judaea had faced long ago.

The purpose of this book, discussed more fully in the chapter to follow, is well captured in the details of this anecdote. In what was undoubtedly the leading issue of his political career, Collins looked to the figure of Pontius Pilate as a sort of behavioural example in reverse, a model of how *not* to conduct himself in this highly fraught moral situation. In itself this is not an especially surprising thing for him to have done, of course – people, in general, and politicians, in particular, have frequently sought guidance from the Bible on what to do or not to do in troubling times. What was unusual in this situation, however, is the way in which Collins had gone about it. 'The title intrigued me because I always thought of the events of those fateful times as working around the trial of Jesus', he told the people of his beleaguered state that evening. 'I never had thought in terms of Pontius Pilate being on trial. But Sherwood in a very logical and in a very reasonable way pointed out that Pontius Pilate was truly the man who was on trial'.[7] If the governor had been looking to Jesus or St Paul for principled instruction, one has to imagine that he would have quoted their words directly. But this was a moment of fundamental political crisis for Florida and for the governor himself, a time of conflict that he realised would call for a full-scale change of mind and change of heart. Speaking about a strange new situation through a new mode of mass communication, Collins appealed to Biblical authority, as might have been expected in the Easter season. In doing so, however, he referred to Pilate not as he is found in the Scriptures, but rather as he was found on the screen.

The Trial of Pontius Pilate had aired on 22 April 1957, Easter Monday, on the *Robert Montgomery Presents* playhouse, as I have noted. To many today, Robert Montgomery will be remembered only for his daughter Elizabeth – an actress regularly featured on her father's programme, who went on to star as Samantha in the 1960s comedy *Bewitched* – but in his day, he had been a well-regarded film actor whose presence as host lent an air of respectability to

NBC's weekly dramatic anthology. *Robert Montgomery Presents* was a staple of Eisenhower-era TV programming and, like so many other showcases for live dramatic work, was intended to satisfy Middle America's taste for higher quality fare. Very often the programmes presented were revivals for the new medium of stage plays, or condensed versions of popular films from previous decades, but each of the networks eagerly sought out new work as well, in order to be able to promote a world premiere. The play about Pilate on Montgomery's programme that had exercised so much influence on Governor Collins's thinking starred Bruce Gordon in the title role. 'With his broad, strong, slightly asymmetrical features', the *New York Times* said of the actor, 'Mr Gordon looked as though he had been carved from stone with a few judicious slips of the chisel'.[8] TV tough guy roles were to fill Gordon's future career. He would become best known as Frank Nitti on ABC's *The Untouchables* (1959–63), and the phrase, 'You're dead', spit through gritted teeth, was to be his catchphrase. Undoubtedly some element of the appealing but menacing bully came into Gordon's depiction of the Roman prefect.

As was specified by Governor Collins that evening in 1960, the play had been written by the multi-talented Robert Sherwood, whose previous credits included three Pulitzer Prizes for Drama, a Pulitzer Prize for Biography and an Academy Award for the Best Screenplay for 1947's celebrated *The Best Years of Our Lives*. In 1952, NBC had paid him the princely sum of $100,000 to produce several teleplays for the network, *The Trial of Pontius Pilate* among them.[9] In his previous work, the figure of Pilate had been a meaningful one to Sherwood. In his award-winning play from 1941, *There Shall Be No Night*, set in Finland two years earlier at the time of the Russian invasion, an American reporter had invoked the Roman character to explain the US policy of isolation: 'It isn't always so completely delightful to be an American, Major. Sometimes even we have an uncomfortable feeling of insecurity. I imagine that Pontius Pilate didn't feel entirely at peace with himself. He knew that he was a good, just man, who didn't deserve death. He was against a crown of thorns on principle. But when they cried "Crucify Him!" all Pilate could say was "Bring me a basin of water, so that I can wash my hands of the whole matter"'.[10] In likening American reluctance to confront military aggression in Europe to Pilate's washing his hands of Jesus' death, it had been the playwright's avowed hope to shame his audiences for their inaction and spur his country to take a bolder, more principled stand in world affairs. The *Times* thought *There Shall Be No Night* was a more well-meaning than well-constructed play, but praised Sherwood for his earnestness – 'there is nothing cynical, cheap or shallow in this portrait of the ordeal of a brave nation', wrote its drama critic.[11] *The Trial of Pontius Pilate* of the 1950s can be imagined to have covered ground similar to *There Shall Be No Night* in the early 1940s, with the Roman governor standing in as a personification of the failures in courage of contemporary American leadership. But, as compelling a message as it contained for viewers such as the governor of Florida, *The Trial of Pontius Pilate* had in fact almost not reached the air.

Without any doubt, Sherwood was a celebrated man of American letters, whose genius had been recognized with numerous plaudits. As an original member of New York's famous Algonquin Roundtable, he had traded quips with Dorothy Parker and Robert Benchley and many others of America's brightest wits. In addition, during the Roosevelt administration, Sherwood been hired as a ghost writer for FDR's addresses. 'It was often suggested that my function in the White House was to *stud the President's speeches with wisecracks*', as he wrote later, with self-deprecation, of the experience.[12] He was a character who had loomed large over the mid-century American cultural scene, quite literally – standing a full six feet eight inches, Sherwood was used to being teased about his height. (Groucho Marx once recounted on his programme *You Bet Your Life*: 'I said to him one day, "Bob, what do you say to people when they ask you how the weather is up there?" He said, "I spit in their eye and tell 'em it's raining"'.)[13] But by the mid-1950s, Sherwood's best work was behind him. Although the network was bankrolling him at enormous expense, his work did not consistently hold the interest of corporate sponsors, and *The Trial of Pontius Pilate* was proving especially problematic in this respect. In the NBC archives at the Wisconsin Historical Society, there exists a file dedicated to the issues surrounding the play, and in the various documents one can discern the discomfort of executives who realised that they had contracted a number of plays from an author of timely dramas who may not be entirely in step with the times.

Together with a copy of the third revised draft of Sherwood's script for *The Trial of Pontius Pilate*, dated to 1953, there is a memo in the file, dated 20 January 1954, from Vernon S. Miller of the corporate sponsor, the Miller Brewing Company. He concluded that much of Sherwood's play 'would be offensive, in my opinion to Orthodox Jews', after listing seventeen specific points that were objectionable. Speaking on behalf of the German-American beer company, Miller was especially sensitive to perceptions of anti-Semitism in the years following the Holocaust. In assessing the potential problems of the play, he had consulted with a number of Jewish scholars, chief among them Rabbi Louis Finkelstein, perhaps the most renowned figure in American Conservative Judaism and the long-time Chancellor of New York's Jewish Theological Seminary. Finkelstein had a longstanding relationship with NBC and had produced a popular programme about Judaism called *The Eternal Light*, which ran from the mid-1940s on radio and would continue to play on TV until the late 1980s.[14] Finkelstein's was a voice that mattered to Miller, to the studio bosses at NBC and to Sherwood himself. Over the next several weeks, the playwright furiously worked on a revision and produced a new draft that ultimately met with the Rabbi's approval. On 18 February 1954, Finkelstein wrote to Sherwood:

> Your revised version of 'The Trial of Pontius Pilate' has been read very carefully by Doctor Davis, Doctor Mandelbaum and myself and we all consider it a real contribution to a better understanding of a difficult period. You will recall the question we raised in our recent discussions, namely, whether it is possible to tell this story in such a manner that we would like our children and grandchildren to listen in. I thought it was impossible, but you have proven that it is quite possible. [. . .]
>
> It was a great pleasure to meet with you in connection with this play and a great privilege to see how you managed to present very profound and intricate theological questions in very simple, beautiful language . . .

Sherwood responded to the Rabbi a week later: 'This letter will always be one of my most treasured possessions. It is no exaggeration to say that it means more to me than any Pulitzer Prize'.

Unfortunately, by the time Sherwood had reworked the script, the controversy hovering over the teleplay had already leaked to the press, a certain death sentence for the production. On the very day Sherwood was thanking Rabbi Finkelstein for his remarks, *Variety* was reporting that 'NBC was apprehensive over reports that Sherwood's "Pilate" contained sensitivities involving the Jewish faith' (24 February 1954). Rather than alienate potential viewers, the network decided to shelve the play, to Sherwood's great frustration. *The Trial of Pontius Pilate*, in the version approved by Rabbi Finkelstein, was not produced until a year and a half after the playwright's death, by which time those same critics and industry insiders were singing a different tune. Considering how unhappy Sherwood had been with NBC in his final years, one unnamed reviewer for the journal *Broadcasting-Telecasting* (29 April 1957) noted that it is 'slightly ironic that he should be resurrected at Eastertime and come off so well. [. . .] In perspective (with the overwhelming mass of Easter shows, religious or otherwise) it was one of the better programs offered'. Whether it was, in fact, one of the better programmes of the season is hard to assess with any certainty, however. Neither the script nor a videorecording of the play that aired that night in the Easter season of 1957 has been preserved.[15]

In lieu of a version written by the playwright himself, we instead have an 'oral tradition' of sorts in LeRoy Collins's recollection of the play, framed consciously or unconsciously to suit the specific political moment he was addressing at the time. 'Pontius was a great, big, strong, politician at the court of the Caesars in Rome. He was a comer. Everybody expected him to do great things and to be given great assignments', the governor began, perhaps unintentionally thinking of the status of his own political career. What followed was a sermon to the people of Florida by LeRoy Collins about segregation, based on the Gospel of Robert Sherwood about Pontius Pilate:

> His wife was one of his greatest boosters. She thought that he would be assigned as the procurator of Egypt which was the most desired post available at that time. But when the day came for Pontius Pilate to get his assignment, it was to the little insignificant country of Judaea. Pontius was furious because he felt that his assignment did not measure up to his capacity.
>
> But he went on, of course, and undertook it just the same. You remember how the events developed toward the time of the crucifixion. The Pharisees got Jesus and they were trying their best to pin something on him the Romans, of course, would feel would authorize his execution. They were having a tough time of it and they were pounding on Pilate's door, and trying to convince him that he should have Jesus executed, and you remember those early days how Pilate said, 'But what's wrong with the man? I don't see, I don't hear anything treasonable about his conduct. Why should you or we be so disturbed?'
>
> And they said: 'He's inciting people to riot and disorder. He's creating insurrection. He's a dangerous and he's an evil man'. And Pontius said to them, 'I was talking to a man who was with him down in the temple yesterday and I asked him about what this Jesus had said, and he reported that somebody showed Jesus a coin and asked him point blank: 'What do you say about Caesar?' And Jesus said in response to that, 'Render unto Caesar the things that are Caesar's and unto God the things that are God's'. Now what's wrong with that?' Pontius asked. The mob then reported that Jesus 'was attracting a lot of people to follow him. He's creating distrust in your government and in your supervision. You've got to do something about it'.
>
> Pontius' wife, Claudia, came into the picture about that time and she said, 'Pontius, think carefully about this thing. I was just down on the street the other day and I saw this man teaching and I went up because I wanted to hear what he had to say and he said very distinctly that, "I came not to establish a kingdom on earth, but a kingdom in Heaven"'.
>
> And Pontius turned to the mob and said, 'How could that be treasonable?' But they insisted, and about that time the growing cry of the mob outdoors could be heard. First it was soft, 'Crucify Him', and then it got stronger,

'Crucify Him, 'and then it got stronger, 'Crucify Him', and then something happened to big, strong, Pontius Pilate.

Hearing the cry of the mob, he went out on the balcony [and the] big man started getting smaller and smaller and smaller in size. And he said, 'Bring me a bowl of water'. And when he got the water, he washed his hands in it.

And he said to that crowd, 'I will not let the blood of this righteous man be on my hands. I wash my hands of it. See to it yourself'.

And they did see to it themselves. They crucified him.

Sherwood's *The Trial of Pontius Pilate* is without any doubt one of the less brilliant products of the author's autumnal period. The script is not included in any volume of the playwright's collected dramas, and biographies pass over the play in silence. Concerning its impact as a work to spur the moral imagination, however, we have one sure witness. On 20 March 1960, LeRoy Collins framed his state's spiritual standing and staked his own political career on a recollection of Sherwood's otherwise forgotten Eastertime drama. Directly after his summary of the teleplay, he continued thus:

Friends, we've got mobs beginning to form now, in this nation, in this Southland, and in this state. The time requires intelligent, careful, thorough study of big problems, and the reaching of solutions that are going to be reasonable and sound and make good sense.

We cannot let this matter and these issues be decided by the mobs, whether they are made up of white people or whether they are made up of black people.

In this state we have extremists on one side, and we have extremists on the other. And we've got the beginnings of a mob too.

But where are the people in the middle? Why aren't they talking? Why aren't they working? They must start working. They must start efforts that are going to bring about solutions if we are going to resolve these problems and clear up these troubles and keep our state growing, as our state should grow.

In the pivot from his synopsis of Sherwood's play, with its reference to the passion of wrong-headed crowds, to the riots taking place at the time in the streets of Tallahassee, Collins connected the events of the Passion to those of the present day and recognized that he had to choose a side. In urging those people in the middle to do more than idly stand by, he recognized that the time had come for him to speak out plainly in favour of the civil rights movement.

In the national press over the next few days, the governor was hailed for the stance he had staked out on matters of race that night, and his name would be suggested as a potential vice-presidential candidate to John F. Kennedy at the Democratic National Convention later that summer. But, although he went on to hold various offices in the Johnson administration, the people of Florida would never elect

Figure 0.1 Former Governor LeRoy Collins, walking with John Lewis, Andrew Young and Martin Luther King Jr during the Civil Rights march in Selma, Alabama, 1965. State Archives of Florida.

Collins to public office again. His principled stand had spelled the end of his political career. Eight years after delivering this TV address, Collins was defeated in his race for US Senate when an opponent circulated a picture of him taken in Selma alongside Martin Luther King Jr (Figure 0.1).

'Do you enjoy being a symbol, Pontius?' The question which serves as an epigraph to this preface comes from an early scene from *The Trial of Pontius Pilate*. It is asked by the prefect's father-in-law, Drusus, an old Roman aristocrat, as he stands with Pilate on the portico of his mansion, sharing a cup of wine and looking out over the crowds that have gathered for the Passover feast days. The scene below is not a peaceful one. Trouble is mounting in the streets of Jerusalem, but Pilate assures his wife's father that there will be no problem keeping the peace, as he has arrived with a suitable show of force. 'I suppose they are truculent, rebellious, like others upon whom we have visited the blessings of our civilization?'[16] Drusus remarks, in an ironic comment about the Pax Romana (and, of course, an ironic comment on the playwright's part about the burgeoning imperialism of the Pax Americana). But Pilate is not in the mood for irony. He has come to the city, so he states emphatically, as a 'symbol of Empire'. In later Western culture, Pilate will come to be the symbol of many other things as well. In *There Will Be No Night*, Sherwood had alluded to him as an emblem of cowardly vacillation, a representative of a nation's failure of nerve at a moment of international moral crisis. But it had needed to be pointed out to the playwright, in a gentle but firm way by Rabbi Finkelstein and not so gently by NBC's corporate sponsors, that if he were not portrayed very carefully, Pilate could also symbolise the anti-Semitism that had given rise to the Holocaust. At the Dexter Avenue Baptist Church, Martin Luther King Jr had thought him an agent of injustice and a monstrous egotist. Watching the broadcast of *The Trial of Pontius Pilate* that April evening in 1957, we can imagine what symbolism LeRoy Collins saw in his ancient gubernatorial counterpart. As the principal Roman figure in this and every other story about Jesus, Pilate is indeed 'the symbol of Empire', whose duty, as the stand-in for Caesar, is to maintain law and order in times of trouble. In pursuit of that goal, however, Pilate had allowed an innocent man to be killed, and in the televised version of the Passion story the governor had watched, the prefect was held accountable for that fact. A few years later, Collins himself was facing civil unrest in the streets of Florida, and although he was not afraid to use force to keep the peace and had permitted water hoses and dogs to be turned against the protesters, his conscience was troubled by the scenes he was witnessing on the nightly news. He then recalled another scene of unrest he had seen on his TV screen, how Pilate had suppressed the riots and had been condemned for it, and Governor Collins decided that he would rather be the symbol of something else. What we find in the issues surrounding Sherwood's play for NBC and the way in which it has ultimately been remembered is a microcosm of the reception of Pontius Pilate on screen generally through the twentieth and twenty-first centuries – we see in it, in other words, the various ways in which Pontius Pilate has been represented as a symbol, to audiences at the movies and on the television sets in their living rooms.

NOTES

1 Sherwood (1953: 21).
2 *Tallahassee Democrat* (22 April 1957) 6 ('Mansion Open House Today') and 12 ('Entertainment Log'). No authors are given for either entry.
3 Wagy (1985: 88).
4 Collins's address is reprinted by Houck and Dixon (2006: 349–56), from which all subsequent quotations are taken.
5 Houck and Dixon (2006: 354). See also Wagy (1985: 101–2).

6   Carson et al. (2005: 168).
7   Houck and Dixon (2006: 354).
8   Fox (2011).
9   Alonso (2007: 315).
10 Sherwood (1945: 122).
11 Atkinson (1940: 25).
12 Sherwood (1950: 821).
13 *Your Bet Your Life* (1949). Groucho's joke can be heard at 2:49.
14 See Weinstein (2007: 109–13).
15 An audio recording of the play is held at the Motion Picture, Broadcasting and Recorded Sound Division of the Library of Congress, Washington DC. Copies of the recording are not permitted, and unfortunately the Covid-19 lockdown of 2020 prevented me from going there to listen to it.
16 Sherwood (1953: 22).

1 *Quod Scripsi Scripsi*

Then said the chief priests of the Jews to Pilate, Write not, The King of the Jews; but that he said, I am King of the Jews. Pilate answered, What I have written I have written.

– John 19:21–22

This is not a book about Pontius Pilate. Not exactly.

The Roman figure who served as prefect of the province of Judaea from roughly 27 to 37 AD is known from numerous ancient works, and while his particular involvement with the Passion narrative is carefully observed, other details about his life remain shrouded in obscurity. The quest for the historical Pilate, like the quest for the historical Jesus, can be a frustrating experience. Although he played only a minor part in it, the story of the Passion occupies so central a role in the theology and history of Christianity that the figure of Pilate has come to take on a significance far exceeding his accomplishments. As the only mortal besides the Virgin Mary to be mentioned in the Apostles' and Nicene Creeds, the prefect's name has, since the fourth century AD, been uttered aloud more frequently than virtually any other from the Roman world, perhaps more often even than Julius or Augustus Caesar. Four of the earliest sources are located, of course, in the New Testament. The Gospels of Matthew, Mark, Luke and John offer a fairly, although not perfectly, consistent depiction of Pilate's interactions with Jesus and the Jewish priests. Earlier still, Pilate had been a subject in the works of Flavius Josephus (Yosef ben Matityahu), the Romano-Jewish historian of the first century AD. In both his *Jewish Antiquities* and *Jewish War*, he discusses the administration of Judaea under Pontius Pilate. It is from Josephus, for instance, that we learn about the civil unrest provoked by Pilate's introduction of Roman standards into Jerusalem and his use of Temple funds to construct an aqueduct – the latter the focus of much cinematic speculation (and the answer to the question asked in *Monty Python's Life of Brian* by John Cleese's Reg: 'What have Romans ever done for us?'). The earliest work to deal with the prefect is *On the Embassy to Gaius* by the Hellenistic Jewish philosopher Philo of Alexandria, who also recounted unrest over Pilate's activities as prefect and referred to him as 'a man of inflexible, stubborn and cruel disposition' (chapter 38). As a historical character, then, Pilate is fairly well attested in the six authors listed above, to which might be added contemporary archaeological evidence likewise confirming his presence in Judaea. Three different coin types are known to have been struck by Pilate, for instance.[1] A copper ring discovered in a hilltop palace in Herodium, furthermore, was recently shown to have Pilate's name on it, and it may well have been one of his possessions.[2] Most significantly, an inscription on a limestone block from a building dedicated to the emperor was excavated in 1961 in Caesarea; it reads '[T]iberieum [...] [Pon]tius Pilatus [Praef]ectus Iuda[ea]e' ('a building in honour of Tiberius built by Pontius Pilate, Praefect of Judea'), thus confirming his title not as procurator (as Tacitus has written in the *Annals*) but as prefect of Judaea, the title by which he will be called for the remainder of this book (Figure 1.1).[3]

A synthetic analysis of this material is no easy task, but there are a number of talented scholars who have engaged in it with great success. A review of the academic literature treating these sources might extend to several pages, but none would be complete that failed to mention Helen K. Bond's *Pontius Pilate in History and Interpretation* (1998), a study that carefully sifts the evidence of Josephus and Philo alongside the Gospels. As Bond concludes, '[i]n each case it has become apparent that the author's portrayal of Pilate has been influenced to a great extent by his own particular theological, apologetic and/or community situation'.[4] Another significant work in this regard is Warren Carter's *Pontius Pilate: Portraits of a Roman Governor* (2003), which indicates that 'History has delivered at least five different verdicts on Pilate'. The spectrum of opinion runs from the very negative to the very positive, and the prefect is seen in turn as . . .

1)   a cruel and anti-Jewish villain,
2)   a weak figure without conviction,
3)   a culturally insensitive Roman official,

Figure 1.1 Limestone inscription bearing the name of Pontius Pilate, Prefect of Judaea, found in Caesarea Maritima in 1961. Commons.wikimedia.org.

4) a sympathetic figure eventually converting to Christianity, or
5) a saint.

From the evidence of the Jewish authors and the Gospels, there are certainly grounds to support any of these interpretations, each of which finds expression in later times. In the Greek Orthodox Church, for instance, Pilate's wife Claudia Procula is considered a saint, while both Mr and Mrs Pilate are canonised in the Ethiopian Orthodox Church. Yet, although it was likely included for the purpose of dating Jesus' earthly life and death, the phrase from the Creeds 'suffered under Pontius Pilate' has lent itself to a more sinister interpretation. The metamorphosis over the course of the Middle Ages of a benevolent Pilate into a more evil archetype, together with its inherent anti-Semitic component, is explored with expert thoroughness in Colum Hourihane's monograph *Pontius Pilate, Anti-Semitism, and the Passion in Medieval Art* (2009).[5] Anne Wroe, the long-time obituaries editor for *The Economist*, had turned her hand to the same topic of the prefect's afterlives with a more lively but less academic account a decade earlier.[6] Wroe handles more modern material, including Bulgakov's *The Master and Margarita*, and has wry insights about some of the films treated in this book. Both Hourihane and Wroe, in their own disparate ways, have set themselves to address, if not to answer, the question that Warren Carter had been led to ask as the title of his first chapter: 'Would the real Pilate please stand up?'[7]

In the cinematic tradition, the portrayal of Pontius Pilate undoubtedly runs the gamut of options outlined by Carter above, for reasons having to do with the nature of drama itself. Whatever else it may be that Jesus has to offer to this world, on the stage he presents a static figure, one whose character and appearance is fairly constant across productions from varying time periods. In *The Bible and Cinema*, noted scholar Adele Reinhartz remarks that Jesus' 'two-dimensional nature' is 'locked into a straitjacket of celibacy and sinless perfection'.[8] In *The Ancient World in Cinema*, this same insight was put still more forcefully by Jon Solomon: 'It is almost easier for a camel to pass through a needle's eye than for an actor to portray Christ with both reverence and dramatic conviction'.[9] While Jesus may be a fixed and unchanging figure at its centre, the other characters of the Passion drama circling around him very often differ significantly from performance to performance. Given that he so often figures as the antagonist, the tendency of the onscreen Pilate is far more inclined toward the villainous than the virtuous. As we shall see, the representations by Hurd Hatfield in *King of*

Kings (1960), Donald Pleasence in *The Passover Plot* (1974) and Vince Regan in *A. D. The Bible Continues* (2015) would be the clearest examples of Pilate as 'the heavy' in films about Jesus. Lowell Gilmore's Pilate in *Day of Judgement* (1953) is a petty bureaucrat of the sort that all right-minded people despise. In *Ben-Hur* (1959), Frank Thring's portrayal of the prefect is memorably comic, but it is a humour of a self-indulgent, cruel sort rather than what we might call good-natured; when he gives a false start to the chariot race which is at the centrepiece of the epic, we know, as he does, that he is the only person enjoying the joke. There is, by contrast, a humourlessness in both David Bowie's version from *Last Temptation of Christ* (1989), as well as Basil Rathbone's from *Last Days of Pompeii* (1935), that one associates with a certain sort of British imperiousness, an efficiency that is relished primarily because of its ruthlessness. Because we see him spending more time with his wife, perhaps, we are more inclined to pardon the resolve of Hristo Shopov in *The Passion of the Christ* (2003), even if we cannot extend such a pardon to the film as whole. Another film that is difficult to admire overall – although its Pilate, Telly Savalas, is likeable enough – is *The Greatest Story Ever Told* (1965), for reasons that will be explained more fully in the pages to follow. Peter Firth in 2016's *Risen* seems to have surrendered to his world-weariness in a way that comes across as understandable, although not entirely forgivable. Of all the Pilates, perhaps only Rod Steiger in *Jesus of Nazareth* (1977) and Barry Dennen in *Jesus Christ Superstar* (1973) are the ones we might describe as sympathetic, even though truthfully neither could be called an innocent. If in fact there is a film production featuring a saintly Pontius Pilate opposing Jesus, it has not come to my attention while writing this book, although I will grant Michael Palin in *Life of Brian* a certain status as holy fool. (Nor does this represent, by the way, a complete listing of the Pilates to be discussed in the book).

As I have noted, this is not a book about Pontius Pilate. It is a book, instead, about what Pilate means, and has meant, in film and television, although it is not a comprehensive study of this character's cinematic presence. Except for *Ponzio Pilato*, the joint Italian-American production from 1962 directed by Gian Paolo Callegari and Irving Rapper and featuring Jean Marais in the title role, Pilate is not the star of any film but a bit player in movies (more or less) about Jesus. According to the Internet Movie Database, the character of the Roman prefect occurs in scores of films and TV programmes. While it is exactly not the case that, 'if they should be written every one, I suppose that even the world itself could not contain the books that should be written' (as the Gospel of John concludes), it still would be a fairly unmanageable work to read, much less write, a study covering the entirety of Pilate's appearances on screen. Undoubtedly, in the pages to follow, some readers will note with regret that a favourite performance has gone without comment, and for such omissions I am sincerely regretful, for I have never come across a performance of Pilate that I did not find fascinating in some fashion. By and large, I have focused my attention on Pilate's major roles, in the big-screen Hollywood movies or on other televised performances of note, as well as those instances that have struck me as having some cultural content worthy of more than passing regard. Some noteworthy films have perhaps been given short shrift, if the performances of Pontius Pilate did not seem to me to merit discussion – glaring instances would be Pier Paolo Pasolini's brilliant but spare Marxist treatment from *Il Vangelo Secondo Matteo* (*The Gospel According to Matthew*, 1964) as well as Mark Donford-May's profoundly moving *Son of Man* (2006), since in each film the prefect appears only briefly. That I have perhaps considered at too great a length performances that otherwise might be considered obscure, I willingly own to be true . . . But what is truth?

'Tell all the truth but tell it slant', Emily Dickinson once wrote, and if moviegoers cannot necessarily place the quotation, they by and large understand the insight. Just as audiences have done since antiquity, viewers go to the cinema or turn to a screen at home with a willing suspension of disbelief about the story they will see and a simultaneous expectation that they will encounter verities of some variety, nevertheless. Perhaps the issues about the historicity of Bible films have no better illustration than the contretemps that followed Pope John Paul II's supposed endorsement of Mel Gibson's *The Passion of the Christ*: 'It is as it was', the pontiff was reported to have said of the film, a remark that led to weeks of dispute in the media.[10] Had the pope really said it? Had the pope really meant it? Did it really matter what the pope had said or meant? Films and TV programmes about Jesus carry a special burden with respect to the truth. Adele Reinhartz speaks of 'the belief, grounded in the Bible's canonical status, that although the Bible tells of things that occurred long ago and far away, its truths – however one understands that term – remain relevant to the present day'. As she goes on to note, however, 'filmmakers use the biblical narrative to address and reflect their own time and place'.[11] There is a similar impulse toward cultural retrojection in movies about classical antiquity, as Maria Wyke has observed in *Projecting the Past*: 'Historians should try to understand not whether a particular cinematic account of history is true or disinterested, but what the logic of that account may be, asking why it emphasizes this question, that event, rather than others'.[12] While accuracy is to be hoped for in historical films set in ancient Judaea, the tendency of the genre is not toward an unimpeachable authenticity of representation, but instead toward a useful allegory about the present.

As figure from ancient Rome situated amid a Biblical story, Pontius Pilate in his onscreen representation suffers from a sort of double indemnity, characterised as he is by a liminality between not just the Greco-Roman and the Judeo-Christian traditions, but between the allegorisations of those traditions as well. More than any other figure on the screen in such films, Pilate is the figure most inclined toward a presentist interpretation – even if he is wearing a breastplate or toga, the Roman in the Passion story often represents the conflicted morals of the modern day. Although he is speaking of the Victorian period, what David Mayer says about the range of possible interpretations in the toga drama applies equally well to productions of the twentieth and twenty-first century: such works allow audiences 'to have it both ways, to select from both sides, to have knowledge of the world and still retain one's innocence, to believe or not believe, and to expect optimistic solutions. Hence the possibility that in a toga drama, *official text and a subversive text*, with alternative readings, coexist'.[13] Insofar as Jesus is a static character in film representing eternal moral integrity, so Pilate is at odds with him, reflecting by contrast the values of the contemporary world. Simply put, the tension in such movies is that between the church and the world outside – between the push of Sunday morning and the pull of Saturday night.

In discussing the various onscreen Pilates over the course of this book, I have tried to consider the political context in which any given film was produced. Movies reflect the anxieties and values of the times in which, and for which, they were made, after all. It is not surprising to find thematic connections between topics in a film and items in the news, and sometimes even one-to-one correspondences. Two months after the February 2004 release of Mel Gibson's *The Passion of the Christ*, for example, the photographs of tortured prisoners from Abu Ghraib were published, leading critics to draw close connections between the two events as reflections of the post-9/11 American mentality.[14] 'He looked like Jesus Christ', one of the torturers wrote about a victim at the time, furthering the comparison.[15] More generally, controversies arising over films about Jesus often reflect, and even stand in for, larger political disagreements. In a famous chat show debate following the release of *Monty Python's Life of Brian* in 1979, the English Catholic intellectual Malcolm Muggeridge accused the movie of being 'a sort of graffiti version' of the Gospels, to which John Cleese responded:

> The sermons that were given, at the age of 11 and 12, I felt insulted my intelligence. When I got into writing this film, we all had exactly the same reaction. We started to discover a lot of stuff about Christianity and I started to get angry, because I started to think, 'Why was I given this rubbish, this 10th-rate series of platitudes, when there were interesting things to have discussed?'[16]

Beneath the young-versus-old argument about the Church of England in general and *Life of Brian* in particular, we hear the language of the charged political atmosphere in which Margaret Thatcher had just come to power as Prime Minister. Still more broadly, larger issues of a cultural nature playing out behind the scenes of a production sometimes find their way into a film, whether it is the Israeli tanks seen in the background of *Jesus Christ Superstar* or the overt ways in which concerns about anti-Semitism influence productions made in the decades immediately following the Holocaust, as is seen in the discussion in the Prologue about Robert Sherwood's *The Trial of Pontius Pilate*.

Another set of considerations I have taken into account in looking at the onscreen performances of Pontius Pilate has to do with the 'office politics' that come up in the midst of production. Where the political matters of the day are often explicitly referenced by movie reviewers and in interviews coming at the time of release, or where they can easily enough be inferred from media accounts of the times, it often requires archival exploration to uncover the production concerns to which virtually any film gives rise. In the yellowing memoranda and handwritten notes as well as the email records of newer films, one sees just how much behind-the-scenes negotiation, bargaining and compromise are part of the work and how much genuine collaboration goes into the making of any motion picture production. I am very grateful for the professionalism and expertise of the dedicated staff-members at the numerous repositories that I visited over the course of my research for this book. In one sense, there is a predictable uniformity about the workings of many of these institutions, but it is the difference in the experiences of them as places that stays with me. The dusty silence of the BBC Written Archives Centre in suburban Reading, interrupted only by the rustle of some other polite researcher's papers, where I read through the pink-coloured pages of notes about Dennis Potter's 1969 *Son of Man*, for instance, contrasts memorably with the splendid subterranean chamber at Brigham Young University, nestled in the mountains of Utah, in which folder after folder with research done for Cecil B. DeMille's *King of Kings* was to be found, as well as a number of his Academy Awards were to be seen (but never touched!). There is nothing quite like the pleasure of being in the Margaret Herrick Library at the Academy of Motion Picture Arts and Sciences in Beverly Hills and turning over a page in the massive file for *The Greatest Story Ever Told* to come across the memo, typed on an IBM Selectric and date-stamped 12 March 1963 (1:35 AM MST), from executive producer Frank Vellani, which reads: 'MR STEVENS WOULD LIKE TO SEE TELLY SAVALAS WITH COMPLETELY SHAVED HEAD'. Since the advent of VHS, DVD and now online streaming platforms, we are able to watch films over and over again, especially if we are scholars looking with a minute critical gaze, until they take on a sort of 'set in stone' quality. The sense that one takes away from perusing the materials in archival depositories, however, is just how much a matter of contingency the numerous details of the productions we ultimately see on the screen genuinely are.

Of special pertinence to this book, sometimes discernible from archival notes, concern the questions of who is being considered for a part, how much they might be paid and whether they will 'fit'. For instance, among casting agent Billy Gordon's papers at the Herrick Library are the lists provided to Owen McLean, the legendary casting director for what would be Twentieth Century-Fox's 1954 CinemaScope blockbuster *The Robe*. On the original memo for the role of Pilate, the names of Howard Petrie, Alan Joslyn, J. C. Flippen, James Robert Justice, Raymond Burr and Roland Winters are listed, and on the final casting sheet 'Robert Douglas' is written in for the part, then crossed out and 'Richard Boone' typed above. It is difficult to say why Boone ultimately got the nod, but in the critical discussions of his small but memorable role, few ever wonder how it might have been otherwise. Imagine if, instead of the hard-bitten American Boone, Pilate had in fact been played by the patrician Robert Douglas, the suave swordsman of 1948's *Don Juan?* How differently might the perception of Pilate have been had the commander to whom Richard Burton's Welsh Gallio answered been a debonair Englishman? What if McLean had gone with the blockish Canadian 'heavy', Raymond Burr, as Pilate? Although Burr had played several Biblical roles for Father Peyton's 'Family Theater' TV series, would there have been a greater sense of menace in the part, especially as the actor would appear as the murderous Lars Thorwald in Hitchcock's

Rear Window around the same time (*Perry Mason* being a few years in the future)? Admittedly, *The Robe* might not feel much different with this change in the casting of Pilate, but we should not dismiss the long-lasting impression that film performances make on viewers – H. B. Warner in 1927's *King of Kings* was the face of Jesus for a generation, just as the blue-eyed Robert Powell in *Jesus of Nazareth* was for another fifty years later. The mass consumption of film images guarantees their long life and long impact, even for bit parts such as Pilate's in *The Robe*.

In considering casting, here too we touch on another idea that will inform some of my discussion. In his ground-breaking work on this topic, British media theorist Richard Dyer elaborated the concept of stardom and its manifold meanings. At the most basic level, Dyer argues, film stars embody dramatic types – the Good Joe, the Tough Guy, the Pin-Up, the Independent Woman – and, if they are to avoid 'type-casting', develop into more specific and complicated 'star images' by a combined reading of media texts in which they feature (as objects of promotional and publicity materials, as performers in film vehicles and as subjects of critical commentary). This combination of texts does not add up to a sum total of some kind, but instead builds up what Dyer calls a 'structured polysemy', which offers a multiplicity of a star's possible meanings. As consumers, we are intended to recognize stars from film to film and to attribute to the enactment of one role an emotional memory of enactments in others in a vaguely intertextual fashion. This engagement with stars means that a specific film performance is more than an end-product in and of itself, and in fact contributes to a larger collection of texts out of which the star's image is fashioned. Generally, this is a broad sort of construction – 'he always plays the bad guy' – but at times can be very particular, with a line or gesture being repeated from another movie in such a way that it gives viewers the sense of being part of an in-joke and deliberately 'breaks the fourth wall' in a way upon which stardom depends. Viewed in this way, a star's later performance might well throw light on a prior one, the subsequent film drawing out more explicitly what was latent at an earlier stage in the star's career. Across this corpus, of course, there is a presumption of consistency, for, as Dyer puts it, 'there must at least be traces of Crawford's flapper in her working women, of Fonda's sexpot in her radical portraits'.[17] Now and again in this book, I have looked to other roles in a performers' careers to get some sense of what they were bringing to their portrait of Pilate. Telly Savalas's playing of the prefect in *Greatest Story Ever Told* offers a fine example of such intertextuality – *Kojak* will be a decade or so in the future for Savalas, but his Pilate has about him the air of the big city policeman, albeit more of the commissioner than the street-smart detective.

In fact, *Greatest Story* is a film that tests the limits of Dyer's sense of stars and their structured polysemy – in his review of the film, Bosley Crowther decried 'the frequent pop-ups of familiar faces in so-called cameo roles' in his *New York Times* review, noting in particular: 'And right at a point of piercing anguish, up pops the brawny Mr. Wayne in the costume of a Roman centurion. Inevitably, viewers whisper, "That's John Wayne!" This sort of conscious intermingling of theatrical personalities with sincere dramatic intentions and occasional stunning effects is the ultimate evidence of distortion in Mr. Stevens's clearly calculated way of handling his familiar material hyperbolically'.[18] Dyer had used Wayne in particular to illustrate his point about star images: 'In some cases, the various elements of signification may reinforce one another. John Wayne's image draws together his bigness, his association with the West, his support for right-wing politics, his male independence of, yet courtliness towards, women – the elements are mutually re-enforcing, legitimating a certain way of being a man in American society'.[19] A famous anecdote about *Greatest Story* is revealing in this respect. At the foot of the cross, Wayne's centurion says: 'Truly this man was the Son of God'. When Stevens asked him to repeat the line, adding some awe to his words, Duke reputedly drawled on the next take: 'Aw, truly this man was the Son of God'. It is not a true story, but it is somehow better than true, because it reveals the workings of Wayne's star persona – his easy-going, indeed casual regard for authority – without the actor actually doing anything at all. Perhaps in this we sense how fully enmeshed we are in a world of predetermined types and tropes when we watch the movies, perhaps never more so than when we are watching movies about our most dearly held myths and most timeless truths.

In trying to gain some sense of the significance that these various portrayals of Pilate in film and television were intended to convey, I have looked for insight from the directors, writers and producers of the films here under study, but above all, I have tried to find out what the actors themselves had to convey about the subject. To find out more about the choices they made concerning specific gestures or intonations of voice in particular, or what frames of mind they adopted more generally, I have consulted publicity materials, memoirs, notes and the like. Most of the actors I have studied here are dead, and of the living many are too busy with their careers to waste time talking to an academic, or, given the battery of publicists and agency representatives, are difficult to reach. But one morning, back in the summer of 2015, when I had made up my mind to go ahead with writing a book about Pontius Pilate in film, I was reflecting to myself on one of my favourite performances, the one on the old Decca album of *Jesus Christ Superstar* which I had fairly worn out from playing so often as a boy. Suddenly it occurred to me: 'Maybe I should try to interview Barry Dennen'. Dennen had played Pilate on the concept album, in the original Broadway production and in the 1973 film. Another voice in my head said: 'How are you going to manage that? You're a classicist in rural Tennessee, far from the glitz of Hollywood. Lotsa luck with that, pal'. But I turned it over in my head and spent the rest of the afternoon giving it a shot. I googled agents and casting companies, shot off emails – all of it kind of pathetic. 'Dear Mr. Dennen, You don't know me but . . .' Toward the end of the day, it occurred to me that, well, maybe he was on Facebook. And, in fact, he was! It was one of those celebrity pages, the kind you cannot post on, but I thought, maybe I'll send a private message. Couldn't hurt. So I cut and pasted one of the pathetic emails I had written earlier, looked at the clock, gathered my things and hopped on my bike home.

My wife and I were having dinner with my sons when the phone rang. She answered it. 'Uh huh. Yes, he's here. Let me get him'. She handed me the phone.

'Is this Christopher McDonough?'

'Yes'.

'This is Barry Dennen. My assistant sent me your message. Is this a good time to talk?'

JESUS CHRIST, I thought. JESUS CHRIST SUPERSTAR. I yammered something, but mostly I was hyperventilating. 'It's OK. I know how it is', he said. 'Take a breath. Tell me a little about your project, and maybe we can find a better time for a longer chat'. And so we talked and then set up a time for a longer chat. Barry was in his 70s, but he still kept up an active schedule as a voice actor for animated shows and video games. Scheduling a time was a bit tricky, but eventually we managed to connect. I really did not understand how Skype worked, but after hitting a few keystrokes, up popped Barry's face onto the laptop screen, the very screen I am looking at now as I type these words. We talked for over an hour, with me furiously scribbling notes the whole time. Some of that conversation has made its way into this book.

The next summer, I travelled to Los Angeles to continue working on the book, for which I now had a contract with Edinburgh University Press. There was a lot of archival work to do, but one evening I went to visit Barry at his home in Hollywood. After finding a parking spot on his hilly street, I climbed the steep stairs to his place. On the door was a funny little sign with his name on it, and a cartoon eye. I rang the door, and out he came and took my hand in his – his hands, the very hands that try to wash off the blood of Christ in a glass bowl so memorably toward the end of the film in *Superstar*. 'So, you found me!' he said and invited me in. By this time, I had a more specific set of questions to ask, but Barry had a discursive way of talking, and most of what I remember of the evening has nothing to do with the questions I had brought. He told me about his life with Barbra Streisand and about his record collection: 'Oh yes, some great old French records, classic stuff from the 40s. I played them for Barbra over and over, and that's where she really learned her singing style from'. At one point, we talked about his own singing, and he told me how he convinced Andrew Lloyd Webber to write 'Pilate's Dream' for him. And then he sang the opening line of the song for me at which point, dear reader, I assure you the hair stood up on the back of my neck. In pursuing this topic, I have talked to quite a few people and been to quite a few places, but not even making my way on my knees up the Scala Sancta, the steep Holy Staircase supposedly of Pilate's praetorium brought by St Helena to the Lateran in Rome, have I felt closer to the idea of who Pilate was.

But this is not a book about Pontius Pilate. Not exactly.

'*Quid ergo Athenis et Hierosolymis?*' the Christian apologist Tertullian once famously asked in the second century AD. 'What has Athens to do with Jerusalem?' This book, to some degree, explores that question. To be more accurate, however, I should say that my inquiry simultaneously alters that question – 'What has Rome to do with Jerusalem?' – as well as widens it – 'And what has Washington, London, or Hollywood to do with all of them?' The chapters that follow proceed largely in a chronological fashion, from the silent period to more or less the present day, and throughout I have been interested in the way in which Faith, Reason and Entertainment have become enmeshed. While reference is made to older films in relation to newer ones, I have resisted the temptation to speak of an emerging sense of representation for the Roman prefect. To my mind, each of the productions I consider is part of a tradition, but each portrayal is a work that stands on its own two feet. In *Saint Joan*, George Bernard Shaw had asked: 'Must then a Christ perish in torment in every age

to save those that have no imagination?' The answer, as the dramatist well knew, was a resounding yes – each generation must have a
Jesus of its own whom it will manage to crucify in its own particular
way. The corollary, it stands to reason, must be that every generation
will also have a Pontius Pilate of its own to preside over its Passion.
On the screen, Jesus will always need to represent the eternal values
of the next world, and Pilate the ephemeral values of the present day.
In writing about this collection of Pilates, I suppose my sense of those
changing principles and changing tastes has influenced me to write
about them in a set of changing ways, varying my tone from the academic to the essayistic to even the colloquial, as the subject moved
me. If that seems capricious, no disrespect to the subject-matter or
the reader is intended. *Quod scripsi scripsi*, Pilate is said to have
replied upon critique: 'I have written what I have written'.

NOTES

1　Bond (1998: 20–22).
2　Amorai-Stark et al. (2018).
3　Bond (1998: 11–2), with further references. Pilate is called procurator
　　by Tacitus, *Annals* 15.44.
4　Bond (1998: 203).
5　Hourihane (2009a).
6　Wroe (1999).
7　Carter (2003: 1–20).
8　Reinhartz (2013: 58).
9　Solomon (2001: 178).
10　Allen (2004) was the first to report the pope's supposed remark.
11　Reinhartz (2013: 7, 10).
12　Wyke (1997: 13).
13　Mayer (1994: 12).
14　Davis (2004) offers one example.
15　Gourevitch and Morris (2008: 52), on which see the discussion in
　　Chapter 10.
16　Muggeridge and Cleese, each quoted from *Friday Night, Saturday
　　Morning* (1979).
17　Dyer (1998: 98).
18　Crowther (1965: 40).
19　Dyer (1998: 63–64).

2 The Silent Pilate

I tell you, if these were silent, the very stones would cry out.

– Luke 19:40

The Internet Movie Database lists dozens of separate entries for actors playing Pontius Pilate, and it is likely not complete. The film tradition about Pilate is an especially rich one, of course, because films about the life of Jesus are as old as film itself: indeed, in America, it is at the movies rather than at the theatre that the idea of the Passion as a drama was first generally formed. In Europe, of course, there had existed a long tradition of staging the death of Christ – Oberammergau's Passion Play, in performance since 1634, is perhaps the best known, although the Benediktbeuern Passion Play can be dated to the 1200s – but such productions were strongly resisted in the US well into the twentieth century.[1] The first theatrical production of the Passion in the US, the brainchild of the energetic young impresario David Belasco and written by the irrepressible Salmi Morse, opened in San Francisco in 1879 and, despite its great popularity, was shut down by local authorities after an outcry among influential church leaders. Attempts to restage the show the following year in New York City met with a similar reaction, and no other Passion Play found its way to the American stage for many decades afterward.[2] Due to the fact that in its early years film was such an obscure medium, however, the sort of protests that hounded Belasco and Morse did not materialise at the movies. As Doris Alexander has noted, those who might have complained about film production 'were sufficiently unaware of what was going on in the hardly respectable novelty of films to raise no serious opposition'.[3]

In 1897, the Klaw and Erlanger company had released a movie called *The Horitz Passion Play*, the initial success of which prompted New York theatre owner Richard G. Hollaman to produce a film of the famous Oberammergau Passion Play. While purportedly shot on location in Germany, Hollaman's movie, employing Morse's script, was shot on the roof of New York City's Grand Central Palace on Lexington Avenue (a fraud exposed by the *New York Herald* at the time).[4] Not to be outdone by these versions, the Philadelphia optician-turned-movie mogul Siegmund 'Pop' Lubin mounted a Passion Play of his own, casting himself as Pontius Pilate. Whether Lubin, a Jewish immigrant from Poland, sensed any discomfort about playing the part is hard to say. As his biographer, Joseph Eckhardt, writes: 'It was a good role for him – a brief appearance in which he could chew the scenery a bit and get some attention. And it was one less actor to pay, not an insignificant consideration for a man making movies on a shoestring in his backyard'.[5] Having produced successful short pieces with titles such as *Horse Eating Hay* and *Daughters' Pillow Fight*, Lubin had been inspired to make longer films by the success of Thomas Edison, with whom he carried out a legendary rivalry. Edison was not above sending out hired thugs to break up Lubin's filming, nor was Lubin above sending out fake camera crews as red herrings for Edison's goon squad.[6] Despite these competing passions, the circumstances under which the production of these films were made highlight the filmmaker's ingenuity. For example, as Eckhardt writes, . . .

> Lubin's backyard had been transformed, by virtue of canvas scenes thrown over Grandma Abrams's clotheslines, into a panorama of Palestine. The mirage of the Holy Land was, according to one account, frequently dispelled by the wind. [. . .] One can only imagine the reaction, in this mainly Jewish neighborhood, the morning they opened their shutters to discover Lubin crucifying Jesus in his backyard.[7]

Much of the experience of these early films about Jesus' life is lost to us, unfortunately. As film scholar Rick Altman has noted, these early film versions of the Passion plays need to be considered in the tradition of the nineteenth-century traveling lecture-and-lantern slide shows out of which they grew. Lubin's *Passion Play*, for instance, was not a single dramatic entity, but had been designed to be shown either in whole or in parts, with various slides interspersed between reels and a lecturer specially hired to supply narrative linking the various still and moving images. It was a specially made point in the adver-

tisements to exhibitors that one could purchase either fifty-foot seg-
ments of Lubin's *Passion Play*, or the entire film (at 'one mile long!').[8]
It is a shame that this specific film is lost.

As film grew in popularity, however, there were some ministers who
saw the new medium's potential for spiritual purposes. The Reverend
Herbert A. Jump, in particular, wrote a significant pamphlet in 1910
on the topic, called *The Religious Possibilities of the Motion Picture*,
in which he outlined the ways in which film might both provide safe
entertainment for Christians and act as a dynamic tool for evangelical and missionary activity. Writing to his fellow ministers, he
argued that Jesus in the Good Samaritan parable and St Paul in his
allusions to racing and boxing illustrated their moral lesson with
graphic examples from their own day. Jump concludes his argument
by observing that . . .

> . . . the crowning possibility of the motion picture, though, is its usefulness
> to the preacher as he proclaims moral truth. It will provide the element of
> illustration for his discourse far better than it can be provided by the spoken
> word. It will make his gospel vivid, pictorial, dramatic, and above all, inter-
> esting. The motion picture preacher will have crowded congregations, not
> because he is sensational but because he is appealing to human nature more
> successfully than his fellow-clergymen, because he is adapting his message to
> the psychology of his hearers, because he is employing a better pedagogical
> method.[9]

As resistance to the medium waned and technology improved, film
began to take a more central place in American culture, including its
religious culture. Over the course of the next two decades, numerous
movies in America and Europe would be made about the life of Christ,
culminating in D. W. Griffith's masterpiece *Intolerance* (1916), which
features a vignette about 'the Judean' (although the Fall of Babylon
episode is the movie's true *tour de force*).

Prior to *Intolerance,* however, came Sidney Olcott's *From the
Manger to the Cross* (1912), the first film that could really be called
a 'spectacular', filmed on location in Egypt and Palestine, far from
the Lubin backyard and Grandma Abrams's clothesline. The Kalem
Company – founded by George Kleine, Samuel Long and Frank
J. Marion (the K, L and M of the company's name) – had sent its
production team across the Atlantic in 1911, to Europe and the
Middle East, in order to make a number of short educational films
and one- or two-reel adventure features. While in Egypt, Kalem's
actress and principal scenarist, Gene Gauntier, suffered a sunstroke
owing to the excessive heat of the filming locations. It was during
her recuperation, so Gauntier recounted years later in the *Woman's*

Home Companion, that she sat up in bed and blurted out in a delir-
ium: 'We're going to make the life of Jesus of Nazareth. We'll go to
Cairo first and take the flight into Egypt at the Pyramids, then to
Jerusalem'.[10] Although originating as a fever dream, the concept
was enthusiastically embraced by the rest of the Kalem company,
and before long they were well on their way to making *From the
Manger to the Cross*, with Gauntier taking the part of the Virgin
Mary. The director, Sidney Olcott, went to London to find actors for
the remaining parts, bringing back Robert Henderson-Bland to play
Jesus, as well as the otherwise unknown Samuel Morgan for the role
of Pilate.

Although filmed in Egypt and Palestine, *From the Manger to the
Cross* is very much a product intended for early-twentieth-century
audiences in Western Europe and North America. All of the films
made by Kalem in the Middle East reflect the overtly imperialist
attitude of the time toward the native Arab population, imagined as
resistant to any historical progress or development. This viewpoint is
expressed not only in productions with exotic titles such as *Captured
by Bedouins* or *A Prisoner of the Harem*, but also in the background
shots for *Moses in the Time of Egypt*, which came from Olcott's turning his camera on the 'chanting breech-clothed fellaheen' behaving,
it was imagined, precisely as their ancient counterparts had. *From
the Manger to the Cross* displays a similar perspective about the
people of its filming locations. 'So unchanged is the East, and especially Jerusalem', Gauntier wrote, that the extras employed to play
the money changers were actual local money changers who required
no alteration of makeup or props. 'They were', she concludes, 'as
they had always been'.[11] Audiences in the West do not seem to have
been troubled by the sight of these timeless locals being driven out
of the Temple by an English Jesus, in any event. Even in 1965, similar sentiments would be expressed in the documentary *Sopralluoghi
in Palestina per il Vangelo secondo Matteo* (*Location Hunting in
Palestine for* The Gospel According to Matthew) by director Pier
Paolo Pasolini. 'The Arab lumpenproletariat is the only thing that
remains truly ancient, archaic', the director remarks after meeting a
young Druse woman on a donkey. It seems clear that Pasolini, much
like the Kalem team half a century before him, had fallen victim
to the Western belief in the 'synchronic essentialism' of the East,
as Edward Said would put it in *Orientalism*. One has to wonder,
however, whose thinking has failed to evolve – that of the native
people of the Middle East, or the Western filmmakers who come to
observe them?[12]

Coupled with this unexamined belief in the nature of the local population is Olcott's own overly deferential attitude toward the source material. In an important discussion of *From the Manger to the Cross*, Charles Keil has spoken of the film's 'stylistic retardation', a term coined to describe the manner in which the filmmakers deliberately represent Jesus' story as a 'visualisation of key events, not a shaping of those events into an integral narrative whole'.[13] Less a 'moving picture' than a series of connected tableaux vivants patterned after well-known Biblical illustrations, the Kalem production particularly made use of the watercolours of the *Life of Christ* by the nineteenth-century French artist James Tissot, which exhibit 'little interest in investigating their principal subject as a knowable psychological being', as Judith Buchanan has remarked. As she further notes, '[i]n adopting Tissot's aesthetics, Olcott also followed suit in keeping anything more intimate about state of mind, psychological dilemma, or human grief largely suppressed'.[14] If *From the Manger to the Cross* comes across in many places as static rather than dynamic, it is a quality ultimately deriving from this constraint placed on the depiction of its central character, Jesus. Whether out of sincere piety or a desire not to offend potential viewers, the Kalem Company had determined at the outset not to take any risks in their portrayal of Jesus and so, by exposing him to neither doubt nor turmoil, ended up with a protagonist who is the object rather than the subject of his own story.

One of the only places in *From the Manger* where this stylistic retardation is challenged, according to Keil, is when the focus shifts away from Jesus to other characters. In the trial before Pilate, the scene is uniquely depicted with interlocking shots filmed from two separate angles. Within his palace, we see Pilate (Samuel Morgan) surrounded by Roman soldiers, with Jesus off to the righthand side of the screen. Behind him is a balcony from which, in the next shot, he addresses the crowd outside. Alternating between interior and exterior shots of the same moment, Olcott artfully depicts differing perspectives of that very scene in a way that the rest of the film has so far resisted. 'Why should the film inject such a relatively involved editing schema into its formal system at this stage?' Keil asks.

> One way to answer this is to view the episode as dependent on an understanding of Pilate's decision-making powers. A less 'familiar' (and sacrosanct) character than Christ, Pilate can be subjected to a more involved stylistic treatment. Hence, at this moment of greatest strain between representing the familiar and speculating on it, the film allows itself the luxury of actually formulating a portion of the Christ story *as story*, manipulating time and space

in such a way as to suggest the strain Pilate endures and depicting his decision in terms of cause and effect.[15]

While the remainder of *From the Manger* unfolds with a reverent lack of surprise, in this scene we have a character whose mental turmoil is uniquely manifested on screen. Deviating from the carefully rendered iconography that has characterised the rest of the film, Olcott has daringly presented his Pilate, nominally the master of the moment, as a man caught in an uneasy position (Figure 2.1).

Is it too much to suggest that, clumsy as it may be, this brief scene in *From the Manger to the Cross* has far-reaching implications for the depiction of Pilate in film? Framed by two different shots that do not entirely fit together well on a visual level, there is a deliberate awkwardness here that encourages the audience to view him as a figure suffering inner conflict. His hesitation is not seen (as it might have been in silent films only a few short years later) in a closeup that shows varying emotions playing across his face; rather, it is seen from a distance, with the sudden exchange of one setting for another. Although Pilate will order Jesus to be flogged and the

Figure 2.1 'Pilate Washing His Hands'. Samuel Morgan as Pilate. Still from *From the Manger to the Cross*, reproduced from Moving Picture World.

film will resume its liturgical style and pace, at this moment the film presents Pilate's uncertainty as though it were not a church service but an actual drama. While in future productions of the Jesus story, the settings may seem distant and even exotic, with characters whose attitudes are thought to be frozen in time, and although the figure of Jesus himself may come across in a pious but predictable fashion, the figure of Pontius Pilate offers screenwriters, directors and actors tremendous space for innovation. Whether the possibilities open to the portrayal of the Roman prefect are exploited to their fullest is a matter to be explored in greater detail in the course of this book, but we can certainly see a memorably performed Pilate, one who wrestles with anxiety and doubt, in the greatest silent-film depiction of the life of Jesus, Cecil B. DeMille's *King of Kings* from 1927.

Few movies had cost so much to make or were released to such celebrity hoopla as *King of Kings*, the last true masterpiece of the silent era. Premiering as the first film ever shown at Grauman's Chinese Theater in Hollywood, *King of Kings* had been shot at tremendous expense over the course of eight months on remote Catalina Island, accessible only by steamer, in order to discourage gawking crowds. Daniel Lord, a Jesuit priest who was part of a group of the film's religious advisors, arrived at the location which he would later describe in his memoir as a 'vast combination of tropic expedition, safari, transplanted Broadway, congress of the nations, great international dramatic stars and recent winners of beauty contests which was the company on location at the end of the lush period of American spending, soaring stocks, and 250-per-cent profit on any well-advertised motion picture'. DeMille himself, so Lord observed with admiration, was 'a strange and fascinating blend of absolute monarch and charming gentleman [...] a Renaissance prince who had the instincts of a Barnum and a magnified Belasco'.[16] Just before filming had begun, DeMille had gathered his enormous cast together to deliver an imperial address on the significance of the film, which was being made, he insisted, for the world's youth who were ignorant of the Bible 'as well as the other class, born with a Bible in their hand, who will criticize and hurl curses if we change an "if" or fail to dot an "i"'.[17] One may well wonder whether the movie's opening scene, in which Mary Magdalene, enraged that her lover Judas is off with Jesus instead of fawning over her, cries out 'Harness my zebras – a gift of the Nubian king!' qualifies as a changed 'if' or undotted 'i'. Watching the rushes of this particular scene, Lord writes: 'I winced. Mr. De Mille patiently explained how essential it was that the Broadway audiences of the world be won over; how they could not be introduced to burlap and desert sands, but must have a sense of luxury and beauty, the kind of life they would themselves like to lead. If they fall in love with Magdalene, then when she leaps into her chariot and says, "I go to find a Carpenter", they will go along'.[18] All of *King of Kings*, and of DeMille's religious epic aesthetics in general, seems to be summarised in this patient explanation: customers will come for the tawdry and over-the-top spectacle and stay for the religious message that follows.

For all of his pomposity, DeMille had a point when he insisted that the 'next generation will get its idea of Jesus Christ from this picture'.[19] The movie was an instant favourite with the public and showed in theatres and church halls at special Easter weekend screenings all over America for decades. Among critics and intellectuals, there was less fervour for the picture, although the poet H. D. (Hilda Doolittle) – a woman of letters writing in the same modernist idiom as T. S. Eliot's *The Waste Land* (and who was at work on her own novel about Pilate's wife at the time) – reviewed DeMille's film for the literary magazine *Close Up* in 1928. She spoke gushingly of *King of Kings* as a cinematic achievement:

> By drawing the Christian tale and poetic drama right into line with the most modern minute-after-next modernity Cecil M. [sic] de Mille has flung it back spiritually into its own setting. The young man Is a young man. He is no bearded and over-robed occult priestling no over-ornate somewhat sheep-like mystic, he Is. The Christ of the *King of Kings* fading out from the little room of the last farewell into the roll of motors, the irregular jag on jag of sky-scrapers, hulks of great boats lying at dry dock is true to utmost convention yet stands unconventionally apart a new reality to be grasped and gratefully re-instated [. . .] 'behold I am with you always'.[20]

The endurance of the film as a cultural touchstone is borne out by an anecdote from later in the life of H. B. Warner, the actor who played Jesus, when he was told by an American minister: 'I saw you in *The King of Kings* when I was a child, and now, every time I speak of Jesus, it is your face I see'.[21] During the filming of the movie, DeMille took pains to ensure that no scandal would undercut the message of his movie. As he notes in his autobiography, '[n]o one but the director spoke to H. B. Warner when he was in costume, unless it was absolutely necessary. He was veiled or transported in a closed car when he went between the set and his dressing-room or when we were on location, his tent, where he took his meals alone'.[22] Despite these precautions, however, off the set Warner seems to have been no saint and had, in fact, started an affair with one of the extras, Sally Rand, the burlesque performer who would go on to later notoriety as the inventor of the scandalous fan dance. The situation with H. B. did not sit well with C. B., who was once prompted to roar: 'Miss Rand, leave my Jesus Christ alone! If you must screw someone, screw Pontius Pilate!'[23]

The part of Pilate in *King of Kings* was played by Victor Varconi, a tall and handsome immigrant with a heavy Hungarian accent. Before arriving in Hollywood, Varconi had starred in dozens of films in Europe, including an Austrian-produced *Sodom und Gomorrah* (1922) directed by fellow Hungarian Michael Curtiz. Seeing Varconi in this picture, DeMille arranged for him to come to America and ended up casting him in numerous films until the arrival of the talkies, when the actor's career would be severely curtailed. During his cinematic career, however, the actor easily fell into the category of heartthrob. As Mrs Lorenzo Stevens of Venice, California, wrote in a fan letter to *Picture-Play*, 'Victor Varconi is an immortal artist without a rival or even a contestant. His polished technique, his charm, his sweet spirituality, his beauty, his depth of drama and color, his ardent pathos, his bewitching capriciousness, and those eloquent eyes of rarest beauty and brilliance make him the outstanding artist of the screen today. [. . .] He is dazzling!'[24] When we first see Varconi's Pilate in *King of Kings*, he is seated in his Judgment Hall beneath an eagle, a symbol of Rome's might, the enormous size of which is only revealed as the camera slowly dollies out from him. The screenplay, authored under great duress by Jeanie MacPherson, offers the elaborate instructions below for this shot, written in the now-extinct language of the silent-film script:

> The head and part of wings of Eagle fill screen. Camera <u>starts</u> opposite the head and slowly <u>DESCENDS</u> along body of Eagle until it rests on ground and shows in the LONG SHOT (on floor) the <u>SMALL FIGURE</u> of the Roman Governor – and several members of his Roman council, group to left and right of him – awaiting TRIAL of Jesus. Pilate (small figure) is leaning forward in his seat – chin in hand – elbow on knee – watching the excitement beyond the Iron Gates (out of scene) at end of hall. No one moves in this scene. It is almost a <u>still picture</u> with great golden Eagle the DOMINANT THING in the scene.[25]

In this impressive opening shot, the eagle seems to sit on Pilate's shoulders, a symbol of his authority, specifically his 'authority to pass sentence of death', as the intertitle emphasises (Figure 2.2).

A few years later, DeMille would make *The Sign of the Cross*, a cautionary fable about Neronian Rome that addressed 'fears that American imperialism was undermining the nation's unifying Christian culture', as Maria Wyke puts it in *Projecting the Past*.

Figure 2.2 Victor Varconi, as Pilate, beneath the enormous eagle symbolising Rome (and the US) in Cecil DeMille's *King of Kings* (1927).

The climax of *Sign of the Cross* juxtaposes the Christian martyrs, who enter the arena bathed in a kindly, cross-shaped light, with Nero (Charles Laughton) lounging in his throne on a raised platform beneath an outstretched eagle. Throughout the movie, Wyke remarks, the eagle and cross are contrasted, so that 'the Roman eagle signifies an oppression and moral decadence which is quintessentially foreign, the triumphant cross a freedom and innocence which is quintessentially American'.[26] It is hard to see this overdetermined symbol behind Pilate in *King of Kings* and not think of the spread bald eagle that has served as the emblem of the US since the adoption of the Great Seal in 1782. Later in his life, DeMille was a right-leaning Republican, and his McCarthy-era insistence on mandatory loyalty oaths and hounding of fellow filmmakers might be called 'red-baiting'.[27] He was not uncritical of American society, however. Several of his early movies in fact had dealt with issues of social justice (notably *Kindling* from 1915), and in 1926, the year before *King of Kings* was released, DeMille's *The Volga Boatman* had given a surprisingly sympathetic portrait of the Russian Revolution.[28] The Biblical injunction that from those to whom much is given, much shall be required (Luke 12:48) was at the heart of those movies, and in *King of Kings*, if the eagle represents anything, it is a symbol of both the might as well as the responsibility of empire. Perched upon his shoulders, the eagle holds Pilate in its very clutches, an indication that it is not power that he possesses, but power that possesses him – he should seem, as we are told twice in the screenplay, 'a small figure' at this moment.

The Roman prefect thus sits in his highly emphatic seat of power as the trial begins. From the right, Caiaphas (Rudolph Schildkraut) enters, exchanging contemptuous greetings with Pilate, and shortly after Jesus (H. B. Warner) is brought in from the right. Interspersed through the remainder of the scene is a shot of the hall's beautiful wrought-iron gates, through which can be seen the growing crowd beyond. The priest flourishes a scroll from which he reads the accusation, although Pilate instead considers Jesus, finally standing up and walking over to him. MacPherson's screenplay here reads: 'As they face each other squarely – they represent <u>completely</u> the TWO greatest powers on earth – the MATERIAL and SPIRITUAL! Both with proud chins raised – both dominant in totally different ways'.[29] Warner's light-haired Jesus wears a simple gown on the lefthand side of the shot and is bathed in a white glow, while Varconi's Pilate, to the right, stands taller in his richly-textured tunic, thumping his chest with a beringed fist. It is a beautifully if unsubtly composed faceoff, the meaning of which H. D. understood implicitly: 'Christ before Pilate was again a sustained and luminous piece of acting and of screen craft. The Roman is all a Roman, heavy yet intelligent, open minded yet conservative, handsome yet limited. The limitless meets the limited, the force of spirit meets the force of earth, earth power at its best Roman law, justice personified in this Pilate, so graciously portrayed by Victor Varconi'.[30] Now and again during this encounter, Pilate looks away toward the world around him – Caiaphas, the crowd, the soldiers, the eagle – but Jesus' unwavering gaze throughout the scene is fixed in an ethereal heavenward direction.

When, bemused by his examination of Jesus, Pilate returns to his chair to declare that he finds no fault in him, Caiaphas is visibly upset. To play Caiaphas and Judas, respectively, DeMille had cast the respected father-and-son team Rudolph and Joseph Schildkraut. The latter would go on to an impressive career, winning a Best Supporting Oscar for his performance as Captain Dreyfus in *The Life of Emile Zola* (1938) and appearing as Nicodemus in George Stevens's *The Greatest Story Ever Told* (1965) for his final film. Rudolph's reputation had largely been built on his stage success as the *Merchant of Venice*'s Shylock: bringing much of that stereotype to his film role, he was understandably the lightning rod of protest among leaders in the Jewish community.[31] For his part, DeMille seems to have sincerely believed in the even-handedness of his presentation, having announced to the cast in his speech on the first day of production: 'The purpose of the story is to treat all classes fairly and particularly the Jew, because the Jew is put in the most unfortunate place of any race in the Bible, because it was not really a matter of the Jew having persecuted Jesus, it was Rome, Rome with her politics and graft'.[32] In response to the outcry from prominent rabbis after an initial screening, DeMille altered some of the title cards so that blame for Jesus' death would be placed on Caiaphas himself directly and on 'the iron heel of Rome' more generally. These measures notwithstanding, there are still many shots of the crowd, now through the gates, rampaging in the hall and protesting – some for, but most against Jesus. Seen from a temporal distance of ninety years, DeMille's *King of Kings* still retains much of the anti-Semitism inherited from its medieval Passion Play source material.

In a conversation recorded many years later, Varconi critiqued Schildkraut's Caiaphas for his overacting, telling an interviewer that the Schildkrauts 'were of the scenery chewing clan of actors' who 'slightly offended the "natural" school of Victor's National Theatre instruction'.[33] Nowhere is the difference in acting styles more evident than in the final moments before Pilate hands Jesus over for his punishment. 'Shall I crucify your king?' he asks, his hands suddenly shooting out in a last-ditch effort to calm the mob. Schildkraut's Caiaphas, noticing the prefect's dubitation, taps him on the shoulder somewhat unctuously and says: 'We have no king but Caesar'. MacPherson's screenplay indicates that the response should be thus: 'Pilate shows that the blow tells! His face loses its defiant expression and begins to look worried. A real FEAR begins to grow in his eyes. His fingers begin to pull at the buckle on his shoulder nervously as if the weight of his cloak were too much! He breathes hard and looks toward Christ'.[34] Despite the very specific instructions here, Varconi does not in fact overplay the scene. After a backward glance at Caiaphas, he slowly turns away, clenching and then unclenching his fist to indicate his sense of defeat. As Gordon Thomas wrote of Varconi's Pilate in his review of the 2006 DVD release of the film, '[h]ere is some screen acting that belies the notion that silent film performances were all hammy overblown gesture and eye-rolling left over from nineteenth-century stage melodrama'.[35] Varconi's manner here, avoiding the exaggerated emphasis on facial expression, is notable for its understatement: his emotions are conveyed not in the kabuki characteristic of the silent-film period – 'All right, Mr DeMille, I'm ready for my closeup', as Norma Desmond would say in the 1950 *Sunset Boulevard* – but by a subtle shifting of the eyes and, significantly, by his manual gestures, from the dismissive wave with which he greets the wearisome Caiaphas at the vignette's opening to the balling of his fist near its conclusion. These are, in fact, the very hands that Varconi's Pilate will wash with great show, just before he signals for Christ's crucifixion.

The trial now reaches its inexorable conclusion. Pilate turns away from Caiaphas and signals to a slave; we cut away to the tumultuous crowd and then back to Pilate, whose retinue has returned with a basin and pitcher. With the enormous eagle framing him in the background, Pilate stands in the centre alongside two servants to his immediate left, one of whom holds the basin while the other pours water over his hands, while further to the left Schildkraut's Caiaphas overtly points to the action. With his hands now washed, three final manual gestures are left for Varconi's Pilate. He first resignedly gestures to Christ, alone on the righthand side of the screen. He then points accusingly at Caiaphas (who, in a longer cut of the film, utters the unbiblical sentiment 'If thou, imperial Pilate, wouldst wash thy hands of this Man's death, let it be upon me – and me alone!' – an intertitle DeMille had later inserted in hopes of minimising the charge of collective Jewish guilt). Finally, Pilate pushes his right arm out toward the crowd – decisively or dismissively? – while he gathers his toga up to his chest ('irritably', is how MacPherson specifies it, although Varconi rather appears uneasy) and walks away to the enormous eagle in the far back. The screen now suddenly fills with members of the Jewish crowd, crossing downstage from stage left to right, and soldiers, crossing from right to left. The staging at this point reads with almost allegorical precision: the eagle as a symbol of worldly power is in the far back, with Pilate immediately in front of it, and an X (or cross?) made by the Jews and Romans cuts him off from the triumphant Caiaphas and the suffering Christ as well as from the viewer.

'He is out of humor with himself and the whole disturbing business!' are the concluding words of MacPherson's screenplay for Pilate, but there is still one final shot of Varconi, only three seconds long, before he exits the picture. Although soldiers are visible in the background, Pilate here is seen at this last glance alone with his decision and with his shame. In just a moment, Judas will rush in guiltily, Jesus will be led away to his death, and the crowd will react with fits of agitation – that is to say, the screen will burst with epic action and overwrought emotion. But first, we have this quiet view of Pilate, a powerful man shattered by his own failure, lowering himself onto his throne with his guilty hands, while behind him the eagle with its enormous talons is off to the side, neither offering protection nor conveying authority. Where Sidney Olcott had filmed Pilate's decision as a difficult one in *From the Manger to the Cross*, he did not, as DeMille does for a few seconds here, invite us to feel some compassion for the prefect. If we are meant to sympathise with Varconi's Pilate here, even briefly, the significance of the moment was not lost upon H. D.:

> The Roman is not brute, de Mille seems to say as the broad minded say to-day with a little stiffening of muscles and stark branching of shoulders, 'the Germans were not altogether to blame'. De Mille says much for Pilate, much for the Roman host, something for the throng and crowd who simply don't know what the whole thing is they shout for. Crucify him they say ignorantly, as more lately 'we want war'. Crucify them, crucify him [. . .] forgive them for certainly they know not what they do.[36]

'De Mille's whole propaganda is explicit', she concludes. 'See both sides, see all sides'. It is worth remembering the cultural context in which she wrote this as we take stock of H. D.'s assessment. The Roaring Twenties, still in full roar when this review appeared, was a time of economic prosperity and societal change, of 'that old-time religion' and Sally Rand's fan dance, of 'flappers and philosophers' (in F. Scott Fitzgerald's phrase). To be sure, H. D. was impressed by the sheer artistic accomplishment of *King of Kings*, but she seems troubled by the morality of the public that made it a hit. Audiences who would go in droves to watch a two-and-a-half-hour-long Passion Play with both a gentle-humoured Jesus and the zebra-drawn chariot of a scantily clad Mary Magdalene not really seemed to know their own mind. They might, she seems to indicate, have some trouble responding to a question such as: 'What is truth?'

To the role of Pontius Pilate in *King of Kings*, Victor Varconi brought a sense of nuance that many of his fellow silent-film actors lacked, and with it a capacity to convey to viewers a sense of fellow feeling for a character intended as one of the feature's villains. In the mid-1970s, an amateur Hollywood historian named Ed Honeck would write together with Varconi a memoir of his career called *It's Not Enough to Be Hungarian*. According to Honeck, '[i]n point of fact, Varconi conceived of Pilate as the first Nazi and that was how he played him'.[37] An insight of this sort, made half a century after the movie was released, might well be taken with a grain of salt, but it is a shame that Honeck did not follow up on this statement to see what precisely the actor meant. If he was thinking about the rise of Hitler during the making of *King of Kings*, there is scarcely any trace of it in film production notes or in the interviews he gave to fan magazines at the time. Perhaps he meant to say that he had modelled his conception of Pilate's role after that of Werner Krauss, who had played the role in Robert Wiene's elaborate German production from 1923, *INRI* (released in the US under the title *Crown of Thorns*). Krauss was, in fact, a Nazi collaborator who would go on to take a leading role in Goebbels's virulent work of anti-Semitic propaganda, *Jud Süß* (1940). Again, it may be that Varconi had in mind a role he played later in his career, after his heavy accent had come to limit his choices: Rudolf Hess, in a pseudo-documentary work of propaganda made in 1944 by Paramount, called *The Hitler Gang*. But it seems most likely that, in this off-the-cuff remark made to Honeck in his Santa Barbara home many decades later, Varconi here was drawing on his own sensibility as a central European. A minor member of Hollywood's Hungarian royalty – which included Alexander Korda, Michael Curtiz, Peter Lorre and numerous others – Varconi would have been well aware of the rise of fascism in the 1920s, even if Americans did not wish to see it yet.[38] To sympathise with the military man beneath an enormous eagle, as despondent as he might have been, might not have been a good idea.

As Jon Solomon notes of *King of Kings* in *The Ancient World in the Cinema*, '[t]he film became so well established that no other major cinematic portrayal of the life of Christ was attempted in America until 1954'.[39] This is not to say that Pilate disappears from the silver screen until then – there will be Basil Rathbone in the role in *The Last Days of Pompeii* (1935), about whom more will be said in Chapter 8. But it is true that, after DeMille's epic production, it would take the film industry a generation or two to gather the courage to remake the Passion narrative, and it would do so under vastly different political and social conditions. Before we go on to consider those mid-century productions, however, it is worth taking stock of the depiction of Pontius Pilate in the silent-film tradition. In the very earliest days of moving pictures, the Bible was looked to as a source of inoffensive story material – if there was any issue, in fact, it only had to do with bringing the characters to the screen in a sufficiently pious manner. The 'stylistic retardation' identified by Charles Keil as operative in *From the Manger to the Cross* has a deadening effect on the portrayal of Jesus, but perhaps allows greater freedom for the filming of Pontius Pilate. Given how early in the industry's technology *From the Manger* was made, it is difficult to say whether more might have been made of the film's only true dramatic moment. As such, we can only imagine how the actor, the otherwise unknown Samuel Morgan, would have capitalised on this opportunity. No such criticism attaches to Victor Varconi's performance. The silent-film era ended almost simultaneously with this film, and the career of Varconi together with it; hence, it is not possible to say more about what influence this particular performance might have exerted going forward. In *King of Kings*, we have the final flowering of a fully formed genre and, in the role of Pilate, an actor whose style has been honed to perfection for this type of production.

NOTES

1 Salzer (1911).
2 See Alexander (1959: 351–66), and Bial (2015: 1–3, 187 n 2, with further bibliography).
3 Alexander (1959: 367).
4 Ramsaye (1926: 8).
5 Joseph P. Eckhardt, personal communication, 19 November 2007.
6 Eckhardt (1997: 48–49).
7 Eckhardt (1997: 29).
8 Altman (2004: 136–38), and Eckhardt (1997: 29).
9 Jump (1910: 24).
10 Gauntier (1929a: 21).
11 Gauntier (1929a: 21) on *Egypt in the Time of Moses* and (1929b: 18) on money changers.
12 Said (2004: 240).
13 Keil (1992: 112).
14 Buchanan (2007: 53).
15 Keil (1992: 118–19).
16 Lord (1956: 278–79).
17 Birchard (2004: 221).
18 Lord (1956: 281–82).
19 Birchard (2004: 222).
20 H. D. (1928: 24).
21 DeMille and Hayne (1959: 276).
22 DeMille and Hayne (1959: 279–80).
23 Hay (1990: 53). Whether Miss Rand ever followed up on DeMille's suggestion is not recorded.
24 Stevens (1927: 114).
25 MacPherson (1926: 221). The name is at times spelled 'Macpherson.'
26 Wyke (1997: 132, 134).
27 Birchard (2004: 343–44).
28 Birchard (2004: 210–15).
29 MacPherson (1926: 228).

30 H. D. (1928: 29).
31 See the discussion of Ohad-Karny (2005).
32 Birchard (2004: 221).
33 Varconi and Honeck (1976: 101).
34 MacPherson (1926: 258–59).
35 Thomas (2014).
36 H. D. (1928: 30–31).
37 Varconi and Honeck (1976: 101).
38 Portuges (2012).
39 Solomon (2001: 183).

3 The Roman in the Living Room: Pilate on TV in the Early 1950s

Christ is one of the 'family' now. I often wonder if God recognizes His own son the way we've dressed him up, or is it dressed him down? He's a regular peppermint stick now, all sugar-crystal and saccharine when he isn't making veiled references to certain commercial products that every worshipper absolutely needs.

– Ray Bradbury, *Fahrenheit 451* (1953)[1]

It was on the small screen of the television set rather than the big screen of the cinema that the most significant dramatisations of Pontius Pilate would next appear in the twentieth century. The success of DeMille's 1927 blockbuster *King of Kings* had precluded the production of another big-budget offering on the topic until Nicholas Ray's 1961 remake, although a listless 16mm colour version of a stage drama, *The Pilgrimage Play*, written by Pittsburgh heiress Christine Wetherill Stevenson, would be released for church screenings in 1949.[2] With the end of the Depression and the victorious conclusion of the Second World War, the circumstances of life for many in America had changed, as had their modes of leisure-time activity. Whereas, at one time, an evening of on-screen entertainment had meant a trip to the movie theatre, most living rooms in Middle America now possessed a TV set. Hollywood continued to turn out pricey epic films on the Old Testament and other ancient topics through the 1930s and 1940s, but it was through the new medium of television that the New Testament would come to the masses in the post-war period. Just as in the early days of cinema Reverend Herbert Jump and others had urged fellow clergy to embrace film as a tool for religious use, so when the new medium first began to emerge, a similar movement arose to make and distribute works about the Gospels for the small screen. By and large, the shows that found their way onto the airwaves in TV's early years for the at-home, family-centred Christian market were made with low budgets and high aims. Equally high-minded and better-funded network programming would likewise turn to the story of Pilate in the 1950s, as was seen in the discussion of Robert Sherwood's *The Trial of Pontius Pilate* in the Prologue. The commercial and cultural context of television would come to exert a unique pressure on the representation of figures from the Passion narrative: the involvement of corporate sponsors, anxieties about Communism, awareness of the unspeakable horror of the Holocaust just a few years earlier, together with a growing dissatisfaction with mid-century domestic arrangements – what Betty Friedan would call 'the problem that has no name' – can all be shown to have influenced televised productions about Jesus, and by extension Pontius Pilate, in this decade immediately following the war's end.

The most prominent productions in the field of 1950s 'Sunday School TV' were those devised and overseen by the indefatigable James K. Friederich, an Episcopal priest from Minnesota, who founded Cathedral Films in 1939 and ran it continuously for the next several decades.[3] Although none of Cathedral's productions achieved anything but modest success, the work of Father Friederich is noteworthy, not only because of the pioneering role that he played in the world of independent American filmmaking, but also for the influence that he and his company exercised in creating what would come to be called the faith-based market. Cathedral's *Living Christ* series, the first mini-series ever broadcast, depicted the life of Jesus from his birth to death and resurrection in twelve half-hour instalments and was aired by NBC on successive Sundays from January through March of 1951, with the final episode showing on Easter Day. Two years later, NBC broadcast another Cathedral production, the made-for-TV movie *I Beheld His Glory*, which presented a version of Jesus' story, told in a series of flashbacks by one of the Roman soldiers present at the Crucifixion; the footage for this movie was largely borrowed and repurposed from the *Living Christ* programs, with a dubbed-in voice-over bridging gaps in the narrative. In 1954, Cathedral turned to the big screen to produce a feature-length film called *Day of Triumph*, directed by John T. Coyle and written by Arthur Horman, just as *Living Christ* and *I Beheld His Glory* had been but reshot at a larger aspect ratio on 35 mm film. There is very little difference between the film and the TV programmes, with virtually identical sets and a script, shortened from the series, reproducing dialogue almost word-for-word in many places for the film. Except for one new role (Pilate's wife is now played by an uncredited Barbara Billingsley, of later June Cleaver fame), *Day of Triumph* uses the same entire cast from the earlier Cathedral productions. As in both television productions, Robert Wilson's Jesus has been made up to resemble Walter Sallman's famous 'Head of Christ' from 1940, although his hair is a little shorter and better kempt. In its initial release, *Day of Triumph* did well with critics, most of whom noted that it was the first cinematic depiction of the life of Jesus since DeMille's *Kings of Kings* a quarter century earlier. *Newsweek* called the film 'a model of simplicity and good taste', while *Variety* praised its 'dignity, restraint, and distinction', although suggesting that it was more suitable for special handling at select venues.[4]

Coupled with *Day of Triumph*'s mainline view of Christianity was a Cold War sense of larger purpose. In announcing the beginning of production for the film, the *New York Times* reported that the film was being made 'largely with a view to aiding in the western world's struggle against the spread of communism' (8 July 1952). This Pax Americana message starts as early as in the opening credits in *Day of Triumph*, which are shown as a book whose pages reveal the historical context within which the film takes place: 'This is a story of the time when Western Civilization was enslaved by the might of Imperial Rome [...] From the Rhine to the Nile, from the Atlantic to the deserts beyond the Jordan, the nations bowed in helpless submission to the legions of the Empire'. Rome, so often described as the foundation of Western Civilisation, here is presented as a thinly disguised allegory for the Soviet Union instead, set at odds with it. When next the page turns, we read: 'Yet in every vassal state, there were men who clung to the dream of freedom, struck back at their oppressors, planned unceasingly to cast off the yoke of slavery ...' These ancient freedom fighters, so we are told, are the Zealots, whose leader Zadok is played by Lee J. Cobb, the film's biggest star who gets top billing over even Robert Wilson as 'The Christ'. As the onscreen action unfurls, we watch one of these Zealots arrested by but then escaping from some Roman soldiers, later sneered at as 'Pilate's dogs'. If we know right away while watching *Day of Triumph* that Rome is the Red Menace whom we ought to root against ('Boo Pilate's dogs!'), it is not immediately clear who we are intended to support. These Zealots, it turns out, may love liberty but their efforts to secure it are ultimately misguided. One of their number, in fact, is a certain

Judas Iscariot, whose subsequent behaviour in betraying Jesus is not meant to gain our sympathy whatsoever.

In its opening montage, *Day of Triumph* presents the Roman Empire as an ancient version of the Iron Curtain, but at other points in Cathedral's work, Rome bears a striking resemblance to the modern US. In the made-for-TV *I Beheld His Glory*, the Passion story is recounted from a soldier's perspectives in setups and sounds that are very American. James Flavin as the centurion Longinus even speaks in a barely contained New England accent when he tells his new partner Cornelius (George Macready) about Jesus entering Jerusalem on a donkey 'walking on a cahpet of robes and pahm branches'. The centurions, patrolling the streets like a pair of TV cops on the beat, see Jesus with a small crowd. 'Uh oh', Longinus notes. 'There go two of Caiaphas' closest aides. Let's stroll over and see what's happening'. What's happening, it turns out, is a Pharisee asking Jesus whether the Jews ought to pay their taxes. 'A very choice trap. If he says pay, the entire crowd turns against him', says one soldier to the other. 'Don't pay, and I arrest him for treason'. When Jesus foils Caiaphas' men by telling them to render to Caesar, the centurions exchange admiring smiles. 'Too bad he's no Roman. We could use men of his cut', they agree. Cornelius and Longinus may be drawn from medieval legends about the Roman soldiers who were among the first Gentile converts to Christianity, but these figures on the screen with their blue-collar mannerisms are meant to appeal to Middle American men in their living rooms. Watching TV instead of going to church on Sunday, they may not see themselves in the immediate crowd gathered around Jesus, but they can imagine getting a positive sense of him as a 'man's man' going about his business over the course of a regular day.

If the Roman soldiers seem by and large to be the salt of the earth, their leader comes across as a fussier and far less congenial sort of character. In the third episode of *The Living Christ* series, for instance, the newly arrived governor, Pontius Pilate (Lowell Gilmore), is droning to his wife about all the concessions that these subjects of his are demanding. 'You'd have thought we were the vanquished and they were the conquerors', he complains and snaps at the servant who is helping him take off his armour. 'Don't paw at me! Get out! Go!' It is hardly an image of gracious or dignified leadership, and the fluctuations of his accent from American to British and back again throughout the series and films heightens the impression of fickleness. When, later in the series (Episode 11), the Jewish leaders arrive to the praetorium to bring him Jesus, the narrator states: 'Pilate, awakened before his accustomed hour, was in a surly mood'. In the corresponding scene from *Day of Triumph*, the prefect asks a guard why this business 'can't wait till a decent hour', and when told that it is the Sabbath, exclaims in exasperation: 'Sabbaths! Holy days! Feast days! They waste more time on one God than we do on a thousand'. We cut then to the breakfast room, where he complains about what he is sure is a plot against him to his wife Claudia (Barbara Billingsley). 'If I had a free hand', he tells her. 'I'd order the Galilean beheaded. All his followers with him. Then I turn the cohorts loose on the temple, on Caiaphas and all the fat cats that surround him'. The entire time while he is indulging this murderous little scenario, he is enjoying a slice of cantaloupe.

A man who likes to sleep in, who rolls his eyes at other people's religious scruples and talks about slaughter with food in his mouth, Lowell Gilmore's Pontius Pilate is meant to be a peevish leader, not as decent as the people who serve under him or as devout as those over whom he presides, and nowhere near the equal to the stoic man he will condemn to the cross. This is hardly the image of the noble prefect played by Victor Varconi for *King of Kings* a generation before. It is hard not to think, watching him shrug and cross his arms, that Gilmore has gilded the lily of Pilate's petulance, almost as if to force the underlying kitschiness of the production's overriding sincerity. Prior to *Day of Triumph*, Gilmore's most notable role had been as the effete Basil Hallward, the painter of the eponymous *Picture of Dorian Gray*, from 1945. Together with George Sanders's charmingly cynical Lord Henry Wotton and the protagonist Hurd Hatfield – who, as it happens, would be the Pilate of the next big-screen Hollywood production about Jesus, Ray's *King of Kings* – the three make up a trio of slightly sexually ambiguous *fin-de-siècle* flaneurs. *Day of Triumph* is no drama by Oscar Wilde, to be sure, but one senses that Gilmore is injecting a bit of Wildean drollery into his performance, exaggerating for humorous effect the essential dullness of his hapless villain in the piece. In his final onscreen moment, as depicted in both *The Living Christ* and *Day of Triumph*, he grumbles to the crowd: 'See to it yourselves'. Washing his hands quickly in a proffered basin, Gilmore's Pilate exits the scene, throwing his towel down in a huff.

On Easter Sunday, 25 March 1951, television viewers in many American cities had their choice between the final instalment of *The Living Christ* series ('Crucifixion and Resurrection') on NBC or the Family Theater's *Hill Number One*, a black-and-white retelling by an army chaplain of the Easter Story, which featured the debut of a young actor named James Dean as Saint John. While Cathedral Films productions were sincere in their belief and straightforward in their presentation, they never impress us with their inventiveness, a charge that cannot be made against *Hill Number One* or any of the other programmes made by the Roman Catholic Family Theater group under the direction of the charismatic Irish priest Patrick Peyton, whose devotion to the cult of the Virgin Mary and praying the Rosary informed his missionary work on radio, television and in live rallies. The scripts of these Family Theater productions were written by James D. Roche, a Jesuit who, Peyton says, had served in the US Navy and worked for a Hollywood studio prior to taking Holy Orders.[5] Where Cathedral always had Jesus at the front and centre of their presentations, he is absent from the productions of Family Theater, which focus instead on the testimony of those who had had personal encounters with him. Earlier in the year, Family Theater had aired *That I May See*, a dramatised testimonial by Bartimaeus (Jeffrey Lynn), the blind beggar healed by Jesus, with Richard Hale reprising the role of Pilate which he had played in both the stage and screen versions of *The Pilgrim Play*. For Easter, Family Theater offered *Hill Number One*, told by a priest to a group of American soldiers about the story of the Passion as it concerned Pilate (here played by Leif Erickson) and other military men like themselves in a play-within-a-play format.

Opening with a volley of cannon fire on a Korean battlefield, *Hill Number One* begins with a group of discouraged American dogfaces on Easter Sunday, a fact that does not impress them. 'Aw, who cares if it's Easter Sunday, Blue Monday, or Dollar Day? Out here, one day's as good as the next, and they're all bad', Batesy (Todd Karns) tells 'Padre' (Gordon Oliver), the army chaplain who has just driven up with some coffee and cigarettes during a break in the fighting. Although they come from different backgrounds, all the men feel this same way, as the chaplain discovers. 'Is there supposed to be a meaning to all this, Padre?' one asks. All day they have been bombing Hill 46, tomorrow it will be Hill 50, three days ago it was Hill 39. 'Why don't you go back farther than that, to Hill Number One?' Padre asks. 'You've got to go back to Calvary, 'cuz if you don't, well, you're right, Batesy, fighting like this has no meaning. It's a mess, and so is everything else'. What will ensue is an inset teledrama involving ancient Roman soldiers, but the theme of the programme is nothing short of the existential crisis of modernity. 'If life is as meaningless as death, if guilt is as questionable as perfection, if being is no more meaningful than nonbeing', the theologian Paul Tillich would ask in 1952, 'on what can one base the courage to be?'[6] It is not too much to say that in *Hill Number One*, we sense that Father Peyton is looking to address the substance of Tillich's haunting mid-century question about the purpose of existence.

As Padre commences his tale, we segue to the praetorium in ancient Jerusalem, where Pilate, in military garb and speaking in the same American accent as Batesy and the other soldiers, is meeting with Joseph of Arimathea (Nelson Leigh, who had previously voiced Jesus in *That I May See* and played the eponymous hero of Cathedral's Saint Paul series). After initially refusing to surrender Jesus' body to him, Pilate eventually relents after agreeing that he did not personally find Jesus to have been a criminal. Joseph tells Nicodemus in the next scene that what had persuaded Pilate was 'his own unsettled mind'. The connection with the Korean War overplot is deftly drawn here: soldiers have doubts about the activities in which they are asked to engage abroad, and it has ever been so. Before the scene has ended, Pilate has also wondered aloud about where his wife Claudia has gone – as we shall find out, she has absconded to become one of the Christians. A centurion named Cassius Longinus (Henry Brandon) now enters to give 'a full report' to Pilate. 'This Jesus we crucified *was* the Son of God', he insists, and a hubbub ensues. 'I'm a soldier, procurator', he continues. 'What's more, a soldier over soldiers. I serve you best when I bring you all the facts'. He tells Pilate of the earthquake that took place when Jesus died, and how, when he drove his lance into Jesus' side, blood and water flowed over his face, healing a squint that had troubled him since childhood: here, it is worth recalling that Father Peyton's devotion to the Virgin Mother stemmed from his own sudden recovery from illness.[7] In addition to these physical proofs, Cassius says, he felt 'a new excitement in my heart', causing him to kneel with the women in worship. 'Ridiculous', concludes Pilate at this effeminate show of piety. 'Didn't the other soldiers laugh?' No one laughed, and in fact others joined him in the mud, Cassius informs Pilate, who then dispatches him – 'fantastic as your story is' – to guard Jesus' tomb. The scene, which has begun with Pilate seated as a figure of authority, ends with Cassius and the commander standing face-to-face on equal footing, in blocking very much like that of the earlier moments with Joseph of Arimathea. The more discussion he has about Jesus, the less Erickson's Pilate seems to be in a position of control.

Pilate's official station is not the only thing that slips away from him in *Hill Number One*. In a later scene, Claudia (Joan Leslie) is seen in a hidden location receiving food from a Christian named

Stephen (Terry Kilburn), who openly wonders why she has joined them, since it is her husband who condemned Jesus to death. 'Because he was weak', she replies, 'and he had the power of might – Caesar's might. When Jesus had been whipped and scourged and beaten, he too was weak. But he had the power of Truth, his own. God now has given me the courage and wisdom to see a difference'. Claudia confirms that she will not return to her husband, prompting Stephen to recall how Jesus said that he had come not to send peace but to bring a sword (Matthew 10:34), although, so he concludes, 'I did not think this sword would cleave Pilate's very household'. In connection with these moments of *Hill Humber One*, it is perhaps worth considering the most significant role that Erickson would play, *Tea and Sympathy*'s coach and housemaster Bill Reynolds, in both the Broadway show (1953) and the Hollywood film (1956): Robert Anderson's drama is set in a repressive prep school, where a new student, Tom (John Kerr), is brutally taunted for his supposed lack of manliness as 'sister boy' by his classmates, as well as by Erickson's coach, whose wife (Deborah Kerr) will comfort the young man and utter the immortal parting line to him: 'Years from now, when you talk about this – and you will – be kind'. It would be too much to push the comparison, of course, but the pattern of a wife who prefers the tender young man to her overtly macho and uncomprehending husband seems like a triangle common to both productions. When next we see Pilate, he is being awakened by Cassius in his bedroom. 'What is it, Cassius? Has Claudia been found? An insurrection?' he asks anxiously, sitting up in his (anachronistic) pyjamas, but the soldier brings him news of none of these things. Instead, he tells Pilate of Jesus' resurrection, which another soldier named Gallicus (Peter Mamakos), previously seen scoffing about Jesus, enters to confirm. 'Truth', Gallicus concludes, with a firm tone in his voice, 'is for those who will hear it'. The look on the face of Erickson's Pilate in this final shot is one of quiet perplexity. Abandoned by his wife and bewildered by the situation, he is no longer asleep but, we wonder, is he truly awake? Probably only a celibate priest like Padre or Peyton could think that the story of a wife leaving her husband would bring a soldier on a foreign battlefield much encouragement, but the point here is, of course, a larger one: what good is worldly power if it cannot protect the innocent? A montage follows, as word of the resurrection spreads, ending with the Virgin Mary who looks up at Cavalry in calm reflection and tells Peter: 'When you understand Golgotha, you will understand Bethlehem and the Eucharist'.

The scene dissolves, and we return to Padre and the soldiers, who have been intently listening during a pause in the gunfire. 'Well, fellas', he says, . . .

> That's the story of Hill Number One. Wheeler, you asked what's the meaning of all this? Well, if you look on Hill Number Forty-Six in the light of Hill Number One, hardship, suffering, self-sacrifice, is never without meaning. Out of these things, many virtues are born. Courage, heroism, love. When good men everywhere so fervently want peace, war is a crucifixion. It shakes the earth, darkens the sun, and makes men search for faith, and meaning, and right. As you're doing by asking, What's it all about? And right's worth defending. The first victory you achieve is always one of faith.

At these wise words from Padre, the soldiers nod their heads in agreement. It is not really the Korean conflict with its series of numbered hills in which they are fighting, nor any specific political cause at all, but a battle 'for faith, and meaning, and right' and, of course, against hopelessness. Up to this point, the story that has been recounted about Jesus has been a fairly ecumenical one, although the centrality of Mary and the recitation of the Lord's Prayer without the doxology do not conform to mainline Protestantism. In these last scenes, the religious sensibility of *Hill Number One* turns hard toward Catholic practice. 'It's all right here in the Rosary', Padre tells the men. Then, as the drama ends, we cut away to Father Peyton himself, in his Catholic priest's cassock and pellegrina, a choral figure urging viewers in his Irish brogue to pray the Rosary. A family of eight is seen kneeling in their living room, as Peyton continues his plea, concluding with his trademark phrase: 'The family that prays together, stays together'.

As a Holy Cross Father, Patrick Peyton's dedication to the Rosary was a deeply held personal devotion, to be sure, but it was one that took on a large-scale political significance in the years that followed his television ministry. 'The Rosary is the offensive weapon that will destroy Communism – the great evil that seeks to destroy the faith', he had proclaimed in a radio address in 1946. Over the course of the next two decades, he would bring his Family Rosary Brigade to Canada, the Philippines, South America and elsewhere, in large-scale rallies that had been secretly organised and paid for by the CIA in an effort to counter Communism and promote American values. When they learned of it, Peyton's Holy Cross superiors were very troubled by the intelligence agency's involvement in his work and informed Pope Paul VI in a letter that stated: 'If the CIA has agreed to furnish money to the Rosary Brigade for its work in Latin America, it is surely not because of any religious motivation, but because it believes that the Crusade, in its work, is a way to promote the American policy of appeasing the popular masses'. Peyton, although put on warning, continued operations as he had done up to that time, until the Pope ordered him to cease his collaboration with the CIA once and for all. 'Tell Father Peyton that I shall say a special Hail Mary for him' was His Holiness's final statement on the matter, but it is not the end of the story. Praying the Rosary, a practice that had been discouraged as too traditionalist in the years following Vatican II, came back into favour with Pope John Paul II, during whose anti-Communist papacy Peyton was nominated for saint-hood.[8] Family Theater Productions in fact released a documentary entitled *Pray: The Story of Patrick Peyton* in late 2020 to a limited number of theatres.[9]

In the Easter season of 1952, American TV audiences were presented with a primetime version of the Passion narrative that focused on the Roman prefect, titled *Pontius Pilate*. It was broadcast live on *Studio One*, CBS's critically acclaimed playhouse series. One of the network's premier primetime shows, *Studio One* was the brainchild of CBS's Director of Program Development, Worthington 'Tony' Miner, an innovator in the field of televised drama. It was Miner's opinion that high-quality drama ought not to be the province of only the wealthy. Speaking before the Theater Guild in Williamstown, Massachusetts, he had observed, . . .

> When we speak of the theater, we speak of one city – New York. Yet even within the confines of that one city, the theater isn't democratic. It is a Park Avenue nightclub, a luxury for a selective few with the price of admission. It is for the rich in the richest city of this country, and I believe this situation is deplored by every author, actor and manager in the business.[10]

Pontius Pilate featured an original script by Michael Dyne (and later revised, as we shall discuss, by the producer with significant consultation) and starred Cyril Ritchard as Pilate and Geraldine Fitzgerald as his wife Procula. Miner felt strongly that bringing drama to the masses was a worthy and indeed patriotic goal, and the particular investment ought to be put into direction 'to give those stories a visual life and a zing'.[11] The dynamism that can be felt in it is very much owing to the direction of Franklin Schaffner, a great talent who later would go on to fame with his 1968 sci-fi masterpiece *Planet of the Apes* and win an Oscar for 1970's *Patton*. As he had for other *Studio One* productions, Schaffner employed a set of moving cameras to give the show an appearance livelier than any of the productions of Cathedral Films or Family Theater with their static cinematography could boast. A technically more proficient production, with a better developed script that gives more nuanced focus to the inner lives of the characters and featuring a cast of highly regarded professionals, *Studio One*'s production of *Pontius Pilate* is a gem from a period and genre that has received too little attention from scholars in the field of Bible and cinema studies.

We hear the shouts of a mob outside and see a worried Procula running to the window as *Pontius Pilate* opens it, very much *in medias res*. To buy himself time to think about how to deal with this sticky situation, Pilate has sent Jesus off to Herod, although his wife tells him that she cannot understand why he has not simply released the man if he is innocent. He recounts to Procula his dealings with the prisoner, whose refusal to answer questions directly and whose mystical invocation of truth Pilate as a judge found to be frustrating. The situation weighs heavily on him, as is evident in Ritchard's performance, and the sound of the crowd heard outside again as they talk only exacerbates his anxiety and irritation. 'My dear', Pilate tells his wife. 'Do you suppose for one moment that that mob of malcontents and beggars that follow him are even remotely interested in the truth? What they would like to do is to storm this palace, string Herod and me up by the neck and put up some crazy revolutionary government of their own'. 'Oh Pontius', she replies in reassurance, certain that he has misunderstood what Jesus stands for. 'Why, he's no more capable of starting a revolution than I am'. The larger implications of what seems to be an innocuous comforting remark will become clearer as the play continues.

In the scene that follows, Caiaphas (Berry Kroeger) and Annas (Richard Purdy) enter to make their case against Jesus on the charge of blasphemy, an idea rejected outright by Procula, who has asked to remain silent. 'Perhaps you do not understand what that means to us, my lady', Annas chides her, although she reminds him that she is half Jewish herself. 'You, a Jewess, defend this man?' he demands of her, to which the prefect's wife replies: 'Because I am a Jewess, I defend justice'. A matter not found in the literary tradition, the Jewish background of Procula is an innovation arising, as we shall see, from negotiations during production with network executives and religious experts. When Procula again disputes with the priests as they argue for their rights as guardians of the law, Pilate silences them and reminds them heatedly that it is he, not they, who represents the law. In another innovation, Herod (Francis L. Sullivan) enters at this point to confer with the priest and the prefect. He points out that Jesus is a problem for all three parties:

We are quite aware that this man represents a threat to all of us. (To the priests) If he proves to be the Messiah, your powers will be considerably curtailed. If he's the hereditary king, I lose my throne. (To Pilate) And if the people rise and join him as seems most likely, it will lead to a revolutionary war with Rome.

Offended by this characterisation of them as acting not out of religious duty but simple self-interest, Caiaphas and Annas depart, leaving Herod alone with Pilate. Looking out the window, he draws Pilate's attention to the crowd outside – ten-thousand strong and many in his pay, against the hundred or so soldiers at the prefect's command – and reminds Pilate that there are only two years left in his term before he can retire back to Rome in good graces. 'This is your moment, Pilate', Herod tells him. 'A crowd is a wonderful thing, a terrible thing, the weapon of power, the anvil of the mighty'. With this threat of civil unrest and personal ruin thrown down as a gauntlet, Herod makes his exit.

'My head is splitting', Pilate says after his departure, another innocuous remark that in fact means far more than it originally seems, for Pilate is indeed finding himself at a breaking point, torn by his private doubts and his public duty. As Procula rubs his aching temples, they speak of the home that they have often talked of building outside Rome – 'the house with the white pillars', an ancient version of the American Dream's one-story ranch with a white picket fence. But this vision of their future life together in the suburbs is one that Procula feels compelled to confront. 'Oh, I have dreamed of the house with the white pillars as much as you', she says. 'But I always thought that if I were faced with a crisis, I could choose what was difficult, even fatal, because I loved you'. His response is to draw a distinction between the private life he will have with her and the public role he must now fulfil:

> You are not called upon to make judgment outside your home. I am not so fortunate. The man I am with you, here in my home, is not always the man I have to be in my courtroom. I live in the world. I am forced to compromise. But the beginning of all wisdom is compromise. It's the basis of all success in government.

Dismissively he concludes by telling her: 'You judge life with the arbitrary intolerance of a child'. This she counters by saying: 'I judge it with the intolerance of a woman who's loved a man and believed in him completely for a long time'. The rest of her remarks demolish his carefully cultivated distinction between public and private selves:

> I cannot believe in you in one room and doubt you in another. I cannot respect you as my husband and question you as a judge. If it's true that you have indeed fought all these years for the principle of justice, then you should be ready to leave this palace with nothing for the sake of your principle.

Thinking of Herod's threats, Pilate doubles down on his role in the public sphere, remarking that she 'has never lived through revolution'. He has, and he has seen the innumerable people killed in such unrest. Emphasising again the distinction between his private and public selves, Pilate then turns back on her to say: 'It's unjust of you to use our marriage as a weapon to sway my judgment'.

Procula's comforting remarks in response at this moment represent only a pause, not an end, to their argument, for she clearly will not be dissuaded by the distinction that he is drawing between his public and private selves, nor by his condescending assurance of knowing best. Their argument resurfaces after she returns from Golgotha, where she has watched the agonising death of the innocent man put on the cross by her husband's command. 'But I saw something else in the midst of this horror', she tells him. 'Suddenly, he was beyond your soldiers with their gleaming breastplates and their spears. There was nothing they could do to him, nothing. He'd passed beyond the thunder and the wind into a silence splendid, terrible, and perfect'. Again, Pilate attempts to dissuade her from the import of the brutality that she has seen and to encourage her to trust in him. 'It is our life together', he tells her, at length, that is the most important thing. 'Do you understand? The walls of our house that shut out the anger and the pain. If I have wrestled with the intrigues and bitter, twisted wickedness of this city so long, it is only that we should retire sooner and lead the life that we've dreamed of'. Her reply to this invocation of their dream life together in the suburbs is devastating. 'Oh', she says quickly, but with a sense of an unshakeable realisation. 'So it is for *me* that you let him die'. At this moment, it seems clear, she has seen through her husband's weakness and self-regard and now refuses to accept herself as the excuse for his cowardly failure to spare an innocent man's life. That Jesus was killed, somehow, on her behalf and for her future comfort is one hypocrisy too many for Procula to bear now.

If we were to leave the description of this Pontius Pilate with a sense only of his hypocrisy, however, it would not be an entirely fair representation of the prefect's story as told here on *Studio One*. While a stifling materialism is front and centre for Pilate's wife in this drama, the experience of war hovers in the background for her military husband. In defending his own decision to put one innocent man to death, Pilate does not silently accept Procula's condemnation, snapping instead that she has never been through a war. 'I have', he reminds her. 'I've seen a city set on fire, buildings burned, and the people pillaged and tortured'. In *Hill Number One*, the Korean battlefield was deliberately set before the viewer as a frame of reference for the Biblical story. How many families watching *Studio One* in their living rooms, we wonder, would have had sons serving in Korea at the time, sons they fervently hoped would make it home alive from the sorts of atrocities that Pilate describes? How many others watching in their living rooms had wartime experiences of their own in Europe or the Pacific, just a few years before? When they were saving the world from fascism, we can imagine at least a few of them thinking, nobody was telling them to turn the other cheek, or discouraging them from dreaming about the suburban houses which they hoped they might own one day, if they survived.

'Do not let this come between us', he tells Procula at the end of the scene. In vain, as it turns out, for when the next scene opens, fifteen years later, we see that Pilate is a governor in Cappadocia with a second wife, Calpurnia. Played with wonderful flamboyance, Madge Elliott was Cyril Ritchards's wife in real life, and their wedding was a celebrity event that many viewers would have remembered. Calpurnia is clearly comfortable in her rich clothing and jewellery, although Pilate himself spends his days signing arrest warrants for the growing number of Christians in his new province, a thing that makes him unbearably gloomy, as Calpurnia tells a friend (Anthony Hawtrey): 'This is a terrible thing to say, Lucius. But I don't believe he wants these Christians to recant. He likes to see them crucified. He thinks that by sentencing them to death that he could stamp out some obsession in himself'. Haunted by guilt, evidently, Pilate's heart has grown hard in the intervening years toward religion in general, and he has become something of a nihilist. 'To deny the existence of God', he tells the same friend, 'is the one honest tribute one can pay him'. At this, Lucius, who has expressed his admiration for the Christians' courage, fiddles with a bracelet, evidently as uncomfortable with Pilate's inflexibility as is his new wife. At this point, an attendant notes that the Christian ringleaders have been apprehended and are awaiting him in his chambers. Who should he see among them but his former wife, Procula, her hair now white but her spirit stronger than ever? They exchange some private words. 'I think it is very fitting that you should judge me', she says, without irony. 'At least I'm certain of a fair trial'. But he is deeply angry with her, more as a husband than as a governor. 'It seems that I was deceived in placing so high a value on the bond of marriage', he tells her, to which she will give the enigmatic reply: 'I never loved you more than when I left you. I had to give up what I loved most in order to learn to love more'. Angry and frightened at her resolve, Pilate demands that she sign the oath of allegiance to the emperor, even as he knows she will not. Having repudiated his authority as a husband, she now refutes him as a public authority as well. The next morning, Pilate can hear the screams of those who has ordered to be killed, seems to rescind his previous command and then agonises before the window dramatically holding out his sword, with the evident intention of killing himself.

The drama ends with this tragic moment for the prefect, but *Studio One*'s programme continues with not one but two framing devices that, as they throw light on the cultural circumstances in which *Pontius Pilate* was made, are deserving of extended comment. After Pilate's final demonstration of his sword, the screen darkens, and a carefully worded condemnation of anti-Semitism follows, delivered by an authoritative narrator over an image of the empty cross slowly dissolving to another of an Old Master crucifixion:

> The crucifixion was done, but nothing was settled. Nothing was ended. The agony goes on and has never been stilled.
>
> Roman soldiers drove the first nails through those hands and feet. Were they the crucifiers? No, not alone. Was it Rome? 1,900 years ago, yes, in part. So in part was the emissary of Rome and a few men in high places who were jealous of their position and who were afraid.
>
> But not the people of Rome, who knew nothing about it, nor the people of Judea, many of whom loved and followed the one who had died on the cross.
>
> But this is not answer enough, for the crucifixion still goes on. Every hour of every day, the agony is reenacted.
>
> This is the season of reminder to look to ourselves. The guilt or innocence is in our own hearts, for anyone today as then who lives in fear, anyone who would secure his own well-being by sacrificing these principles, anyone who would still his conscience to his own gain, anyone who would by false dealing or false report cause hurt to another, anyone who would throw the blame for Jesus' death on another man, another race, or another people, is himself crucifying Christ again.
>
> Look to ourselves. It is only we every hour of every day who cause the agony to go on.

This is an expressive and poignant declaration. In seeking to place blame for the crucifixion on 'ourselves' – what W. H. Auden had called 'the normal human heart' in *September 1, 1939* – it emphatically distances *Studio One*'s production from the traditional anti-Semitism associated with the Passion play narratives. As such, however, these remarks were not an original part of Michael Dyne's screenplay.

The circumstances behind how these sentiments came to be appended to the (near) end of *Pontius Pilate* was discussed decades later by producer Tony Miner, who called it something about which 'I was made to feel deeply ashamed at the start. [. . .] It was a matter of sudden revelation; it was a matter of unpardonable ignorance'.[12] In an interview in 1985 for the *Director's Guild of America Oral History* series, Franklin Schaffner, the director of *Pontius Pilate*, spoke with Miner to get the story-behind-the-story of the producer's reckoning with the anti-Semitism of the Passion Play tradition. Miner noted that, although Dyne's script had been unsolicited, he could tell immediately that it was the work of a writer 'of unmistakeable quality' and would be perfect for the Easter season. Handing it to the CBS head office after light editing, he was surprised to hear soon thereafter that the network had some issues with the script. They had been contacted by representatives of B'nai B'rith and asked Miner to consult them. Meeting with a small delegation at the Commodore Hotel, the B'nai B'rith spokesman (whose name Miner cannot recall) acknowledged *Pontius Pilate* to be 'an enthralling document'. Yet, he was troubled by the plan to air it during Passover week, noting 'the fact that some eighty-five to ninety percent of all pogroms' took place close to Passover. It was a matter that could not be treated lightly, he told the producer: 'It is too persistent a part of our history'.

Miner was mortified to hear all of this, telling Schaffner: 'Having been brought up in an atmosphere of casual, but nonetheless inexorable anti-Semitism, I fully understood, I thought, the apprehension of any Jew toward the mention, no matter how oblique, of their 2,000-year persecution'. While he had felt that he had shed his prejudices in this regard, 'it came as a stunning shock that I had yet failed to recognize the monstrous threat this script presented'. He offered to cancel the show right away, stating: 'One television show seemed a trivial matter in the shadow of such inhumanity'. But the B'nai B'rith spokesman did not feel such a drastic response to be necessary, telling him: 'Don't give up so soon. We've dredged our way out of worse than this'. And then in an almost casual tone he asked: 'Have you ever met Moses Jung?" A prolific writer for the Jewish popular press as well as a professor of Comparative Religion at Columbia University, Jung was an expert on interfaith dialogue and would be the co-author of a 1963 volume entitled *Relations Among Religions:*

A Handbook of Policies and Principles. Miner had not heard of Jung but, upon their meeting a few days later, 'I fell in love with him on the spot'. After some good-natured ribbing at Miner's expense, the eminent Professor Jung agreed to look over the script and offer some revisions. 'I am no Savonarola', he told the grateful producer. 'My mission is not to torture, but to soothe'. When they next met, Jung suggested that the heart of the problem in the original script was the depiction of Annas and Caiaphas – Dyne had depicted them as leaders of the Jewish state, but, as Miner notes, the 'moment they were depicted as Quislings, they at once became the enemies of the Jewish people and the Jewish state'. As painful as it was to have his biases pointed out to him, Miner concluded that this had ultimately been an instructive episode for him:

> As we know, all prejudice is at a minimum in theatre. Anti-Semitism is all but nonexistent; yet the roots of bigotry run deep. Too often our native prejudices are betrayed by some sin of omission, rather commission. Every man's history is part of mine. We have an obligation to explore the legends of good and evil alike, of those we have reason to cherish, as well as those we have reason to shun.

With the relevant portion of the script revised to reflect Jung's suggestion, all subsequent obstacles were swept away, and *Pontius Pilate* made its way to broadcast, 'far more effective dramatically than it had been before'.[13]

Far more dramatic undoubtedly, but nonetheless, the contextualising material that surrounds *Pontius Pilate* points to larger issues in the presentation of the programme. In *Fahrenheit 451*, the famous dystopian novel he would publish in 1953, Ray Bradbury had imagined a time in which Jesus would appear on TV 'making veiled references to certain commercial products that every worshipper absolutely needs'.[14] As religious programmes, Father Friederich's *The Living Christ* and Father Peyton's *Hill Number One* had both been presented without advertisements – unless one were to conclude that the programmes themselves were advertisements for the churches which had funded them. But by contrast, *Studio One* was heavily bankrolled by the American manufacturing company Westinghouse, whose overriding interest in *Pontius Pilate*, as with any other programme in the *Studio One* showcase, was as a vehicle for promoting its products. Corporate executives, hoping not to look like Philistines, had clearly given some thought to the appropriate way to handle this matter, and so *Pontius Pilate* opened with a voice-over intoning: 'Because of the nature of tonight's program, Westinghouse does not wish to interrupt the story with commercial messages. Therefore, our product demonstrations will precede and follow the play'. And so, just before the agonising tale of Pilate wrestling with his conscience came on the air, viewers turned to official Westinghouse spokeswoman Betty Furness touting the company's new 21-inch screen television set with 'the amazing development called the electronic clarifier' on sale for $299.95 (a TV ad for a new TV that could hardly be a more apt illustration of Marshall McLuhan's famous adage 'The medium is the message'). An even clumsier transition came at the end of the programme: 'It is only we every hour of every day who cause the agony to go on' run the final lines of *Pontius Pilate*, as we have noted – a brave indictment of the production as well as of its viewership who might well have taken from it a moment for self-reflection. A darkness of four seconds follows, and then a jarring trill of cheerful music brings Betty Furness back again in 'Jane's Twins Arrived!' – a short vignette about the delivery of a brand-new matching set of washer and dryer. She walks over and shows us how simple the machines are to operate, with nothing more required than the setting of a dial and the press of a button. 'Now then, isn't that just the easiest way you ever heard of to cut out all of the work of wash day?' she asks. There is a quip to be made here along the lines of 'cutting out all of the work of wash day' and 'Pilate washing his hands', of course, but it is worth avoiding the ironic detachment of a too easy pot-shot in order to look instead into the ideological paradox that the very awkwardness of this ad reveals (Figure 3.1).

'Why, he's no more capable of starting a revolution than I am', Procula had said of Jesus earlier in the programme; she should indeed be considered a revolutionary figure, perhaps even more so than the sponsors of the *Studio One* play had intended. When Joseph of Arimathea had sought the body of Jesus after the crucifixion, he explained to Pilate his need to make amends, because he had been told to sell all his things and not done so. In response to Lucius' query about whatever became of Procula, Pilate responds that she disappeared suddenly, 'without warning, without a word to anyone, she left everything – her home, her family, her future, everything'. The most noble figures who appear onscreen in *Pontius Pilate* are those who feel that, in order to do the will of Jesus, they must renounce their claim to the things of this world. It is one thing to watch figures from the Bible walking away from their material goods, but it is another thing altogether to see a housewife who has long dreamed of owning a suburban home 'with white pillars' tell her husband that she no longer wants anything to do with him, the house, or any of the things they own. What should the husband and wife watching at

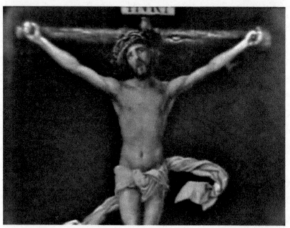

Figure 3.1 Concluding images from Studio One's production of *Pontius Pilate* (1951). Pilate (Cyril Ritchard) prepares to kill himself, followed by an Old Master print of the Crucifixion, and then by an advertisement for a washer and dryer set.

home make of such a programme? If it is hard to reconcile Betty's enthusiasm about her new washer and dryer with Procula's desire to renounce all of her worldly possessions, it can only be because those things cannot be reconciled, four-second darkening of the screen notwithstanding. In the midst of unprecedented material prosperity at the dawn of the Pax Americana, there is nevertheless a sense of spiritual dissatisfaction nagging at all three of the productions about Pilate that we have considered here. *Day of Triumph* perhaps seems least troubled by any internal conflicts, and its Mr and Mrs Pilate seem a fatuous pair, enjoying as bland a middle-class lifestyle as Barbara Billingsley would do later on *Leave It To Beaver*. But in *Studio One*'s *Pontius Pilate* and *Hill Number One*, the marriage of Pilate and his wife is not strengthened by their encounter with Jesus, but in fact destroyed by it. In considering her husband and the materialism he represents, it is almost as if these versions of Pilate's wife had been reading an advance copy of 1963's *The Feminine Mystique*. 'After the loneliness of war', Betty Friedan would write there with great compassion, 'and the unspeakableness of the bomb, against the frightening uncertainty, the cold immensity of the changing world, women as well as men sought the comforting reality of home and children'.[15] Indeed, it might very well seem like a communist idea to suggest that there is any problem with being a homeowner with a television set, a lover of worthwhile drama, a liberally-minded opponent of anti-Semitism and, of course, a discriminate purchaser of quality Westinghouse products.

NOTES

1 Bradbury (2003: 109–10).
2 'The Pilgrimage Play', *American Film Institute: Catalog*, https://catalog. afi.com/Film/26192-THE-PILGRIMAGEPLAY (accessed 1 December 2020).
3 See generally Suit (2018).
4 Suit (2018: 151).
5 Peyton (2018: 335).
6 Tillich (1952: 174–75).
7 Peyton (2018: 77–90).
8 Wilford (2008: 182–196).
9 See https://www.praythefilm.com/ (accessed 1 December 2020).
10 Fraser (1982).
11 Schaffner (1985: 195).
12 This and all subsequent quotations are taken from Schaffner (1985: 236–43).

13 In connection with this, some networks had refused to air Cathedral's
   I Beheld His Glory in 1951, on the grounds that the production was
   anti-Semitic, so notes Suit (2018: 126).
14 Bradbury (2003: 109–10).
15 Friedan (2001: 268–69).

4 Mrs Pilate: Claudia Procula and Clare Boothe Luce

While he was sitting on the judgment seat, his wife sent word to him, 'Have nothing to do with that innocent man, for today I have suffered a great deal because of a dream about him'.

– Matthew 27:19

From this single sentence in the Gospels, a rich set of legends has grown about Pontius Pilate's spouse, named Procla or the more Roman-sounding Procula in the tradition. Although it is brief and not physical in nature, Matthew portrays her suffering as aligned and in sympathy with Jesus' own suffering. As a consequence of her perceived participation in Jesus' passion, the belief arose as early as the second century AD that she was the first Gentile woman to convert to Christianity and, as such, she has been canonised in the Greek Orthodox and Abyssinian Churches. That the dream of Pilate's wife closely seemed to resemble that of Caesar's wife, Calpurnia, before his assassination suggested a Roman aristocratic background, and later commentators connected her with the Claudia mentioned in Second Timothy (4:21). By the Renaissance, her name had been filled out to Claudia Procula, and she was further imagined to be a member of the Julio-Claudian family, perhaps a niece or even daughter of Emperor Tiberius. Whether Pilate's wife ever actually existed may not be known – although there is, in fact, archaeological proof of a woman in the later first century BC buried near Beirut with two golden bracelets on which the name Claudia Procla has been inscribed in Greek – her legend developed for those audiences of Gentile Christian women to whom such a figure would have had much appeal.[1]

As brief as her anonymous mention is in the Bible, the afterlife of Pilate's wife in the later tradition is extensive, and she features in genres as varied as New Testament apocrypha, late antique legends, medieval art and drama, Romantic poetry and contemporary novels. Her character, likewise, runs the gamut of portrayal: a major figure in the 30th York Mystery Play, for instance, where she is called Percula and her dream is inspired by the devil, she speaks highly of her husband – 'my duke doughty', she calls him – and of herself says: 'All welle of all womanhede I am, wittie and wise'. In the early Victorian era, Charlotte Bronte imagined a less happy marriage for the unnamed spouse in *Pilate's Wife's Dream* (1846):

> Forced to sit by his side and see his deeds;
> Forced to behold that visage, hour by hour,
> In whose gaunt lines the abhorrent gazer reads
> A triple lust of gold, and blood, and power;
> A soul whom motives fierce, yet abject, urge –
> Rome's servile slave, and Judah's tyrant scourge.
>
> How can I love, or mourn, or pity him?
> I, who so long my fetter'd hands have wrung;
> I, who for grief have wept my eyesight dim;
> Because, while life for me was bright and young,
> He robb'd my youth – he quench'd my life's fair ray –
> He crush'd my mind, and did my freedom slay.

In fictional depictions, the story of Pilate's wife has been vastly expanded upon in sometimes wildly innovative ways. In a novel written in 1929 but only published posthumously in 2000, H. D. (Hilda Doolittle) gives her protagonist the name Veronica and imagines her not just a follower of Jesus but in fact his saviour, rescuing him from the cross by administering an opiate that gives him the appearance of death, from which he is resurrected three days later. More recent treatments continue in this creative tradition. Antoinette May's *Pilate's Wife* (2007) is a standard romance novel in which the heroine routinely has prophetic dreams because she is a clairvoyant (not unlike the celebrity psychic Sylvia Celeste Browne, whose memoir May had co-authored just a few years earlier). The self-published 2014 novel *Claudia Procula: Wife of Pontius Pilate, Friend of Mary Magdalene* by Kris Darquis reveals, according to the press's website, that Jesus married Mary Magdalene and that Claudia helped 'both of them to escape to Languedoc, where [she] had been brought up, in today's town of Narbonne'.[2]

The imaginative treatment of Claudia Procula in the popular literature found similar expression in the small-screen dramas of the mid-century, as was noted in the last chapter. From this same period comes perhaps the most intriguing portrait of Claudia, although it was a production that never made it from the page to the screen. From March of 1951 through the spring of the following year, Clare Boothe Luce worked diligently on a concept for RKO Pictures to be titled *Pilate's Wife*, which told the story of the Passion from the perspective of the prefect's new spouse, Claudia. As the eighteen-year-old niece of Emperor Tiberius, Claudia develops over the course of the story from a spoiled young aristocrat interested in nothing but her own amusement into a figure of keener spiritual depth. The discussion of *Pilate's Wife* given below is based on Luce's sixty-one-page screen treatment of the story, dated 25 September 1951 and now held in the archives of the Margaret Herrick Library in Beverly Hills. (While the Library of Congress does possess, among the vast trove of Luce's papers, a later version of the concept, a 199-page screenplay dated 29 April 1952, much of this is the work of Nicholas Ray, who had been hired by the studio to rewrite Luce's original; RKO would commission yet another version by Robert Wilder in 1954.) Although the 1951 treatment is bald in its descriptions, it seems to represent best the author's original idea for the story of Claudia. What it lacks in terms of the wit for which Luce was famous, it more than makes up for as a critical document of the time when the Catholicism to which she had converted was making its way into the mainstream of American life and when post-war American women were moving slowly toward second-wave feminism. It is this sense of the life of a modern woman like herself seen 'through a glass darkly' of an ancient Roman woman's story that gives particular significance to this unique and unfortunately never-produced Gospel according to Luce.

Clare Boothe Luce was, by any measure, one of the most remarkable women of the twentieth century. Over the course of seven decades, she was by turn an actress and socialite, an editor at *Vogue* and *Vanity Fair*, the author of the enormously successful and enormously catty play *The Women* (later to be made into a film starring Norma Shearer and Joan Crawford heading an all-female cast of over forty), a highly regarded journalist and war correspondent, an Oscar-nominated screenwriter, a Congresswoman from Connecticut, the Ambassador to Italy, a seriously considered vice-presidential candidate and, in 1983, the recipient of the Presidential Medal of Freedom. The elements that made Luce famous are easily sensed in the maiden speech she delivered before the House of Representatives in February 1943. Reacting to Vice President Henry Wallace's proposal for opening

American airports up to free international access, she praised the innovativeness of his approach, although memorably concluding: 'But much of what Mr. Wallace calls his global thinking is, no matter how you slice it, still "globaloney"'. As such a remark shows, she was a dependable member of the Republican establishment, and it was for her dedication to a conservative ideology that the Heritage Foundation's highest honour – bestowed upon Margaret Thatcher, Ronald Reagan and William F. Buckley Jr, among others – was named for her in 1991. But the 'globaloney' quip, which instantly made her a darling of the press and the public, highlights Luce's ready way with words. 'They say that women talk too much', she once remarked. 'If you have worked in Congress, you know that the filibuster was invented by men'. The only person to ever outmatch Luce's rapier wit was her ardent enemy, Dorothy Parker. As one famous but probably apocryphal story goes, the two women were once trying to exit through the doorway of a New York building at the same time. Luce gave way to her, cracking: 'Age before beauty'. Sweeping forward, Parker replied within earshot of all: 'And pearls before swine'.[3]

Clare Boothe Luce was also, as it happens, married to Henry R. Luce, the founder of the Time-Life magazine franchise and one of the century's most influential men. Theirs was not a happy marriage. Not so much a union of like minds as an alliance of supremely vaunting ambitions, the Luces' partnership can perhaps only be compared to Franklin and Eleanor Roosevelt, or still better, to Zeus and Hera. As formidable a figure as Clare Boothe Luce was, there is a way in which she was overshadowed throughout her impressive career by her powerful media magnate husband. In the late 1930s, for instance, the couple had visited London – he to inspect Time-Life's British headquarters, she to see the West End production of *The Women*. While in town, she arranged through a friend to carry out the lifelong dream of meeting George Bernard Shaw and was introduced to him by her maiden name, Clare Boothe, the name under which her play was listed. They had a very pleasant lunch and the next day, as she recounted, . . .

> I received a postal card from Shaw, written by his very own hand. I read it, and propped it up in front of the clock on the mantel piece. When my husband came in, I, very proud, said, 'Darling, I got a postal card – a postal card from George Bernard Shaw. Over there. Read it'. Very triumphant. He read,
>> 'My dear Clare Boothe,
>> In the delirious pleasure of our visit yesterday, I quite forgot to inquire if there was anything I could do to make your stay, and Mr. Boothe's, more pleasant.
>> G. B. S'.

Harry's face fell. I feel sure that Shaw knew that my husband was Henry Luce. [. . .] I think that that postal card was sheer Shavian impishness – what would be called today, a 'put-down' of my husband. Or, perhaps, knowing how much more important my husband was than I, he was trying to build me up. Anyway, that was the first and last time in my life I met anyone of importance who didn't know – or pretended not to know – who my husband was.[4]

Imagine what that must have been like: to have a play running con-currently on Broadway and in the West End, to lunch with George Bernard Shaw himself, to have sitting on your mantel piece a post-card praising the 'delirious pleasure' of your company signed by the same and yet somehow to have the anecdote be about the feelings of your husband.

It seems clear enough that, in many respects, *Pilate's Wife* is a roman à clef for the life of the Publisher's Wife (Figure 4.1). The contentious dealings between the partners of the American Century's premier power couple suggests an important lens through which to view the work, but the kernel of the story undoubtedly grows from Clare's decision to become a Roman Catholic in 1946, shortly after the death of her only child from a previous marriage, the twenty-one-year-old Ann Brokaw, killed in a car-crash during her senior year at Stanford University. For Clare, the story of *Pilate's Wife* was one of deep fascination and identification. As she wrote at the time, '[a]lmost from the day of my conversion, I knew I had to do this picture in Hollywood. [. . .] My mind teems with ideas and thoughts. What is clearest, just now, is that this must not be a 'Spectacle' – a technicolor orgy. [. . .] It must be pitched at a *psychological* level – for its interior rather than visual impact'.[5] The psychological dimension was a complex one indeed. Henry nominally supported Clare's con-version but, due to his Protestant missionary upbringing, was himself unwilling to become a Catholic. 'Of course her great interest is that I should follow her', Luce once said of his wife's new religion. 'But that won't happen. I have what has been called, "The Presbyterians' invin-cible ignorance"'.[6] But there is a still more complicated element to the story of Clare's conversion: the deep-seated unhappiness which char-acterised the Luces' marriage resulted in frequent infidelities on the part of both spouses. Henry, too cowardly to ask for a divorce from Clare and worried about the effect on his reputation, had evidently encouraged her embrace of Catholicism in order to force a breakup of the marriage. After his lawyer had visited Clare at home in July 1946 to say that she 'owed it' to Roman Catholicism to leave her husband, she wrote Henry a long, bitter note, concluding: 'But mostly

Figure 4.1 Clare Boothe Luce and Henry Luce in New York City, 1954. *World Telegram & Sun* photo by Phil Stanziola. Commons.wikimedia.org.

you aided me into the church [...] because you believed my conversion would mean *your* legal freedom'.[7] A husband's reluctance to accept his wife's sudden but sincere embrace of a new religion, the manipulations within the marriage of a powerful couple and, of course, the adultery were all matters that Clare felt to be as true for Claudia in the first century AD as they were for herself in the mid-twentieth.

The film, as noted, was never made, although not for lack of interest on the part of RKO Studios chief Howard Hughes, who sent a payment to Luce of $11,250 for a detailed outline of the project in May 1951. Over the course of the next year or so, as Luce worked to craft the story and fill out dialogue, the film was promoted by RKO's publicity department, who suggested that either René Clair or Curtis Bernhardt might direct and that Laurence Olivier and Vivien Leigh might star, although Luce herself expressed her preference that Jean Simmons take the title role. Various other projects vied for Luce's attention during the early years of the 1950s, however, including (but not limited to) the planning and dedication of Saint Ann's chapel in Palo Alto in memory of her daughter, the writing and staging of a new religious play, *Child of the Morning*, and, above all, her dedicated campaigning on behalf of Dwight D. Eisenhower for the presidency, an effort for which she would be rewarded with the appointment as Ambassador to Italy in 1952. In the end, Luce herself never returned to the project, and *Pilate's Wife* remains a great what-if in the history of American mainstream religious cinema.

As Luce's script opens, we see Pilate as an old man in his apartment in Rome writing a manuscript, the title of which is 'The True Facts Concerning the Trial of Jesus of Nazareth, by C. Pontius Pilate, a Knight of the Equestrian Order and Procurator of Judea by Tiberius Caesar in the 15th year of his reign . . .' (1).[8] The scene dissolves to a map of Palestine, which is revealed to be lying on the captain's desk of the ship that is bringing Pilate to the province to which he has been newly appointed. On board along with him is his new bride, Claudia, whom Luce describes as 'sensual, impetuous, willful, and amoral, like most privileged young pagans of an empire and civilization in decline'. A sort of first-century flapper, she is unimpressed with the province, called in the screen treatment 'the Roman sticks', but finds consolation in the thought of the fortune he will be able to make here. 'She is cheered even more', the treatment continues, 'by a glimpse, in the garden below, of two handsome young men: the dark Ben-Ezra, and the fair Antonius. She conceals this from Pilate: we see he is jealous, and she is a flirt' (4). Insofar as Claudia has any motivation in the early part of the story, it is to keep herself entertained in her otherwise unexciting surroundings by carrying on dalliances with the younger men of her acquaintance and trying to keep her husband wrapped around her finger. She is talking with Antonius and Ben-Ezra coquettishly in a later scene but, just as they 'get going' (as it is put in the treatment), notices that the imperial standards are not being carried in procession. This irritates her as a scion of the Julio-Claudian household, and she lets her husband know it, but Pilate explains that he has been advised against doing so by his staff, for fear of antagonising the local population. 'But Claudia needles Pilate' into a display of Roman power that will ultimately backfire, 'in order to show who is master of Judea (and who is the mistress of Pilate)', as the treatment concludes (6).

The characterisation of Claudia in these early scenes seems to be equal parts Lady Macbeth and Lady Chatterley – she is ruthless on behalf of her spouse's career but at the same time dangerously flirtatious with his subordinates. An exchange between the pair early in the script outlines the situation clearly:

CLAUDIA:
Should I not be ambitious for you? Is not that a virtue in a wife?

PILATE:
Not the greatest.

CLAUDIA:
What then?

PILATE:
(A pause). Fidelity.

CLAUDIA:
But fidelity is no longer the fashion in Rome.[9]

The Luces were, like the Pilates, a highly accomplished couple, but they were highly adulterous as well. Affairs litter the pages of the biographies of each, and unsurprisingly adultery is a major theme in *Pilate's Wife* as well: 'After one look at Jerusalem', as the treatment makes plain (9), 'it is clear to Claudia that her only amusement will lie in flirtation'. Just as Claudia is instantly attracted to Antonius – whose name suggests Mark Antony, the great Roman general forever associated with his affair with Cleopatra – so had Clare a fateful weakness for soldiers throughout her life. 'For the most part, her attraction to men-at-arms was visceral and intellectual rather than merely sexual', writes Sylvia Jukes Morris in her authorised biography of Clare, 'and they were beguiled by her understanding of their missions, as well as by her extraordinary personality and looks. Generals in both theaters were confessedly in love with her – Lucian Truscott in Europe and Charles Willoughby in the Pacific, not to mention Ray Stecker and the long list of officers, American and British, who at least found her irresistibly beautiful'.[10] In this regard, the parallels between Clare and Claudia are striking. At one point, Antonius is showing a view of Jerusalem to Claudia, who is 'bent on trying to make Antonius kiss her', although he, while 'plainly tempted by her loveliness and availability', rebuffs her advances out of 'loyalty to his chief' (13). The general of *Pilate's Wife* shows a greater respect for Claudia's marriage vows than some of the generals of her acquaintance did for Clare's.

Rejected by Antonius, Claudia nevertheless allows herself to be seduced later by Pilate's more cynical political Jewish advisor, Ben-Ezra, and ends up going with him into the city to carry on their affair. Afterwards, as the leave their secret love nest – 'a house "where people go" [. . .] even in Jerusalem' (22) – they come upon a woman being dragged away from the same place by a group of Pharisees. Clearly the woman taken in adultery from the Gospel of John (8:3–11), she is being brought to 'the Man', as Jesus is called here and for most of the story. 'Claudia, herself dressed as a Jewess', writes Luce at this point, 'emotionally identifies herself with the woman, and is horrified by what is about to happen to her', for she imagines that she will be stoned to death (23). Something more than curiosity compels her to follow, but the sudden sight of Herod's attendant Chusa and his wife Joanna, both of whom she has met before, frightens her. Has she been recognized, despite the disguise? Will her infidelity be revealed? She rushes home in fear, ignoring the reassurances of Ben-Ezra, and has just taken off her costume when her husband enters her room.

Cheerfully, Pilate has come to tell her that a great honour has been bestowed upon them. They have been invited to Herod's birthday banquet, although she is loath to attend, as an earlier encounter with Herodias, whom she considers 'an Arab slut' (17), had gone poorly. But her husband's surprise gift of some spectacular jewellery changes her mind as, 'womanlike, the opportunity to parade her jewels and impress Herodias overcome her fears' (24). Despite the occasion to flaunt her new baubles, the banquet does not go well. Relations between the two 'first ladies' of Judaea are not good to begin with, and to make matters worse both Antonius and Ben-Ezra happen to be present, as are Chusa and Joanna. Claudia, already uncomfortable, grows bored with the entertainment and prods her hostess into displaying John the Baptist, the prisoner about whom she has heard so much. John is presented to the dinner party, but he is far from the entertaining floor show that the guests had expected, and when he loudly denounces the adultery of Herodias and Herod – it is a scene derived directly from the Gospels (Matthew 14:3–4, Mark 6:17–18, Luke 3:19–20) – Luce's Claudia feels the sting of his words as well. Salome dances to cheer up the 'drunk and maudlin' Herod and, at Herodias' suggestion, demands John's head in response to the king's foolish promise that she be granted whatever she wants. When Herod quails at keeping this pledge, Claudia, who up to this point has been distracted, needles the king as she had her own husband earlier over the display of the Roman standards, although she does not seem to know what it was that Salome requested. John's head is subsequently brought out on a platter, at which Claudia reacts strongly and begins to quarrel with her hostess. The scene reaches its heated climax, as Luce writes, when 'Herodias accuses Claudia of being partially responsible for the beheading (which is true) and, being no better morally than Herodias herself, which is also true' (26–27). The argument between Herodias and Claudia at this point is certainly melodramatic and indeed might even be described as sensational, but it also represents Luce's story at its most allegorical. As is discussed more fully below, there is a simplistic metaphorical framework derived from Catholic tradition that juxtaposes Herodias and Claudia as feminine archetypes. On the one hand is Herodias, 'the Arab slut' (as Luce's Claudia calls her), who represents the loose morals of the East; on the other hand, Claudia, often depicted as her counterpart, is a symbol of Western marital fidelity and, for her inter-cession on Jesus' behalf, a saint in some churches. Working within and against this tradition, Luce seeks to complicate the allegory of *Pilate's Wife*, not by brightening the character of Herodias (who remains an unsympathetic figure) but by darkening the character of Claudia.

If there is a rock bottom that Claudia must hit before she ascends to the heights of prototypical feminine virtue, it comes in the scene to follow, which takes place in her room in Herod's palace. 'Now Pilate, at the end of his patience with Claudia, piles it on', the treatment reads. 'Claudia has certainly "bitched" everything between him and the Herods' (27). He is furious that she has interfered in the delicate political affairs of the region and furthermore gives voice to his suspi-cions about her fidelity. 'What did Herodias mean by insinuating that Claudia's morals were no better than her own?' Pilate jumps to the wrong conclusion at this moment, however. 'She referred to Antonius, didn't she?' Claudia, rattled by the accusation but relieved that her husband has miscomprehended, now gives in to her worst impulses to preserve her reputation before her husband. First – taking a cue from Phaedra or Potiphar's wife – she accuses Antonius of being the one to have made advances toward her, which she rebuffed time and again, but kept to herself out of the regard that she knew Pilate to have for his general. And then, to give her lie greater credibility, she blames her maid – a young Jewish woman named Rebecca, whom we have met in an earlier scene – of 'spreading untrue "backstairs" gossip to Herodias' maids'. She then summons Rebecca, accuses the innocent woman to her face and slaps her, adding that, 'if she were a Roman slave, she would be flogged'. She fires Rebecca, as Pilate leaves the room to confront Antonius and demote him to the rank of centurion. Her cynical lover Ben-Ezra later enters to comfort Claudia by telling her that 'she did right to brazen it out'. They resolve to find out whether Chusa and Joanna in fact know of their relationship, and if so, to find some way to keep them from revealing it (28).

In the following scene, the reversal of Claudia's fortune takes place after Chusa and Joanna are brought to her that evening. She asks them to join her staff, given that she has fired Rebecca, and offers other enticements as well, but the couple seem unaware that they are being bribed. Chusa excuses himself, for he must now go to speak about John's death with Jesus, whom he has not seen since the day that the woman taken in adultery was carried off to him. Luce imagines Claudia's reaction and the subsequent conversation (29):

> Claudia freezes. Now what she feared is coming. Chusa goes on: did Claudia hear how <u>that</u> incident turned out? No? Well, the Man said, 'Let him who is without sin cast the first stone' [. . .] and then He said, 'Go and sin no more'. Bowing respectfully, Chusa leaves.
> Claudia bursts into tears of mingled relief and shame.

Here is the crux of the story for Luce's Claudia, the '*psychological level*' and '*interior rather than visual impact*' for which the author has been striving throughout. As we read just a little later, '[s]he feels that He has forgiven <u>her</u> thru Chusa'. Undoubtedly, the identification of Pilate's wife and the publisher's wife at this moment is complete, as the sin of adultery is washed away through an act of indirect divine mercy. When Claudia asks Joanna by whose authority Jesus forgives sins, the older woman begins to tell her the entire story. As they look out the window at the stars, she says: 'He was born on a night like this, in a cave . . .' (30).

The scene dissolves into a montage, as we see John's body taken away by Chusa and others, Caiaphas and the Pharisees conferring, and groups of sick people coming to an offscreen Jesus, including one of Pilate's own centurions. Over this, Luce imagines in the treatment, we hear a voice-over from Pilate narrating the rise of Jesus' power with the people and his own growing sense of concern. Even some of his own soldiers have gone to him, he notes. We then cut to him looking out from his balcony to see Rebecca in the courtyard meeting with Claudia. He feels that his wife must be trying to bribe her former maid, but, in fact, it is quite a different conversation transpiring, as Claudia haltingly tries to apologise for what she has done. Rebecca makes it easy on her. She has 'been with the Man', as Luce writes, so she now 'turns the other cheek, and Claudia kisses it'. The sense of relief and happiness is instant and deep for both of them, and Claudia begins to speak more fully to Rebecca, whom she now increasingly finds a source of trust. Claudia confesses to Rebecca – the Catholic concept is one very much in Luce's mind here – her adultery with Ben-Ezra and seeks the maid's counsel, asking whether she should tell Pilate. As the treatment continues, 'Rebecca thinks not: what good would it do? The truth would cut him off from both her and Ben-Ezra and leave him with no one. Claudia must try to regain Pilate's confidence; he needs her' (32). It is a very curious sort of confession, accompanied by no act of penance, but Rebecca is a curious confessor, and a Hollywood screenplay is a curious confessional. Perhaps, given Luce's own frequent adultery, we might see this moment as a rather self-serving and even hypocritical one. But in any event, we can be certain that Pilate's wife has repented of her sin, and we should leave judgment of the publisher's wife to some higher authority. As the scene ends, Rebecca tells Claudia that her brother, a tax collector, has begun to follow Jesus, who has changed his name from Levi to Matthew (that Pilate's wife is only known from Matthew's Gospel likely suggested this to Luce). Jesus has also given Rebecca herself a new name: Veronica, which Claudia tells her is Greek for 'true image'. What this new appellation means neither of them can say, and they fall into good-natured laughter.

If Claudia is not quite up to an honest conversation with her husband about her infidelity, she at any rate goes on to break off her affair with Ben-Ezra. In the midst of the conversation with her lover, she asks him whether he thinks that she is in fact any different from Herodias. 'Oh, much more beautiful!' he replies, but Claudia is looking for something other than flattery; as result, Ben-Ezra reveals his low opinion of most women, and most men as well, including her vacillating husband. 'People are what they are in a dog-eat-dog world. Who can make them clean or whole?' (33). The cynicism which Ben-Ezra expresses here and which Claudia initially found so attractive now leaves her cold, and in the scene that follows, she tries harder to be a good wife. The following day, she and Pilate are eating dinner, but he is 'taciturn, broody', and although Claudia 'is being gentle, patient', it is still 'uphill going'. His anxieties about Jesus are mounting, and when she suggests that perhaps he 'should throw the weight of Rome behind the people's desire' and make him king, 'Pilate blows his top' (34). Despite his anger, Claudia persists, even suggesting that the two of them go incognito to listen to Jesus for themselves, for she understands him to be full of love and mercy. 'Why he even forgives the blackest sins', she insists, to which he replies with suspicion: 'What black sin has <u>she</u> got that a carpenter's son can forgive?' Claudia does not respond to this, evidently content to give advice about foreign matters, but unwilling still to engage in any open conversation about domestic affairs (35).

The rest of the story unfolds with Jesus in the background of the action but in the foreground of everyone's thinking. Pilate has built the aqueduct, and a procession that he is leading with Herod to inaugurate its unveiling is interrupted by quite another one – it is Palm Sunday, and Jesus is entering the city to the cheers of the crowd. Antonius is still sought out for advice by a flummoxed Pilate, but his more ruthless replacement, Flavius, 'itches to get his hands on the mealy-mouthed Galilean'. As Luce continues, 'the Man would have a chance afterwards to see if He could raise <u>Himself</u> from the dead' (39). Later, the elderly Jewish priest Annas comes to Pilate's house and manoeuvres him into agreeing to try Jesus if it can be proven that he is a threat to the Roman order. Claudia is not much more than a witness to these events which, by and large, follow the outline of the Gospels in a fairly straightforward fashion. Only after the arrest in the garden of Gethsemane is she once again involved as a principal figure. Rebecca and her brother Matthew come to inform Claudia that Jesus 'is being tried by a "kangaroo court", at Caiaphas' house' (42), but when she tries to get Pilate to intercede, he is out of reach to her. She and Antonius go to Caiaphas' house but are denied entrance, although they meet 'a stern, vigorous young man' coming out. It is Saul of Tarsus, who denounces Jesus' blasphemy and will ride to Damascus to inform the community there of the events transpiring in Jerusalem. Claudia witnesses these things herself all firsthand, and would tell Pilate about them, but to no avail. When she returns home, Pilate orders her confined to her room under lock and key (44).

The Passion narrative proceeds now without significant variant for the next section of the treatment, with the only exception that Claudia is able to convince Ben-Ezra to convey to Pilate that she has had a dream concerning these events of which he must take heed. But take heed he does not and, as he must, Pilate orders Jesus to be scourged. When he at long last finally comes to her in her room, she is distraught and overcome. He asks her about the dream, and she reveals that she has dreamt of a man who washed his hands

in a bowl of blood, 'and the blood flowed out of the bowl all over
Jerusalem and dyed the blue sea red, and flooded the brown Tiber –
and rose so high it drowned Rome and all that the Caesars had built
there!' Her words leave Pilate shaken, and she continues: 'Jesus is not
being judged. He has been sent to judge all of us – the evil in every
heart: the avarice of Caiaphas, the lust of Herod and Herodias, the
weakness and vacillation of Pilate himself'. When Pilate asks her
whether she herself will be judged, she says – and it is striking how
Luce once again postpones any admission on Claudia's part here
of wrongdoing – that she is guilty of ambition and selfishness, 'and
other sins she will tell him about sometime' (51–52).

At this moment, Flavius appears at the door: the scourging is
over, and Pilate must present Jesus before the crowd. The release of
Barabbas, the order for the crucifixion, all of it follows along. When
it has all been handed over to Flavius and his soldiers to be carried
out, Pilate silently returns into his house. He passes by Claudia's
door, thinks to enter, reconsiders and goes out onto his balcony.
At this moment, as he looks out over the courtyard, we hear an
exchange, based on the Gospel of John (Chapter 18):

PILATE'S VOICE
Are you the King of the Jews

A WHISPERED VOICE THAT IS AN ECHO
Do you say that I am?

The exchange continues, as Pilate again and again tries to ascertain
the situation and, again and again, the voice refuses to give him a
straight answer. Finally, the echo says: 'Everyone who loves the Truth
hears my voice'. 'What is truth?' Pilate replies harshly, according to
Luce's treatment (54–55).

Pilate withdraws back into his room and 'feverishly draws all the
curtains to blot out the distant view of Golgotha'. In the meantime,
Claudia discovers that the door to her chamber is open – Pilate had
intended to speak with her on the way to his chamber, but never got
any further than unbolting the lock – and she begins to leave with
Rebecca to follow Jesus as he makes his way to the cross. In the
courtyard, they meet Ben-Ezra who himself is leaving, although his
intention is simply to get away, stating that there is nothing more he
can do for Pilate. Realising that her cynical adviser is abandoning
her husband at his moment of greatest need, Claudia turns back to
the house. 'Her duty is with Pilate', writes Luce, and she makes her
way into his chamber, where he is absent-mindedly playing with dice.

Outside, the weather has become stormy, and the curtains throughout the scene billow in the wind, revealing intermittently the activity on Golgotha seen in the far background. Claudia tries to engage her distracted and morose husband, begging him 'to trust her', but it is without avail for he is beyond listening. At this moment, she begins to offer a 'straight-forward confession to Pilate', but the sudden arrival of a message about the arrival of troops from Syria disrupts the conversation. He laughs at the futility of it all, but we understand that Claudia will not be deterred from admitting her infidelity to him (56). The confession is not heard onscreen, but implied instead, as the wind continues to kick up and eventually tears the curtain of the chamber. When at last the storm subsides, we see Pilate and Claudia sitting together. He continues to throw the dice, but Luce gives no indication of his frame of mind.

At this moment, Joseph of Arimathea, Nicodemus and Matthew enter seeking permission to bury Jesus' body, which 'jesting Pilate' allows. With them has come Rebecca who, after an embrace, shows Claudia the scarf with which she had wiped Jesus' face as he carried his cross. Antonius now comes into the room, looking to join Joseph and the others in the burial, for, having heard Jesus' final words on the cross, he has become a believer. Rebecca exits with Antonius, leaving Claudia alone with her husband and the stained veil. 'If I had only seen his face', she says ruefully to Pilate and then looks down at the veil, on which is 'the imprint of the Man's face: "Veronica – the True Image!"' (58). Overcome by this miraculous answer to her wishes, she falls to her knees and holds it for her husband to see. 'We think, for a moment, he is convinced', Luce writes. 'Then his eyes grow clouded, he half smiles . . .

PILATE'S VOICE:
And yet, what was it, but a rag with the imprint on sweat and blood on it? (59).

With these as the last words, the scene in Jerusalem ends, a slow dissolve taking us next to Pilate's apartment in Rome many years later. He is much older now, and before his hearth is writing a manuscript. There is a bang on the door, and several soldiers enter, curtly telling him not to keep the courts of Caligula waiting any longer. 'He throws his script in the dying fire. As it blazes up, he "washes his hands" – an old gesture now with Pilate'. Hauled off before the emperor, himself now the defendant rather than the presiding magistrate, he is made to answer for his time in Jerusalem. Numerous charges are read out against him, including his seizing of funds from the Temple to be wastefully spent on 'some self-glorifying, utterly useless building project'. A deposition is also introduced from Herodias, indicating that Pilate had badly mistreated his wife, 'who sold her jewels to give them to the lepers, beggars and prostitutes, and made the riff-raff of Judea her companions'. Claudia had died of a foul disease, Herodias continues, in the house of Mary Magdalene – a scene that 'should be dramatized', Luce notes parenthetically. At the end, Pilate asks: 'Does it say anywhere in that indictment that he tried and crucified a Man called Jesus of Nazareth?' The magistrate looks blankly at him. 'What does one killing of one Jew mean to the world?' he asks, before sentencing Pilate to life in exile. The next case brought in is a certain Saul of Tarsus, whose own letters, although written under another name, prove that he is a follower of Christ, while Pilate looks over his shoulder as he is dragged away (60).

Pilate's Wife never saw production, of course, but it is worth taking a moment to consider what might have been the movie's impact had Luce seen the script through to completion and RKO committed itself to filming. Given the industry-wide concerns about competing with television, it is difficult to imagine that Howard Hughes would not have mounted *Pilate's Wife* as the 'technicolor orgy' that Luce was initially eager to avoid. The rumours that floated in the press of Vivien Leigh in the title role spoke to the level of spectacle that the studio heads had in mind for the production. Even Luce's own privately expressed hope that Jean Simmons might play the part instead did little to deflate expectations, given her co-starring role as the Roman aristocrat Diana in the 1953 religious blockbuster *The Robe*. A look at the broad plot outlines of both *The Robe* and *Pilate's Wife* invites further comparison, in fact. Each is a story of legendary figures peripherally connected with but deeply affected by Jesus and his sufferings, with the conversion of each of the central characters coming at a one-step remove from Jesus himself: *The Robe* centres on the effect of the magical nature of Christ's garment on Richard Burton's centurion, Marcellus Gallio, while Claudia's own turn originates with hearing about Jesus' pardon of the woman caught in adultery. Indeed, as we consider a possible reaction to Luce's screenplay, it is reasonable to think that audiences might have responded to a *Pilate's Wife* in the same way in which they had to *The Robe*, which ended up being the highest-grossing film of 1953. A Biblically inspired epic rendered in some heavily marketed, over-the-top technique such as CinemaScope clearly was to viewers' tastes in the early 1950s.

Beyond questions of box office return, it is worth asking, too, how Luce's film might have figured into wider cultural conversations, particularly about the state of American marriage. 'But fidelity is no longer the fashion in Rome', Claudia says to her husband in the opening exchange of *Pilate's Wife*, a remark that undoubtedly would have caught audiences' attention. The second highest-grossing film of 1953, after *The Robe*, was *From Here to Eternity*, which featured the famous roll in the surf of the adulterous lovers Burt Lancaster and Deborah Kerr. In the very same years as Luce was working on her screenplay, the national dialogue about sex and marriage was given a pair of seismic jolts by the release of the two Kinsey Reports, *Sexual Behavior in the Human Male* in 1948 and *Sexual Behavior in the Human Female* in 1953. Of the married women surveyed by Kinsey's team for the latter book, 26 percent disclosed that they had engaged in extramarital coitus by the age of forty, a figure which the authors indicated might actually be too low, given the period's tendency to underreport socially disapproved sexual activity.[11] Although the numbers for unfaithful men reported by Kinsey were higher, this particular statistic provoked disbelief and outrage in the popular press: could it really be the case that every fourth wife in America was carrying on an affair behind her husband's back? Widespread accusations of faulty methodology on Kinsey's part followed, as did suggestive remarks about the nature of the survey pool, but behind the handwringing and fingerpointing lay the fact that marriage in the post-war period was a more complicated matter than the culture had previously allowed itself to believe.

Discussions about marriage in the 1950s cannot be separated from the growing emancipation of women from conventional gender roles during the period, and in this screenplay we have a significant document concerning Luce's ardent if socially conservative support of women's rights. 'I had always been what you now call a women's liberationist', she told Gloria Steinem during a panel discussion of *The Women* in 1971. 'When I was 16 years old, I was throwing handbills for women's rights from an airplane over Buffalo'.[12] But while Luce had long fought for equality in public life, she also argued that, within the home, women ought not to stray too far from their traditional responsibilities as mothers and wives. Having converted to Catholicism in the late 1940s, Luce looked to ground these commitments within the tenets of her new-found faith which, as it happened, dovetailed with her fervent opposition to Communism. Concerning motherhood, for instance, she had declared as the commencement speaker for a Catholic girls' school around this time that 'the proper role of women in our Atomic Age is – in obedience to the will of God – to mother the children of the Crucifixion'. This is not a uniquely conservative position, of course – Adlai Stevenson's commencement speech at Smith in 1955 contained similar sentiments, as Betty Friedan notes in *The Feminine Mystique*.[13] But concerning wifehood, Luce had less to say overtly, likely due to the troubled state of her marriage and her own frequent infidelities. Nevertheless, much can be gleaned about her thinking on the topic of spousal duty from the way in which she has portrayed Claudia in *Pilate's Wife*.

In conceiving the plot for the film, Luce had been greatly influenced by Monsignor Fulton Sheen, who had been her spiritual adviser as she made her personal 'swim across the Tiber'.[14] An expert apologist and media-savvy evangelist, Sheen was a fitting religious counsellor to Luce, and not for nothing had he been featured by *Time* magazine on its cover (14 April 1952). For two decades, Sheen had hosted a weekly Sunday night radio show on NBC, called *The Catholic Hour*, during which he addressed the pressing issues of the day. In the 1950s and 1960s, there followed a primetime television programme called *Life is Worth Living* for which Sheen would win an Emmy. In the Easter season of 1946, the monsignor had delivered a number of addresses on *The Catholic Hour* about the people of the Passion narrative. These dealt with the figures of Judas, Peter, Pilate, Barabbas and, most significantly for Luce, Claudia and Herodias, whom Sheen spoke of as 'the prototypes of all women who have a role to play in the social and political life of the world'. A printed copy of this specific address is filed together with the screenplay for *Pilate's Wife* among Luce's papers at the Library of Congress. In the ancient lives of Claudia and Herodias, Sheen had written, could be seen role models for modern women torn between the materialist impulse of Communism and the spiritual call of Christianity. As he continued, . . .

> Women will be either the daughters of Herodias, wrecking their own homes by divorce, educating their children like Salome in the false wisdom of how to solicit men to do their worst, aligning themselves with any political leader who will further their own interests or pamper their own ambitions, who will never forget the just rebukes of modern Johns. [. . .] Or women today will be the daughters of Claudia, challenging politics when it would send righteous men to death; urging the path of highest duty when indecision, cowardice and compromise allure; being to a husband an unfailing preacher of righteousness; his counselor and his saviour; ever braving stern law rather than be unfaithful to conscience; and never scrupling to talk about the just and righteous Christ even when its penalty might well be the spurning of love.[15]

Perhaps Sheen has made too much about Claudia's character from the paltry evidence of one single line in Matthew, but the manner in which he balanced her as a figure of virtue against Herodias as a corresponding figure of vice is without a doubt artful.

It is easy to see how Luce, with this particular pairing in mind, went about building on Sheen's insights in the passionate dramatic exchange between the women following the beheading of John the Baptist. Although she denigrates Herodias, Luce's Claudia has been rendered as an adulterer herself – when she is confronted by her hostess, it is in front of her lover (Ben-Ezra), her deceived husband (Pilate), as well as the parties who have witnessed her infidelity (Chusa and Joanna). While it is not a plot point that has been particularly well-constructed, Claudia herself is at least in part guilty for the decapitation of John the Baptist. Not even Claudia herself, so Luce seems to be indicating, was always the moral paragon praised by Sheen, and she captures with some pain the mortifying moment when Claudia must come to terms with just how much like Herodias she herself has been in her unfaithful behaviour and self-justification. In *Pilate's Wife*, Claudia is not the static, indeed iconic figure of holiness idolised by Fulton Sheen, but a flawed individual whose journey from self-involvement and frivolity to commitment and conversion, although unsteady, follows the path of a traditional saint's life. Indeed, it seems worth noting that, during the same period as she was working on *Pilate's Wife*, Luce was editing *Saints for Now*, a collection of essays for Sheed & Ward about different saints by eminent writers such as Thomas Merton, Evelyn Waugh, Rebecca West and Whittaker Chambers. 'The very meaning of the lives of the saints for us lies in the fact that they were sinners like ourselves trying like ourselves to combat sin', she writes in her introduction. 'The only difference between them and us is that they kept on trying'.[16]

Claudia, in this respect, should be remembered as yet another saint (of the Eastern Orthodox Church), and if she was a sinner who kept on trying to combat the sin of adultery, Clare was waging similar combat, but with less success. In late 1949, a year or so before she began writing *Pilate's Wife*, Luce had taken a trip to Italy. While there, she personally met with Pope Pius XII, who had called her 'a great apostle and a great orator'; a week or so later, she encountered by chance Carlos Chávez, the distinguished Mexican composer and conductor, in front of Botticelli's *Birth of Venus* in the Uffizi Gallery in Florence, in what was destined to be the very romantic beginning of a twenty-eight-year-long relationship.[17] At the time she began working on *Pilate's Wife*, while she was publicly brandishing her Catholic identity, she was privately struggling to live up to the ideals of marital fidelity that her new faith demanded. In the introduction to *Saints for Now*, she singles out Augustine as a particular favourite, and what she has to say of this saint reveals a great deal about herself, as undoubtedly she knew:

> The conflicts that raged in his bosom between the tangible pleasures of paganism and the intangible joys of Christianity, between doubt and faith, self and God, also rage in ours. From birth, Augustine was a great – one would almost say greatly gifted – sinner. [...] In young manhood he recklessly pursued self-gratification, self-advancement, self-expression. He was the liveliest, most sensual, most brilliant, and no doubt the most egotistic student in the University of Carthage. In Carthage where, he wrote, 'shameful love bubbled about me like boiling oil', he read the wrong books, expounded the wrong ideas, embraced the wrong loves – and made a triumphant 'success' of all of it.[18]

As with everything she wrote, there is much here in Luce's discussion to consider, not least the association of Augustine's turmoil with that of the modern age, by which she means of course her own inner turmoil. It is the line with which she concludes this discursus about Augustine that perhaps is most instructive. 'Lust and sophistry were his twin idols', she writes, and it is hard to decide how much truer such a statement is of the brilliant, beautiful, successful and hypocritical Clare Boothe Luce herself.

The figure of Claudia Procula was never again to find such moral complexity on screen as she did in the unrealised production of Luce's *Pilate's Wife*. In film productions, portrayals of Claudia are far more dramatically circumscribed, for understandable reasons. These big-budget movies are focused on the life of Jesus, after all, and if even Pontius Pilate is a secondary figure in them, how much more peripheral is his wife to the story? Mel Gibson's *Passion of the Christ* (2004) offers an interesting case: Claudia Gerini plays the role of Pilate's wife memorably, although it is a minor part. She and Hristo Shopov's Pilate speak intimately in Latin about the situation as they sit together in their home. Later, as the trial of Jesus unfolds, Pilate looks up at her from his seat on the praetorium, evidently recalling what she has said to him earlier that day. Gazing out from a window back at him, Claudia represents her husband's private life and his conscience, and the height of the perch from which she looks out would seem to indicate this notion. But he turns away from her, and she from him, as he casts his glance back to the crowd in order to pronounce his sentence and seal his fate. It is a subtle moment in the unsubtle Gibson vehicle, but for all the subdued intensity that Gerini brings to the part of Claudia, there is little in this twenty-first-century production that was not already to be found in the part played by

Majel Coleman in DeMille's *King of Kings* (1927): each of these wives recounts her dream, reacts to Pilate's resistance and returns to her room. In mainstream movies of the mid-twentieth century, some notable actresses have languished in the part of Mrs Pilate: Barbara Billingsley, later to find fame as June Cleaver, is largely wasted in Cathedral Films' *Day of Triumph* (1954), while Angela Lansbury is little more than an adoring appendage to Telly Savalas's Pilate in *Greatest Story Ever Told* (1965). In the 2015 NBC miniseries *A. D. The Bible Continues*, Joanne Whalley appears as a shrewish Claudia, a fitting partner to Vincent Regan's equally unpleasant prefect. In other instances, Pilate's spouse does not appear at all. Frank Thring is notably without partner in *Ben-Hur*, as is Basil Sydney in *Salome*, while an incidental reference to Claudia in the first draft of the script for Martin Scorsese's *Last Temptation of Christ* was removed before shooting. In *Jesus Christ Superstar*, an uncredited Ellen David makes a brief appearance as Claudia at the very end of the song called 'Pilate's Dream', which Andrew Lloyd Webber and Tim Rice have ascribed to the prefect himself, completely effacing the wife from the story.

Found in a research file among Clare Boothe Luce's papers at the Library of Congress is a clipping of an article titled 'A Letter from Pontius Pilate's Wife, Rewritten by Catherine Van Dyke'. Published in the *Pictorial Review* in April 1929, the so-called letter is addressed to a friend named Fulvia in Rome and purports to offer an account of Claudia's life with Pilate before and during the time of the Passion. Written from a vantage point many years later, while she and her disgraced husband are living in exile in Gaul, Claudia begs for her friend's sympathy, telling her that, 'if even here children slink away from us and women draw their veils closer, let me believe that somewhere some woman will understand even as she, the mother of Jesus, would have understood'.[19] We go on to read that the couple had been unhappily married, and that, although Pilate was ambitious, his cold 'philosophical' nature left Claudia feeling emotionally abandoned until sometime later when she would give birth to a son who 'became my life, my love'. Despite the article's title, it is as a parent and decidedly not as a wife that Claudia feels happiest, a point immediately emphasised by her invocation of Mary as the mother of Jesus. But in addition, it is evident enough that 'A Letter from Pontius Pilate's Wife', running in a leading women's magazines, was designed for readers who might feel a similar conflict between their identities as women. As it appeared in the *Pictorial Review*, the final page of the piece was centred between an ad on the lefthand side for Glostora hair gel, featuring models with fashionable flapper hairstyles, and another on the righthand side for Vanta Baby Garments, under the banner 'Mother, keep your baby safe from loose pins and buttons'. Luce, herself once a women's magazine editor, had a clipping of the story from the *Pictorial Review*, but the letter was published later in 1929 as a pamphlet by the Bobbs-Merrill Company of Indiana, with a dedication to long-time *Ladies' Home Journal* editor Edward W. Bok. It has been reprinted by several other publishers for niche markets subsequently.

Ostensibly a translation from an ancient manuscript, Claudia's letter details the frustrations of a modern married woman seeking more from life than simple devotion to and from her spouse. 'Altho the flute-players pleaded all night before my bridal chamber', Claudia writes of her wedding night, 'they did not know I lay alone, for Pontius had put me from him saying, "I seek truth, the truth of life"'. He spends his evenings not with her but poring over the books in the library, although five years later she becomes 'wife enough to be a mother' to an otherwise unattested lame son named Pilo who, like Tiny Tim, 'was so bright in his smile that the very slaves looked up when he passed'. Pilate is proud of his male offspring, we read, but chagrined by his son's disability. When later he is assigned a magistracy in Jerusalem, Pilate is a dutiful public servant who debates the matter of truth with the Pharisees and the synagogue leader Jairus, but at home remains aloof. 'Austere and very just in his judgements here', Claudia remarks, 'yet my husband judged not the ache in my heart nor turned to me then as to a faithful servant. Had it not been for my boy, Pilo, I would have died of loneliness in Jerusalem, even in all the dazzling circumstance with which Rome upheld our court'. Neglected by Pilate, Claudia comes to befriend Jairus' wife, Salome, from whom she is thrilled to hear about Jesus and learn of his miraculous ability to cure the lame. She mentions Jesus' healing powers to Pilate, but he is dismissive. 'I want truth not any trickery', he sniffs. 'Hold thyself Claudia Procula, very high; thou art a Roman's wife'. When Jerusalem is afflicted that summer by a plague, Pilo becomes gravely ill, and Salome's daughter, Smedia, dies. Jairus writes Jesus to come to their child and, despite the jeering mob that follows him, he raises her from the dead. Seeing this, Claudia falls to her knees in wonder, before in the crowd she loses sight of Pilo, whom she has brought with her to Jairus' house. She is sick with worry, but then hears him calling out to her: 'Mother, Mother!' As the text continues, '[t]hrough all the multitudes sprang Pilo into my arms. Pilo, erect and firm, without any sickness in him. And more,

nay more. He dragged no withered foot. My Pilo leaped, walked, danced, all sound. His feet were as lovely as his face. Pilo, my son, made whole'. As the episode concludes, '[b]efore I had asked of Jesus he had heard. More than I had asked, he had granted'.

From this miraculous healing in summertime, the scene passes quickly to the following Passover season. Pilate tells Claudia that his friend, King Herod, has informed him of Jesus' imminent arrest, and perhaps is even responsible for it. Overhearing this, Pilo implores him: 'But, Father, you will save Jesus, of course'. But rather than answer his son, Pilate sends him away and furthermore refuses to converse even with Claudia on the topic. That evening, she has a dream of Jesus together with all the children he has healed, singing 'a canticle of unceasing beauty', while apart from them, 'wrapped in a swollen angry cloud', are many bitter and old people, cursing and crying, 'and Pontius the philosopher was among them'. Awaking in a sweat, she rushes to find her husband presiding over the trial of Jesus, whose wounds she describes at length. It is clear to her that Pilate has lost his nerve and, although he asks Jesus 'What is truth?', he 'stayed not for any answer' (again the phrase borrowed from Bacon). Pleading with her husband to intercede, she tells him: 'Pontius, it is Pilo's dear Jesus, he who healed our boy'. It is of no use, however. The guards have taken Jesus away for scourging, and even though Pilate is upset by situation, he does not intervene in the subsequent crucifixion. The ramifications of his indecision follow swiftly:

> When Pilo returned and heard his father had condemned Jesus to death, he fell and was dead. Nor did I wish him to live, for never could my child have forgiven his father, for he loved Jesus very dearly. Then Herod, for whose fear Pontius had delivered Jesus, spoke against Pontius privately to Caesar and had his own cousin appointed at Jerusalem. And Pilate was judged and sentenced by the Senate at Rome unjustly, for there were false witnesses.

Stripped of his position and of his precious library, Pilate is sent with Claudia into exile in Gaul. Hated by his neighbours and wracked by remorse, he is a broken man, but as Claudia tells Fulvia in her concluding remarks: 'In his weakness is my hope'. She ends with an earnest exclamation to Fulvia, and all readers: 'Ye who pray, pray now for Pontius'.

Although quite obviously a work of fiction, Claudia's letter was nonetheless presented in the *Pictorial Review* as though it were a true document from antiquity that Catherine Van Dyke had simply translated (or 'rewritten'). The Editor's Note below ran as preface:

> This is rewritten from an old traditional manuscript first found in a monastery in Bruges, where it had lain for centuries. When Madame de Maintenon became consort of Louis XIV of France she had this letter read every Good Friday before the Court assembled at Versailles. In some of the older communities in Europe its reading follows the washing of the feet of the poor on Good Friday, in remembrance of Christ's washing the feet of His Disciples. A copy of the original letter was also found among the private papers of the last Czarina of Russia, and was given by her in trust to a friend to keep until the Czarina expected to return from the fateful last journey to Tsarskoe Selo.

Here we see the trope of the 'found manuscript', long a feature of romantic fiction, which gives an air of credibility to the story of Claudia's letter, as well as lending to it the seductive charm of a long-undisclosed secret now being revealed. The exotic details – Madame de Maintenon! Versailles! The Czarina! 'The fateful last journey to Tsarskoe Selo'! – all pile up to reinforce the sense of a secret society of illustrious, tragic women speaking directly from the past to their female counterparts of the present day. The popularity of 'A Letter from Pontius Pilate's Wife', as well as the belief in it as genuine document written in the first century AD, continued unabated for decades. In 1945, Robert L. Odom, a leading figure in the Seventh-Day Adventist Church, set out to get to the bottom of the matter of the letter's authenticity in an article for *The Ministry* and, after consulting with a patristics scholar and cataloguers at the Library of Congress, found Mrs Van Dyke's address and wrote to her himself. She replied to his inquiry:

> I saw the copy of the manuscript at Bruges. It was in very old French (medieval). I also saw the copy the czarina had. It was translated in Russia and shown to me by Princess Troubetskoy in London. The copy from which I rewrote my story belonged to the nuns at the Sacred Heart Academy at Manhattanville, New York. It was very badly translated from the medieval French, and terribly interlarded with long talk on manners and morals to the young ladies of the French court. I was told Madame de Maintenon (wife of Louis) read it to his children regularly. I had to greatly rewrite and simplify the entire story, but kept to the true main theme.

Unconvinced, Odom systematically set out his many objections to Van Dyke's claim and concluded his investigation: 'The thing is a piece of fiction, and is unworthy of serious use by any Seventh-day Adventist minister. Let us give it no circulation whatever, for its use would certainly discredit us before men and women of intelligence'.[20] As subsequent researchers online have indicated, Van Dyke's work seems to have been cribbed heavily from a piece by Éveline Ribbecourt, called 'La Mort du Juste', originally published in the *Journal des Demoiselles* in 1846 and reprinted in the nineteenth century several times thereafter. Ribbecourt's story contains no mention of Pilo, however, which likely was Van Dyke's own contribution to the so-called letter.[21]

Whatever its ultimate origin, Odom's emphatic rejection of its authenticity ought to have put the matter of 'A Letter from Pontius Pilate's Wife' to rest for English-speaking audiences, but as is so often the case with pious claptrap, a lack of truth need not be a hindrance. Having performed a dramatic narration of the story in various Southern Californian churches to some success, the actress Marjorie Lord, best known for her role as wife Kathy Williams on CBS's popular *The Danny Thomas Show*, in 1962 released a recorded version of van Dyke's story on vinyl under the title *Claudia's Letter*. Melodramatically delivered and sensationally scored with shimmering violins and booming kettledrums, as *Time* magazine noted, the album enjoyed instantaneous hit status in various Christian markets:

> Biblical soap opera it may be, but *Claudia's Letter* is boffo in the California city of Pomona. This week, so the city fathers have decreed, the record will blare each noontime from loudspeakers along Pomona's new nine-block downtown mall. At least 15 Pomona churches plan to use it during Holy Week and Easter Services, and some clergymen are treating it like a new Gospel.[22]

As the anonymous article goes on to say, 'Kelley Norwood, president of the company that recorded the letter, stoutly claims "there is no question about its authenticity"'. That Norwood was not an expert in first-century manuscripts but an orchestra leader who had had minor hits with 'Too-Soon' and 'The Doodle Song' passes without mention. As to why Lord herself made the recording, she is quoted by *Time* as saying: 'For one thing, I really love the letter. For another, I need some recognition outside *The Danny Thomas Show* for my career's sake'. Close to sixty years later, autographed CDs of *Claudia's Letter* are still available for purchase on Lord's official website, although she herself passed away in 2015.[23] Copies of Lord's recording uploaded on YouTube have been viewed thousands of times, and despite the spurious nature of the letter, it is clear from the online comments how moving the story remains for many.

NOTES

1 Hourihane (2009b) and Boxall (2018), each with references to primary and principal secondary sources. On the bracelets of Claudia Procla, see Smith (1984: 107).

2 https://www.valwineyardpublishing.com/claudia-procula (accessed 1 December 2020).

3 Harriman (1941: 22).

4 Weintraub and Luce (1974: 56).

5 Morris (2014: 284).

6 Martin (1991: 288).

7 Morris (2014: 192, 195).

8 Luce (1951). This, and all subsequent parenthetical citations, are to Luce's screen treatment now in the Margaret Herrick Library in Beverly Hills.

9 Morris (2014: 285), quoting the script now among Luce's papers at the Library of Congress.

10 Morris (2014: 136).

11 Kinsey et al. (1953: 416).

12 Klemesrud (1971: 42).

13 Friedan (2001: 112–13).

14 See Morris (2014: 150–58).

15 Sheen (1946: 67–68).

16 Luce (1952: 8).

17 Morris (2014: 253–55).

18 Luce (1952: 10).

19 This and all subsequent quotations of 'A Letter from Pontius Pilate's Wife' are taken from Van Dyke (1929).

20 Odom (1945: 8).

21 See Paul Smith, 'Claudia Procula, "pays des Rhedons" & Narbonne: Supplementary Information', (12 January 2019), http://www.priory-of-sion.com/rlc/claudia-procula-pays-de-rhedones-narbonne.html (accessed 10 May 2020).

22 *Time* (1963: 52).

23 http://www.marjorielord.com/shop.html (accessed 10 May 2020).

5 Pilate in CinemaScope, or Notes on Roman Camp

Speak the speech, I pray you, as I pronounced it to you, trippingly on the tongue: but if you mouth it, as many of your players do, I had as lief the town-crier spoke my lines. […] O, it offends me to the soul to hear a robustious periwig-pated fellow tear a passion to tatters, to very rags, to split the ears of the groundlings, who for the most part are capable of nothing but inexplicable dumbshows and noise: I would have such a fellow whipped for o'erdoing Termagant; it out-herods Herod: pray you, avoid it.

– Shakespeare, *Hamlet* 3.2

In the 1950s and 1960s, as is noted in the last chapter, television brought drama out of the theatre and into the living room, and those teleplays involving figures from the Passion took on something of a domestic nature – Mr and Mrs Pilate are seen in their breakfast room in *Day of Triumph*, discussing Jesus while sharing cantaloupe, whereas a more troubled homelife formed the background of Family Theater's *Hill Number One* as well as Studio One's *Pontius Pilate*. Marshall McLuhan would call television a 'cool medium', one drawing the viewer into a private experience, while cinema was a 'hot medium' engulfing audiences with its scale and scope.[1] If the coolness of TV showed Pontius Pilate in a more intimate light, a depiction more overblown and distancing would be found in the overheated genre of Hollywood film. In the big-screen performances of the mid-century, we have already seen Lowell Gilmore's turn as a figure of comic relief in *Day of Triumph*, the actor giving a twist of the risible to his role as chief antagonist. Over the course of the 1950s, the figure of Pilate would grow more baroque and brash. Richard Boone in *The Robe* may act his part in a candid and straightforward manner, and there is an ironic quality to the Pilate of Basil Sydney playing a first-rate third wheel to lovers Rita Hayworth and Stewart Granger in *Salome*. With Frank Thring in *Ben-Hur* at the decade's end, however, and Hurd Hatfield in *King of King* at the beginning of the 1960s, we find performances of the Roman prefect that are notable for their exaggerated gesturing and stagey affectation. If they do not 'out-herod Herod', as Hamlet would have it, they certainly out-Pilate Pilate.

'Will television kill the cinema?' was the question of Spyros P. Skouras, head of the Twentieth Century-Fox studio in 1954, in a speech preserved among his papers at Stanford University. In this big picture look at the challenge of the small screen, Skouras noted how the rise of TV in post-war America had 'had a disastrous effect upon motion picture attendance because the average citizen could turn a dial and tune in any one of a number of stations' for entertainment that, although inferior in quality, was 'convenient and free'. If cinema were to survive, he concluded, '[o]bviously it was imperative that some way be found to make motion picture entertainment so attractive that people would return to the box office and pay admissions to see motion pictures instead of remaining at home before their television sets'.[2]

The particular irresistible attraction that Skouras had in mind was the innovative format known as CinemaScope, the projection of film through an anamorphic lens onto a special wide screen to create a more all-encompassing viewing experience, the very essence of McLuhan's idea of the 'hot medium'. Such technology lent itself to films of a grander scale and sweep, the sort that could entice families out of their living rooms and into the movie theatre. Just as filmmakers had in an earlier day, Twentieth Century-Fox turned to the Biblical epic as a way of putting bums on seats, following the trend set by MGM with its release in 1951 of the enormously successful *Quo Vadis*.

The film that Twentieth-Century Fox opted to make to counteract the small-screen threat was *The Robe*, based on Lloyd Douglas's widely popular novel of the same name from 1942. Henry Koster was chosen to direct and Richard Burton to star as Marcellus Gallio, the young aristocratic soldier who, in a noisy dice game conducted at the foot of the cross, wins Jesus' robe (Burton would win the Oscar for his performance). The subsequent interactions of Marcellus and the robe with various Roman emperors and early Christians thrilled viewers onscreen just as they had readers of the original book, in which Pontius Pilate had played a larger role than in the film. In Chapter VI of Douglas's novel, for instance, Marcellus (here a legate rather than a military subordinate) critiques the execution of the innocent Jesus, prompting a disgruntled Pilate to question him about the day's proceedings.

> 'A strange person, indeed', agreed Pilate. 'What did you make of him?' he asked, lowering his voice confidentially.
> Marcellus shook his head.
> 'I don't know, sir', he replied, after an interval.
> 'He was a fanatic!' said Pilate.
> 'Doubtless. So was Socrates. So was Plato'.
> Pilate shrugged.[3]

Their discussion is interrupted by a drunken centurion's demand that the robe which Marcellus had won in his gambling be brought forward and put on him. It is under the pressure of the watchful scrutiny of the prefect – whom Douglas calls at different points in the passage 'coolly derisive', 'sardonic' and 'contemptuous' – that Marcellus dons the garment which will cause him to have a nervous breakdown and subsequent spiritual awakening. In the film version of *The Robe*, by contrast, Pilate's role was substantially curtailed. As played by Richard Boone, he is a gruff commander who summons Marcellus and orders him to guard the cross, where he predicts that there will be unrest. He tries to downplay how evidently troubled he is by the day's events, and it is a credit to Boone's acting that we feel this is uncharacteristic of Pilate. 'I've had a miserable night. Factions. No one agreeing with anyone else. Even my wife had an opinion', he says more to himself than to Burton's Marcellus, whom he dismisses with an unconvincing 'Good luck'. At the beginning of the short scene, as Anne Wroe has noted, 'his wrists were so heavy with bangles, and his fingers were so encrusted with jewels, that he could hardly squeeze the absolving water between them'.[4] At the end, he calls for water to wash his hands. 'But you just washed them, my lord', replies his servant, as we have seen when the scene opened. 'Did I?' he replies, looking at his hands. 'So I did'. In a sort of trance he departs, but we feel Boone's Pilate will never cease calling for water in compulsive guilt for the rest of his life. We can easily imagine him sleepwalking in his guilt along with Lady Macbeth, asking: 'What, will these hands ne'er be clean?' (*Macbeth* 5.1).

Given the extraordinary gamble that Twentieth Century-Fox was making on *The Robe*'s CinemaScope filming, it is understandable that less effort was invested in developing the role of an admittedly minor figure. What might be made of the character had been demonstrated by Basil Sydney's performance in the Rita Hayworth vehicle *Salome*, released by Columbia six months before *The Robe* came out. Also conceived on an epic scale – a 'gee-whiz picture', as the *Washington Post* called it, and 'a whale of a spectacle'[5] – the film garnered an impressive return at the box office, largely the result of Hayworth's Dance of the Seven Veils, which, although it seems prim today, was an event much hyped for the contemporary male gaze. A trained Shakespearean actor of some versatility, Sydney himself was not an unknown quantity at the time, even though perhaps not so well remembered today. He had given a credible performance as Captain Smollett in Disney's *Treasure Island* in 1950 and, still more memorable, in Olivier's noirishly Freudian *Hamlet* two years before as the unpleasantly appetitive Claudius, first seen swigging from a goblet and leering at Gertrude. In *Salome*, where the Roman presence in Judaea plays an important backdrop for the story, Sydney's Pilate has been appointed governor because of his soldierly accomplishments elsewhere in the Roman Empire. 'We need peace in the East. That is of great military importance', Tiberius (Cedric Hardwicke) tells Pilate, who appears before the emperor in full armour in the court at Rome. 'I am depending upon your reputation. But this time, use it like a glove not as a spear'. This is a Pilate who, like King Claudius, is in need of some restraint, or so we are at first led to believe.

Pilate is ordered to sail for Judaea the next evening, on a ship that will likewise convey Salome, as he discovers just before the departure. As a princess newly banished from Rome, Hayworth is late and must be waited upon by everyone. 'Well, why is she not here?' Pilate, the great military man, says in a tone that can only be called sputtering. 'I follow orders and I expect others to'. Some members of the audience must have wondered whether Captain Smollett would have put up with such lollygagging as the *Hispaniola* was about to weigh anchor. When Salome finally saunters aboard, astounding all those along the way with her beauty, she snubs Pilate, whose quarters she instantly takes over with her retinue. The prefect is irked by this turn of events, but his lieutenant Claudius (Stewart Granger) has a better sense of how to handle the capricious princess, and before long he is bickering with Salome and then passionately kissing her without her consent in a match modelled after Petruchio and Kate in *Taming of the Shrew*, *sans* the Shakespearean banter. The screenplay is otherwise competent, the work of journeyman Hollywood scriptwriter Harry Kleiner, who is evidently borrowing heavily from Henry Denker's 1952 potboiler novel *Salome: Princess of Galilee*.[6] In the film, Pilate's activity in Judaea centres on dealing with Charles Laughton's sybaritic King Herod, whose attention to his stepdaughter Salome is lascivious and inappropriate (one wonders whether Laughton is ever so slightly paying homage to Sydney's Claudius from *Hamlet* here, in fact). When Pilate first appears in full betoga'd pomp to bring Caesar's felicitations to the king at his court in Galilee, Herod pays him no mind and only has eyes for Salome, who has just sauntered in. Once again, the Roman prefect finds himself outplayed by the princess. 'Does *she* always take precedence over me?' Pilate asks Claudius later in the scene, as though anybody making that inquiry in a film starring Rita Hayworth would ever receive a different answer.

Overall, Galilee is not a happy place for the king, bedevilled as he is by John the Baptist (a hollow-eyed Alan Badel in camel's hair-garb) who, in addition to exhorting his listeners to prepare the way of the Lord, laces his sermons with insults about the royal marriage as well as virulent anti-Roman rabble-rousing. Pilate orders the prophet to be killed, but this command is countermanded by Claudius, who argues that his death would bring on a rebellion. Secretly, however, Claudius has been converted to John's way of thinking, as soon Salome will be, and eventually he reveals the truth of the situation to Pilate. Although he encourages the prefect to think of the immortality that he would achieve were he to join them – 'Your name will be enscrolled on the pages of history!' – Pilate dismisses this 'idiotic nonsense' and expresses disappointment at his junior officer's treason. At this moment in Henry Denker's novel, Pilate has the commander (called Cornelius here, not Claudius) punished for his insubordination with blinding, but in the film it is Pilate who turns a Nelson eye to the situation and decides only to relieve him of his post. As Claudius leaves the palatial chamber, Pilate calls him back to look him in the eye, exchange one final grasp of the forearm and say: 'Sorry, Claudius'. If Jesus Christ had struck as handsome a profile as Stewart Granger, one wonders, might the prefect have let him off, too, with just a handshake?

Understandably enough, a Pilate who gouged out a main character's eyes might have been too much for a moviegoing audience to bear, especially one that was being lured off its couches back to the cinema to gawk at a rerun of Gilda's striptease. But there are larger issues involved in the conversation of Pilate and Claudius than might appear at first glance. As *Salome*'s Roman figures, Basil Sydney and Stewart Granger may speak with British accents, but the sentiments they espouse are those of the Pax Americana. Audiences watching the film in the US might well have heard echoes of contemporary rhetoric about foreign policy in some of the dialogue between the prefect and his commander.

CLAUDIUS:
Rome cannot go on as it has, ruling with a sword and a whip. If we are to survive, we must recognize that a new force is coming into the world.

PILATE:
New force?

CLAUDIUS:
The religion of this prophet. It will bring hope to the conquered. It will bring peace to all men by teaching every man how to live at peace with his neighbors. This faith will march across the world and win men where Rome could only conquer them.

PILATE:
Caesar is the only faith possible for a Roman.

Only a few weeks after *Salome* was released, Josef Stalin would die, and a new American president would seize the opportunity of a change in Soviet leadership to try to take the Cold War in a new direction. With the delivery of his 'Chance for Peace' speech, Eisenhower attempted to outline a way toward a more secure basis for international peace. 'This world in arms is not spending money alone', he pointed out in this heart-felt address. 'It is spending the sweat of its laborers, the genius of its scientists, the hopes of its children'. One modern heavy bomber, he noted, cost the same amount of money as thirty modern schools, two electric power plants, or half a million bushels of wheat. As Eisenhower famously said of this state of affairs, '[t]his is not a way of life at all, in any true sense. Under the cloud of threatening war, it is humanity hanging from a cross of iron. These plain and cruel truths define the peril and point the hope that come with this spring of 1953'.[7] As the Supreme Allied Commander in Europe, Eisenhower had overseen the unconditional surrender of the Axis Powers. Just as the Pilate of *Salome* had been encouraged to use his military prowess 'like a glove, not as a spear', Eisenhower had to reflect on how best to keep his mighty nation from carrying out a modern crucifixion as he himself made the transition from five-star general to commander-in-chief. Even though a Pontius Pilate constantly upstaged by Rita Hayworth in a 'gee-whiz' Hollywood movie might have been deaf to it, the question of how he would be 'enscrolled on the pages of history' mattered a great deal to the new US President in the spring of 1953.

Beyond these oblique connections with the politics of its time, *Salome* likewise charted out new possibilities for the genre of the

Biblical epic. In *The Robe*, Richard Boone's Pilate is an officer in an occupying force disconcerted by foreigners who seem to have gotten the better of him. As a soldier who, even though his 'military reputation precedes him' (as Tiberius explicitly states), throughout the film is undermined by the beautiful princess, Basil Sydney plays his part in *Salome* instead with a tilt toward the ridiculous – a Mars undone again and again by Venus. Both Boone's and Sydney's performances build on the contradiction inherent in the persona of the prefect as portrayed in drama: in the onscreen world of the Passion, Pilate may be the story's most powerful figure, but viewers are well aware from the mere mention of his name that he is destined to be a flop.

This intrinsic paradox of the prefect's character and its potential for, if not outright comedy, then at least a little understated humour, finds its fullest expression in the mid-century depictions of Pilate with Frank Thring Jr's performance in William Wyler's 1959 extravaganza *Ben-Hur*. A beloved character actor in his native Australia, Thring would go on to develop a cult of personality that made him a beloved icon of the international gay community in the decades to come. It was his affected sense of stage presence, a calculated world-weariness, more than anything else, that had gotten him the part of Pilate. 'Are you sure you don't want me to do anything?' Thring had asked Wyler about his dropping a silk handkerchief to signal the beginning of the race. 'No', was the reply. 'Just sit there and give one of your looks'.[8] Thring improvised a false start, looking deviously off to the side first before dropping the hankie with the called-for glower. It is a shot that gets lost in the shuffle just before the race that the crowd both onscreen and in the audience all have come to see in widescreen Panavision splendour. The world is waiting for Pilate, in other words, and he makes it wait just a bit longer, so he can enjoy his own private moment of wicked pleasure.

Ben-Hur features glorious set pieces in the form of large-scale sea battles and cinema's most famous chariot race, of course, but at other times it settles into a stodgy churchiness. As the anecdote above reveals, Thring's jaded turn as Pilate was intentional, leavening the lump of the production's grandiosity as a whole. 'They are at no point in danger of lawsuits for impersonating real people', critic Dwight Macdonald had said, unkindly if not unjustly, of the main characters' performances in his review of *Ben-Hur*. No such criticism could be levelled against Thring. Never trying to seem like a real person in the first place, his Pilate was an understated masterpiece of what we would now call camp. 'One is drawn to Camp', Susan

Sontag famously stated only a few years later, 'when one realizes that "sincerity" is not enough. Sincerity can be simple philistinism, intellectual narrowness. [. . .] Camp introduces a new standard: artifice as an ideal, theatricality'.[9] In the midst of this four-hour film, there is genuine relief in being able every now and again to take a break from the 'hot medium', with its overwhelming Panavision and overacting from Charlton Heston, to arch an eyebrow at all the hubbub with Pontius Pilate.

When we first meet Thring's prefect, it is at a banquet in Rome celebrating Judah's chariot victory earlier that day (Figure 5.1). Bedecked in a costly maroon-and-gold mantle fastened by an ornate brooch, he wears an elaborate bracelet on his wrist and a dandyish beard on his face. From a lowered brow, he shoots 'one of his looks' up at Heston's Judah Ben-Hur, standing higher in the shot to the left, and tells him: 'Before you came to this city, my horses always won'. Our instant impression is of a man of leisure, not used to challenge or hardship of any sort whatsoever. He then asks about Judaea where, he has just discovered, he is to be made governor. 'I asked for Alexandria', he tells Quintus Arrius (Jack Hawkins), the fellow Roman aristocrat who is Judah's adopted Roman father. 'But it seems the wilderness needs my particular talents. The scorpions and holy prophets can't get on without me'. The stage direction for this line reads 'ironic humor', and it is the key to understanding his character.[10] Throughout *Ben-Hur*, Pilate is the film's principal and perhaps its only ironist, and the aloofness he maintains throughout is in marked contrast to the overriding earnestness of the rest of the production. Pilate ends this initial scene by taking a proffered goblet and rolling his eyes slightly upward in good humour. 'Goats and Jehovah!' he says, and off he walks not to be seen again for another hour or two. Alone of all the characters in *Ben-Hur*, Pilate seems not to care very much about the Judeo-Christian God in this over-wrought and unsubtle 'Tale of the Christ'.

There is a story that, just before the filming of the great chariot race in *Ben-Hur* was to begin, the director's tired voice could be heard over the loudspeaker, saying: 'Would Pontius Pilate please remove his sunglasses?'[11] At another time, Thring told a version of his disruption of the movie's most elaborate scene in even more picturesque detail:

> With a 20 camera set-up, the race began. Frank, seated on a throne and wearing a full toga, watched as the race was building to its final dramatic moment. From behind the throne and hidden, Wylder [sic] whispered: 'Frank, stand up'. Never one to disobey his director, he leapt to his feet. From the folds of his toga tumbled sun-glasses, pieces of chicken, a bottle of brandy,

Figure 5.1 Frank Thring as Pilate in *Ben-Hur* (1959).

eye-drops, and the other necessities required to help you though a day of
filming a Roman chariot race.[12]

Is either of these versions, or any of the others he used to tell,
factual? Who can say? *Quid est veritas?* Thring was a practiced
raconteur who would regale talk show hosts and others with back-
stage tales from the set of *Ben-Hur* for the rest of his life, and
he could expand or contract details depending on his audience's
tastes. What we can take away from his various recountings, however, is that sense we have of *Ben-Hur*'s Pilate as an ironic persona
onscreen emanates ultimately from Thring's actual ironic persona
offscreen.

Something of this irony comes through in at least one particular
niche viewing experience of *Ben-Hur*. The non-straight appreciation
of mainstream movies by gay audiences explicated in the 1995 documentary *The Celluloid Closet* evidently encompassed *Ben-Hur* as
well, centring particularly on Thring's performance among fellow
Australians. In one oral history of the period, an interviewee named
David recalls how a gay cinema manager in a Melbourne theatre
in the early 1960s would arrange special late-night screenings of
various Hollywood epics, the more over-the-top the better. As David
tells it, . . .

And so that would be a very gay, a very camp audience that would go. . .
and so he would show, sort of, you know, *The Pride and The Passion*, or
um, one of those films about Roman life or the early life of Jesus or something, and we'd all sit there giggling and going through it. And so he developed, also, um – there was an Australian actor called Frank Thring from
Melbourne, who had appeared in one of those historical dramas as Pontius
Pilate or something like that, and so, no matter what film we were watching,
at some point, it would be interrupted while this scene with Pontius Pilate

condemning Jesus was played (laughs). And so we'd all wait for that. It's a little bit like sort of going to, you know, *Rocky Horror* and singing along. We were all waiting for that bit of Frank Thring to say, 'I condemn you to death', you know, so silly.[13]

In fact, Thring never says 'I condemn you to death' in *Ben-Hur*. The only moment when he encounters Jesus is the wordless handwashing scene that Judah and his family watch from the crowd. Two years later in Nicholas Ray's *King of Kings*, however, Thring would play the part of Herod Antipas – 'a grimacing and gaudy grotesque', as Bosley Crowther called him in the *New York Times* – before whom Jesus, the handsome young Jeffrey Hunter, is brought for judgement. Garbed in elaborate Eastern dress, his hair coifed and beard meticulously curled, Thring rises from his chair to prowl around the blue-eyed blond Messiah before demanding a miracle. When Jesus fails to comply, a disappointed Thring resumes his chair. 'Take this faker back to Pilate', he concludes, looking away and biting his thumb in mock indignation. 'Tell him Herod was not . . . pleased with his performance'. Earlier in the film, Thring's Herod Antipas had watched his father Herod (Grégoire Aslan) collapse before his throne; climbing over him to get into it, he gave the old man a vicious kick down the platform stairs. Whatever the factual accuracies may or may not be of David's cinematic experience in Melbourne referenced above, one can easily imagine cheers going up from an audience of moviegoers who had come to see not the King of Kings, but the Thring of Thrings.

It has only been in the last several years, in fact, that Nicholas Ray's *King of Kings*, the re-make of DeMille's silent era blockbuster, has begun to receive the attention it deserves. Critics at the time of the film's initial release took turns scourging it: in a review called '$ign of the Cross', for instance, *Time* magazine decried the film's high budget and went on to call it 'the corniest, phoniest, ickiest and most monstrously vulgar of all the big Bible stories Hollywood has told in the last decade'. In particular, *Time* savaged the casting of the heart-throb Hunter in the main role by saying that the movie ought to have been called 'I Was a Teenage Jesus'.[14] *King of Kings* is not a movie without flaws, it should be noted, many of them inflicted by overly involved MGM studio heads who increasingly wrested creative control from Ray. A new script with a new major character was introduced halfway through filming in Madrid (only to be discarded entirely in editing), scenes were re-cut with new 'quieter' dialogue, and the film's overall lack of coherence was finally papered over by a last-minute faux-Biblical narrative written by Ray

Bradbury and 'intoned by the great intoner, Orson Welles' (to quote Dwight MacDonald). Too many cooks may have ended up spoiling this Biblical broth, but the baby ought not to be thrown out with the bathwater. It is worth considering the film we actually do have, and not the film that it might have been or that the critics insisted it was. Ray was a director of numerous eccentricities – the wearing of an eye-patch on set, so as to look like a pirate, for example – but, as the director of 1955's iconic *Rebel Without a Cause*, he was one who thought deeply about the mid-twentieth-century culture of youth that put John F. Kennedy in the White House. 'I will be personally satisfied', he told an interviewer, 'if our film can establish the fact the story of Jesus and the men and women who were first attracted to His teachings is essentially a story about, and for, young people'.[15] If Hunter's Jesus – the square-jawed, blue-eyed son of a loving Irish mother (Siobhán McKenna) – is a stand-in for JFK in this New Testament story for the New Frontier, the Pilate who confronts him is an elegant and malevolent scoundrel, decidedly of the old school.

'I had a whale of a time as Pontius Pilate, who I played as most fastidious in *King of Kings* [1961], directed by that wonderful madman Nick Ray', Hatfield would tell an interviewer many years later of a performance which is, to quote MacDonald again, 'right out of Grand Guignol'.[16] Without any doubt, he is the heavy in the piece, the bad guy whose stylish onscreen villainy may have only been matched in 1961 by *One Hundred and One Dalmatians*'s Cruella de Vil. Hatfield's performance of Pilate is informed by the most prominent role that the actor ever played, the title character of the 1945 MGM classic *The Picture of Dorian Gray*. Charming and debonair, the handsome aristocrat had hidden his malevolence behind the frozen smile of his un-aging face. Although Hatfield would spend his entire career dogged by *Dorian Gray*, his Pilate is suffused with a similar pettiness, cruelty and narcissism, and it was this sense of patrician disregard that led Ray to cast Hatfield in the role. In fact, Pilate is not the first cruel Roman commander whom we see in *King of Kings*. When the film opens, Pompey has brought his troops through a burning Jerusalem and mounted the steps of the Temple on his horse. 'Where no pagan had ever set foot, in the court of the priests', Orson Welles intones in the voice-over, 'most irreverent Pompey stood himself down'. After having the high priests shot, the general enters the Holy of Holies in search of gold, only to discover a scroll parchment by Moses. He hands it to a beggar, but we have to imagine that his successor, Pilate, would have been just as inclined to toss this holy item into a bonfire instead. Likewise leading a large army on horseback when he enters the film, Pilate is outfitted in dazzling armour of gold and white, although his heart, as we soon realise, is as black as his hair. His first words in the film come when he is told that there is fresh water ahead. Should the soldiers take a break after their extensive march, a subordinate asks. 'Not too long', he says, taking a big gulp from a wineskin. When his wife chides him, he responds with a sly smile: 'I enjoy it'. Throughout the film, this is a Pilate who sees no reason to sympathise with other people's suffering and, from his position of privilege, smirks at anything resembling weakness.

'Judaea. A fine wedding present your father gave me', Pilate remarks as he finishes his wine. A brief exchange follows, from which we right away understand what a curious set of wrinkles have been worked out for *King of Kings*' Pilate and wife by Philip Yordan's screenplay.

CLAUDIA:
My dear Pontius, it is said whoever can govern Jerusalem can govern anywhere, even Rome.

PILATE:
Do you think Tiberius really has me in mind as his successor in Rome?

CLAUDIA:
I wish I knew my father's mind as well as I know my husband's ambition.

The Emperor Tiberius, to begin with, is evidently Claudia's father, making Pilate not, as he is sometimes represented, some minor bureaucrat serving out his days in a provincial backwater, but rather a figure very close to the centre of imperial power. Although he has been granted Judaea, Pilate has ambitions, and without a doubt we are meant to think of him as a sort of twin to Thring's Herod Antipas, one who might be just as likely to dropkick his father-in-law off the throne. But the perhaps most curious wrinkle of all is Claudia herself. Played by Viveca Lindfors, the actress speaks in her native Swedish accent, the foreignness of which is no accident in a film that stars an all-American Jesus. While Hatfield's polished quasi-British accent points to the 'aural paradigm' of Anglo-American relations (discussed more fully in Chapter 8), other associations come to mind when we realise that this princess in her elaborate garb is not a native English speaker. The analogy drawn openly between Rome and Russia in the opening titles of 1954's *Day of Triumph* is here more subtly hinted at concerning the alien nature of Roman rule. The Cold War context gives a point to the scene that follows, as Pilate demands that the likenesses of Tiberius be hung in the temple, as though they were the oversize banners of an Eastern Bloc leader cult of personality.

When John the Baptist (Robert Ryan) subsequently leads the people in protest against these imperial images, their chants can be heard outside the palace where Pilate is preparing to feast with Herod and his family. 'Why must he agitate beneath your window?' Pilate asks in a bit of before-dinner banter, and the diners head over to the balcony to see what the fuss is all about. 'You! You there! Speaker!' Pilate calls out, and from the crowd's perspective we look up at him from an extreme low angle shot. Most of what can be seen at this angle are the protective walls of the palace that keep its wealthy occupants at a far remove from the lower classes. If the likenesses of Tiberius had seemed like Communist propaganda, the behaviour of Pilate at this point can only be called 'capitalist pig'. He tosses a coin down to John and shouts, with a disdainful chuckle: 'Now be gone!' John picks up the coin and, evidently deciding to render unto Caesar that which is Caesar's, hurls it back at him, while the crowd cheers. Pilate, regarding this coolly, instructs a guard: 'Bring the beggar in'. We have a classic Hollywood slobs-versus-snobs confrontation when John is produced before him: the prefect stands in his elegant ancient evening wear before a torch-lit scene arrayed in crimson, purple and gold, while the bearded prophet is unkempt in his earth-tones. 'Judging from your appearance', Pilate quips, 'your God seems to be a rather unprofitable master to serve'. The rows of slaves roasting pigs over open fires in the distant background behind Pilate and Herod reinforce this distinction in class. But they also remind us that Herod does not keep a kosher household (we have been told in the prologue that the Herods were not Jews but Arabs, evidently ones who consume pork): Herod Antipas may be a king over his subject people, but he is not one of them.

Is Herod even the king of his own castle? What is most striking in this scene with John is the provocation of Herod throughout it, a reflection of mid-century male anxiety and a favourite theme of Nicholas Ray's. When John insults Herodias (Rita Gam) – 'Woman, is not your cup of abominations full enough?' – and is in turned taunted by Salome (Brigid Bazlen), Thring's character is called upon to act. 'Do you intend to do nothing with this man?' Pilate goads him, and a browbeating Herodias follows up: 'Herod, Pilate has asked you a question'. The assaults on Herod's manhood come from all sides, and to have his wife and niece act up in such a fashion – while the boss is over for dinner, no less! – seems like a nightmare not out of ancient Jerusalem but rather suburban America. Ray's portrait of a hen-pecked Herod seems to fit in with larger anxieties of the period. 'There are multiplying signs, indeed, that something has gone badly wrong with the American male's conception of himself', Arthur Schlesinger Jr had written in a famous essay about the so-called crisis of masculinity for *Esquire* in 1958. Herod certainly seems to be bearing the brunt of the overly aggressive females in his family, which Schlesinger identified as part of the problem. At a later banquet, Pilate will be there again to witness Herod's humiliation as Salome initially refuses to dance. 'You are not enough of a king!' she yells at Herod. 'You keep the man who reviled my mother in a dungeon when he should have died months ago!' The camera quickly cuts to Pilate for a reaction shot at this moment, and the amused look on Hatfield's face is priceless – 'Well, this *is* juicy', he seems to be thinking. As the film's most powerful figure, the Roman governor is in a prime position to judge the failures of all the characters lower in the social hierarchy than himself, and oftentimes, he will do so with a snicker.

The pleasure that Pilate takes in watching this family argument unfold, as great as his delight in the salacious dance to follow, is part of what makes him the villain of the piece. But in a larger sense it speaks to the way in which virtue and vice are figured in *King of Kings*, in terms of deviancy – another constant of Nicholas Ray's oeuvre – all forms of which the tyrannical Pilate takes a cruel pleasure in observing, taking part in and, as the occasion moves him, punishing. The sense of menace created by the prefect's position as arbitrary judge, jury and executioner can be felt in the scene that follows. Although it was not Pilate who gave the decapitation order, Ray artfully juxtaposes John's death with Pilate's first learning about Jesus – the executioner is just striking the Baptist's neck with his scimitar as we dissolve to a private chamber in which Pilate's barber is attending to his master. Herod is there as well, and their conversation about Jesus continues as Pilate is shaved. It is a scene that deliberately seems to allude to the moment in John Huston's 1948 masterpiece *Key Largo*, when arch-gangster Johnny Rocco (Edward G. Robinson) outlines the workings of his criminal enterprises during a shave – a scene on which Brian DePalma will also draw to establish the character of Robert DeNiro's Al Capone in 1987's *The Untouchables*. Rather than act rashly, Pilate dispatches his lieutenant, Lucius (Ron Randell), to spy on Jesus and report back to him whatever he learns. 'If he utters a single word treasonable to Rome, you'll have to act', Pilate says as he grabs the wrist of the barber holding the razor over his neck, in the same way that Rocco had (and DeNiro's Capone will). Ray is pointing the allusion here, but even if viewers do not recognize it completely, they unmistakably sense that the prefect is the picture's kingpin. Even when the blade is at his own throat, Pilate is the most powerful character in the world of the film.

In a recent discussion of *King of Kings*, Jason McKahan noted: 'Always lurking in the background of cold war discourses on masculinity was the threat of demonic femininity, variously embodied in the homosexual, the femme fatale, or the female enemy agent'.[17] Certainly, Herodias and Salome captured the film's concern with dangerous feminine behaviour, but Ray also gives us various moments of homoeroticism. When Judas (Rip Torn) betrays Jesus in the Garden, for instance, it is not the chaste peck on the cheek that Joseph Schildkraut had given H. B. Warner in DeMille's original *King of Kings* from 1927, but rather a face-to-face kiss that only at the very last moment turns to the side. It is not just Jesus' betrayer who displays such behaviour. Prior to Jesus' trial, so we read in the Gospel of Luke (23:12), Herod and Pilate 'had been enemies', but throughout Ray's *King of Kings* they are the very best of buddies. As the movie proceeds, the intimacy between them grows, and when news of Jesus' behaviour is brought to them several days later, they are drinking wine together in a steam bath, wearing nothing but their towels. The inference here is unmistakable, and not at all minimised when Lucius tells them: 'He spoke of peace, love, and the brotherhood of man'. Having delivered his message, Lucius turns on his heel to leave these half-naked men to whatever hedonistic pleasure the audience imagines they were engaged in before he got there. (It seems likely that Ray is alluding here to the 'snails or oysters' bathing scene between Tony Curtis and Laurence Olivier in 1960's *Spartacus*: although the suggestive remark was altered before the film's worldwide theatrical release, the original scene had been screened several times before studio heads insisted on its deletion, only being restored when *Spartacus* was re-released in 1967).

As a point-of-view character, Ron Randell's Lucius stands in stark contrast to the leaders whom he serves throughout the film. Early in the movie, we see him in the court of Herod the Great as a Roman soldier reluctantly helping to carry out the Slaughter of the Innocents. Later, he will meet Mary and the young Jesus and then actually attend the Sermon on the Mount. But unlike the soldiers of the Cathedral Film productions and *Hill Number One* or Stewart Granger's Claudius in *Salome*, whose conversions are instantaneous and complete, Lucius' journey is not so smooth. When he informs Pilate and Claudia that he plans to remain in Jerusalem after his retirement, he cannot precisely tell them why. Pilate is, as is his wont throughout *King of Kings*, dismissive of such wavering. 'Personally, I suspect you found our Roman gods too cruel', he says, adding with a chuckle. 'Are you also awaiting the coming of the local Messiah?' In another movie about Jesus, we might expect some intimation of imminent conversion at this point, but Lucius instead responds with a far bleaker profession. 'To believe in the Messiah, one must believe in God. What I've witnessed in my years on earth is proof enough that there can be no God', he states. It is a surprising expression of atheism in a movie with an American Jesus. By 1961, the American embrace of Christianity was a distinct part of Cold War ideology, a way of drawing a distinction between the West and 'godless Communism'. The phrase 'under God' had been officially incorporated into the Pledge of Allegiance in 1954, and 'In God We Trust' had been adopted as the official motto of the US in 1956. Yet, even in the midst of these patriotic professions of faith, there could be heard a secularist backlash, even at the highest levels. Just three months before *King of Kings* was released, the Supreme Court ruled in *Torcaso v Watkins*, a landmark case about the separation between church and state: 'We repeat and again reaffirm that neither a State nor the Federal Government can constitutionally force a person "to profess a belief or disbelief in any religion"'. By the movie's end, of course, the solider will indeed kneel at the foot of the cross and proclaim: 'He is truly the Christ' (as the Biblical epic genre requires). However, in his discussion with Pilate, Lucius gives voice to an honest scepticism born from his own lived experience that many in the moviegoing audience must themselves have felt.

In the trial of Jesus before Pilate, Lucius furthermore performs another unique and decidedly non-canonical role, serving as the accused's court-appointed advocate. It is not the only deviation from Scripture in the scene. Jesus stands before the tribunal off to one side as Pilate and Lucius make their entrance on a long red carpet – undoubtedly, it is intended to foreshadow the blood that Jesus will spill in this same courtyard after he is scourged, but it is also a symbol of Pilate's celebrity status. For the director, the image of the side-lined Jesus suffering in silence as others proceed along the red carpet might well have captured his own sense of alienation from Hollywood itself and the mainstream American culture that shunned him and would damn his *King of Kings* in the most virulent of terms. In as clear a contrast as possible for this first meeting of protagonist and antagonist, Jesus is dressed in white on the righthand side of the screen, while downstage from the left Pilate proceeds, wearing a black mantle. Neither the crowd nor the high priests appear – after the servants who have cobbled together this tribunal have left, the only people present are Jesus, Pilate, Lucius and, curiously, a court stenographer.

'You have been interrogated by Caiaphas', Pilate says as the trial begins, only to dismiss the religious decision of the Sanhedrin and take the political charges into his own hands. 'They've judged you guilty on two counts: Blasphemy and sedition. This court takes no cognizance of your blasphemy. But the charge of sedition is a major offense', the prefect intones. The background to this statement is worth discussing in greater detail. In putting together research for *King of Kings*, Ray had conferred extensively with Reverend George Dunbar Kilpatrick, the Dean Ireland's Professor of Exegesis of Holy Scripture at the University of Oxford, whose lecture titled 'The Trial of Jesus' had been published a few years earlier. MGM had made much of this consultation in its publicity, prompting *The New Yorker*'s Brendan Gill to write a satiric poem about it:

Matthew, Mark, Luke, and John,
Bless the reverend Oxford don

Hired by Metro-Goldwyn-Mayer
To bring a scholar's mind to bear

On the news you scribbled in bits and pieces.
It takes a master of exegesis

To clarify what you left dark.
Careless Matthew, hasty Mark,

Unjournalistic John and Luke.
But count it not as a rebuke

If M-G-M turns what was crypt-
ic into a clear-cut shooting script.

Doubtless you did the best you could
Two thousand years pre-Hollywood,

And details in need of beefing up
(What kind of bread? What shape of cup?

How brightly did the candles glow?)
Can be inserted now to show

Our Lord's Last Supper in terms theatric,
Thanks to Professor George Kilpatrick.[18]

Lampoons notwithstanding, Kilpatrick seems to have been of material help to the director in conceptualising this part of *King of Kings*. In a letter to his producer in February 1960, in fact, Ray maintained that 'thanks to Kilpatrick, he had solved the dramatic problem of the trial of Jesus'. While it does not seem likely that the Professor of Exegesis of Holy Scripture suggested that either a court-appointed advocate or stenographer was present, the particular charges that Pilate investigated probably were suggested by Kilpatrick who, in explaining a crux in the Gospel of Mark, remarks: 'Jesus was brought before Pilate by the Sanhedrin on a political charge, namely that he claimed to be the king of the Jews, not on a charge of speaking against the Temple, which would not have impressed Pilate'.[19] It seems clear enough that, in the post-Holocaust age, Ray was eager to avoid as best he could any anti-Semitic element in his film, and it is for this reason that the trial of Jesus before Pilate proceeds without reference to any religious matters and strictly along political lines.

As noted, Lucius is appointed by Pilate to represent Jesus, who has refused to respond to any of the prefect's questions. Doing his best as a public defender for his silent client, Lucius parries with Pilate over the various charges brought about Jesus, and the film at this point turns into a courtroom drama.

PILATE:
During the past three years, the accused has in acts and speeches disturbed the people, condemned the payment of tribute, and claimed himself king. And spread the word that his kingdom has precedence over and above Roman jurisdiction.

LUCIUS:
The defendant has only spoken of the Kingdom of God. He's never attempted to usurp Roman jurisdiction over Judea.

PILATE:
The implication is the same. There can be no division of authority in Judea. A nation can have only one master.

The unlawful assembly of the Sermon on the Mount is then introduced, when Jesus 'advised people to dispose their possessions and follow him', Pilate maintains. 'How can Rome levy taxes on the people if they follow his teaching?' When Lucius then submits that the charge against Jesus be reduced to tax evasion, Pilate abruptly switches tactics, demanding to know if he is a king. 'Whoever believes in the truth will listen to me', Jesus replies, prompting Pilate to ask whether there can be more than one truth. 'My lord, the court deviates from the issue', Lucius interjects. 'Truth is not on trial here, but a man named Jesus, from Nazareth'. Being reminded of Jesus' Nazarene background, Pilate realises that he can send Jesus off to Herod and, with that, swiftly brings the case to its close.

In many ways, it is not surprising that Ray has chosen to present the trial of Jesus as he has, in the form of a courtroom drama (Figure 5.2). No stranger to the genre as a director, Ray had made the Humphrey Bogart vehicle *Knock on Any Door* in 1949. In the late 1950s and early 1960s, however, legal battles constituted quite a few of the highest-grossing films: for instance, *12 Angry Men* and *Witness for the Prosecution* had both come out in 1957, *Anatomy of a Murder* and *Compulsion* in 1959, *Inherit the Wind* in 1960 and *Judgment at Nuremberg* in 1961, to name just a few (and of course 1962 would see the release of one of the finest specimens of the genre, *To Kill a Mockingbird*). The courtroom drama has an illustrious history that can be traced back to Aeschylus' *Eumenides* in 458 BC, but its appeal for mid-century Americans is likely connected to the heightened judicial activity of the Supreme Court under Chief Justice Earl Warren. Cases dealing with freedom of speech, reproductive rights, the separation of church and state, and, of course, civil rights had all been adjudicated by the Warren Court. Increasingly in this period, the courts were seen as the preeminent venue for hammering out the day's thorniest moral issues, and so it is unsurprising that Ray decided that Jesus ought to be tried in an actual courtroom; even if the impartiality of the judge could not be guaranteed, he would have had a competent public defender by his side. Looking to sidestep the anti-Semitic overtones of the received tradition, Ray situated his trial of Jesus before Pilate in a courtroom far more contemporary.

As was noted earlier in this chapter, *King of Kings* now turns to the court of Herod and a scenery-chewing finale on Frank Thring's part, but the last full scene with Hurd Hatfield's Pilate takes place just after

Figure 5.2 Hurd Hatfield sits in judgment over Jesus in Nicholas Ray's *King of Kings* (1960).

Jesus has been sent back to him. Although he is reclining at dinner with his wife, he is furious to have to deal with Jesus one more time and yells at a subordinate: 'Scourge him! Loosen his tongue! Make him confess!' Claudia cannot understand why her husband is so angry, and he struggles to answer her.

CLAUDIA:
What would you want him to confess, Pilate?

PILATE:
His conspiracy.

CLAUDIA:
What conspiracy?

PILATE:
Take the miracles.

CLAUDIA:
What is his crime there?

PILATE:
He is different and refuses to behave like the others. If he can influence even Caesar's daughter, he is dangerous.

Although we will see Pilate a few times afterward, observing the beatings and watching Jesus in his crown of thorns being led away to death, these are the prefect's last words in the film. If there is a single line that captures not just Nicholas Ray's sense of the story of Jesus but the sentiment of the entire body of work from the director of *Rebel Without A Cause*, it might well be: 'He is different and refuses to behave like the others'. He is irritated by the miracles (which he has earlier called 'utter nonsense'), by the conspiracy, by the unlawful assembly and by the tax implications of the wholesale selling of worldly belongings, but in the end what Hurd Hatfield's Pilate in *King of Kings* really hates about Jesus – what he considers to be Jesus' actual crime – is his failure to conform to the expectations of society.

Despite the unfair reviews it received upon release, Ray's film has failed to hold up as a document of its time, not simply because of the staggering budget, the butchered screenplay, or the pompous voice-overs of the great intoner Orson Welles, but perhaps for reasons that can reasonably be extended to all the films considered in the chapter. As challenging a representation of the Gospel as *King of Kings* has presented here, was it really the case that a countercultural Jesus in 1961 was nothing more than a surfer turned philosopher? Never mind that even the Beach Boys themselves in 'Fun, Fun, Fun' would soon be poking fun at *Ben-Hur*'s chariot race, unfavourably likened to a free-spirited woman's joyride in her T-bird. The problem of the presentation of Christ and Christianity in *King of Kings* – as it is also in *Ben-Hur*, *Salome* and *The Robe* – is that it is simultaneously far too extravagant and far too insufficient: so much effort and expense had been put into bringing these stories of Jesus to the screen and so little thought about what might have been attractively radical about him in the first place. There is no real sense in these big-budget films of what the protagonist has at stake, and so Pontius Pilate, his antagonist, ends up being nothing more than a stage villain twirling a moustache (or, in the case of Hurd Hatfield, threatening the barber), a 'motiveless malignity' like Iago, but without the Shakespearean dialogue. The sense had been growing through the 1950s that Christianity was in need of some fundamental updating – in 1959, Pope John XXIII famously articulated the concept of *aggiornamento*, 'modernisation', and announced the formation of the Second Ecumenical Council to work toward this end. When asked by a papal dignitary about this council's intentions, the Pope is said to have walked over to a window, which he then opened, saying: 'What do we intend to do? We intend to let in a little fresh air'.[20] For both Hollywood and the Holy Catholic Church, the hope of putting more bums in the seats was paramount, and a sincere need to look beyond the stained glass seemed to have been in order.

NOTES

1 McLuhan (1964: 40–49).
2 Chrissochoidis (2013: 22–23).
3 Douglas (1942: 105).
4 Wroe (1999: 39).
5 Llewellyn-Jones (2017: 210).
6 Denker's novel, long out of print, is summarised by Streete (2018: 114).
7 Eisenhower (1953).
8 Fitzpatrick (2012: 415).
9 Sontag (1966: 288).
10 Tunberg (1958: 94). In fact, the page dated '9-19-58' originally read Cyprus for Alexandria but was probably altered due to the political violence associated with the island throughout the year.
11 Connor (2018).
12 Fitzpatrick (2012: 415.)
13 McKinnon (2011: 209).
14 Quoted by McKahan (2014: 219).
15 McGilligan (2011: 417).

16 Bawden (2017: 354); MacDonald (1969: 428).
17 McKahan (2014) 224.
18 Gill (1960: 38).
19 Kilpatrick (1953: 14).
20 Cousins (1963: 20), evidently the first person to cite this famous story.

6 Finding Meaning in the Middlebrow: Pilate in the 1960s

The great American proposition is 'religion is good for the kids, though I'm not religious myself'.

– John Courtney Murray, S. J.,
quoted in *Time*'s 'Is God Dead?' issue (8 April 1966)

'Of the three most recent stabs – *le mot juste,* I think – at the Christ story', wrote Dwight MacDonald in his review of *The Greatest Story Ever Told*, 'Nicholas Ray's *King of Kings* is lowbrow kitsch, Pier Pasolini's *The Gospel According to St. Matthew* is highbrow kitsch, and the present work is the full middlebrow, or Hallmark Hall of Fame treatment'.[1] We will come to George Steven's *Greatest Story* later in this chapter – and perhaps come to the same conclusion about its value as a film as well – but before we proceed to consider further these various Hollywood versions of Jesus and company, it is worth stopping to take the full measure of MacDonald's scorn into account. 'It seems to be impossible for this Christian civilization to make a decent movie about the life of its founder', the critic began this particular review, even as a few years earlier he had said of Ray's *King of Kings*: 'The genre is hopeless and that's that'.[2] For MacDonald, what was offensive about the big-screen Biblical epics was that they were entertainment of the lowest-common-denominator variety, made at an unjustifiable expense for the sake of still more unjustifiable profit. In his eyes, they were an offense against good taste. Now, perhaps it would be churlish to point out that these holier-than-thou pronouncements did not appear in *Partisan Review* or some other highbrow journal but in the decidedly middlebrow *Esquire* – where,

on the page after his review, there ran ads for elevator shoes and a
brand of boxers called 'Ah Men!'[3] Yet, there can be no doubt that
MacDonald was one of the most significant cultural commentators
of his day, one who, in insisting that mass culture deserved serious engagement, almost singlehandedly invented the concept of the
'public intellectual'. To hold even the most popular of art forms
to the highest of critical standards was not a duty ever shirked by
MacDonald, whose witty reviews influenced filmmaking in general
and the reception of particular films for decades to come. Certainly,
he earned his reputation as 'the greatest American hatchet man', as
Franklin Foer put it in a review essay of *Masscult and Midcult* half
a century later.[4] It can be difficult, admittedly, after reading what
MacDonald has to say about these films, to resist the urge to pick
up a rock and join in the stoning. But, as amusing as he undoubtedly
can be, this critic owed it to his readers to understand the works
under review for what they were, rather than indulging himself in
snobbery – which is *le mot juste*, I think.

'I'm just so sick of pedants and conceited little tearer-downers I
could scream', says one of the main characters in Salinger's *Franny and
Zooey*, a book topping the *New York Times* charts for twenty-seven
straight weeks in 1961 and 1962. She is speaking about college
professors rather than film reviewers here, but Franny's observation
holds true for both. As a student as well as an actress, she is suffering a spiritual malaise for which the mid-century's sanctimonious
aesthetic criticism offers little solace. Her brother Zooey, himself
an actor, labours mightily to comfort her, although the long-winded
tirades which make up most of the book's second half seem almost
by design not to be much help. In the end, however, he recollects the
enigmatic advice that their older brother Seymour had given him
when he was just a child on the radio, that he should remember the
Fat Lady before every performance. 'He never did tell me who the Fat
Lady was', he remarks, before going on to tell Franny:

> I don't care where an actor acts. It can be in summer stock, it can be over a
> radio, it can be over television, it can be in a goddam Broadway theatre, com-
> plete with the most fashionable, most well-fed, most sunburned-looking audi-
> ence you can imagine. [. . .] There isn't anyone anywhere that isn't Seymour's
> Fat Lady. Don't you know that? Don't you know that goddam secret yet?
> And don't you know – listen to me, now – don't you know who that Fat
> Lady really is? [. . .] Ah, buddy. Ah, buddy. It's Christ Himself. Christ Himself,
> buddy.[5]

As we proceed, perhaps it might make sense to consider these productions not with the condescension of a Dwight MacDonald, but

with the less cynical yearning of Franny and Zooey Glass. Granted, the temptation to indulge oneself in Olympian ridicule of mid-1960s Bible-based entertainment is tremendous, but somewhere out there in the audience were people like Seymour's Fat Lady who were not laughing up their sleeve about it all.

The people who went to see the shows about Jesus covered in this chapter, after all, were the very same people who had put *Franny and Zooey* at the top of the *New York Times* bestseller list, and whose collective naïveté did not necessarily mean that they were precluded from the early 1960s sense of spiritual longing. They were, in other words, the very same people who, in their unsophisticated way, might have found something meaningful in the middlebrow story of Barabbas in 1961, whether it was the, yes, *Hallmark Hall of Fame* treatment that aired on NBC in March, or the epic film produced by Dino DeLaurentiis and starring Anthony Quinn which premiered that December. The story of the Biblical prisoner whose sentence Pilate commuted as part of a supposed Passover tradition came to popular attention in the twentieth century, following the success of the 1950 novella by Pär Lagerkvist, who won the Nobel Prize for Literature the following year. Originally published in Swedish and translated into numerous other languages shortly thereafter, *Barabbas* was a statement of post-war spiritual anxiety not unlike *Franny and Zooey* (although it featured far fewer 'goddams'). After his release, the eponymous hero ends up in Rome as a slave, not forgetting his encounter with Jesus but uncertain what to make of it. Later asked by a Roman official about the pendant disk he wears, on which a fellow slave has carved *Christos Iesus*, he denies being a Christian. He wears it, he tells the incredulous Roman, 'because I want to believe'. In 1953, a Swedish film adaptation by Alf Sjöberg premiered at Cannes, but English-language audiences would have to wait until the next decade to see a screen version of the Barabbas story, and even then the works were palimpsests of Lagerkvist's slim but profound book.

Written by the prolific Henry Denker, *Give Us Barabbas!* was staged for Hallmark by the renowned George Schaeffer who, out of his sixty-plus years of directing experience, called it 'an almost perfect live television drama'.[6] The teleplay explores the barrage of emotions felt by Barabbas (played by James Daly, although Laurence Olivier had been considered for the part) in the hours and days that followed his release, as his bliss turns to bewilderment. His lover, Mara (Kim Hunter), tells him that people in the crowd were paid to shout for his freedom and the crucifixion of Jesus, an idea that disconcerts her. Had Barabbas gained his freedom by informing on his friends, Mara openly wonders, even as many of his comrades among the Zealots were certain of his collaboration with the Romans? Breaking into his house, they find a sack of Roman coins, planted there by one of his enemies, and kidnap him in order to conduct a kangaroo court trial. Barabbas is determined to be guilty – none of them can get past his claim that the crowd was given bribe money not 'to free me but to convict' Jesus, a person whose fate nobody can imagine is all that important. Sentenced to outcast status, Barabbas agonises over the enigma of his release. First going to Golgotha, where he meets a Roman centurion who tells him that 'Pilate doesn't want anybody asking any questions', Barabbas ends up rapping on the Roman guardhouse door and demanding to see the prefect, played by Dennis King.

Primarily a stage actor of musical comedies in London as well as on Broadway, King had often been cast as a romantic lead when a young man and in more comic roles later in his long career. He had played the title role in a televised version of Gilbert and Sullivan's *Mikado* (starring Groucho Marx as Koko) earlier in 1961, but it is a very different sort of potentate that he portrays in *Give Us Barabbas!* – his final TV appearance. From the first moments of their encounter, we have a strong sense of the inner turmoil plaguing King's Pilate: he is holding his head in his hand when Barabbas first approaches him. 'Why is he here?' he asks a soldier. Barabbas demands to learn why he has been set free and Jesus sent to the cross, to which Pilate replies loudly: 'I crucified no one!' A nerve has clearly been touched, and throughout the scene King comes close to and backs off from revealing how troubled he is. When Barabbas presses him on why Jesus died, Pilate answers him testily: 'Because he talked in riddles! ... He spoke of truth, but I asked what truth was, you could get no straight answer'. Turning away, he then adds quietly: 'At least, I could get no straight answer'. The prefect beckons Barabbas to come closer, and reveals an unexpected anguish:

PILATE:
You know, to keep peace, you do strange things. You condemn prophets and let thieves go free. And all the time, it's like trying to scoop up wine from a shattered jug (holding out his hands helplessly toward the ground) with only your hands for sponges. It's like trying to push back the blood ... Have you ever been in battle?

BARABBAS:
My kind of battle.

PILATE:
I mean civilized battle. It was the campaign in Gaul, a beautifully organized battle (non-diegetic trumpet music is heard) until my closest friend was run

through with a sword. I knelt down beside him (holds out his hands again) trying to push back his blood into the open wound, trying like a fool to push back the blood so that he might live. He looked up at me as if I were mistaken. He was dying, and yet he was more rational than I.

 Well, it's the same thing with rebellion here. You do insane things, but they seem sane at the time. But it's all for nothing. (Getting up from his chair.) Nothing! Nothing. (He walks across the room to a stand with a bowl and ewer, and pours water over his hands.) Too much soot in your city. It's your temples, burnt offerings. Impossible to keep one's hands clean. [. . .]

Following this, Barabbas will arrange for the freedom of a close friend (who, like the Zealots, will misunderstand his motives) and end up in the company of the more sympathetic Apostles, but truthfully the drama is all downhill after this encounter with the Roman prefect. There is something deeply affecting about watching King's Pilate remember a friend's bloody combat death – it is not too much to think of him as suffering from post-traumatic stress disorder here – and seeing him wrestle with the existential void that grew from it. While the dots do not all connect in his narrative – how exactly is his friend's rational acceptance of death the 'the same thing' as rebellion? – the disconnectedness of his thoughts is the very point. The psychological truth of Pilate's frame of mind can be felt in the way in which King's voice trails off throughout the passage. John P. Shanley wrote in his *New York Times* review: 'As the irresolute, troubled Pilate, who first sought to avoid and then was distraught by the decision that sent Jesus to the cross, Dennis King provided a moving portrait'.[7] In Pilate, King could hardly have found a more fitting role as the swansong to his television career, the portrait of a man in pain that is all the more convincing because of its subtlety.

Figure 6.1 Arthur Kennedy's Pilate is dwarfed by the architecture in the opening scene shot at a 'Dutch angle' of *Barabbas* (1962).

Subtlety is hardly the word to be used in connection with the more famous screen version of the bewildered ancient prisoner's story released in 1961. DeLaurentiis's *Barabbas* opens with an enormous wide-angle view of the colonnaded praetorium, specially built for the movie at the outdoor studio south of Rome which tabloid wags called Dinocittà. The film's initial shot is shot at a 'Dutch angle', one in which the horizon line does not match up with the bottom of the frame. The disorientation caused by such a shot immediately conveys a sense of tension – things are off-kilter, nothing seems right – and the size of the building, so immense that it nearly blocks out the sky, reinforces the immediate feeling of oppressiveness. As Mario Nascimbene's deliberately unsettling theme music dies down, we can just discern Pontius Pilate (Arthur Kennedy) making his way forward to address the crowd. The camera dollies up to take him in, lifts higher so that we can see Jesus and some guards behind him and then turns to the right to scan over the mass of people that has gathered at the foot of the imposing staircase. Following this will be an establishing shot of the building as a whole and the entire forum, in which not a single individual can be discerned. The epic nature of the filming did not escape Saul Bellow who, in his brief stint as a film critic for *American Heritage*'s arts magazine *Horizon*, wrote: 'They do not resist the allure of "the most spectacular period in history" and there is nothing restrained or austere about their "intimate spectacle". [. . .] they are about to put Golgotha and the Circus Maximus in our laps'.[8] The architecture in this opening scene simply overwhelms Kennedy, as it does everybody else in the shot – it will be a great tribute to Anthony Quinn in the main role as Barabbas, with his larger-than-life persona and Popeye-style delivery, that he is not dwarfed by this grandiose set. It is hard to say what purpose director Richard Fleischer was pursuing with these imposing architectural shots – was he so impressed by the locations that he wanted to get everything in all at once? – but the sense of institutional oppressiveness is very immediately conveyed in these initial moments. (The next year Quinn and Kennedy would trade in the stifling soundstage of suburban Rome for the sweeping Arabian vistas of David Lean's *Lawrence of Arabia*) (Figure 6.1).

'This man has been brought to me as one who misleads the people', pronounces Kennedy's Pilate, suitably attired in a purple-bordered toga, although we are so far from his face that it is not possible to make out his expression. 'He is accused of sedition and blasphemy, for which he should suffer death'. A member of the crowd points out the custom of releasing a condemned person during this season; after a loud protest, Pilate agrees to release Barabbas. Quinn emerges from a bulkhead before the temple into the blinding light and, looking up, can just see Jesus being condemned. As he backs up, he bumps into the cross and finally walks off, dazed. In the background, we see Pilate being brought a basin and are then given our first close-up of Kennedy, who begins to wash his hands. We then switch to Barabbas, now outside the forum, washing his own hands in a nearby fountain. We are meant to draw an association here between the two figures – the Roman prefect with power to decide between life and death, and the criminal whose life has been spared by some odd turn of luck – both of whom, for reasons unstated, feel the need to be purged of this moment.

Following his release, Barabbas makes his way to his paramour, Rachel (Silvana Mangano), who has become an outspoken Christian, a circumstance that the Jewish high priests consider blasphemous. They arrange for and oversee Rachel's stoning, an overwhelmingly horrific depiction of organised mob violence, which is perhaps the film's most powerful moment. In his subsequent fury over this, Barabbas attacks the priests as they are later transporting the funds of the temples and is then abducted by Roman soldiers who bring him before Pilate. The scene that unfolds, not found in Lagerkvist's novel, is largely the work of Christopher Fry, the well-regarded British poet and playwright who wrote the screenplay:

PILATE:
It seemed to me at the time, Barabbas, when you were given your liberty before it wasn't a fortunate exchange. They were calling for death and disorder when they called your name. This is what I thought and this is what has occurred. They put the scourge back into the fist. By that I mean you and your life. And many men have suffered and died in consequence.

BARABBAS:
The other man, too. They're dying because of that.

PILATE:
This is a local matter, which I hope will soon be adjusted. The shock and fear of an unreasoning fanaticism will pass. But the appetite to destroy which, alas, the human being shares with the wild beast, is always with us. And it has rigorously to be disciplined in the name of civilization and according to the law.

We are meant to see the connection between the brutal stoning, all done according to the law, and Pilate's 'by-the-book' attitude toward crime and punishment. There is a moral callousness to Pilate's remarks here, and his insistence on the rectitude of legality seems particularly unconvincing when punctuated by the insincerity of his 'alas'. Kennedy's Pilate makes his case with all the flinty assurance of one whose privilege has protected him from any serious test of his principles. Barabbas objects to his self-congratulatory tone. 'My knife may have bitten a few throats, but what about your weapons? [. . .] Your armies have looted and raped across continents, and have been called the glory of the earth for doing it'. Although roughly put, the argument Barabbas is making here is a straightforward one: it is easy to claim to be civilised when you also happen to be strong. The mise-en-scène here powerfully reinforces Barabbas' point. He is a lonely figure in chains, even at one point prostrate on the ground, while all around him is the pomp of the Roman court and, of course, numerous armoured guards with drawn spears. Pilate continues: 'Unfortunately for you, Barabbas, the law is indispensable. The law is the pass and permit to life in this world. You were without it'. He then adds, in a line that is not historically accurate but has the value of moving the plot along: 'However, the law here tells me that a man released by the will of the people at a holy festival cannot thereafter be given a capital punishment'. Released from his chains, Barabbas asks with (justifiable) incredulity: 'You can't kill me?' Like Spartacus, however, Barabbas will go on to become a gladiator and in the end die on a cross, the Roman death penalty evidently unavoidable despite the prefect's decision.

'Pontius Pilate met Pontius Pilate in Rome last week', reported Sheilah Graham in a widely circulated item from her syndicated Hollywood gossip column in October 1961. 'Jean Marais, who portrays the Roman procurator in Irving Rapper's *Pontius Pilate*, had lunch with Arthur Kennedy, who portrays the same character in *Barabbas*. May the portliest Pontius win the Oscar!'[9] Neither actor was especially portly, as it happened, nor were the two ever seriously in the running for an Academy Award. There the similarities end, however. While Dino DeLaurentiis's *Barabbas* would go on to become a worldwide sensation, with Kennedy's performance receiving serious if limited critical approval, the fate of *Pontius Pilate* – a joint Italian-American production featuring an international cast including Jeanne Crain as Claudia, Basil Rathbone as Caiaphas and John Drew Barrymore in the dual roles of Judas and Jesus – is one of far less success. Although, as Graham notes, it was being filmed in Rome at the same time as the DeLaurentiis epic, *Pontius Pilate* saw only limited release in Europe the next year (under the name *Ponce Pilate* in France and *Ponzio Pilato* in Italy), but would not be screened in the US until December 1967, when it opened in the decidedly off-market venue of Detroit.[10] The film was never shown in a British or Australian theatre, but for several Easter seasons in the 1970s played on late-night TV in various English-speaking countries, with almost always the same description. 'Depicted are the political struggles of the Roman governor and events from the time of Pilate's arrival in Palestine until he is recalled to Rome after Christ's death'. The description was often accompanied by a two-star rating – diverting enough for those insomniacs with nothing better to do. My summary below is based on a watching of a bootleg DVD copy of the dubbed English version on VHS, purchased online from a dealer in the Netherlands.

Pontius Pilate was one of a number of films about classical antiquity that were made in Italy in the early 1960s, where lower production costs allowed epics with pretensions of grandeur to be shot on far more stringent budgets, while simultaneously offering the ready-made marketing cachet of being 'filmed on location'. The cast for such movies would often include well-known European actors whose lack of facility with English could be smoothed out in postproduction. Writing about this very matter for *Pontius Pilate*, the film critic for the *Boston Globe*, Marjory Adams, noted at the time: 'As the American market is the one in mind, there will be at least three languages used. By skilful dubbing, it will be possible for an actor like Jean Marais, for instance, as Pontius Pilate, to speak in French for the French version and mouth the English and Italian versions'.[11] When done well, the technical manipulation of an actor's voice (a process known in the industry as 'automatic dialogue replacement' or ADR) can indeed improve the overall experience of a film; when not done well, however, the results can be ludicrous. That audiences and critics will dismiss a film out of hand for what are only superficial problems of sound quality is not fair, of course, but neither is it incomprehensible. Viewers do not like to have their money wasted on subpar products, and critics are never happier than when venting their spleen. Exploiting the phenomenon of the poorly dubbed foreign film, Woody Allen struck comedy gold with his first feature-length film *What's Up, Tiger Lily?* (1966), a Japanese spy flick deliberately rewritten and revoiced to preposterous effect. The low pleasure that Allen finds here arises from watching an ambitious work of cinema betrayed by its shoddy production values – the sort of movie of which 1962's *Pontius Pilate* is a prime example, alas.

It may be that Irving Rapper and Gian Paolo Callegari's film about the Roman prefect is more deserving than the two-out-of-four-stars that TV critics awarded it, but any reconsideration needs to take into account the sort of work that it is. The overriding aesthetic of

Pontius Pilate is that of the mid-century sword-and-sandal variety –
the expectations for such movies are not especially high, of course,
as the peplum genre features as a leading draw the physiques of its
stars, most of whom are dressed in kitschily revealing outfits vaguely
suggestive of classical antiquity. The overt attractiveness of the main
actors in such films, rather than whatever inherent dramatic talent
they might possess, is a given feature of the genre. At times, even genuine talent is dismissed due to the genre. The star of *Pontius Pilate*,
Jean Marais, was a notable figure of European cinema whose most
immediate previous starring roles had been in the Franco-Italian
period drama *Le Bossu* (1959) and the remake of *Captain Blood*
(1960). A charismatic actor with an almost absurdly handsome profile, Marais was often compared to his Hollywood contemporaries
Burt Lancaster and Kirk Douglas, but this Gallic Adonis possessed a
far greater depth than his swashbuckling roles might otherwise suggest: the long-time lover of noted artist and director Jean Cocteau,
for whom he memorably starred in the classic *La Belle et la Bête*
(1946), Marais played numerous roles over the course of his varied
career and was for many the very face of dashing twentieth-century
European sophistication (Figure 6.2). When the actor died in 1998,
President Jacques Chirac remarked ruefully: 'Today, many French
have lost a bit of dream and youth'.[12]

Of the many parts that Marais played, it must be said, Pontius
Pilate is not among his finest, but he nevertheless brings an intensity
to the role of the Roman prefect that merits some measure of critical
attention. As the film opens, Pilate is at the end of his career, and
he stands before Caligula (Charles Borromel) in the Roman senate
to answer for accusations of cruelty against the Jewish people. As
a hostile judge, the new emperor walks menacingly around Pilate,
an appointee of the late Tiberius, as he makes his charges and even
produces the wooden INRI sign as evidence against him. 'You wrote

Figure 6.2 Jean Marais as the title character in 1962's *Pontius Pilate*. Commons.
wikimedia.org.

this?' he asks in mock incredulity. 'You're guilty of lèse majesté!' Finishing up his examination, the emperor lounges among the senators, demanding that he answer. Pilate refuses to reply, however. 'Speak!' Caligula bellows, slamming his hands down on the sides of his chair, but Marais's Pilate only clenches his square jaw, a faraway look visible in his eye as the scene dissolves to the day when he first led his army into Judaea. As an opening scene, there is an effective irony about this moment: it is Pilate whom we see here on trial, in the same situation that we know Jesus had faced, although now it is the prefect who stands mute before the brutal workings of Roman justice.

Our sympathy for the traditional villain of the piece thus encouraged, we look up at Pilate from below in the scene that follows, as he rides through the streets of Caesarea on horseback in full military regalia. The crowd staring at the Romans is unfriendly, but the new prefect does catch sight of the beautiful Sarah (Letícia Román) looking out at him. 'With all these hostile faces here, it's refreshing to see a pair of beautiful eyes', says Pilate, his first words in the film telegraphing clearly enough that he is destined to have an affair with her. There follows an exchange of greetings with Caiaphas, played by Basil Rathbone in one of the B-movie roles that characterised so much of his later career – a far cry from the noble Pontius Pilate he played in 1935's *Last Days of Pompeii*. But the courteous relations between the Romans and Jews is shattered by a sudden attack by the Zealots, in which Pilate receives an arrow wound to the wrist. 'I hope it's not serious', says an anxious lieutenant to his bleeding commander, who waives away the concern. Even though he later jokes that it is his 'first decoration in Palestine', the audience readily infers that the wound prefigures the blood that Pilate will need to wash from his hands following Jesus' trial.

A fracas follows the initial attack, but when the Romans begin to chase after the Zealots, Pilate orders them to stand back. 'I came here to build, not to destroy', he tells his subordinates, and much of the film will depict the construction of the massive aqueduct in Jerusalem, over the objections of the Jewish elders whom he has consulted. When he orders a new tax to pay for building costs, they also reveal that a certain wealthy merchant, the otherwise unattested Aaron El Mesin (Roger Tréville), has been instrumental in a plot among the moneychangers to devalue Roman currency – that this Aaron is also the father of Sarah, she of the refreshingly beautiful eyes, will not be surprising. Pilate feels strongly about the aqueduct, and in the following scenes many laborers are to be seen toiling away on its erection. During an inspection, Pilate instructs the Roman foreman: 'I want you to see to it that all the workers are given ample food and water'. The sight of so many ancient Hebrews working away on a monumental structure might call to mind the construction of Seti's monumental city in Cecil B. DeMille's *The Ten Commandments* from 1956, but the prefect is not by nature like Pharaoh, as we are meant to understand. When Caiaphas later confronts Pilate at the worksite, telling him that the temple funds that he has seized are not intended for use such as this, the prefect tells him that it is the Jewish people who will benefit from the aqueduct. The high priest refuses to understand and organises a work stoppage – a reminder, perhaps that the film was produced in Italy? – and relations grow increasingly ugly, although the Roman's intention is entirely altruistic.

'When they ask you what sort of man is Pontius Pilate, admit at least he is a just man', he tells Sarah who has been apprehended in a previous scene. She will go, over the course of about three minutes, from pounding his chest yelling 'I hate you!' to holding his hand and kissing him in his tent after visiting the aqueduct worksite. Their dalliance is punctuated with thematic explication, however. 'You fill our lives with art, with philosophy, even with power', Sarah tells him, as he caresses her cheek. 'We live only for God. All our thoughts begin and end with him'. When, later on, Claudia (Jeanne Crain) arrives in Judaea with their children, the reception between husband and wife is decidedly chilly, while from a nearby rooftop Sarah casts hateful glances with her refreshingly beautiful eyes toward her rival, the not yet suspecting Roman spouse. Claudia's jealousy is soon provoked, however, but quickly assuaged after a chance overhearing of Jesus preaching one day by the seaside. 'Judge not that you be not judged', she hears the young preacher say, while her children gather with others at his feet and listen in spellbound silence. When later Claudia forgives him for his infidelity, Pilate is astounded by her magnanimity, although what she knows of his affair has never actually been depicted and Sarah disappears from the movie straightaway. Plot holes such as this run throughout the film, unfortunately. While some effort was made in the script to develop the characters, at various points *Pontius Pilate* loses its focus as the producers attempted to pad out the plot – the prefect watches a *naumachia* that is made more artificially thrilling with the insertion of stock footage of alligators, for instance, while a celebration of Tiberius' birthday necessitates a night-time display of exotic dancing and torch-juggling. And of course, now and again, a towel-clad Marais issues stern orders while receiving a massage.

The film regains its footing after the high priests reluctantly permit the Zealot leader Barabbas (Livio Lorenzon) to attack the caravan which is carrying the temple funds to Pilate for the construction of the aqueduct. In the face of such outrageous banditry, Pilate rides to Jerusalem with his army and orders the Roman eagles to be raised over the Temple itself. The sacrilege draws the people out of their homes to the square in lamentation, and a public confrontation between Pilate and Caiaphas ensues. While keening fills the background, the prefect and priest face off. Although Rathbone delivers the lines like the old pro that he was, Pilate remains unpersuaded. Never will he allow the eagles to be removed and set at the feet of a foreign people! Back in the praetorium, even though Claudia begs him to show clemency, Pilate realises that he will need to use force. He commands his troops to be deployed in the square and watches them move out in military formation from his balcony. The tension builds in the scene, as the Romans draw their swords, the Jews kneel, Claudia implores, and the music rises. Finally, Pilate raises his hands and, in what is a genuinely dramatic moment, addresses the people in the square:

> Put away your swords! People of Israel, Roman swords will never be stained with your blood. There are people who wish to destroy the pact of friendship which binds us, but they have not triumphed today. The sole victor is my love for the people. Go back to your homes in peace. Although the protection of Rome will remain with you always, I promise, the Roman eagles will be removed!

Cheers rise from the crow below, as Caiaphas raises his hands to God in thanksgiving. On the balcony above, Pilate turns away with a swing of his cape. For many viewers, unaware of the incident of the standards related in Josephus, it must have seemed an unexpected moment in the narration of a story with few dramatic surprises otherwise. The Zealots are the only ones displeased with the outcome of the standards affair, it seems, and the film moves full speed toward various battles between the Romans and the Jewish rebels, complete with flaming projectiles shot from catapults.

The moments of warfare are juxtaposed with the appearance of Jesus who enters Jerusalem accompanied by a heavenly choir. When at the Temple Jesus drives out the moneychangers, Pilate and Claudia are watching from their balcony once again, but the Roman figures have little involvement in the scenes of the Passion narrative that follow. Pilate disappears for a good while from the film that bears his name, as Judas (played by John Drew Barrymore) hands over Jesus (also played by John Drew Barrymore) to the agents of the

Sanhedrin. But rather than the usual villainy from Caiaphas at this point in the traditional narrative, there is a tenderness in Rathbone's portrait, speaking gently at this moment to Jesus 'as an old Rabbi to a young one', which might even have become famous if *Pontius Pilate* had been a better-made film. Looking into Jesus' eyes, which now fill the screen with a piercing gaze, Rathbone's Caiaphas turns away uneasily. 'Go then', he says, in quiet resignation. 'For I have no other recourse than to return you to Pilate's guard'. The film moves swiftly through the rest of the Gospel story to its conclusion. Back at the praetorium, Claudia rushes in to tell her husband of her dream – 'I saw the sky blackened, the earth tremble, an eagle swoop down on a helpless lamb!' she says – but as she begs him to listen, a subordinate enters to let Pilate know that the Sanhedrin has sent Jesus to him for judgment. When he emerges to the trial, Pilate will ask: 'What is truth?' But it is one of the high priests who answers: 'The truth is that he came down from Galilee preaching rebellion!' Pilate has Jesus sent off to a jail cell while he deliberates.

As the prefect paces nervously in the praetorium, a lieutenant remarks that this is not the first time he ever has had to pass a death sentence. Pilate perches anxiously as he replies: 'The other times it was all so clear – the crime, the punishment to be given, and my personal conviction! And this time, it ... it all escapes me!' As he says these lines, Marais gestures wildly with his hands before his face – we cannot help but think of what those hands soon will do. He returns to the portico of the praetorium to render his fateful decision. We have been watching this sentence pronounced from a perspective somewhere behind Jesus, whose side we are thus encouraged to take. To this aggressive new wrinkle in the trial of Jesus yet another is immediately added. We see a shot of a perplexed Caiaphas looking around at the crowd which, rather than loudly calling for crucifixion as they do in the Gospels, instead stands in shocked silence until someone shouts out in protest: 'Let us judge him!' When Jesus and Barabbas are brought out, again someone in the crowd yells out: 'He is one of us! Let the Sanhedrin decide!'

Earlier in the scene, Pilate had turned away after the sentencing, asking a subordinate: 'Why are they acting like this?' Truthfully, he is not the only one who is confused about what is going on at this point in the movie. There is no help coming from Jesus in resolving the situation, at any rate. 'Behold this man', Pilate says, pointing to him. 'If he is innocent, why does he not speak?' With little other option at this moment, the prefect calls for a basin of water in which to wash his hands – in it, we see the reflection of Jesus' eyes just as Caiaphas had seen them a little while before, 'an interesting and imaginative cinematic touch', as Peter Malone has called it, although it seems to have little effect on the prefect's behaviour.[13] Paying far less attention to these eyes than he had to Sarah's at the film's beginning, he plunges his hands into the water. A servant holds out a board on which Pilates then paints *Iesus Nazarenus Rex Iudeaorum*, and although Caiaphas complains, he intones: 'What I have written, I have written'. Events move swiftly toward their conclusion. The earthquake that follows the crucifixion destroys the praetorium, and amid the rubble Pilate finds Claudia who lives just long enough to die in his arms, asking him to make others believe as she now does. Looking around the ruins with a bewildered look, we dissolve back to the opening scene of the film. 'Do you know I have the power of life and death over you?' Caligula roars at Pilate, standing once again in the Senate chamber where he is on trial. 'The highest of all judges is not seated here', Pilate calmly replies. 'And it is for his infinite mercy that I am praying, not yours. Divine judgement comes from a higher sphere, Divine Caesar. "For mine is the kingdom of Heaven . . ."' The camera pans upward to an oculus in the ceiling through which light shines forth, as the music of a celestial choir rises dramatically and the words THE END appear on screen.

All in all, it seems, the television critics of the 1970s were right in their two-star assessment of *Pontius Pilate* – as a bit of entertainment, it is diverting enough, for those insomniacs with nothing better to do late at night. Certainly, some fine actors grace the cast, of whom Marais and Rathbone might particularly be singled out, and the sets of the Cinecittà studio were among the grandest available for movies about ancient Rome. But there is something off-kilter about this film. We are inclined to want to like Pilate as the film begins, for surely there is no way that a man whom Caligula is browbeating can be anything other than our hero. Marais looks debonair in his cuirass and helmet, and there is something admirable about the way in which he restrains his troops after the initial attack of the Zealots. His flirtation with Sarah may perhaps be pardonable – indeed, his own wife forgives him, so why shouldn't we? – and he manages to walk back the disastrous erection of the standards on the Temple in what can be seen as a noble act of humility. But when the original concepts found in the screenplay begin to be grafted onto the Biblical material, the tension starts to tear at *Pontius Pilate*. Eager to avoid blaming Caiaphas and the Sanhedrin for the death of Jesus, the producers need to transform their sympathetic title character into the villain of the piece. There is just no way to square these inconsistent dramatic conceptions with one another, much as Marais may wring his hands in existential dread. The mismatch between the actor's moving lips and the dubbed voices that come out of their mouths might be the best metaphor for this well-intentioned but poorly executed film.

Upon release, *Pontius Pilate* languished in obscurity, quite unlike the reception that met *The Greatest Story Ever Told*, released three years later to widespread negative critique. George Stevens's mammoth depiction of the life of Christ starred Max von Sydow as Jesus, Charlton Heston as John the Baptist, Telly Savalas as Pontius Pilate and a host of others in walk-on roles. As discussed in Chapter 1, the most famous anecdote about this film concerns John Wayne who, asked to repeat his line as the centurion at the foot of the cross, adding some awe to his words, intoned: 'Aw, truly this man was the Son of God'. Amusing though untrue, this anecdote tells us a lot about the hostile reception of *The Greatest Story Ever Told*. Shot at great expense among the mesas and buttes of Utah and Arizona, the film is as much a love-letter to the landscape of the Southwest as it is a narrative of the ancient Middle East. But just as Joseph Mankiewicz's *Cleopatra* (which had come out a year before it) had been and just as John Huston's *The Bible* (which came out the year after) would be, Stevens's *Greatest Story* was an exorbitantly expensive blockbuster that fizzled at the box office. After the financial failure of these three films, the epic film set in classical antiquity for all intents and purposes would be a dead genre, until Ridley Scott made *Gladiator* thirty-five years later. 'To everything there is a season', the Byrds would sing in one of the year's biggest hits. A 1950s-style spectacle out of place in the mid-1960s, *Greatest Story* was a product of Eisenhower-era earnestness that had the bad fortune to be released during the Johnson administration, at a countercultural moment suspicious of traditions both religious and cinematic. It is a film one *wants* to like for many reasons (the heartfelt religious sincerity, the desire to address monstrous injustice, the painterly beauty of its landscapes), but for just as many reasons (its overreliance on clichés, its shallow sensibility, its turgid pace) one cannot. But before we dump *The Greatest Story Ever Told* onto the heap of mid-1960s middlebrow mediocrities, it is worth reflecting on the journey, itself no less epic, that brought director George Stevens to make this particular film. This will help explain, as well, the particular way in which his Pilate is presented.

As a director Stevens's career can be divided neatly into two distinct categories. There were the light comedies he made before the Second World War: shorts with Laurel and Hardy, *Alice Adams*

(1935), *Penny Serenade* (1941), *Woman of the Year* (1942). And then there were heavier message movies that came after: *A Place in the Sun* (1951), *Shane* (1953), *Giant* (1956), *The Diary of Anne Frank* (1959). What came in between was Stevens's wartime work with the branch of the US Signal Corps known as the 'Hollywood Irregulars', a group of accomplished directors (John Ford, John Huston, William Wyler and Stevens) working under the leadership of Frank Capra to produce films for use by the US Army. The remarkable story of this group has recently been told in *Five Came Back*, a book by Mark Harris (2014) that has subsequently been made into a three-part documentary of the same name for Netflix (2017). The work of Capra's group was significant in the production of Allied propaganda abroad and newsreels for the domestic market. After D-Day, Stevens and his filmmaking unit went with General Omar Bradley across France into the collapsing Germany, capturing among other things the first meeting of American and Russian soldiers at Torgau. But, without any doubt, the most important documentary footage he shot was the liberation of the Dachau concentration camp in May 1945. 'It was like wandering around in one of Dante's infernal visions', as he put it.[14] The experience was to have a profound impact on the director and his work for the rest of his life.

As they came upon the heaps of corpses and the hundreds of emaciated people resembling corpses at Dachau, Stevens and his unit documented the horrors with grim determination. This work would be of extraordinary importance for the prosecution of the Third Reich war criminals at Nuremburg. When the war ended, the other Irregular members returned to their civilian livelihoods: Capra made the pivot back to Hollywood with particular success, directing *It's A Wonderful Life* in 1946, as did Wyler, sweeping that year's Oscars with *The Best Years of Our Lives*, while Huston and Ford, both initially stalled in the post-war period, would resume their careers and go on to make films of great renown. But for Stevens, the duty of being the world's witness to the atrocities of the Final Solution came at a great personal and professional cost. He had taken to drinking and grown understandably withdrawn and morose. Katherine Hepburn and others urged him to make comedies again, a genre for which he had shown true genius, but Stevens was unable to do so. 'After the war', the director told an interviewer in 1962, 'I don't think I was ever too hilarious again'. Capra knew the heavy burden under which his colleague suffered. 'None of us were the same after the war, but for him . . .', he said, trailing off, when asked about Stevens years later. 'The films that he took of Dachau, the ovens, and the big, big piles of bones that nobody could believe existed. [...] He had seen too much'.[15]

When he did eventually make his way back to directing, Stevens was a very different man. A seriousness had entered his films, informed by his unspeakable wartime experiences. In the 1950s, the Academy would award him two Oscars for Best Director and nominate him for two others, but – and this is a painful thing to say about a filmmaker who was trying so hard to grapple with the evil that he had encountered in the Nazi death camps – Stevens's work over the years had become increasingly sententious. Film scholar Marilyn Ann Moss sees *The Greatest Story Ever Told* as the 'logical next step' in his development as a filmmaker, 'another way that Stevens continued to create art from his experiences in the war. His view of Dachau left an indelible imprint that seemed to drive his aesthetic forward to the ever-larger expression, as if he were trying to gain on the enormity of life-changing images he saw in the war'.[16] Viewed as a way of processing the atrocity of his Holocaust experiences, Stevens's story of Jesus comes into sharper view, not just as a retelling of the Passion narrative but as an attempt to confront the virulent anti-Semitism at its core. Only a few months after *Greatest Story* was released, a similar theme would be sounded by Pope Paul VI in his encyclical *Nostra Aetate*. 'Furthermore, in her rejection of every persecution against any man', the pope stated forcefully, 'the Church, mindful of the patrimony she shares with the Jews and moved not by political reasons but by the Gospel's spiritual love, decries hatred, persecutions, displays of anti-Semitism, directed against Jews at any time and by anyone'.[17] This categorical statement was deemed ground-breaking in a papal encyclical, but the same sentiments in a mainstream movie simply seemed churchy. Critics were cruel, but Stevens was content that he had accomplished what he hoped to do in what would be his last significant Hollywood film.

In an opening scene from *Greatest Story*, the Herod who orders the slaughter of the Innocents had declared to the Magi 'I am an Idumean not a Judean', just as the Herod of Ray's *King of Kings* had been described in the voice-over as an Arab – each, it is clear, acts as a client-king for their Roman overlords. Both Stevens and Ray are eager to brand the wide-scale murder of these Jewish children early on in their Jesus narrative as a decision made by non-Jewish leaders. Stevens, in fact, goes further in his association: casting Claude Rains as Herod in his final film appearance, the director knew that few filmgoers could fail to associate the star with his best-known role, the charming Captain Renault in 1941's *Casablanca*. Rains's Herod is hardly a charmer but, like the captain, he is a collaborator with unseemly anti-Semites, and when he dies, the people cry out: 'The old Herod is dead! Death to the new one! Long live Israel!' (a statement one cannot imagine in a film made before 1948). After a crowd tears down the symbol of his Roman-derived power, a Roman eagle intentionally designed to look like the swastika-wielding Nazi *Parteiadler*, it is restored by goose-stepping Romans who, we are told, now intend to maintain order by governing the region directly.

The Roman governor assigned to bring this order is, of course, Pontius Pilate, played here by Telly Savalas, the actor who would go on to far greater fame a decade later as the hero of CBS's hit detective show *Kojak*. It is nearly impossible, at this distance, to watch Savalas in this role and not think of the 1970s celebrity whom *Newsweek* once called on the cover of its international edition 'TV's Global Superstar' (16 August 1976). Surveying his career in an obituary, *People* magazine identified 'some inexplicable combination of telegenics and testosterone' that made Savalas 'a star and an improbable sex symbol'.[18] Given the trappings of tabloid machismo in which he later arrayed himself – the emblematic lollipop, the 'Who loves ya, baby?' tagline and the overall Rat Pack manqué persona – one forgets that Savalas was actually a talented performer. He would be nominated for an Oscar, two Golden Globes and an Emmy over the course of his career, although he had never had any formal training as an actor. As he said to Billy Boggs in 1976, Savalas regarded his success as a matter mostly of good fortune, as is evident from a conversation he recounts with his mother after being cast in Stevens's film:

> 'Telly', she says, 'that's wonderful. You'll make a great Jesus'. 'Hey ma, I'm playing Pontius Pilate'. Well, there was a dramatic pause on the other side and she says, 'Well, all right Telly, but make sure you play him sympathetically'.[19]

In a film that explicitly looks to exonerate the Jews for Jesus' death by overtly casting blame onto the Romans, Savalas's Pilate is a decidedly sympathetic figure, one who despite his tough-guy exterior finds the sentencing of Jesus a matter of some inner anguish. But there is a complexity to the character that goes beyond sympathy as such.

When Pilate makes his initial appearance onscreen in *Greatest Story*, he is seen first from the rear – subordinates scattering out of his way, he marches in, wearing a heavy leather cuirass that accentuates his broad torso, but what we notice right away is Savalas's bald head. In fact, it was for this very role that the actor adopted the look that would become his trademark. In the same interview with Boggs,

Savalas recounted his discussion with the director about this hairstyle decision:

> 'Mister Savalas, forget about how you conceive Pontius Pilate in the past. But it would give me a feeling of power, a feeling of . . . of course, the man was a governor and a general and he ruled the land with an iron fist, I'd like to shave your head. How do you feel about that?' I says, 'I don't mind, I'm free of any feeling, but I do have small children at home. It might be traumatic for them for Poppa to come home looking so different'. He says, 'Well, why don't you bring them in. They'll watch the ceremony'. I says, 'It's a good idea'. So I brought my kids in, my nieces and nephews in, I brought the whole neighborhood in. They never even noticed, they couldn't care less. And the next picture was waiting, and the next picture was waiting, and I could never let it grow. So I figured, well, it's comfortable this way, just a lot more face to shave.[20]

Given the emblematic place that Savalas's bald head would hold in the 1970s celebrity pantheon, it is (as noted in Chapter 1) quite a thing to read the memo that says: 'MR STEVENS WOULD LIKE TO SEE TELLY SAVALAS WITH COMPLETELY SHAVED HEAD'. It is like seeing a note that reads 'SANTA TO BE DRESSED IN RED SUIT' or 'GEORGE WASHINGTON TO WEAR WHITE WIG'. Who knew that there might be an actual piece of paper on which the decision for an iconic image was proclaimed for the very first time?

George Stevens wanted Telly Savalas to shave his head in order to play Pontius Pilate, that much is clear – but why? That is something for which there exists no evident documentary testimony about which we might be justified in speculating. In a well-known chapter from *Mythologies*, Roland Barthes had written about the 'insistent fringes [that are quite] simply the label of Roman-ness' on the heads of all the Romans in Joseph Mankiewicz's *Julius Caesar* (1953). Perhaps Stevens and his hairstyling consultants were looking to buck the tradition of insistent fringes, as they are not much in evidence in *Greatest Story* – indeed, the Roman men's hair in the film is generally more mid-1960s contemporary. Barthes goes on to note that, in films about antiquity, 'the bald are not admitted, although there are plenty of them to be found in Roman history'.[21] It may be that Stevens was aware of this, although it seems more likely that the imagery of Benito Mussolini, who had employed his bald head much as Hitler had done with his moustache, as a quickly-identified emblem in the imagery of his personality cult. Also, in the background of this decision to shave Savalas's head might have been a desire to suggest some symbolic connection with the appearance of Yul Brynner's Ramses from *The Ten Commandments*, Cecil B. DeMille's 1956 blockbuster about Moses. Like Pilate, Ramses is the civil authority whom the

holy man confronts – and, of course, Brynner had a strikingly original look in that film due to his baldness. Perhaps we can suggest,
beyond any particular allusion, that Stevens thought that the phal-
lic suggestion of a bald head would lend his Pilate the 'feeling of
power' he was seeing. In the end, it is hard to say whether the Pilate
of *Greatest Story Ever Told* was portrayed as bald out of a desire
to draw on associations from political propaganda or earlier film
imagery, but the effect certainly is to make him stand out amid the
numerous celebrity appearances in the film.

As the movie progresses, we see Savalas's Pilate with the Nazi-
esque *Parteiadler* eagle visible in the distance behind him, while he
himself is often seated behind a large desk. Rod Steiger's Pilate would
likewise appear as a desk-bound official in 1977's *Jesus of Nazareth*,
but for Savalas here, there is a suggestion of something beyond the
general sense of being overworked. Jesus, we are given to understand, is one more item in his morning's inbox, to be dispatched as
efficiently as possible, without evident interest or malice. It is because
of the very absence of interest or malice, in fact, that this representation of the prefect takes on its most unsettling aspect. In the spring
of 1961, as the production for *Greatest Story* was coming together,
the world watched the televised trial in Jerusalem of Adolf Eichmann,
the civil servant who became the official chiefly responsible for the
Nazis' deportation of European Jews – we may be certain that among
its most avid viewers was George Stevens, whose footage from the
concentration camps was used as evidence in the trial. Surely the
1960s version of the ancient trial in Jerusalem was bearing some
connection to the actual trial in Jerusalem earlier in the decade.
Eichmann's defence had been that, while he was personally troubled
by the bloodiness of the Final Solution, he was simply following the
orders and so was free from responsibility for its horrors. The decisions had been made by his superiors and, at the infamous Wannsee
Conference, communicated to him at the level of a mere functionary.
'At that moment', Eichmann told his Israeli interrogators, 'I sensed
a kind of Pontius Pilate feeling, for I felt free of all guilt'.[22] The
term *Schreibtischtäter*, 'desk murderer', was later coined to describe
Eichmann and other such bureaucrats who sought to hide their com-
plicity in mass murder behind a veneer of dutiful uninterest for which
their large impersonal desks were a perfect symbol (Figure 6.3).

As Savalas speaks, he raises his voice but does not bark at the
people presented to him – this is not a hot-headed Pilate, as Hurd
Hatfield had been in *King of Kings*, or an especially ironic one, as
Frank Thring was in *Ben-Hur*, or even an especially world-weary

Figure 6.3 Telly Savalas as Pilate behind a large desk in *The Greatest Story Ever Told* (1965).

one, as *Last Days of Pompeii*'s Basil Rathbone had been. 'I care noth-ing for your superstitions or your God', he tells his Jewish advisers, in reference to the trouble caused by John the Baptist. 'I'm here to keep order in this desert land, and that I will do. I want to hear noth-ing more about this troublemaker or anyone like him'. Throughout his initial scenes in the film, Savalas's Pilate holds the collar of this leather cuirass in a way that, although not evidently historical, gives an impression of aggressiveness.[23] When next we see Pilate in a his-torically more accurate toga, he is conferring with Herod Antipas (José Ferrer) after Jesus' Palm Sunday arrival to Jerusalem, as a com-mander enters to tell him that the crowds are growing unruly. 'Clear the streets, close the gates, and maintain the peace', Pilate tells him. 'And bring the Nazarene to me!' He takes his place at the large desk, while a number of large dogs can be seen in the chamber behind him (these are surely meant to be intimidating, although now and again they can be seen wagging their tails). On the desk is an inkstand and other small items neatly arranged, as well as an incongruous little vase of red flowers which, together with the stripe of Pilate's garment, offer the only hint of colour in the shot. It is a moment that, but for the toga, looks like the office of a big city mayor reassuring business leaders that the protests will be dealt with smoothly and that all will be well again soon. The eagle in the distance, fasces in its talons, is framed in such a way that it seems to sit on the prefect's shoulder. 'He's actually telling people to, uh, love their enemies', Pilate says, his face breaking out into a grin. At this Herod smiles back, while the scene dissolves into the next, a shot of Roman soldiers lining up and linking shields. It is now night-time as we cut to Jesus, who is addressing a fire-lit rally. 'I have come as a light into the world', he says, holding high above his head a torch. He addresses his followers, reciting lines from the Bible which they repeat, as the soldiers begin to move out of their barracks.

In a film that sometimes seems hopelessly outdated, the moment of confrontation that transpires at this point seems to capture with stunning accuracy the spirit of the tumultuous 1960s. The shield-bearing Romans march forward in riot formation toward a peacefully assembled crowd. 'We only pray', one of them says to the commander, who tells him to step aside and then slaps him across the face. We hear swords drawn. It is a tense moment, as the soldiers charge with weapons in hand into the unarmed crowd. Directed by Jean Neguelesco while Stevens was filming on location in Utah, the scene was shot in the summer of 1963 and looks it.[24] Through the spring of that year, all eyes were riveted upon events in Birmingham, Alabama, where Martin Luther King Jr and the Southern Christian Leadership Coalition were leading a series of non-violent protests against the city's Jim Crow laws. Commissioner of Public Safety Eugene 'Bull' Connor, determined to maintain order, released police dogs and turned firehoses on the protesters – tactics which, when they appeared on TV and in print, shocked viewers around the globe. On Good Friday, Connor arrested King, who at this time would write his famous 'Letter from a Birmingham Jail'. An agreement was signed to bring formal segregation to an end in mid-May, and shortly thereafter King travelled to Los Angeles to raise funds for further civil rights work, notably the March on Washington. On 26 May, he addressed a gathering of over 40,000 people at the now-demolished Wrigley Field, with numerous figures from the film industry in attendance. 'Birmingham or Los Angeles, the cry is always the same', King told the crowd. 'We want to be free'.[25] Two weeks later, Medger Evers was killed in Jackson, Mississippi, and his funeral procession was met by police in riot-gear. It was during this time that Neguelesco filmed the scene of centurions rushing like cops with batons at the RKO Lot in Culver City. Only ten miles away is Watts, where soon after the movie's release a week-long race riot would erupt (events that form the background of Joseph Wambaugh's police novel and later film *The New Centurions*). King would later attend a special screening of *Greatest Story* at Hollywood's Cinerama Dome, a benefit hosted by George Stevens to raise money for the Freedom March.[26]

After this large and violent riot scene, the film switches gears to a quieter register. The very evening that Jesus is with the Apostles at the Last Supper, Pilate is enjoying a tranquil evening at home star-gazing with Claudia (Angela Lansbury). 'Do you hear it?' he asks her. 'I don't hear anything', she replies. 'That's what I mean. It's the best sound of all'. This silent night is hardly a holy night, however. The camera scans over the Jerusalem square where the altercation has taken place hours before and lingers on a few scattered corpses in the streets. The peace that the Pilates are enjoying has, we understand, been purchased with blood – and it is the meaning of blood that Jesus is simultaneously discussing with his disciples. Later that night, Jesus will be brought before Pilate, who has just woken up and is wearing a hooded garment of some sort. 'What has he been found guilty of that it cannot wait until a decent hour?' he asks, but not in the spirit of petulance that had been shown by Lowell Gilmore's Pilate in 1954's *Day of Triumph*. In the previous scene, Jesus is arrested in the garden, asking the arresting Roman soldiers: 'All my life I have walked in the light and spoken in the light. Why now do you come and take me like a thief in the night?' This night-time activity is characterised as shameful and cowardly, and it finds its culmination in the appearance before the prefect, who looks small behind his enormous desk. 'You claim to be the son of God. Which one, hmm?' he asks with slight derision, although he hardly seems the master of the moment. He points to the statues of Mars, Jupiter and Hercules behind him, where the eagle can also be seen, even though all of these also are framed to appear small. On the lefthand side, the figure of Jesus seen from behind dominates the screen. The Roman façade is indistinct in the early morning twilight, and only a few curious touches can be made out: the vase once again incongruously sits on the prefect's desk, and in the background by the statues there is a sleeping guard dog.

Pilate's interrogation of Jesus is played here by Savalas with sur-prising subtlety – surprising, that is, if one comes to it expecting a detective browbeating a suspect, Kojak-style. Throughout, we hear the tone of mocking disdain in Savalas's voice, but it is not entirely convincing, least of all to himself. Again, the composition of the shot emphasises Pilate's lack of control – where we get repeated close-ups of Von Sydow's radiant face with his glistening blue eyes, Savalas is nothing more than a little flesh-coloured scalp abob in a widescreen sea of grey. At the inevitable 'What is truth?' moment, he breaks off his stare at Jesus and looks down, fidgeting with a pen. Claudia now appears, half-concealed at the top of a staircase, and Pilate goes to her, remaining a step below her as they engage in a brief moment of what the closed-captioning subtitle calls 'indistinct talking'. Pilate returns, but this time he is filmed from far behind, and the statues of

Hercules and Mars that he has facetiously gestured to a moment ago now loom in the foreground, framing the shot. 'I find no guilt in him', he states, the least significant figure on the screen at this moment. We now return to a view from the front, as Pilate orders Jesus off to Herod. He crosses his arms, once again striking a pose of defiance, but now that he is not in his leather cuirass, it is far less forceful. Jesus in his robes is a dignified figure; Pilate in his bathrobe is not.

José Ferrer's Herod sends Jesus back to the Romans in Jerusalem, with none of the campy fanfare that Frank Thring displayed in *King of Kings*. Once again, Jesus is brought before Pilate, who this time is seated in the middle of the praetorium, which is shot from far above on a dolly – if he had seemed small before, Pilate is miniscule now, seated on the platform of the theatre-like building, from the grated windows of which members of the heckling crowd are hanging. Throughout the scene, Pilate is filmed through this grillwork, looking as though he is the one who is caged. From the reverse shots, he looks out at Jesus and a thin red band of soldiers; dominating the screen, the crowd is vast and intimidating. 'Play him sympathetically', Mrs Savalas had told her son, and it is hard not to feel sorry for this Pilate at this moment, as the barely contained mob jeers at him and his soldiers are barely in sight. We have a close-up of Savalas's face as he looks to Jesus for some help with the situation – 'Have you no answer for these things they accuse you of?' – but it is no use. 'My kingdom is not of this world', are the only words he receives. When he orders Jesus to be crucified, there is one more close-up of Savalas who has a blank look – it is not exactly the face of Eichmann's impassivity, nor exactly of contrition. A voice-over can be heard reciting the words from the Apostles' Creed: 'Suffered under Pontius Pilate, was crucified, dead, and buried'.

As the words of the Creed are intoned – it is unclear by whom – the impression is that audiences would recognize them as part of the church's tradition. But how many moviegoers in the mid-1960s were in fact churchgoers as well? Although he will appear once more before the end, to grant permission for the guard of the tomb, it is this penultimate scene with Savalas's Pilate that demonstrates what is the problem of *The Greatest Story Ever Told* and the others of its ilk. These movies fell flat for any number of reasons, Dwight MacDonald's carping remarks among them no doubt, but surely the biggest unexamined assumption of them was the declining consensus about Christianity itself for much of the culture. The people who saw a film on Saturday night increasingly were not the same people reciting the Creed on Sunday morning. Almost one year after *Greatest*

Story's premiere, *Time* magazine ran its famous cover story titled 'Is God Dead?' (8 April 1966), a wide-ranging survey on the decline of religion in America. Discussing church attendance in particular, the article remarked:

> Plenty of clergymen, nonetheless, have qualms about the quality and character of contemporary belief. Lutheran Church Historian Martin Marty argues that all too many pews are filled on Sunday with practical atheists – disguised nonbelievers who behave during the rest of the week as if God did not exist. Jesuit [John Courtney] Murray qualifies his conviction that the U.S. is basically a God-fearing nation by adding: 'The great American proposition is "religion is good for the kids, though I'm not religious myself"'. Pollster Harris bears him out: of the 97% who said they believed in God, only 27% declared themselves deeply religious.

Increasingly, Americans were voting with their feet about church, despite (and in some cases, because of) the modernising tendencies of most of the mainstream denominations. This did not mean a loss of faith, necessarily. The *Time* article noted that Protestant chaplain of Yale, William Sloane Coffin, reported that 'a girl said to me the other day, "I don't know whether I'll ever believe in God, but Jesus is my kind of guy"'. It disapprovingly continued: 'But a Christ-centered theology that skirts the question of God raises more questions than it answers. Does it not run the risk of slipping into a variety of ethical humanism?' But it is just such an atmosphere of distrust in institutions, doubt about metaphysics and morality, and a search for personal connection that the story of Jesus, and thus of Pilate, would be told in the decade immediately to follow.

NOTES

1 MacDonald (1969: 431).
2 MacDonald (1969: 430, 427).
3 Don't believe me? Look at *Esquire* 54.1 (July 1965): 122, https://classic.esquire.com/article/1965/07/01/the-greatest-story-ever-badly-told (accessed 1 December 2020).
4 Foer (2011).
5 Salinger (1961: 17, 202).
6 Schaefer (1996: 80).
7 Shanley (1961: 53).
8 Bellow (1963/2016: 147).
9 Graham (1961).
10 *Detroit Free Press* (1967: 8).
11 Adams (1961).
12 *Los Angeles Times* (1998).

13 Malone (2012: 51).
14 Harris (2014: 370).
15 Harris (2014: 418).
16 Moss (2004: 269).
17 Paul VI (1965: sec. 4).
18 Levitt (1994).
19 Boggs (1976).
20 Boggs (1976).
21 Barthes (1972: 24–26).
22 Arendt (1964: 114).
23 Costumer Nino Novarese almost quit over Pilate's inaccurate wardrobe, according to a letter in the Margaret Herrick Library (15 March, 1963).
24 Moss (2004: 285).
25 Boyd-Pates and Bythewood-Porter (2018–19).
26 Moon (1997: 118).

7 What Is Truth? Pilate as 1970s Moral Relativist

The view of all three of us [President Nixon, Attorney General John Ehrlichman and Haldeman] through the whole period was that the truth must be told, and quickly, although we did not know what the truth was.
— H. R. Haldeman, White House Chief of Staff,
Testimony to the US Senate Select Committee on Presidential Campaign
Activities, 30 July 1973[1]

If the popular conception of Pontius Pilate in the 1970s has any specific moment of origin, it can probably be pinpointed to the December 1968 release of a song by the Rolling Stones.

The first track of their bestselling album *Beggar's Banquet*, 'Sympathy for the Devil' was an enormous hit for the Stones, certified gold in Germany and the UK, and its recording in a London studio was the subject of an avant-garde film by the noted auteur, Jean-Luc Godard. Taken together with the title of their previous album, the relatively poorly selling *Their Satanic Majesties Request*, 'Sympathy' planted the idea for many in the period that Mick Jagger and company were practicing occultists. This sinister impression was cemented a year later when, during the playing of 'Sympathy for the Devil' at the unruly Altamont Free Concert for which the Hell's Angels had been hired as security, a fight broke out in the audience, which ultimately led to the stabbing death of a fan, a moment captured in yet another film about the Stones, *Gimme Shelter*. But, as understandable as the inference may be, the composition of 'Sympathy for the Devil' was not in fact based on Satanism at all. As Mick Jagger told an interviewer years later, '[t]he "Sympathy" character is much more complicated because my inspiration for that came from Baudelaire and *The Master and Margarita*, so I had all these things going on. It's very much of the time. It's got the violence of the time'.[2] A copy of *The Master and Margarita*, a novel written by Mikhail Bulgakov in the Stalin-era Soviet Union and newly translated into English in 1967, had been given to Jagger by his then-girlfriend, Marianne Faithful.[3]

The Master and Margarita is discussed more fully in Chapter 9, but it does not require much more than a passing knowledge of the novel or the Stalinist period in which it was written to appreciate the Stones' 'Sympathy for the Devil' for the masterpiece that it is. Inspired by and reflecting the turbulence of its own era, the song opens with an individual introducing himself and boasting of the destruction he has wrought during his long life; having witnessed Jesus Christ's hesitation, the speaker tells us, he made certain— damned certain, in fact—that Pilate would implicate himself in the crucifixion. As we are invited to guess at numerous points, the name of the speaker is Lucifer, though over the centuries he has taken many forms. In what is the song's most pointed contemporary reference, Jagger's Satan invokes the assassination of the Kennedys, and implicates even the listener in their deaths. What we hear in 'Sympathy' are the words of a devil who, we come to understand, is not an otherworldly figure of incarnate evil, but rather a character for whom we feel sympathy because he ultimately represents our most wicked and least forgivable inner selves. If we cannot understand this, it is due to the confusing nature of evil itself. The song breaks up into ad-libbing and a monosyllabic chorus of woo-woos without ever addressing the fundamental question of *why* the various wars and acts of widespread atrocity referred to in the lyrics take place. Although the ramifications are clear and damnable enough, the motivations behind them remain unfathomable, buried deep in a musical heart of darkness. Seen in this context, what are we to make of this devil's line about Pilate's handwashing? Whose fate are we to imagine that this act has sealed – that of Jesus, or the prefect's own? Or both?[4]

The representations of Pontius Pilate in the films and televised productions of the decade to follow all seem to participate in this same ambiguity laid out by Bulgakov and the Rolling Stones: if Pilate is no saint, he is at least a sinner deserving some measure of sympathy. As noted in the previous chapter, when Telly Savalas had agreed to take the role of the prefect in *Greatest Story Ever Told*, his mother had advised him to 'make sure you play him sympathetically'; however, the film's ponderousness robs him (as it does most of its many characters) of any genuine sense of fellow feeling from its viewers. In films about Jesus in the 1970s, the characterisation of Pilate is that of a conflicted figure, less authoritative in his actions and more inclined to display uncertainty, irritation, or outright incompetence. In *Jesus Christ Superstar*, for instance, we find in Barry Dennen's performance a brittle Pontius Pilate who, haunted by a dream, knows even as the story is unfolding that there is no way out of his destined role and the consequent blame that future generations will cast upon him. It is a more unscrupulous prefect whom we see in *The Passover Plot* played by Donald Pleasence, for whom holding on to power is paramount, even though that power is pointless and glaringly illegitimate. Just a few years later, Rod Steiger's Pilate in *Jesus of Nazareth*, the made-for-TV production directed by Franco Zeffirelli, will be not as apprehensive as he will be beleaguered, a mid-level military functionary trying to dispatch one last difficult matter before the weekend. Taken as a whole, the onscreen Pilates of the 1970s present a very different sort of idea of authority than had the corresponding figures in earlier films. Whether tormented, underhanded, or exhausted, the Pilates of the 1970s reflect the difficult politics of their period in the fragmented America of the Vietnam and Watergate era as well as the Britain suffering through its pre-Thatcherite Winter of Discontent, and they openly wonder whether truth is a thing for which they have much regard.

At the end of the 1960s, the Stones had been encouraging sympathy for the devil, but there were others in the music scene at the same time moving in an emphatically different direction. Norman Greenbaum declared that he had a friend in Jesus in 'Spirit in the Sky' from the spring of 1969, a song reaching number three in the US and number one in the UK. 'My Sweet Lord' was the name of a George Harrison song the following year, which went to number one in both nations. Other hits along these lines were 'Put Your Hand in the Hand' by Ocean in 1971, 'Jesus is Just Alright' by the Doobie Brothers in 1972 and 'Morning Has Broken' by Cat Stevens in the same year. The Country and Western charts for the same period would give many more examples. Attendance at mainstream churches in the late 1960s may well have been declining, but sales of Christian music were going through the roof, and record companies were making it a point to serve both God and Mammon. 'Jesus and religion were having a bit of a vogue in pop culture', writes Andrew Lloyd Webber in his memoir; never one to let a trend go unexploited, he and Tim

Rice set out to capitalise on the burgeoning interest in Christianity by releasing a song in late 1969 sung by Murray Head and backed by the Trinidad Singers, Joe Cocker's Grease Band and a full orchestra. 'It was called "Superstar"', Lloyd Webber notes, 'and its chorus was destined to become the best-known three-chord tune I have written'.[5] Of the lyrics, Rice remarks: 'They were at once shocking yet respectful and unforgettable'.[6]

Whether they were respectful is a matter perhaps best left to individual listeners, but shocking and unforgettable seems like an accurate description of the lyrics. Where the Jesus Movement in the pop music of the late 1960s and early 1970s had an air of earnestness about it, 'Superstar' was a song steeped in irony. Although not coined by Rice, the word 'superstar' itself caught fire right away, featuring in the titles for hit songs by the Temptations and Karen Carpenter within a year or so afterward, and entering the lexicon in a myriad of media references ever since. From virtually no usages before 1969, the phrase had grown in popularity by over 600 percent in the half century or so since the song came out, while '#superstar' has appeared over seven million times on Instagram as of the time of this writing.[7] Whatever the term might suggest today, Rice's description of Jesus Christ as a 'superstar' tapped into a contemporary idea of celebrity that was not entirely flattering. 'In the future, everyone will be world-famous for fifteen minutes', Andy Warhol had famously quipped in 1968, summing up the idea of fame as an essentially ephemeral and empty enterprise (as it happens, *Superstar* was the title that filmmaker Chuck Workman gave to his 1990 documentary about Warhol). By insinuating that his superstar fell into the same category of celebrity as short-lived fads and one-hit wonders, Rice suggested that Jesus' message was, if not the work of publicists and press agents, then one that had been co-opted by parties prizing style over substance. What is one to make of Head's Judas' open question about why Jesus came in a time before mass communication? The lyrics to the song do not preclude a sincere and respectful reading, of course, but their postmodern self-referentiality suggests a figure beset by tabloid paparazzi and struggling to escape the slick packaging of his admirers – and perhaps even of his creators.

Executives at the respectable old record label Decca had been uncertain about the viability of Lloyd Webber and Rice's offering, but when the marketplace responded to the single with a building zeal that could only be called religious, they greenlighted the commissioning of an entire double album based on the song. Over the course of the next few months, the composer and lyricist worked furiously to complete the writing and recording of the album that would be called *Jesus Christ Superstar*, in which the trends of the 'relevant' musical such as *Hair* came together with the new rock opera format of The Who's *Tommy*. It is not too much to say that the album proved to be both enormously popular and enormously controversial. By and large critics raved: 'nothing short of brilliant' (*Newsweek*), 'every bit as valid as (and to me more moving than) Handel's Messiah' (*London Sunday Times*) and '[p]otentially the single most important recording since Edison waxed his first cylinder' (*Los Angeles Free Press*) were some of the accolades.[8] Those who disliked *Jesus Christ Superstar* were equally hyperbolic, and Archie Bunker spoke for many when he bellowed at a 'Jesus freak' in a 1971 episode of *All in the Family*: 'Jesus Christ I dig, and I dug him a long time before you weirdos turned him into a superstar!' As the scene continues, Archie's ire grows, and he fulminates at some hippies dancing to the Lloyd Webber-Rice song:

> Let me tell you something. Christ don't want you turning on to him. He wants ya coming to him on your knees, not wigglin' and jigglin' till your parts fall off. [. . .]
>
> What's the use in talking to yas! What a generation! We try to learn ya something, try to teach ya some religion, drags ya off to church, and what do ya do? You give us back the Son of God like he's some sort of 'Englebert Whatshisdink'.[9]

Amid such controversy, the LP reached the top of the charts in US sales in February 1971 and again in May, and it was the bestselling album of that calendar year.

In finding the voices for the album, the producers kept Murray Head in the part of Judas. The lead singer of the rock band Deep Purple, Ian Gillen, would be Jesus, and the otherwise unknown Yvonne Elliman was selected to sing the part of Mary Magdalen. When it came to casting the part of Pontius Pilate, however, Rice and Lloyd Webber were looking for a seasoned singer with genuine acting ability. 'Would Barry Dennen, the actor who had made such an impression on me as the MC in *Cabaret*, conceivably consider us?' asks Lloyd Webber in his autobiography, knowing Dennen from his performance in the original London production. 'I knew at once his highly distinctive voice was what we needed'.[10] In a conversation I had with him, Dennen recounted his side of this story:

> In 1968, I was in London playing the MC in *Cabaret* alongside Judi Dench. Andrew came to see me in it in London, and he wanted me to listen to what they had written so far for *Superstar*. It wasn't quite finished, all they had

at this point was a demo. So I listened. When I didn't respond right away, Andrew was dyspeptic. 'Well, what do you think?' I told him I thought it would be either an enormous failure or an absolute phenomenon. I thought it was going to be a smash, and we'd be talking about it for decades. Then I told him, I would do anything, including killing somebody, to be in it.[11]

The only person he would need to kill, of course, was Jesus Christ. Dennen went on to sing the part on the original album issued by Decca in 1970, known to fans as 'the brown Bible' (with its famous logo of two praying angels, designed by Ernie Cefalu). Together with Elliman, he was the only member of the original cast who would go on to appear in the subsequent Broadway show in 1971 and Norman Jewison's film version of 1973.

Pilate does not appear until late in the opera's first act which is dominated by the figure of Judas singing caustic indictments against the Apostles ('Heaven on their Minds') and Mary Magdalene ('Strange Thing Mystifying'), followed by the Apostles' own hapless rejoinder ('What's the Buzz?'). In the pair of songs that follow, Mary consoles an agitated Jesus ('Everything's Alright'), while the high priests express their murderous concern over his rising popularity ('This Jesus Must Die'). The plot thickens in the next episode, which is introduced by the gospel-like number of Simon Zealotes and a large crowd, pledging the full measure of their loyalty to Jesus in exchange for some small but specific endorsement of their avow-edly anti-imperialist political principles. In the stage show as well as in the film, Simon Zealotes' song is accompanied by an energetic dance number that features dozens of figures leaping and twirling in highly stylised hippie choreography – Busby Berkeley meets, well, Berkeley. Thematically, 'Simon Zealotes' introduces into *Superstar* an opposition to Rome that had only been mentioned incidentally by the high priest and will be typified in the person of Pilate, soon to be seen and heard from onstage. This anti-government sentiment, very much in keeping with the late 1960s and early 1970s zeitgeist, is not of interest to Jesus, however. In a song addressed to the city of Jerusalem itself, Jesus quietly indicates that Simon and his frenetic devotees do not understand what power or glory are at all. This song, 'Poor Jerusalem', intoned by Jesus almost to himself, smoothly flows into 'Pilate's Dream', another soliloquy immediately follow-ing, which shares the same melody. As Scott Miller aptly notes in *Sex, Drugs, Rock & Roll, and Musicals* of this transition, '[t]hese twin pieces show us the anguish, apprehension, and ambiguity of both Jesus' and Pilate's situations, and joining them melodically also provides a strong segue between scenes. After spending time with Jesus, we delve into his inner thoughts, then cross-fade into the related inner thoughts of one of Jesus' antagonists'.[12] The connection between the protagonist and Pilate is artfully made here, for just as in 'Simon Zealotes', Jesus has been hemmed in by the demands of the mob, so his Roman counterpart likewise foresees himself forced by popular pressure into actions contrary to his will.

As noted in Chapter 4 concerning Claudia Procula, the attribution of the dream to Pilate was a liberty that the composers took with the text of Matthew's Gospel for artistic reasons. During an interview with the cast of *Jesus Christ Superstar* to promote the album's release in 1970, Dennen told David Frost: 'Bible readers everywhere know that Pilate never really did have a dream, it was his wife who had the dream, as my wife pointed out to me during the casting, but we put it in really'. At this, Frost cracked: 'Have Women's Lib complained about your taking away the dream? . . . Why did you do it, you pigs, why did you do it?'[13] The sexist joke lands flat today, but Frost was right to point out that *Jesus Christ Superstar* is a musical featuring few enough female roles as it is (as with so many films even of the most 'liberal' variety, they fail the Bechdel Test miserably). Rice would later note that 'we had no At Home With the Pilates number' for no reason other than an economic one, and given the expense of a large cast and a full symphony orchestra, such cost-cutting measures seem sensible enough. The dramatic effect, however, was to heighten the prominence of the only woman in the show, Yvonne Elliman's Mary Magdalen, whose solo 'I Don't Know How to Love Him' would be the biggest hit single from the album. But, in addition, 'Pilate's Dream' focuses the listener's attention squarely on the procurator himself, who was thus given an opportunity to express his inner anguish more fully. He has dreamed of meeting a Galilean whose appearance perplexes him deeply but who will respond to him when spoken to; following this, the room is filled by an incensed crowd which falls upon the man, only to vanish and be replaced by a vast multitude of mourners, all of whom blame Pilate himself for the man's death.[14] As Rice remarks, 'his Dream is one of the best tracks on the album, understated and sensitively delivered by Barry Dennen'.[15] For the actor himself, the dream became the key to understanding Pilate's entire character. 'Imagine if you met someone in a terrible dream', he told me. 'And then, the very next morning, you were to meet that person in real life? What would that be like? That is how I played the role'.[16]

That Pilate is utterly bewildered by the dream and will be influenced by it in the second half of the show seems clear enough, but it is worth thinking through the issues raised by the lyrics to the song. Although not labelled as such, anxiety dreams were as common in antiquity as they are now – frequently considered prophetic in nature, they were believed to come from without, as divinely or demonically delivered messages describing an imminent external reality. The Gospel of Matthew presents the dream of Pilate's wife in just such a way: 'Have nothing to do with that innocent man, for today I have suffered a great deal because of a dream about him' (27:19 NRSV). She here intuits the catastrophic consequences that will ensue from the unjust trial of Jesus, the suffering of her dream foreshadowing the suffering of Christ to come and, perhaps, the loss of her husband's reputation as well. In Telly Savalas's portrayal in *The Greatest Story Ever Told*, the line from the Creed 'suffered under Pontius Pilate' is intoned by a voice-over just after he condemns Christ to the cross. As terrible as it might be to carry the burden of an everlasting shame such as this, the stakes for Dennen's Pilate in *Jesus Christ Superstar* are somehow even higher. As Lloyd Webber and Rice were aware, it makes for better drama if it is Pilate himself who experiences this dream, and thus he is fully aware of the implications of his decisions even as he is making them. The song does not simply invoke later people mentioning the prefect's name and blaming him but, significantly, that he *hears* them doing so. Rice's lyrics depict a Pilate who, with this foreknowledge, evidently suffers from a persecution complex: he vastly minimises his future involvement in the death of Jesus, and imagines thousands of millions castigating him, far out of proportion to what he has claims to have done. The melodies of 'Poor Jerusalem' and 'Pilate's Dream' are the same, as noted, and this encourages us to think of the parallels between the situations of the two characters. But there is an inescapable element of projection in this dream, as well. Pilate, as the Roman administrator in charge, will indeed give the order for the death of this Galilean, but in this nightmare he frames his situation as that of a hounded victim of injustice rather than its perpetrator. It is much to Dennen's credit that in his delivery of the song, we are left finally with a greater impression of pained sympathy with Jesus than of pity for himself (Figure 7.1).

While a more detailed analysis of the sound of his voice singing 'Pilate's Dream' is to be found in Chapter 8, Barry Dennen is filmed performing the number just before dawn in Norman Jewison's 1973 film version of *Jesus Christ Superstar*. The implication of his first appearance in the film shot at the so-called 'golden hour' is significant for the audience's sense of Pilate's character. Although the 'golden hour' is hardly an hour long – closer to twenty minutes,

Figure 7.1 Barry Dennen as Pilate in *Jesus Christ Superstar* (1973).

depending on the time of year, latitude and weather – the soft and rich quality of light just before sunrise and just after sunset bathes subjects in a radiant hue, even as it renders shadows more indistinct. The lighting is indeed a central element of the 1973 movie version of *Jesus Christ Superstar*, which director Norman Jewison chose to film on location in Israel, and in his review of the movie, Roger Ebert had been impressed by the cinematography which offers 'a color range that glows with life and somehow doesn't make the desert look barren'.[17] Later in the film, Pilate will appear in the harsh light of the Negev, looking hot and uncomfortable in his purple Roman regalia, a visual analogy of the heat which he is feeling from the situation and the spotlight under which he feels himself. But in this first glance of the prefect, the viewer is invited to look upon him with sympathy, as in the cool of daybreak he gives voice to the anxieties he has experienced the night before. Whatever presuppositions we may have about the figure of Pontius Pilate beforehand, we are encouraged to put them aside and to view him in a more positive light.

Dennen was evidently instrumental in bringing Jewison into the film project. 'That record of yours is just all over the place in New York', the director had told him in Yugoslavia during one of the long winter breaks in the shooting of the *Fiddler on the Roof*, in which Dennen was playing Mendel, the rabbi's son. 'Do you have the number of Andrew and Tim? I think I know a way to make the show into a movie'.[18] Rice was pleased to be approached by a big-name director – Jewison's most recent films, *In the Heat of the Night* and *The Thomas Crown Affair*, had all won multiple Oscars, as would of course *Fiddler* – and when he was hired to write the screenplay, he set out his vision for a grand epic, described with a certain tongue-in-cheek humour in his memoir:

> I set about this with great enthusiasm and minimum concern for budget, certain that a massive *Ben-Hur* kind of treatment was essential. Tens of thousands of extra would soon be thanking me for a boost to their incomes. After all, *Superstar* has not got where it had by excess subtlety or by its creators thinking too small. Obviously all the words were already in place . . . so it was merely a question of pointing out which massive visual effect accompanied which song. Should the procession of camels enter from the left or the right of the frame? What was the best marching formation for the Roman legions?[19]

The desire for a more traditional look for the film was understandable, perhaps, given director Tom O'Horgan's trippy staging of the Broadway show, complete with a large silver chalice that rose up and out of the floor to open up into a flower with Jesus at its centre. For good reason *New York* theatre critic John Simon had called it 'a Radio City Music Hall Show into whose producers' and designers' coffee cups the gofer has slipped some LSD'.[20] Jewison was not interested in correcting the psychedelic excesses of the stage show, however, by mounting an old-fashioned Technicolor extravaganza for the screen. Dismissing the desire of Rice and Lloyd Webber for greater conventionality, he remarked: 'They had this very modern concept for the music but when it came to the visuals they lapsed right back to sheer Hollywood '30's'.[21] The picture that the director had in mind was a far different affair, one influenced by Pier Paolo Pasolini's spare Marxist fable *The Gospel According to Saint Matthew*, but situated in a political context less timeless and more timely.

Jewison's involvement with *Jesus Christ Superstar*, it must be noted, helped to alleviate the widespread allegations of anti-Semitism against the project, which were frankly not without basis: as contemporary a sound as the rock opera had, its roots in the medieval Passion Play tradition, with its ingrained image of Jews as 'Christ-killers', were undeniable. Protests against the play had been lodged by the Anti-Defamation League and other prominent Jewish organisations, much to the consternation of Rice and Lloyd Webber, who seemed oblivious to the issues. Jewison had good ties to prominent figures in the Jewish American community as well as Israel, and when he confirmed to Haim Bar-Lev, the Israeli minister of trade and industry, that the film would be entirely free of anti-Semitic material, the latter replied: 'I trust you on account of *Fiddler on the Roof*'.[22] Whether such reassurance ought to have been sufficient is a debatable matter, of course, and the same concerns about the album and stage show were raised about Jewison's film, particularly in the representation of the high priests, whose all-black costumes and enormous headpieces seemed simultaneously cartoonish and ominous, the very essence of the anti-Semitic caricature. Yet, if Jewison's film failed to address the problems of Jewish stereotypes at the heart of the Passion Play tradition, his insistence on filming in Israel was intended to confront the way in which the origin story of Christianity interacted with the hot-button issues of the present-day Middle East.

The decision to film on location in Israel put *Jesus Christ Superstar* into a tradition stretching back as far as Sidney Olcott's *From the Manger to the Cross*, the silent masterpiece of 1912, and encompassing more recent mainstream Biblical epics such as DeMille's *Ten Commandments*. While such films gained an ersatz authenticity with audiences for being shot 'in the Holy Land', it was rather as a contemporary cultural landscape that the setting of *Superstar* derived its impact. To film in Israel in the early 1970s was to summon consciously images of the war-torn Middle East: this was the period of extensive PLO terrorist activity, as well as the Six Days' and Yom Kippur Wars, after all. Jewison deliberately allowed fighter planes and tanks to be seen in the background at various points, as a comment on the depressingly familiar nature of religious conflict. But perhaps the most powerful use of the modern military vehicles had nothing to do with politics: when Judas (Carl Anderson) is crouching in regret over his betrayal of Jesus, to the opening guitars strains of 'Damned for All Time', he suddenly looks up to see five Israeli tanks cresting a hill and bearing down on him. He begins to run away frantically, a nightmarish image of futile escape in the face of his overwhelming sense of guilt.

In this region of contemporary conflict, Jewison consciously shot many of the scenes on ancient archaeological sites. The trial before Pilate, perhaps most prominently, takes place in the ruins of a Roman theatre: according to Jewison in his DVD director's commentary, it is the theatre in Caesarea Maritima (the very building, as a matter of fact, in which the so-called Pilate stone had been discovered), although when looking at the location, it seems rather to be the theatre of Beit She'an, ancient Scythopolis. The thirty-plus years between the commentary and the movie's making – a production 'helped along by a healthy quantity of pot, which was relatively easy to obtain in the Middle East', as the director writes – is probably to account for the mistake.[23] The decision to film the trial before Pilate in an ancient Roman ruin stranded in the desert wasteland is certainly suggestive: like the massive Roman eagle which stands behind DeMille's Pilate in *King of Kings*, the theatre points to the grandeur of empire but, even more pointedly, to its downfall. Before the trial even gets underway, then, the scene has been set for us along the lines of Shelley's *Ozymandias*, the 'king of kings' by whose broken statue 'boundless and bare, / The lone and level sands stretch far away'. The ruins in the desert have the feel of a ghost town in a Western, one in which Pilate somehow has gotten stuck being the sheriff with a lynch mob on his hands. In another sense, they suggest not just the demise of Roman civilisation but the collapse of all authority, political or otherwise. While the album and stage show of *Superstar* had been products born of 1960s idealism, the movie instead reflects the cynicism of the 1970s and the breakdown in trust that characterised the Watergate era. In questioning Jesus, Barry Dennen's Pilate defensively elaborates upon John 18.38 ("What is truth?"). Far more than the 'jesting Pilate' of Sir Francis Bacon who 'would not stay for an answer', Dennen here seems to be an anxious representative of the moral relativism described by Allan Bloom a decade later in *The Closing of the American Mind*.[24]

Throughout the trial scene, it is as though Dennen's Pilate possesses a mystic vision, and so is able to see what nobody else but Christ can – the fact that it is an empty ruin over which he presides. In this final scene, as Dennen's Pilate implores Jesus to talk to him, the faint music of 'Pilate's Dream' (and 'Poor Jerusalem') can be heard non-diegetically in the distance. At this moment, Pilate, realising that he must make a decision to either spare Jesus and face a riot or put an innocent man to death, hits upon a middle path that will neither win him friends nor rid him of enemies by having him flogged.[25] The insufficiency of his response to satisfy the demands of either mercy or security captured the sense of disillusionment that many Americans felt in 1973, caught between the hawks and doves of their political leadership. As a matter of performance, Barry Dennen's Pilate in *Jesus Christ Superstar* is likewise wedged in an awkward spot between more well-defined dramatic types: on the darker side of the spectrum are the sinister machinations of Caiaphas, rendered in full *basso profundo*, while on the decidedly lighter side there is the show-stealing vaudeville number by King Herod, played in the movie by Josh Mostel, Zero's son, with all of his father's clownishness. It is much to Dennen's credit that he finds an edgy space between *Superstar*'s Caiaphas and Herod, even if it consists primarily of a corner from which he cannot escape.

The finale is now at hand, beginning quietly and building to a fever pitch. Approaching Jesus after the thirty-nine lashes, Pilate speaks to him plaintively, begging for any word that could alter the situation.

The tone would be one of reassurance, if either the one speaking or the one listening were not themselves already sure that the situation is far beyond either one's control. The melody is derived from Mary Magdalene's 'Everything's Alright', but significantly it is sung in a minor key.[26] In the end, as the chorus cries over and over again 'Remember Caesar' and 'Crucify him', Pilate is brought to the very crux of the situation. A clear Pyrex bowl is brought out and, shot from below, we see a grimacing Dennen throw his bloody hands into it, splashing water everywhere. Now he struts frenetically before the crowd, growing more and more agitated, and we realise why it was that Rice and Lloyd Webber had so badly wanted Dennen and, in moving from album to stage to screen, never sought to replace him, because in the role he 'was prepared to take real vocal chances'.[27] His final words to Jesus are delivered with vehemence and – there can be no other word – passion.

When you sing these final lines, I asked Dennen when we met, what is it that is going through your mind? Are you scared, or angry, or is it some other emotion? What is your Pilate thinking as he commits the act for which he will always be remembered and which he himself will never forget? He thought about it for a few minutes, and then replied:

> At that moment, I am feeling a complete loss of control, in a froth, like the top of my head is about to explode. I have felt that way every time I've done the scene. I have this feeling of a loss of control, and to get rid of it, I have to kill this guy. The scene has never wrecked my voice, and it's never felt forced or untrue to do it that way.

'Untrue'. It was only sometime later, as I went back over my notes of this interview in preparation for writing this chapter, that I realised I had failed to follow up on this lead he had left me. If only I had thought to ask at this moment: What is truth?

'My part, from end to end is only twelves minutes long, but it is jam-packed with awe, fury, and mystery'. So Dennen said in offering a final reflection on *Jesus Christ Superstar*'s Pontius Pilate. He would continue to act in the years to come, mostly in minor roles (in *The Shining*, for instance, and *Titanic*), and he voiced parts for countless animated shows and video games right up until his death in September 2017. But of all that he had accomplished in his career, it was playing Pilate that had been the most important to him. When we met in Los Angeles the year before, he told me, among other things, about how he had toured with *Superstar* in Italy in the mid-2000s:

> We did the show in the Roman amphitheatre in Verona, an incredible place. Afterwards this young man approached me, tentatively. And he took my hands and said, 'This play means everything to me'. And he paused, and then he said, 'You are my myth'. Can you imagine that? Being somebody's myth? I nearly lost it. No, I'm sure I lost it.

Sometimes, in the writing of this book, I have wondered to myself what it must be like to have somebody like me track you down to talk about something you had done over forty years ago. Truthfully, would that not be irritating? If it were me, the association of my face and name with the suffering of Jesus Christ is a burden I would be glad to get out from under. But I got the distinct feeling from Barry that he was happy to have been Pontius Pilate and to have borne the symbolic weight of the role for an entire generation. The number might not have reached 'thousands of millions' invoked in 'Pilate's Dream' of course, but he knew that for many he had occupied a significant place in their spiritual lives. He understood, in other words, what it meant to be somebody else's myth. Barry Dennen is buried in the Hollywood Forever Cemetery, and beneath his name on his gravestone is written 'Star of Stage & Screen / Loving Father Brother Friend', under which is inscribed the Superstar logo of two praying angels. *Requiescas in pace*, Barry. May you rest in peace.

Before we move on from *Jesus Christ Superstar*, it is worth looking at a legal decision made in the US District Court for the Southern District of Ohio, Eastern Division, which serves as a curious codicil to the film as a whole and to the song 'Pilate's Dream'. In late December 1972, Leeds Music Limited and the Robert Stigwood Group Limited, as rights-holders for Rice and Webber, filed an injunction in Columbus, Ohio, against a certain Pierre Robin and his corporation, the Repertory Company of America, who had plans to produce their own filmed version of *Jesus Christ Superstar*, claiming the musical was 'pirated from *The Passover Plot*', a book in which they had a proprietary interest. The matter would ultimately be adjudicated in favour of Leeds and Stigwood for *Superstar* the following May by Judge Carl B. Rubin, in a decision which considers the relationship of the one work to the other in a manner simultaneously serious and witty.

The Passover Plot was a work of mid-1960s pop scholarship by Hugh J. Schonfield, a prolific author of trendy books about Judaism and the New Testament. Setting out to counter the traditional picture of Jesus as the God-Man of Christianity, Schonfield declares in *The Passover Plot* (1965) that 'the "inside story" of Jesus and his early Jewish adherents is the Jewish struggle with Rome', which was 'the arch-enemy of God and his people'.[28] In fact, a political rebel in sympathy with the aims of the Zealots, Jesus declared himself the king of the Jews, sent to free his people from the Romans, and had worked out an elaborate scheme to fake his own death at their hands, through the use of a drug that would give him a corpse-like appearance. As Schonfield expostulates, one of the bystanders at the cross had been sent by Joseph of Arimathea to administer this drug in the vinegar-soaked sponge mentioned in the Gospels. 'If what he received had been the normal wine vinegar diluted with water the effect would have been stimulating', Schonfield writes. 'In this case it was exactly the opposite. Jesus lapsed quickly into unconsciousness. His body sagged. His head lolled on his breast, and to all intents and purposes he was a dead man'.[29] This carefully worked-out plan failed, unfortunately, when a Roman soldier pierced Jesus' side with a lance. The tendentious nature of this argument – made with many a 'must have' and 'would have' – is not especially convincing, of course, but it was extremely popular.

That Schonfeld's book bears very little resemblance to *Jesus Christ Superstar* is obvious enough from this summary of its argument, of course, but obvious facts do not always prevent expensive lawsuits from being filed, and they did not do so in this case either. At issue was the question of plagiarism, a matter that Rubin dismissed out of hand, as each work had the Gospels as their ultimate source material. Concerning the defence's further argument that 'evidence of piracy can be inferred because of similarities in the depiction of certain key characters in both *Plot* and *Superstar*', the judge chose to reply by focusing on the representation of Pilate and particularly his first song in the opera. As Rubin writes, ...

> The defendants' reactions to the assignment of the song, 'Pilate's Dream', to Pilate is clear from the outset. They are outraged that this song, which they describe (and in which description the Court concurs) as 'one of the loveliest in the play', and as one possessing a 'sweet and moving melody', (in which description the Court once again concurs) should be sung by Pilate who is described as 'a cold and ruthless despot'.

Whether the song is lovely or Pilate's nature despotic is beside the point, Rubin observes, as none of this has anything to do with the issue of the piracy of the one work from the other. He notes that he has reviewed over twenty pages from the defence 'of highly personalized and subjective analysis (which the Court can barely fathom, much less concur with)', including a chart reprinted in the footnotes of the lyrics of 'Pilate's Dream' juxtaposed with vaguely similar passages from *The Passover Plot*. In the end, however, Rubin points out that Schonfield had followed the Gospel of Matthew in assigning the dream to Pilate's wife rather than to Pilate himself, as Rice and Webber did. He then concludes that . . .

> [f]rom what we have said above, it should be obvious that, in our view, by allowing the Pilate of their play to sing the 'sweet and lovely melody', 'Pilate's Dream', the plaintiffs have created no inconsistency with the biblical record. Furthermore, the scripting of the song for Pilate raises absolutely no inference of literary piracy from *The Passover Plot*. Our representative analysis as to the role of Pilate applies with equal force to the remaining alleged similarities of character and general setting between *Jesus Christ Superstar* and *The Passover Plot*. We therefore conclude that the ideas embodied in *Jesus Christ Superstar* are derived from an independent source in the public domain, namely the Bible. Consequently, the defendants' contention that the underlying conception of *Superstar* was pirated from *The Passover Plot* is lacking in merit and must be rejected.

Thus, the matter was definitively settled by Judge Rubin, appointed to the bench by Richard Nixon just a few years earlier and going on to a long and illustrious career. He noted that, in making this decision, the court had carefully read the extensive briefs, affidavits, exhibits and analyses submitted by both parties to the suit and 'been generally briefed by its own teenage children on the place of rock opera in the counter-culture'.[30]

Summary judgment by the Southern District of Ohio notwithstanding, *The Passover Plot* was not to pass away entirely into the annals of forgotten history, and in 1976 a film version of Schonfield's book would be released which, although it would earn an Academy Award nomination for Best Costume design, did not achieve mainstream appeal. 'The physically handsome production drains the vitality out of the Christ story through verbiage and overacting' was *Variety*'s assessment (31 December 1975), but even today it retains the status of a cult classic with a dedicated following. As a film of the mid-1970s, *The Passover Plot* has to be seen as part of the genre of conspiracy dramas so popular in the period. In highly successful movies such as *The Conversation* (1974), *The Parallax View* (1974), *Chinatown* (1974), *Three Days of the Condor* (1975), or, of course, *All the President's Men* (1976), to name just a few, one thing we can be certain of is that, even though the details of any important story may be correct, their official explanation is often deliberately misleading. Writing in the wake of 1964's Warren Commission report and the widespread distrust that it engendered, historian Richard Hofstadter remarked: 'If for every error and every act of incompetence one can substitute an act of treason, we can see how many points of fascinating interpretation are open to the paranoid imagination'.[31]

This trend was brilliantly satirised by the Firesign Theatre comedy troupe, whose 1974 album *Everything You Know Is Wrong* opened with a listing of alternative truths: 'Dogs flew space ships! The Aztecs invented the vacation! Men and women are the same sex! Our forefathers took drugs! Your brain is not the boss!' Audiences who felt that JFK's assassination had been whitewashed or that the moon landing was a fake were certainly open to paranoid readings on any number of things, and an exposé about 'who *really* killed Jesus' was right up their alley.

By and large, the film has a deliberately perverse quality to it, with all the assumptions about the traditional Passion narrative being turned inside out. It is difficult to see who is supposed to be the hero. Zalman King as Yeshua – all the Jewish characters have Hebrew names – resolutely confronts the Romans and particularly Donald Pleasence as Pontius Pilate. The province he governs is a tinderbox, Pilate says apprehensively to a soldier, and 'the only thing that prevents it from bursting into flames is this crazy, bickering jealousy among the Jews'. Bullying his subordinates and engaging in underhanded tactics, Pleasence's Pilate is a modern dictator more than an ancient proconsul. After local authorities confront anti-Roman demonstrators, Pilate berates a hangdog Herod (Peter Frye) whose forces have overreacted. 'You cut off the head of the Baptist, and up springs another rabble-rouser to take his place!' Encouraging him to take greater advantage of spies, Pilate offers a final word of advice to his client-king. 'If you must kill, kill only the weak'. Likewise, he confers with his military aide, demanding 'a dossier' on all of Yeshua's followers and suggesting 'an ordinance against public meetings of more than six people'. This is a Pilate for the Watergate era, one with his own handbook of dirty tricks, but it is not as if Yeshua is above reproach – with his retinue in tow, he encounters a blind man in his first public outing. He spits in the man's eye, as is recounted in the Gospel of Mark (8:23), but here it is a contemptuous rather than a curative act. 'What did you do that for?' the man yelps, staring at Yeshua now and clearly not really blind at all, prompting a sly smile from Shimon (Simon Peter, played by William Burns). 'A miracle', he cynically intones and then begins to shout it, as a crowd gathers to hear what else Yeshua has to say. Pilate may be paranoid, but this Messiah and crew are truly opportunistic about stirring up political trouble.

Concerned about a military uprising, Pilate leans on Caiaphas (Hugh Griffith), a surprisingly sympathetic figure, to use his temple police to patrol the streets and to find some trumped-up charge against Yeshua. In the world of this political thriller, however, the prefect and high priest are falling right into the Messiah's trap – by pre-arrangement, Judah hands Yeshua over in the Garden to the authorities who bring him in for a hearing. When Caiaphas announces the charge of blasphemy, his fellow priests are loud in their incredulity. 'That is what Pilate ordered', Caiaphas explains, ignoring cries of protest. When Yeshua is cleared of this charge and then asked whether he claims to be the Messiah, members of the Sanhedrin object. 'I am sure the High Priest is aware that it is no crime to claim to be the Messiah', says one, to which another adds, when the Messiah does come as prophesied: 'How will we know he is the king unless he tells us?' Yeshua affirms that he is in fact the Messiah – when it is pointed out to him that this is considered high treason by the Romans, he responds: 'I am what I am'. Pilate is disgusted with Caiaphas' inability to handle the situation and decides to take matters into his own hands.

After a bailiff formally announces that the court is in session, Yeshua is brought before the tribunal in chains. At first, the dialogue follows the lines from the Gospel of John, but Pilate soon loses patience with the Biblical source material:

PILATE:
Do you declare yourself to be the king of the Jews?

YESHUA:
Yes.

PILATE:
Then you are guilty as charged.

YESHUA:
Yes. I am guilty. I am guilty of speaking the truth.

PILATE:
Truth? What truth? (Chuckles, then angrily yelling) What is truth? The empty-headed ravings of a lunatic, a madman! One prophet more or less will not be missed. You'll be forgotten by sundown. In ten days, only your bones will remain to say you ever existed. What shall we do with him? Hmm? What do you say, all of you?

There is none of the hesitation that Pilate ordinarily shows in the Passion narrative to be found here, and nothing like 'I find no crime in this man' (Luke 23: 4) is to be heard. But once again, in this version, Yeshua is way ahead of Pilate in this game of cat and mouse. By predetermined agreement, his followers murmur that he should be crucified. 'The people have spoken', Pilate says and orders him to be taken away and beaten before he is crucified. 'It is finished! Done'.

Everything is going precisely according to Yeshua's plan, right down to taking the death-simulating narcotic – that is, until a soldier spears him in the side while he is on the cross, the one detail he evidently failed to account for.

During the trial, Pleasence's Pilate nibbles on some small titbits for breakfast, every so often licking his fingers, which he gives a wipe with a napkin in our final glimpse of him. If he is washing his hands, it is only to clean them of crumbs. Throughout the film, there is a similar deployment of moments from the Gospels – Yeshua's spitting, Judah's betrayal, 'It is finished!' – in new and highly imaginative rearrangements. The suspicion that things are not what they seem pervades *The Passover Plot*: from the dust kicked up by the horses breaking up a riot, to the blinding sun of the desert and the flickering shadows cast by torches in the Temple, the film presents scene after scene of occluded vision. Well might we feel that somebody is spitting in our eyes, too. The only thing that we can trust in these conspiracy films is our inherent distrust, and in *The Passover Plot* that distrust centres on the man with the most power and the least principle, Pontius Pilate, a familiar modern type wearing an Oscar-nominated toga. With his balding pate and piercing blue eyes, Pleasence brought an unnerving intensity to all of his roles, from his memorable performance as arch-villain Ernst Stavro Blofeld in the James Bond film *You Only Live Twice* (1967) to his cold-eyed Heinrich Himmler in the action-adventure film *The Eagle Has Landed* (1977) and, of course, the bit part of Satan in *The Greatest Story Ever Told*. The same unsettling quality of these parts can be felt in his turn as the petty tyrant of ancient Judaea. This Pilate never does uncover Yeshua's Passover plot, but he gets the Messiah killed off anyway, and in the end his hands are as clean as they reasonably can be after a quick breakfast. 'I don't go to people for my feelings about a part. I always go to animals and birds', Pleasence once said of his acting style, noting that for one part 'I thought of myself as an alley cat'.[32] If there was an animal after which Pleasence modelled *The Passover Plot*'s Pilate, it seems most likely to have been a jackal, the loping scavenger who hunts alone and possesses an uncanny instinct for survival.

In the summer of 1973, *Jesus Christ Superstar* would be released and become a worldwide hit, but already that year another Jesus movie, also filmed on location in Israel, was playing to moderate success in theatres across the American South – this was *Gospel Road*, a documentary of sorts about the life of Jesus, produced and narrated by the country singer Johnny Cash, who with others also sang a number of thematically-related songs for the soundtrack (released simultaneously as a double LP). As Jewison had been with *Superstar*, Cash was eager to bring his story of Jesus into modern times, and during the crucifixion the background changes from an imagined ancient Israel to a number of contemporary American cities, complete with smokestacks and traffic jams. Robert Elfstrom, who directed *Gospel Road*, also played the role of Jesus, and the singer's sister Reba played the Virgin Mother. June Carter Cash, as Mary Magdalene, offers a cover of John Denver's 'Follow Me' that is perhaps the most heartfelt performance in the entire film. The part of Pontius Pilate was portrayed by the Reverend Jimmie Snow, son of country star Hank Snow and a good friend of Cash's. His Pilate appears for only about a minute, in the company of Caiaphas and Herod, who all look upon a suffering Jesus as Cash begins to sing 'The Burden of Freedom', a recurring song in the score.

The inspiration for the movie was Billy Graham's visit in early 1970 to Cash's home in Hendersonville, North Carolina. His son, the evangelist said, was a wayward boy and a fan of Cash's, and he had come looking for the singer's help for his own child and all the other troubled young people he had seen on his travels. Graham challenged him to use his talent to write something 'that would inspire people to sit up and take notice of religion and Jesus', Cash recounted in an interview. While the eventual product of this challenge from Graham would be *Gospel Road*, more immediately – the very next morning, in fact – Cash was led to write the song 'What is Truth?'[33] As he said of the composition, 'I'd read a book on Pontius Pilate and wanted to write a song on what is truth [. . .] I got up at 6:30 and the wheels were still turning, so I made some coffee and sat and wrote the song. It just came real fast, as long as it take me to write it down'.[34] The lyrics of the song, growing from the line addressed by Pilate to Jesus in the Gospel of John (18:38), address the very issues of the day that Graham had come to talk with Cash about – that is, the disillusionment of the American youth and the uncaring response it had provoked in the older generation. In fact, as he recounted later, he ended up writing twelve stanzas for the song. Released a few months later, the song was to be Cash's biggest crossover hit since 'A Boy Named Sue'.

When Cash was invited to give a special live performance before an invited audience at the White House a few months later, President Nixon had specifically requested that he sing two 'anti-hippie' songs by other artists, Guy Drake's 'Welfare Cadillac' and Merle Haggard's 'Okie From Muskogee'. As is recounted on a recent episode of

Netflix's *ReMastered* series titled 'Tricky Dick and the Man in Black', the singer declined to perform either of Nixon's requests, instead making a point of singing 'What Is Truth?' Nixon squirmed in his chair as he listened to his guest, the Man in Black, who had refused to join the chorus of the silent majority, instead calling for giving those hippies protesting in the streets a respectful audience. Others who were in attendance felt that there was special significance in Cash's choice of song. As one said, '[e]vidently, John knew something or picked up on something, and I think he was trying to say powerfully to President Nixon, "You need to think about what you're doing and you need to be truthful". Who would have ever thought that that song would have been so prophetic?'[35] So seemed the piece built on Pilate's line from the Gospel of John to the Reverend Jimmie Snow. Within two weeks of Cash's performance at the White House, Nixon would order the bombing of Cambodia, thus expanding the war despite his promises to end it, and in the subsequent protests four students would be shot dead by National Guardsmen at Kent State. 'Nixon lied not only to America but to our soldiers', concludes Snow, who would go on to play Pontius Pilate in *Gospel Road* a little over a year later.

The sense of incipient moral ruin felt in both the US and UK in the early 1970s would only grow worse as the decade wore on. 'At a moment of universal crisis in the West', Lew Grade wrote to Franco Zeffirelli in 1976, trying to convince him to direct his projected television miniseries about the life of Christ, 'a crisis of all traditional values and of all ideals, with this film we can perhaps remind people what they are foolishly and wickedly losing'.[36] *Jesus of Nazareth*, a joint Anglo-Italian production, aired on Radiotelevisione Italiana (RAI) and Britain's ITV over the course of six weeks in March and April of 1977, to tremendous acclaim. Although protests from American evangelicals had caused General Motors to withdraw its sponsorship early on in production, the miniseries went on to become a worldwide sensation, rebroadcast in many places during the Easter season to this day. Filmed on location in Tunisia and employing an intelligent screenplay by novelist Anthony Burgess, *Jesus of Nazareth* was produced at great cost by the British media giant Grade, but it is above all the abiding vision and flair for grandeur on the part of director Zeffirelli that gives the miniseries its particular appeal. The director's previous work had included staging opulent classical operas and bringing lavish versions of Shakespeare to the screen, notably the Elizabeth Taylor and Richard Burton vehicle *Taming of the Shrew* in 1967 and, in the following year, the award-winning sensation *Romeo and Juliet* – 'the most exciting film of Shakespeare ever made [. . .] because it has the passion, the sweat, the violence, the poetry, the love and the tragedy in the most immediate terms I can imagine', as Roger Ebert had put it.[37] In 1972, he turned to religious themes, releasing *Brother Sun, Sister Moon*, about Saints Francis and Clare of Assisi, a film which coupled a hippie sensibility with the ethos of Vatican II in the filmmaker's now familiar lush style. Zeffirelli next flirted with the idea of a movie based on Dante's *Inferno* but, after intense courting by producers in Britain, was convinced to take on *Jesus of Nazareth* as his next project. 'The time allotted for the television script will allow you to develop the narrative in unprecedented depth', Grade told him. Thus, with a sense of high-minded cultural purpose and the promise of an enormous budget, Zeffirelli set out to film the story of Jesus, not as a blockbuster for moviegoers on the big screen but rather as an intimate narrative to be viewed in the privacy of their homes by believers and nonbelievers alike.

In addition to Zeffirelli's direction, of course, much of the series' success can be attributed to its big-name cast, which included Sir Lawrence Olivier, Anne Bancroft, James Mason and a host of other well-known actors. As casting choices became known during pre-production, the publicity among critics was sceptical – was this to be a Cecil B. DeMille-style extravaganza, long on Hollywood razzle-dazzle and lacking in religious substance, or a rerun of *The Greatest Story Ever Told*, festooned with celebrity appearances like an episode of *Love Boat*? While fears that *Jesus of Nazareth* might suffer from a parade of overly familiar faces were very real, Zeffirelli's insistence that actors be cast for roles despite rather than because of their name recognition went a long way toward blunting the issue. Furthermore, in hopes of reining in runaway egos, most of the cast was paid far below their usual fees. 'The only star of this production is the Star of Bethlehem', the director made clear. 'We are all at his service'.[38] Of the many fine performances in the series, it was that of the hitherto-unknown Robert Powell in the central role of Jesus that was far and away the most memorable. Indeed, Powell's lanky face, with his piercing blue eyes, remained the image of Jesus in the mind's eye of many Christians in the later twentieth century, just as the face of H. B. Warner, the Jesus of Cecil B. DeMille's *King of Kings*, had been for a generation fifty years before. What is striking about the composition of the cast as a whole is that the Jewish figures by and large are played by British actors and the Romans by Americans, a decision starkly in contrast to the traditional 'Brits-as-Romans' casting of older Hollywood films about Jesus and early

Christianity. To what degree this was a conscious matter by casting director Dyson Lovell is hard to say, but the effect of the Americans as Romans is palpable on viewing, a matter discussed more fully in Chapter 8.

For the role of Pontius Pilate, Zeffirelli's original choice had been Marcello Mastroianni, but when the Italian actor pulled out of the project over a salary dispute, Rod Steiger was asked to play the Roman prefect in his place. In his memoir, Zeffirelli said of the interaction between the prefect and Jesus: 'It must have been something like Monday morning in any city magistrates' court, when the weekend miscreants are rushed through, while the justice of the peace hardly looks up as he sentences the usual line of drunks and brawlers to a small fine or a day or two in jail'.[39] Steiger had made a career in the 1970s, playing complicated leaders such as Napoleon and Mussolini in big-budget films (although he had stupidly turned down the title role in *Patton,* thus allowing George C. Scott to become a megastar instead). The role of Steiger's that perhaps most informs his Pilate, however, was his performance in Norman Jewison's *In the Heat of the Night* as Bill Gillespie, the town's gum-chewing racist sheriff. Set in the Deep South in the late 1960s, *In the Heat of the Night* was a classic film about contemporary race relations which juxtaposes Steiger with Sidney Poitier as Virgil Tibbs, a black homicide detective from Philadelphia, with whom he uneasily attempts to solve a murder in the small Mississippi town. The most famous scene of the movie comes as the pair arrive at the plantation manor of a wealthy white suspect who, affronted by Tibbs's audacity in questioning him, slaps the detective across the face. Not inclined to turn the other cheek, Tibbs slaps him right back – 'this was the slap heard round the world', as Jewison put it, one of the most highly-charged cinematic moments of 1967.[40] When the rich white man demands to know what Steiger's Gillespie intends to do about it, the sheriff freezes. Unable to square the town's racist code with what he understands is Tibbs's perfect right to respond, Steiger's Gillespie glimpses in this moment the legacy of discrimination to which he has been wilfully blind all his life. 'I don't know', he replies, his gum-chewing halted. For his depiction of a lawman coming to a hard-fought but inescapable realisation about the nature of racial injustice, Steiger would win the Academy Award for Best Actor, concluding his acceptance speech – given two days after the assassination of Martin Luther King Jr – with the words 'We shall overcome'. That sense of budding epiphany on the part of an official charged with upholding the law if not necessarily carrying out justice hovers over Steiger's Pilate in *Jesus of Nazareth*, although we do not entirely feel the light breaking through in ancient Judaea as we had in backwater Mississippi.

As the title suggests, *Jesus of Nazareth* is concerned largely with the Jewish context of the story, and so the Romans are less central to this version of the life of Jesus as they had been in others. Zeffirelli had given some serious consideration to assigning Rome a larger place in his production. 'In fact, my scenario had included an opening sequence in the palace of Augustus at Rome and emphasised the aloofness with which the emperor regarded that remote corner of the empire', he wrote, going on to explain that he had to excise these scenes from the final screenplay for budgetary reasons:

> The film was already exceeding the most generous time limits. I had to abandon that sequence and another, too, in which Augustus, on his deathbed, transferred the imperial power to the man who was to succeed him, Tiberius. This was a painful sacrifice, and I deeply regretted not being able to fully delineate the context of the Roman world in the confrontation with the Hebrew.[41]

Unable to give a more complete sense of the imperial circumstances in which the story of Jesus takes place, the director opted instead for a thumbnail sketch that might stand in for the whole so that, insofar as the Romans are depicted at all, they come across as little more than a menacing presence. In one of the earlier episodes, a troop of mounted soldiers enter a defenceless Nazareth, with the young Jesus present, and roughly appropriate goods from the villagers, including the food from their tables. 'I did not want to give this callous raid by Roman soldiers too violent or vicious a tone', wrote Zeffirelli of the scene. 'I wanted, rather, to show how, in the face of Roman arrogance – ruthlessly snatching family provisions and the very bread of the Nazarenes, and laughing at their angry reaction – the people's sense of humiliation was inversely proportionate to the insults and scorn they received'.[42]

If the Roman Empire as a whole is cast in a negative light, at least one individual Roman is portrayed with considerably greater sympathy. Our first sustained encounter with a Roman figure comes with the centurion who asks Jesus to heal his slave, an episode drawn closely from the Gospel of Luke (7:1–10). Played with wide-eyed earnestness and uncomplicated countenance by Ernest Borgnine, the centurion seeks out Jesus in person rather than sending for him because, as he says, 'I am not worthy to have you come under my roof'. Borgnine's sincerity in the role is palpably unaffected, never more so than in a later scene when he is standing at the foot of the cross during the crucifixion. As he would relate in an essay for the Christian magazine *Guideposts* in 1989, the filming was a moment of intense significance for the actor. Because Jesus was not to be seen in the shot, Powell was not present and so the centurion's remarks were to be addressed to a chalk mark placed on a board beside the camera mounted above. To help put the actor in the right frame of mind, Zeffirelli read the words of Jesus on the cross from the Bible, and Borgnine allowed himself to imagine the centurion's emotions as he stood in that location. 'As I stared upward, instead of the chalk mark, I suddenly saw the face of Jesus Christ, lifelike and clear. It was not the features of Robert Powell I was used to seeing, but the most beautiful, gentle visage I have ever known', Borgine recalled, adding that he began to sob uncontrollably at the sight. 'Whether I saw a vision of Jesus that windswept day or whether it was only something in my mind, I do not know. It doesn't matter. For I do know that it was a profound spiritual experience and that I have not been quite the same person since'.[43] If one compares this anecdote with the cynicism of the famous albeit apocryphal story of John Wayne's portrayal of the centurion – 'Could you give it a little more awe, Duke?' 'Aw, truly this was the son of God' – perhaps we can forgive the sentimentality oozing from Borgnine's overidentification with the Roman soldier.

If Rod Steiger felt a similar sense of personal affinity with his part in *Jesus of Nazareth*, he seems to have kept it to himself. No interviews can be found in which Steiger discusses how he felt about playing Pilate, nor is there any substantive discussion to be found in any of the retrospectives that followed the actor's death in 2002. That he came with a particular concept in mind about how he would play the prefect is clear enough from Zeffirelli's memoir, however. 'As a veteran of the Actors' Studio, the centre for "method acting", he had meticulously prepared his role before he arrived', writes the director. Steiger had determined that 'Pilate was a tortured man thrust to the centre by a powerful historical destiny', but Zeffirelli felt that this was a conception that 'hardly fitted our interpretation of the Gospel story in its Hebrew setting'.[44] He asked the actor to reconsider his idea for the part, suggesting that he read 'The Procurator of Judaea' written by Nobel laureate Anatole France in 1902. In this short story, Pilate is an elderly man living in Marseilles who happens to meet an associate from his time serving in Judaea many decades before. As they reminisce about the old times, the friend asks about Jesus. As France writes, 'Pontius Pilate contracted his brows, and his hand rose to his forehead in the attitude of one who probes the deeps of memory. Then after a silence of some seconds: "Jesus?"

he murmured, "Jesus – of Nazareth? I cannot call him to mind".[45] Steiger altered his interpretation accordingly, the director noted: 'Rod took the point and Pilate's slightly bored, unconcerned attitude that is slowly unnerved by Christ's presence was the perfect interpretation'. The way in which Steiger's portrait of Pilate is built on the one found in 'The Procurator of Judaea' makes for an instructive contrast with the thoughts running through the mind of Barry Dennen, who also had looked to the short story for guidance. 'To me', Dennen had said, 'this was the absolute opposite of how I played the part'. Where the Pilate of *Jesus Christ Superstar* finds himself haunted by his encounter with Jesus, for France's Pilate – and, by extension, Rod Steiger's as well – the Passion is just one more item to be handled on a provincial governor's overcrowded agenda.

When we first see him, Steiger's Pilate is in military gear riding up on horse through a crowd shouting for the Romans to free Barabbas. Greeted by a commander as he dismounts, he retorts angrily: 'Welcome! I leave for one week and I come back and find a mob clamoring in the street and you dare to say to me "Welcome"!' With the ferocity of a bulldog, he shoots the assembled soldiers a furious stare before marching off, demanding from a subordinate named Quintilius (Tony Lo Bianco): 'Who's this Barabbas they've been shouting about?' Pilate makes his way through the praetorium, a quiet and cool building, although the sounds of the roaring crowd in the background can be heard throughout the scene that follows. He sits at his small desk, covered with various scrolls all promising headaches, and puts his hands on his face, as the same subordinate approaches him: 'I'm afraid there is another case with which I must trouble you'. 'Another one?' Pilate replies wearily. He rises in clear exasperation, uninterested in any of the Jews' preachers or prophets, and walks over to a basin, where a servant pours water over his hands: it is a significant moment of foreshadowing, the first moment he hears of Jesus pointing to the last moments he will spend with him. Quintilius continues: 'The Sanhedrin, whose cooperation have been very useful to us, they consider it extremely important . . . even urgent'. The prefect wipes his hands and face, loses his composure for a moment and then regains it, and this struggle for control, too, has an important symbolic meaning. Quintilius notes that the delegation from the Sanhedrin is in fact waiting outside, led by Zerah (the fictional scribe devised by Zeffirelli to avoid charges of anti-Semitism and played by Ian Holm). They want this preacher whom they have brought to be judged by Pilate, although he has no desire whatsoever to get involved in their religious disputes.

QUINTILIUS:
I think it's wise not to offend them unnecessarily. I think you should see them.

PILATE:
Well, have them brought in. (Quintilius delays) Don't stand there. Bring them in.

QUINTILIUS:
Uh, Pilate, I regret . . . I'm afraid that we must go out to them.

PILATE:
We must go to them?

QUINTILIUS:
Yes. According to their beliefs, uh, they cannot come into the house of a Roman. Not on Passover. They would be defiled.

Steiger's Pilate hears this last remark with an incredulity that, though brief, is wide-eyed, before he looks down to give a small laugh. 'Defiled', he repeats and then after a pause says: 'I forgot about that. . . . Alright. We'll go to them. Bring them to the Great Hall'. Quintilius exits to inform Zerah and company, but the camera lingers on the prefect's face, looking off into the middle distance, as he asks himself: 'How does one govern such a people?' Throughout the scene, Steiger registers weary disbelief while his subordinate is manoeuvring him into a reluctant acceptance of how the matter with the Sanhedrin must be handled. At several points, we hear Quintilius' voice but are watching Steiger's jowly, expressive face, as looks of surprise, fatigue and resignation cross it in unhappy recognition about what he is being required to do. In these tight close-ups, we sense how much of an unpleasant duty it is that Pilate confronts, one he does not feel comfortable with or entirely understand – 'No. No, no, no', he tells Quintilius when told he is expected to render a judgment – but there is no sense that he has any control over the situation in which he finds himself. 'How does one govern such a people?' he asks, rather than 'How do I govern such a people?' Although officially he is the one in charge of Judaea, the question of what he himself may want or be able to do hardly seems to arise.

In the composition of the scenes that follow, the cinematography stresses with subtle effectiveness this sense of Pilate's power as something merely nominal in nature. Speaking with the priests, for instance, he is not installed commandingly at the centre of the praetorium's Great Hall but rather sits off to one side in an awkward *sella curulis*. Against a background of busy scribes working away without looking up, the moment feels less like a tribunal rather than a hastily arranged meeting to which the prefect has been summoned. Pilate is petulant at being unable to extricate himself from this situation and demands to know whether this Jesus has spoken against Rome. 'Well, not directly', he is told, to which he replies: 'Not directly? Then he's *your* problem. You'll have to judge him according to *your* law'. When it is pointed out that he has called himself King of the Jews, a treasonous claim as Quintilius notes, Pilate rubs his temple – this is a matter that will not be easy to get out of. 'Alright, alright. I'll talk to him. Your Jesus', he says with irritation. The shot cuts away to another angle, with the priests standing off to one side of the image and the Romans to the other, while between them we can see Jesus framed to look very small as the central door of the hall opens; the shot then cuts back quickly from a perspective behind Jesus, who now looms over the priests and Pilate. 'Is this the man you think so dangerous?' Pilate asks jokingly.

In the *Blackwell Companion to the Classical Tradition*, classicist Karl Galinsky had called Steiger's Pilate 'undersized and pudgy', and while it may be that anybody placed alongside the lean Robert Powell, with his gaunt face and unblinking blue eyes, would suffer by the comparison, the impression is one deliberately constructed by the camera work.[46] In fact, both Steiger and Powell were the same size – 5'9" tall – but the angles from which each is presented in the subsequent interview gives a different impression, with Steiger shot from slightly above and Powell from slightly below. When Jesus tells him that '[a]ll who can accept the truth hear my voice', Steiger's Pilate asks in a highly mannered fashion, pointing his finger and opening his eyes wide: 'And what is ... the truth?' The camera cuts back to Jesus and then slowly moves in for a tighter closeup – *It's Jesus!* Zeffirelli indicates unsubtly. *Jesus is the Truth!* – but when we return to the reverse shot of Pilate, the prefect drops his finger and slightly shakes his head. 'Hmm', he says and walks away, the light not breaking through. 'No, this man's no criminal'. He orders Jesus to be taken away and flogged – 'That should wake him up!' – and is then approached in his official capacity by a self-composed Zerah, who assures him that the Sanhedrin have always shared the same aim as Rome, the peaceful administration of the people. 'As long as they obey, we care as much about your children of Israel as we do about the mob in Rome', Pilate tells him with a swagger, his hand on his hips to reveal his leather cuirass. Before the scene ends, however, he asks Zerah confidentially why the Sanhedrin find Jesus dangerous and is told: 'Oh, perhaps for the same reasons as you, Procurator, if you knew him as well as we do, you would also find him dangerous'.

We cut back to Pilate who is poring over the various papers at his desk. A dim figure, backlit and indistinct, is seen in the doorway, which gradually can be seen to be Jesus, walking slowly toward Pilate. He has just been scourged by the mocking soldiers, and in the low lighting it is hard to see just how much physical damage he has borne. Fifty wordless seconds pass as Jesus comes increasingly into focus before him, but if Pilate is troubled by the sight, he shows no sign of it. 'Ecce homo', he says to the priests and then, turning to Jesus: 'Well, what have you got to say for yourself now?' The moment of recognition that had given pause to his racist Southern sheriff in *In The Heat of the Night* does not quite rise to the level of troubling the conscience of Steiger's Pilate. The suffering of Jesus is not especially unique to him, and we feel that he has had a lot of time to become hardened to such things. Speaking of this, Zeffirelli had put the matter well:

> Far from being a monster whose hands are stained with the blood of the innocent, Steiger gave us the representative of a civilization whose ethics bend under political pressure: a figure truly representative of our own time, rather than some neatly divided tale of good and evil that probably has never existed.[47]

When eventually he presents the choice of prisoners to the crowd, Quintilius is incredulous. 'Pilate, you're not going to free Barabbas? An assassin, and enemy of Rome?' he asks. Steiger's Pilate looks again at Jesus and replies: 'I wonder. Who is the real enemy?' The dubious battlelines that made up so much of the politics of the 1970s were well expressed in this moment, as a not unsympathetic official consigned a young man to death, not out of anger or fear, and certainly not out of moral certitude (Figure 7.2).

When he leaves the scene and the jeering crowd, Steiger's Pilate looks back over his shoulder, and the door closes – no handwashing takes place, nor is there a sense that any handwashing is necessary. It may be as perfect a symbol of the end of the decade, even as the Stones' 'Sympathy for Devil' had been a serenade for the 1960s. To be sure, in both Britain and the US, the 1970s concluded on a note of despair. *Jesus of Nazareth* may have been a worldwide hit, but there was a generation of angry young people who preferred the I-am-an-Antichrist sentiments of Johnny Rotten and the Sex Pistols' 'Anarchy in the UK', released around the same time. The bitterly cold months of January and February 1979, together with a series of nationwide strikes, pointed to the Labour government's failure to lead, and Prime Minister James Callaghan's assertions to the contrary were deeply unconvincing, as *The Sun*'s headline – 'Crisis?

Figure 7.2 Rod Steiger's Pilate confronts Robert Powell's Jesus in *Jesus of Nazareth* (1977). Powell is filmed to appear taller than Steiger, although the actors are the same height.

What Crisis?' – indicated. That summer in the US, President Jimmy Carter delivered his infamous 'malaise speech', as well as a similar one a few months later, which the left-leaning *Boston Globe* labelled 'More Mush from the Wimp'. There was a widespread sense that the grey men the in the grey suits in Westminster and Washington were too out of touch to do their jobs. Carter and Callaghan faltered, while Reagan and Thatcher waited in the wings to take their places on the global stage. It was during this time, in one of the year's biggest movie hits in both countries, that Michael Palin as Pontius Pilate stepped out before a crowd to assure a jeering crowd: 'People of Jewusalem! Wome is your fwiend'.

NOTES

1 Watergate Hearings (1973). At 1:17:49, Haldeman can be watched saying this on the American Archive of Public Broadcasting website.
2 *Crossfire Hurricane* (2012).
3 Hardeman (2018).
4 You may well wonder, dear reader, why I have not simply quoted the words of the song here. Alas, the reprinting of song lyrics is not covered

by a fair use provision, and when I wrote to Alfred Music, who handles
the permission for this item, I was informed, 'We do administer print
licensing for this song on behalf of ABKCO. They have a minimum fee
of $1000 USD for lyric print licensing. If you wish to proceed, please let
us know and we will can secure approval from ABKCO for this usage'
(October 8, 2021). Given that you probably already know the words to
'Sympathy for the Devil' or can Google them easily enough, I decided
not to spend the money. The Stones are rich enough.

5 Lloyd Webber (2018: 112).

6 Rice (1999: 173).

7 Google Books Ngram Viewer, 'superstar', 1969–2009, https://books.
google.com/ngrams/graph?content=superstar&year_start=1969&year_
end=2009&corpus=15&smoothing=3&share=&direct_url=t1%3B%
2Csuperstar%3B%2Cco#t1%3B%2Csuperstar%3B%2Cco (accessed
1 December 2020). My thanks to Thomas Lakeman for this reference,
and for the Instagram figures.

8 Nassour and Broderick (1973: 80–81).

9 'Archie in the Lock-up' (1971). Archie's remarks were written by Paul
Wayne, Michael Ross and Bernie West, with 'Englebert Whatshisdink'
improvised by actor Carroll O'Connor.

10 Lloyd Webber (2018: 128).

11 Dennen, interview (26 July 2016).

12 Miller (2011: 103).

13 Braun et al. (1972: 109–10, although note that the book is unpag-
inated), reprinting transcript of David Frost's interview with the
Superstar cast.

14 Reader, believe me, I would have dearly liked to quote the lyrics to
'Pilate's Dream' at this point. But after many months of waiting for
permission and getting only perfunctory replies, I had to rewrite the
passage with the bald summary you see here.

15 Rice (1999: 204).

16 Dennen, interview (26 July 2016).

17 Ebert (1973).

18 Dennen, interview (26 July 2016). Rice (1999: 283) confirms this
account.

19 Rice (1999: 284)

20 John Simon, quoted in Nassour and Broderick (1973: 206).

21 Nassour and Broderick (1973: 228).

22 Nassour and Broderick (1973: 227–28). It is worth noting that Jewison,
who was raised as a Methodist, is often thought to be Jewish because of
his name. In fact, when the producers of *Fiddler on the Roof* asked him
to direct the film, he claims to have thought: 'Oh my God, they think I'm
Jewish!' See Jewison (2005: 13).

23 Jewison (2005: 188).

24 Bloom (1987: 25–43).

25 See Wroe (1999: 244–45) on Pilate's ancestor, Gavius Pontius, making a
   similar decision.
26 Miller (2011: 109).
27 Lloyd Webber (2018: 128).
28 Schonfield (2005: 192).
29 Schonfield (2005: 167).
30 All quotations from Rubin (1973).
31 Hofstadter (1964).
32 Ross and Ross (1962: 267).
33 Streissguth (2007: 179).
34 Banister (2014: 159).
35 Snow, quoted in 'Tricky Dick & the Man in Black' (2018).
36 Zeffirelli (1984: 5).
37 Ebert (1968).
38 Zeffirelli (1984: 21).
39 Zeffirelli (1986: 282).
40 Quoted by Abele (2011).
41 Zeffirelli (1984: 29).
42 Zeffirelli (1984: 30).
43 Borgnine (1989/2012).
44 Zeffirelli (1986: 282).
45 France (1908: 26).
46 Galinsky (2007: 403).
47 Zeffirelli (1986: 283).

8 *Michael Palin's Accent in* Monty Python's Life of Brian, *and a Few Others*

       – Geoffrey Chaucer, 'The Miller's Prologue',
             The Canterbury Tales

As much as fun as it would be to start this chapter with 'And Now for Something Completely Different', the fact of the matter is that *Monty Python's Life of Brian* is not really all that much at odds with the Biblical film tradition.[1] The film owes quite a lot to *Jesus of Nazareth* (of which it is something of a parody) and was shot in many cases on the very same sets in North Africa and with the very same extras as the ITV miniseries had been just a few years before. 'I had these elderly Tunisians telling me, "Well, Mr Zeffirelli wouldn't have done it like that, you know"', director Terry Jones joked about the production in an interview some time later.[2] *Life of Brian* is about many things, of course, and the Python troupe's usual buffoonery is everywhere to be seen in the film, but there is a consistent engagement throughout with the concept of empire. The well-known and hilarious 'What have the Romans ever done for us?' episode is a send-up of contemporary anti-imperialist movements set in ancient Judaea, of course, but it is also addressed in some wider fashion to the protests of its present day. All of the Pythons were children of Britain's decline, who in their formative college years strongly felt the 'Winds of Change', as Prime

Minister Harold Macmillan had famously called Britain's stepdown from its own empire. In many ways, the entire *Monty Python* project can be seen as a madcap made-for-TV version of *The Waste Land*, a gathering of *disiecta membra* from the cultural past rearranged and reconsidered in a startlingly innovative format.[3] If empire broadly imagined is a matter at issue in *Life of Brian*, then it makes sense that the representation of Pilate, as the chief agent of empire in the film, will be an especially important character to ponder. Michael Palin's depiction of Pontius Pilate in the movie is much in keeping with the broader cinematic tradition of the role, but in its absurdity also represents a sort of meta-commentary upon the way in which the Roman prefect has customarily been presented.

Palin's Pilate is a figure of fun, but also of serious considera-tion, never more so than in the moment when he speaks in public. From high above on the praetorium's elevated balcony, accompanied by gleaming trumpets and armoured soldiers, Pilate addresses the people below in a forum where further soldiery, elaborate columns and nude classical statues are to be seen. The mise-en-scène is faith-fully patterned after the traditional depiction of imperial appearance found in every movie set in Roman times. Visually, the scene has been set out to majestic effect, all of which is undercut when Pilate opens his mouth to talk: 'People of Jewusalem, Wome is your fwiend! To pwove our fwiendship, it is customawy at this time to welease a wong-doer from our pwison! Whom would you have me welease?' 'Welease Woger!' says a man in the crowd (Terry Jones), imitating Pilate's speech impediment, at which the whole crowd hoots uproari-ously and begins to chant: 'Welease Woger!' At this, Palin's Pilate, not recognizing the mockery to which he is being subjected, responds: 'Vewy well, I shall welease Woger!' The centurion by his side (John Cleese) lets him know: 'Sir, we don't have a Woger, sir'. Pilate, inform-ing the crowd of this fact, is then greeted with the demand to 'welease Wodewick', also non-existent, and also followed by unruly laughter. 'Are they wagging me?' Pilate asks, finally sensing that he is the butt of the joke and, although the centurion denies it, 'wagging' him is precisely what the crowd has been doing. 'Centuwion, why do they titter so?' Pilate wants to know, and the remainder of this chapter will be dedicated to giving a long answer precisely to that plaintive question (Figure 8.1).

In thinking about Pilate in the film tradition, it had not ever occurred to me to ask how Pilate might have sounded until by chance I was re-reading Geoffrey Chaucer's *Canterbury Tales*. There is a moment just after the knight has concluded his story,

Figure 8.1 'Centuwion, why do they titter so?' Michael Palin's hapless Pilate in *Monty Python's Life of Brian* (1979).

and it is not clear who will go next. Robin the Miller drunkenly speaks up and, as the poet writes, *in Pilates voys he gan to crie*, 'he began to cry aloud in Pilate's voice'. The tale that the miller tells is among Chaucer's most famous, although the phrase 'Pilate's voice' is obscure. The phrase has been authoritatively glossed to mean 'in a loud, commanding voice', like that of Pilate in the mystery play tradition.[4] For Chaucer, the braying loudmouth of the medieval stage was an archetype of the cruel and petty official justly relegated to his place in the Creed as a perpetrator of suffering. Already in the medieval dramatic tradition, we see, there is a customary way in which the role of Pilate must be acted and how his voice ought to be heard. On the cold page, the inflection or accent that Pilate might have used was a matter of interpretation for individual readers to ascertain on their own. The prefect might be dismissive, derisive, curious, or kind – the adjectives pile up, and various options can coexist. Once his words are said aloud for dramatic purposes, however, choices have to be made and a single intonation employed. As with stage performance, a set of dramatic customs is likewise at play in the representation of Pilate in film and on television. Onstage and especially onscreen, the voice communicates to an audience in a subtle but powerful manner the way in which the prefect's character ought to be understood and tells us just as much about the external cultural moment in which the production takes place. The critical bibliography on the place of voice in drama is extensive, and the number of onscreen Pilate performances available for review is long, so we must be selective about particular vocal performances to appraise. Nonetheless, as we proceed, we will be considering not so much *what* Pilate has to say in any given production but rather *how* it is he says it. In the movies we have been considering, the question of Pilate's place in the story is a thorny one. Is he the villain of the piece, an officious fool, a misunderstood saint, or something else altogether? The manner of the actor's delivery, in every film since the silent age, contributes meaningfully to the perception of the character's personality and place in society. When Pilate speaks, what do we hear beyond his words? What is the symbolic value of his delivery, and how does this develop from performance to performance? In this chapter, we will consider the range of 'Pilates voys', charting both its intonation and accent, as a way of understanding broader matters of characterisation.

There are some preliminary historical questions to ponder before we proceed to look at – or rather listen to – individual dramatic portrayals. To begin at the very beginning, how do we imagine the historical Pontius Pilate himself actually to have sounded? In the Gospels, there is no description whether Pilate was in fact loud, as Chaucer would have him, or quiet, nor do we have any sense of what Roland Barthes called the 'grain' of his voice, 'the materiality of the body speaking its mother tongue'.[5] Without such specific personal information, however, we can nonetheless make some guesses about the tone and tenor that the prefect might have struck as a matter of education and training for someone of Pilate's governing class. Stuttering, lisping, even having the wrong pitch of voice were all obstacles that had to be overcome if there was any hope for social advancement. For the rhetorically minded Romans, there was a close connection between the speaker and their settings, each of which had its proper mode of address. These situations can be divided broadly into two categories, in Cicero's view: there is speech in public, which is called *contentio*, 'oratory', and private speech, which is called *sermo*, 'conversation'. As he remarks, '[o]ratory is the kind of discourse to be employed in pleadings in court and speeches in popular assemblies and in the senate; conversation should find its natural place in social gatherings, in informal discussions, and in intercourse with friends; it should also seek admission at dinners'.[6] Can this classical distinction drawn between oratory and conversation help us better to hear the historical Pilate upon whom the Pilate of the dramatic tradition is based? In the Gospel of John's depiction of the trial of Jesus, we see 'Pilate shuttling back and forth between Jesus and his accusers, acting on two stages as it were, a front stage and a rear stage'.[7] The register of Pilate's his voice will change accordingly between *contentio* and *sermo*, depending on whether he is speaking to the crowd or in a less formal situation.

How might Pilate have sounded in private? Whether the Roman prefect in fact conversed with a native of Galilee one-on-one, as is so often portrayed in literature and onscreen, can never really be known, although there are those who surmise they spoke together in Koine Greek.[8] The likelihood of the language barrier separating Jesus and Pilate provides Mel Gibson in *The Passion of the Christ* (2003) with an ingenious moment for representing their initial exchange, as based on John (18:33–34). When Jesus is brought before him, Pilate offers a drink that is refused and then asks:

> PILATE: (in what appears to be broken Aramaic)
> Tan' est melek yehudayyah? ('Are you the king of the Jews?')

> JESUS: (in Church Latin)
> A temetipso hoc dicis, an alii dixerunt tibi de me? ('Does this question come from you? Or do you ask this because others have told you that is what I am?')

Most viewers, unable to comprehend either spoken Latin or Aramaic, will be reading the subtitles as they watch the film and not notice any difference between the ancient languages. But others, perhaps upon a repeat viewing, will observe that, when Jim Caviezel's Jesus responds in Latin to the question he has been asked in Aramaic, Hristo Shopov's Pilate furrows his brow slightly. In the quick cutaway shot following, Pilate's lieutenant Abenader (Fabio Sartor) registers more overt surprise. For the devout, of course, the point of the exchange is that, because Jesus is not just the broken victim before Pilate but also God in all his omniscience, he can speak whatever language he so chooses. Although it is a subtlety hidden in the subtitles, Gibson cleverly alludes in this exchange to the response of those later hearing the Apostles filled with the Holy Spirit at Pentecost (Acts 2:7–8): 'Amazed and astonished, they asked, "Are not all these who are speaking Galileans? And how is it that we hear, each of us, in our own native language?"' Most film versions follow the Gospels closely and, sidestepping the issue of linguistic hurdles, assume that Jesus and Pilate can understand each other without intermediary. Following Cicero, then, we should expect Pilate's interview inside the praetorium to have been conducted in the manner of the *sermo*, although even this still leaves us in some uncertainty. In the most famous of these private moments, Pilate asks Jesus: 'What is truth?'

(John 18:38a). Yet, we do not know in what tone of voice he asks this question, and the lack of response from his interlocutor is no help in figuring it out. 'Jesting Pilate', Sir Francis Bacon wrote of this remark in the opening line of his essay *On Truth* (1625), 'would not stay for an answer'. Bacon imputed to Pilate's question a 'delight in giddiness', a flippancy which is the very opposite of that most fundamental of Roman qualities, gravitas. Two and a half centuries later, Friedrich Nietzsche gives the question an entirely different cast, imagining 'the noble scorn of a Roman, before whom the word "truth" was shamelessly mishandled'.[9] Most Biblical commentators have tended toward some middle ground between Bacon's and Nietzsche's interpretations, and the film tradition has followed suit. In Jeanie MacPherson's script for Cecil B. DeMille's *King of Kings*, the scene is described in this way: 'Pilate listens to this and lets the full meaning of it SINK IN! He is simply staggered (HOLD LOOK). These are not the words of a common rebel – these are the words of the greatest "savant" he has ever listened to'.[10] With the consummate facial acting characteristic of the times, DeMille's Pilate, Victor Varconi, milks this moment, looking down and away in reflection, then dutifully up toward the enormous eagle by his throne offscreen and finally back toward Jesus (H. B. Warner), before he asks (silently of course) with a slight smile: 'Truth?' Taking the word seriously but not overly so, Varconi manages to tread the line between Bacon's giddiness and Nietzsche's scorn.

How does this interaction between public and private voices play out in the movies we are considering? An excellent example of the interplay is to be found in MGM's *Ben-Hur* (1959). Toward the end of the film, after his victory in the well-known chariot race, Judah (Charlton Heston) has been summoned to the palatial hall of Pilate (Frank Thring). We see Judah from a high long shot enter on the right through a set of massive doors that dwarf him; dominating the lefthand side of the shot is a large Roman eagle and raised platform with a tribunal chair, alongside which Pilate in his toga makes his dignified entrance. Straightaway, we are cued to see Judah as small and out of place, an impression furthered by his rustic attire in red and brown earth tones, jarringly at odds with the colour palette of gold and royal purple that otherwise predominates in this Roman space. The contrast between the characters is set up visually – right versus left, high versus low, gold/purple versus red/brown – and reinforced vocally throughout the scene. Descending the stairs, Pilate comes to Judah's level to tell him about an offer of Roman citizenship that has been arranged through Arrius Senior, the Roman aristocrat by whom

Figure 8.2 Frank Thring as Pilate and Charlton Heston as Judah Ben-Hur speak man-to-man in *Ben-Hur* (1959).

Judah was adopted when he lived in Rome. Throughout the scene that follows, Pilate and Judah are filmed at eye level, an indication of their equal social status in the dialogue (Figure 8.2).

JUDAH:
You sent for me?

PILATE:
I hope I bring you a good conclusion to your victory.
I have a message for you from the consul, your father.

JUDAH:
I honor him.

PILATE:
As you may honor yourself. You have been made a citizen of Rome.
Do you say nothing to this?

Pilate's tone, although tinged with noblesse oblige, is nonetheless warm here, calculated to reduce the sense of inequality in their relative positions. Judah's corresponding silence, perhaps meant to recall Jesus' before Pilate in the Gospels, catches the prefect off-guard – how can he be rejecting so great a gift? – and a discernible frostiness enters his voice. When Judah tells Pilate about the suffering of his family and even his rival Messalla at the hands of the Romans, Pilate bristles into an even more impersonal tone, saying: 'Where there is greatness, great government or power, even great feeling or compassion, error also is great'. Calling him 'Young Arrius' in an attempt to draw him closer into the Roman sphere, Pilate once again extends the offer of citizenship, but is cut short by the response: 'I am Judah Ben-Hur'. At this moment, Pilate draws himself up, and his remarks point emphatically to the distinction between *sermo* and *contentio:* 'I cross this floor in spoken friendship, as I would speak to Arrius. But when

I go up those stairs, I become the hand of Caesar, ready to crush those who challenge his authority'. Judah listens and, as a final personal renunciation of the offer, gives Pilate his stepfather's ring to return for him. The prefect takes it, looks at Judah and, raising his chin slightly, warns him: 'Even for Arrius' sake, I cannot protect you from personal disaster if you stay here. You are too great a danger'. He then turns on his heel and slowly mounts the platform. A full seventeen seconds elapse in silence – thus long does it take to transform from potential friend and social equal back to official representative of Caesar – at the end of which Pilate proclaims with great stateliness: 'Leave Judaea'. These final two words echo with solemnity in the hall as no other part of the conversation has. Throughout the scene, we watch Thring's Pilate adjusting his manner and hear him modulating his voice to fit the social setting that his character is hoping to frame, from bearer of good tidings, over fatherly surrogate and chiding superior, to, finally, the emperor's resonant mouthpiece.

Concerning Pilate's manner outside, before the crowd, we can deduce from roughly contemporary evidence how Pilate, as a member of the Roman elite, might have spoken in more formal surroundings. Our best information on the principles and methodology of public speaking current during Pilate's lifetime is to be found in a handbook from the later first century AD called *Institutio Oratoria* (*The Education of the Orator*) by the Roman rhetorician Quintilian. Among his extensive set of instructions for the Roman orator's voice and delivery, Quintilian dictates that 'the tone must be agreeable and not harsh', that the 'voice [be saved] from dwindling to the feeble shrillness that characterises the voices of eunuchs, women and invalids', and that speaking should be 'fluent, clear, pleasant and "urbane", that is to say, free from all traces of a rustic or a foreign accent'. Above all, he notes, 'the first essential of a good delivery is evenness. The voice must not run joltingly, with irregularity of rhythm and sound'.[11] Although, as noted, we have no specific information about how Pilate spoke, we must imagine that principles such as these were a part of his educational background, as they would have been for any person of status in his day. We can well imagine Pilate coming out of his headquarters into public view and proclaiming in the urbane and even tone recommended above by Quintilian: 'Take him yourselves and judge him according to your laws' (John 18:31). And yet – and this is perhaps a clue as to the insufficiently forceful nature of the prefect's voice – we know that the high priests do *not* behave as Pilate has bid them but in fact insist that the Romans take him into custody. When he addresses the crowd directly, attempting to get them to release Jesus instead of Barabbas, they resist him and do the opposite of what he wants (John 18:40). The political situation of first-century Judaea is thorny, as we know, but even so it is hard not to conclude that, in spite of the rhetorical education, the commanding tone that the Roman prefect employed on various recorded occasions was not really all that commanding or persuasive.

Are there traces in the cinematic tradition of a Pilate whose voice, while polished, is nonetheless ineffective? The performance of Barry Dennen in *Jesus Christ Superstar* (1973) provides a ready illustration: as a musical, the movie features vocal performances as a primary element, and in Dennen we have a singer with a highly trained voice capable of conveying foreboding as well as failure. We first hear him in *Superstar* singing 'Pilate's Dream', not exactly in soliloquy (distractedly, he passes by a soldier and at the end is approached by his wife), but in a decidedly detached and introspective manner. Accompanied only by an acoustic guitar, Dennen's tenor is clear and articulate as he begins the number, singing in *recitative*, the informal 'speaking style' of light opera, conveying here not an easy-going but rather quite uneasy frame of mind. As the anxiety in the dream that he is recounting builds, the instrumentation beneath his voice begins to swell, but Dennen's vocals remain the song's central focus right through to the end. Pilate is clearly upset by this night-time vision, but the tumultuous events it depicts have yet to unfold – for the present, he remains in at least tentative control of his life and the political situation of Judaea, a fact emphasised by his wife's bringing him a golden wreath at the song's conclusion. With a look of dismay on his face, Dennen's Pilate silently takes up the wreath, a symbol of Rome's authority, while a non-diegetic chorus sings his name, followed by the opening electric guitar riffs of the frenetic next number, 'The Temple', a cue for the coming turmoil. When we next encounter Pilate in *Superstar*, Jesus has been brought before him by the high priests. It is a public setting, and Pilate, wearing his wreath, stands on a rocky outcrop meant to stand for his praetorium. He is filmed from far below at an extremely low angle and, in like fashion, his voice is unnaturally elevated, quite different from the more informal tone of his first song. With his nightmare coming to life before him, Pilate seems incapable of managing his tone, even as he knows he will be unable to manage the unfolding situation. As he asks who this wretch is before him, he sings at a far higher pitch than he had previously, jarringly enunciating every syllable in direct contradiction of Quintilian's dictate about evenness of tone. Where in 'Pilate's

Dream' Dennen had sounded edgy but natural, here the artificial cadences he adopts in the hopes of sounding menacing come across as shrill instead. His political antagonist Caiaphas (played by Bob Bingham), in the meantime, sings in an exaggerated *basso profundo*, the deepness of his delivery suggesting an authority that stands in stark juxtaposition to the halting screeches of Pilate. When he goes to examine Jesus (Ted Neeley), furthermore, all Pilate gets are barely audible answers to his increasingly agitated questioning. In his last scene, with Jesus' fate hanging in the balance – as well as his own, as he knows from his dream – Pilate begins to ridicule and harangue the crowd, who respond to him in loud unison demanding crucifixion. With the steady voices of the priests and crowd on the one side, and the quietly understated replies of Jesus on the other, this Pilate is hemmed in vocally, an apt aural depiction of his uncomfortable political and dramatic situation.

In *Jesus Christ Superstar*, Pilate's voice can be heard in at least two different registers – that of his privately expressed dream and that of his public proclamations – a distinction corresponding to the genres outlined above of *contentio* and *sermo*, oratory and conversation. A far greater distinction than that between Pilate's public and private voices is the marked difference in British and American English, employed in not only this film but the entire film tradition depicting early Christianity. If I may add a personal insight here, it only occurred to me early on in this project that there *was* a tradition of Pilate's having an English accent when I conducted a phone interview with Barry Dennen, the Pilate of *Jesus Christ Superstar* discussed above. In the film as well as on the old Decca LP of the Broadway show (where he had originated the role), he speaks with an upper-class British accent, but talking to me on the phone he was clearly an American. Dennen had a great intuition about voice-work – even into his late seventies, he kept up a busy schedule voicing commercials and videogames – but he had trouble framing an answer to my question about why he had chosen to play the part that way. 'I don't know', he replied. 'It was not Andrew Lloyd Webber's suggestion, but he was happy with what I did. It just seemed right that he should be British. It separates Pilate from everyone else on stage. It suggests nobility, gives him a tony reality. He's upper class'.[12] The aspect of Pilate's being a member of the elite is well brought out in the scene where Jesus is first brought to him: as noted before, his diction is brittle and artificial here, but the soldier's response, voiced in an exaggerated cockney accent on the 1970 Broadway soundtrack, emphasises the difference in class.

In the scene from *Ben-Hur* discussed above, Judah speaks with Heston's distinctive American inflection, entirely appropriate for the point-of-view character in a movie made for a primarily American audience, while Frank Thring (despite being one of Australia's best-loved character actors) employs Received Pronunciation, the agreed-upon accent of the British elite, in his portrayal of Pilate. As critics have noted, *Ben-Hur* is characterised by a near consistency of what Charlton Heston once succinctly called director William Wyler's 'Americans-as-Jews, Brits-as-Romans cast'.[13] This broad distinction between American and British English is a long-standing cinema tradition, the use of which Michael Wood described in his 1975 study *America in the Movies*. 'But I do want to insist on another aspect of the casting of these movies, and that is the distribution of American and English actors in them', he writes, going on to note, . . .

> The heroes are American [and are often] military men, or slaves, or Jews, and the *other* men, the ruling class, are again almost invariably English . . . I don't mean to suggest, of course, that this pattern is intentional, merely that it reveals some interesting assumptions, since it clearly hints at a famous old transatlantic story: The English have manners and purity while the Americans have life; the decadent English, like the rotten Romans they so often portray, have a wonderful past while the energetic Americans, like the Christians and Jews in these stories, are promised a fabulous tomorrow. [. . .] It is the colonies versus the mean mother country.[14]

Discussing this phenomenon in her study of movies about antiquity, *Projecting the Past*, classicist Maria Wyke coined the term 'aural paradigm'.[15] It was only after Al Jolson's *The Jazz Singer* heralded the advent of the 'talkies' that voices began to matter for cinema (although non-diegetic music had long been a staple of the film experience) and that Wyke's aural paradigm began to emerge. As anybody who has watched the downfall of the squeaky-voiced Lina Lamont in *Singing in the Rain* knows, the shift from silent movies to sound had a decisively negative impact on the careers of many actors.[16] Not just those stars graced with less than dulcet voices were affected, but likewise others such as Victor Varconi (Pilate in DeMille's *Kings of Kings*) who spoke with a foreign accent. The arrival of the talkies begged the question: could the same accent work in domestic markets such as New York, as well as in international markets such as London or Sydney? Would what played in Peoria play likewise in Praetoria? 'The British public will never submit to American-made films in which performers speak in the nasal twang of the Yankee', opined one British newspaper of the day.[17] It was during this transitional period in film history, when conventions about sound were beginning to be formed, that Cecil B. DeMille decided to cast for his 1932 remake of *The Sign of the Cross* the English character actor Charles Laughton as the decadent and languid Nero, set against the forceful Marcus, a Roman commander and convert to Christianity, played by Frederic March, who speaks with a mid-Atlantic American accent. With one deft decision, DeMille had thus found an efficient way to represent broader differences of status and ethnicity between the Roman emperor and the Christian commoner by a simple distinction in English pronunciation.

Laughton's Nero was a fortunate piece of casting both for DeMille and the tradition of films about early Christianity as a whole, and yet, such a singular piece of casting does not an aural paradigm make. There would need to be another, and here we must look to Basil Rathbone as Pontius Pilate in *The Last Days of Pompeii* (1935), the first Pilate in a talkie, as the lynchpin to Wyke's aural paradigm. Sharing little beyond a title with Edward Bulwer-Lytton's 1834 novel, *Last Days* had been intended by its producer, Merian C. Cooper, to be a moneymaking spectacle along the lines of his previous blockbuster, *King Kong*. Despite the elaborate attention given to set design and special effects, the movie fizzled rather than exploded, never able to make back its expensive budget until becoming drive-in fare twenty years later; nevertheless, Rathbone was singled out at the time by numerous critics for his memorable performance. *Variety*, for instance, observed: 'Basil Rathbone comes very close to stealing the picture with his playing of Pontius Pilate, the aristocrat not entirely without a conscience who washes his hands of the blood of Jesus while tossing Him to the mob'. *The New York Times* likewise praised his prefect as 'a fascinating aristocrat, scornful in his hauteur and sly in his reasoning'.[18] What made Rathbone seem so aristocratic was not just his suave manner and aquiline nose but also the crisp upper-crust accent, perfected through his long Shakespearean apprenticeship on the London stage, with which he delivered his lines.

Indeed, Rathbone's accent is a matter of studious application rather than natural delivery. Having been born in Johannesburg, he informed journalist Tony Thomas decades later in an interview on an album called *Voices From the Hollywood Past*: 'I was told when I first went into the English theater that I had what was then known as a "colonial" accent. Now this interests me very much indeed, because I had to correct my speech'. His further thoughts in this conversation on accents, which he regards more a matter of class than region, are worth noting in this connection as well:

'I maintain that there is no such thing as an English accent, and there is no such thing as an American accent. There are inflections used by speakers in both countries which differentiate – I think it would be interesting to hear [British Prime Minister] Mr Eden speaking to [US President] Mr Roosevelt, and I don't think any of us could say which spoke the better English'.[19] Rathbone would go on, of course, to become the silver screen's quintessential Sherlock Holmes (starring as the detective in over fourteen films), but due to his clipped and even supercilious manner, he was often cast as villain; despite this onscreen reputation, he was universally regarded in the industry as a 'nice guy' who was always on time, knew all his lines and hit every mark. Because of his professionalism, Rathbone remained very busy, and in 1935 alone appeared not only in *Last Days of Pompeii*, but also in *David Copperfield*, *Anna Karenina*, *A Feather in Her Hat*, *Kind Lady*, *Tale of Two Cities* and the brilliant swashbuckler *Captain Blood*. For all that he brought to the part of Pilate, Rathbone was only cast very late in the process, as can be seen from the cast list dated 29 May 1935, now in the archives at Brigham Young University: while all the other major roles have been assigned, the name of the actor to play Pilate is blank.[20] One can only wonder what might have happened to the 'Brits-as-Romans' aural paradigm had an American actor been selected for the part.

In his initial appearance in *Last Days*, Rathbone's Pilate is seated in an elaborately carved chair behind a large desk. He strikes a stately figure, imposing and imperial in his appearance and, as we shall hear, in his voice as well. A servant ushers in Marcus (Preston Foster) and his young son, Flavius (David Holt), both of whom give an awkward Roman salute. Marcus then gives Flavius a scroll to hand to Pilate, who looks it over and finds it to be without significance – as he impatiently says, . . .

> PILATE:
> My good man, what is all this? There's nothing important in this, yet you insist on seeing me. You bring a child, and you both watch me . . . as though you expected me to burst into flames.
>
> MARCUS:
> I'm sorry, Excellency. I thought it would do no harm to help the prophecy come true.
>
> PILATE:
> Prophecy? What prophecy?

The revelation of the prophecy that 'the greatest man in Judaea' will somehow help his son, as well as the subsequent arrangement that

Pilate and Marcus strike to steal some horses from an Ammonite chief across the Jordan, are not as significant for the purposes of this analysis as is the sharp contrast in their manner of speaking and behaving. In his regal-looking chair, this Pilate is at ease in front of Foster's lower-class American Marcus but, quick to anger at the apparent waste of time, brusquely addresses him with the Britishism 'my good man': it is a condescending expression, as noted by the *Oxford English Dictionary*, which cites versions of the retort 'Don't "good man" me' as early as 1846.[21] As with the conversation between Frank Thring and Charlton Heston in *Ben-Hur* discussed earlier, the difference in accent stands for a difference in status, with Romans represented by British actors and Christians (as Marcus will be by the film's end) by Americans. In both content and manner of his speech, Rathbone's Pilate radiates disdain.

While William Wyler would draw on the aural paradigm of the 1930s cinema for casting decisions in *Ben-Hur*, as we have seen, it was not universally the case in mid-century films that Romans spoke only with British accents. In *The Robe*, for instance, Henry Koster's 1953 Cinemascope spectacular, we see the American actor Richard Boone playing Pontius Pilate and Richard Burton as his subordinate. It may seem strange to have an officer with a rich Welsh baritone answering to an American superior, especially one who would go on to play the troubleshooting TV cowboy Paladin in CBS's *Have Gun – Will Travel*. Perhaps we are meant to recall the multi-ethnic nature of the ancient Roman army or the coordinated military arrangements of the Allies in the Second World War and NATO. On the other hand, perhaps not: according to the list kept by *The Robe*'s casting director Owen McLean, now at the Academy's Margaret Herrick Library, most of the actors being considered for Pilate's role were Americans (including Raymond Burr). However, on the final casting sheet, the name of British actor Robert Douglas is typed in and crossed out, with 'Richard Boone' scrawled above it (his salary, a mere $850 a week alongside Burton's $1 million, probably tells us everything we need to know about Boone's selection for the role). Another film of the period, 1954's *Day of Triumph*, discussed more fully in Chapter 3, enjoyed modest success in the US market (even being held over for additional screenings in Texas), but fared poorly in the UK, where audiences found the picture too American in its outlook as well as its sound. A critic for the Manchester *Sunday Observer*, for instance, wrote that he 'curled up a little bit inside' when he heard Robert Wilson's Jesus pronounce, in an American accent, 'Lissun – a sower went out to sow his seed' at the movie's beginning.[22]

If we fast-forward a few decades, the aural paradigm of *Last Days of Pompeii* and *Ben-Hur* can be heard at work in Martin Scorsese's 1989 *Last Temptation of Christ* (a film to be considered more fully in Chapter 9). Here, once again, we see a British Pontius Pilate (David Bowie) facing not an American Christian convert, but an American Christ himself (Willem Dafoe). One gets the strong sense that Scorsese has the Rathbone-Foster scene from *Last Days* in mind in his depiction of the meeting between Bowie's Pilate and Dafoe's Jesus: although in this scene Scorsese's Pilate is standing rather than seated, as Rathbone had been, the differential in power is framed visually. According to the director's commentary on the DVD, Scorsese had wanted his Pilate to be 'young and imperious' and endowed with a certain amount of charisma. Unsurprisingly, much of the authority of this Pilate is conveyed by Bowie's voice which, like Rathbone's, is delivered in the 'cut-glass' Received Pronunciation of the British elite. He is paired off against Willem Dafoe's Jesus, who speaks with a broad Midwestern intonation, as can be heard clearly, for instance, when he says 'God' with the flat short 'o' typical of American pronunciation. When Jesus refuses to answer his questions, Pilate drops his tongue-in-cheek stance and commands him to 'say something'. After a long pause, he insists: 'You *had* better say something'. The emphasis is worth noting. As with Rathbone's 'my good man' in *Last Days of Pompeii*, there is a condescension to the phrasing: 'had better', a modal expression articulating a threat or warning, is often used outside of Britain in the clipped form 'better', without 'had'.[23] The pointed use here of the full expression in its proper form has an imperialist edge to it, an insistence on the British way of doing things rather than the colonial. Uncowed by the authoritative tone, however, Jesus continues in his silence. Moving away from commands, Pilate sighs in exasperation and changes tactics. 'All right. Tell me what you tell people on the streets'. Having failed to persuade Jesus to speak *up* to him in the language of the empire, Pilate instead coaxes Jesus to speak *down* to him, as he would to the crowds, not an imperial official. As the scene progresses, Bowie's Pilate takes a seat beside Dafoe's Jesus, descending to his level to talk with him in a more informal, even fraternal, manner – these moments resemble Cicero's *sermo* far more than *contentio* – but when the interview is over, he rises to resume his patronising attitude and pedantic grammar: 'You do understand what has to happen? We have a space for you up on Golgotha. Three thousand skulls there by now. Probably more. Guard! I do wish you people would go out and count them some time. Maybe you'd learn a lesson . . . No, probably not'. Throughout the scene, we have heard Bowie alter the register of his address, much as Frank Thring had done in *Ben-Hur*, from the supercilious to the sociable. But like Rathbone's in *Last Days of Pompeii*, the archness of Bowie's intonation is the audio equivalent of the ruins in *Superstar* or the eagle behind Varconi in *King of Kings* – the sound of the superstar's voice here is a symbol of empire.

In hearkening back to an older 'Brits-as-Romans, Americans-as-Jews' casting concept, Scorsese may have been looking to certain broader traditions of movies about early Christianity as a way of blunting criticism of his controversial Jesus movie. If that was the case, it did not work: *People* magazine acidly commented that 'the film is marred by clashing acting styles and stilted language. Harvey Keitel's Brooklynese Judas and David Bowie's clipped Brit of a Pontius Pilate are just two that jar the ear'.[24] What is notable about Martin Scorsese's decision to employ the older aural paradigm is that, by the late 1980s, it was nothing more than a cinematic convention entirely without any corresponding contemporary reality. When Basil Rathbone had played Pontius Pilate in the 1930s, the British Empire was still a global force with vast holdings in Asia and Africa and considerable sway in the Middle East. By the late 1980s, when *The Last Temptation of Christ* was released, Great Britain was a far paler world power than it had been half a century earlier, its overseas holdings reduced greatly in number and its imperial status mostly a memory. As much as we may admire David Bowie's brief performance as the Roman magistrate, the imperious manner and highborn accent with which this Pilate speaks is an empty cinematic gesture, a nod to a tradition that had long since lacked real-world correlation. If in the 1930s Rathbone's performance as Pilate in *The Last Days of Pompeii* called to mind larger-than-life figures such as Lawrence of Arabia, Bowie's performance seems more indebted to *Lawrence of Arabia*, the 1962 epic starring Peter O'Toole.

We now come to *Jesus of Nazareth*, released by Britain's ITV and Italy's RAI production companies as a joint venture (discussed more fully in Chapter 7). Of the accents here, critic Jeffrey Richards aptly observes: 'Zeffirelli reversed the "aural paradigm" by having the leading Romans played by American actors'.[25] The reversal is a significant one, political as well as cinematic in nature. Alongside their suave British counterparts, the Americans Ernest Borgnine and Rod Steiger, as the Roman soldier and Pilate, respectively, come across as brusque and uncultured, a sly commentary on the part of the European makers of the series on American manners and heavy-handed foreign policy. We sense this in the crispness with which both

Zerah, the Jewish priest played by Ian Holm, and Robert Powell's Jesus articulate their points, starkly in contrast with Steiger's halting, uncertain questioning. Seated uncomfortably in his chair – how different Steiger looks in comparison to the easy manner struck by Basil Rathbone in *The Last Days of Pompeii* – this American Pilate angers at the patronising attitude of the Jewish officials talking down to him in Received Pronunciation. One defensive exchange is particularly revealing: a Jewish priest explains that Jesus 'calls himself the Christ, which means the Anointed One', at which Pilate chafes, replying, 'Thank you. I too know some Greek'. Just after Pilate says this, the camera cuts quickly to a medium close-up shot of Zerah, on whose face is a slight, supercilious smile from which we read his reaction. *How charming it is that this boor,* he seems to think, *who happens to be in charge, also pretends to be learned.* It is a smile that also offers subtle recognition of a rearranged political dynamic. In the years preceding *Jesus of Nazareth*'s premiere on British television, relations between the UK and US had come to be irrevocably inverted, with the former on the wane and the latter on the rise. British Prime Minister Harold Macmillan had famously employed a classical analogy to outline British responsibilities in this time of geopolitical change: 'You will find the Americans much as the Greeks found the Romans – great big, vulgar, bustling people, more vigorous than we are and also more idle, with more unspoiled virtues but also more corrupt. We must run [things] as the Greek slaves ran the operations of the Emperor Claudius'.[26] In the decades following the Second World War, the power in the West had shifted towards the Americans, who looked to older models in both Rome and Britain for an imperial example. But by the mid-1970s, the 'special relationship' between the US and the UK was at a particularly low ebb, with differences over relations in the Middle East being a primary bone of contention. The gaunt Powell and the shrewd Holm speak knowingly in this ancient Middle Eastern scenario, while the heavy-set Steiger stumbles through his part. *Jesus of Nazareth*'s trial of Christ before Pilate is as much a portrait of British-American relations in the 1970s as it is of Roman-Judaean relations in the first century AD.

All of these considerations – aural paradigms and altered political conditions – form the background for Michael Palin's indelible performance in *Monty Python's Life of Brian.* As noted earlier, the connection of *Life of Brian* with *Jesus of Nazareth* is a very close one, but where the convention concerning accent had been inverted in *Jesus of Nazareth*, so that the Romans spoke with American rather than British voices, *Life of Brian* up-ends the tradition altogether.

Both Jews and Romans have British accents, since all the members of the Python troupe are from Britain. Yet, Palin's Pilate speaks with an exaggerated rhotacism – an inability to pronounce the letter 'R' – to preposterous effect, as in the scene noted at the beginning of this chapter, when he offers the crowd the choice of setting a prisoner free for Passover. In the *Life of Brian Scrapbook*, Palin had spoken of his particular inspiration for this vocal performance:

> Pontius Pilate was a legitimate historical character, part of the Bible story, [therefore] he had to be dealt with. How do you deal with this man? I must have felt: ruling class, British ruling class, very often distinguished through some aristocratic inbreeding by vowel difficulties of some kind, or vocal distinctions I think it might have come from there.
>
> Pilate never acknowledges that he has a problem at all. This is the wonderful thing, again I think this just came in my mind from listening to Violet Bonham Carter or people like that, the English aristocracy. They have vewy stwange ways of tawking, and they doughn't think eet's vewy extwawdinawy at awl![27]

As Palin suggests here, the manner of speech that he adopted for his Roman aristocrat on film is a skewering of the overly refined way in which British aristocrats were heard to speak in real life. In his recent exhaustive commentary on *Life of Brian*, furthermore, Dale Larsen observes that the Pythons were lampooning two significant politicians of their day, who spoke with this speech impediment: the first was the intellectual and long-time Labour Party eminence, Roy Jenkins (routinely mocked as 'Woy Jenkins' by the satirical magazine *Private Eye*), while the other was Margaret Thatcher, the well-known Tory leader who would become Prime Minister just as *Life of Brian* was being released.[28] Although neither Jenkins nor Thatcher had come from aristocratic backgrounds, as Bonham Carter had, the simple fact of their holding powerful positions made them seem ripe for even the most puerile of ridicule.

But while we hear in Pilate's r-challenged speech a critique of British aristocracy broadly and of particular politicians specifically, another hapless figure of fun seems to lurk in the background as well. In the carnivalesque world of Warner Brothers' Looney Tunes cartoons, there is perhaps no bigger chump than Elmer Fudd, Bugs Bunny's nemesis, whose speech is replete with the same mispronounced Rs that we hear from Pilate. 'The influence of American animation on the Pythons and especially their use of speed, violence, and gaggery can be seen throughout [*Flying Circus*]', Larsen notes.[29] Voiced not by Mel Blanc but by Arthur Q. Bryan, Elmer with his slow, sad manner of speaking instantly conjures up his status as an utter loser, even though with his rifle and the occasionally maniacal look on his face, he nevertheless had a slight air of menace about him. During the Second World War, evidently, audiences associated the spunky Bugs with the American GI and Elmer with the Axis powers, and the connection is understandable enough.[30] How better, at the height of the Fascist threat, to cut the menace down to size than by imagining a hunter who can hardly hold his gun or say the name of his prey? 'Be vewy, vewy qwiet', says Elmer, sneaking along with his rifle. 'I'm hunting wabbits'. Perpetually he is met by the blasé Bugs ('What's up, Doc?') who chomps a carrot and makes a fool of him every time. In *Life of Brian*, Pilate shouts 'Siwence!' to his guards as well as the crowd, issuing the command in a way that guarantees everybody within earshot will *not* be silent, but instead dissolve into fits of uncontainable laughter. Neither the might of the empire at Pilate's command nor the shotgun that Elmer holds are sufficient to their circumstances for maintaining either silence or control. As soon as they open their mouths to speak, they each find themselves subject to merciless ragging. Once the representative of a great power whose word was law, the British figure here speaks before a crowd that listens only to laugh at him.

It is worth observing, in this connection, that the contours of the British-versus-American aural paradigm was territory that Palin and his fellow *Life of Brian* star, John Cleese, would explore for comic purposes a decade later with the American actor Kevin Kline in the comic heist send-up *A Fish Called Wanda*. At the end of the film, which features many a screwball situation, Cleese's English barrister Archie Leach has a final showdown with his American counterpart, Kline's Anglophobic petty criminal, Otto West (an Oscar-winning performance for Kline). The two hurl insults at each other that, going far beyond the personal level, involve the stereotypical perceptions of one another's countries:

WEST:
You English, you think you're so superior, don't you? Well, you're the filth of the planet. A bunch of pompous, badly-dressed, poverty-stricken, sexually-repressed football hooligans. Goodbye, Archie.

LEACH:
Well, at least we're not irretrievably vulgar.

WEST:
You know your problem? You don't like winners.

LEACH:
Winners? Winners like North Vietnam?

WEST:
Shut up! We did not lose Vietnam! It was a tie!

LEACH: (affecting an American accent)
I'm tellin' ya, they kicked some ass there! Boy, they whupped your hide real good!

WEST:
Oh, no, they . . . Shut up!

LEACH:
Gonna shoot me?

WEST: (affecting a British accent)
Er, yes. Yes, 'fraid so, old chap. Sorry!

In this exchange, we hear many of the buried elements of the 'Brits-as-Romans, Americans-as-Jews' vocal casting found in such Biblical movies as *Ben-Hur*, here exposed to typical Python-esque lampooning. The British are imperial and imperious, but their prime is long past; Americans, by contrast, possess vigour and youth, but also an insufferable arrogance about their prowess. The confrontation ends when Palin's Ken Pile, a figure whose stuttering has been the butt of frequent brutally unfunny remarks by West, runs over the American with a steamroller as an act of revenge and, as result, loses his speech impairment. 'I can speak!' he says in amazement. 'Ha ha! How much wood could a woodchuck chuck if a wood chuck could chuck wood?' Ken's triumph notwithstanding, various disability support groups protested *A Fish Called Wanda* about the ridicule of Ken, although Palin maintained that the performance had been inspired by his own speech-impaired father, in whose honour in 1993 the actor would establish the Michael Palin Centre for Stammering Children in London.[31]

As an important supplement to this discussion, let us consider now the juxtaposition of British received pronunciation and Irish brogue in scenes of Jesus and Pilate. During Holy Week of 2008, the BBC aired a four-part miniseries, *The Passion*, produced by Nigel Stafford-Clark with a script by the Irish author Frank Deasy. As the title indicates, this Passion was intended to be a response to Mel Gibson's *Passion of the Christ* from 2003, with greater attention to the ministry of Jesus as well as his humanity. In hopes of making the story feel more immediate and less remote, the producers deliberately decided against using the Latin and Aramaic which Gibson had employed and opted for a very contemporary English instead. Deasy had wanted his Jesus to sound like a regular guy 'coming from Newcastle' rather than a classically trained Shakespearean actor. 'We thought long and hard about the issue of accents', Stafford-Clark remarked in a Q&A session available in the BBC Online Archive. As he continued, . . .

> One of the most important aims for us was to make the story seem as real and as immediate as possible. And when you go out on to the streets in your everyday life you are not surrounded by people speaking RP [Received Pronunciation]. So to use it would be to insert a sense of distance, a historicism you might say, that would run counter to what we were trying to achieve.
>
> We therefore decided to be 'accent blind' – to allow the actors to speak in their natural voices, just as they would have done at the time.
>
> Palestine in 33 AD would have been rife with regional accents, even with different languages. We were very happy with the results for us it helped to make characters like the Disciples and Barabbas feel more like real people and less like figures from history.[32]

There is indeed a vast array of British accents on display in *The Passion*, in some ways not unlike the variety of American accents heard in Scorsese's *Last Temptation of Christ* (1989). But while the choice to forego a standardised accent had given the BBC's production a greater relatability for its British viewership, it was understood that those outside the UK would probably be less capable of distinguishing a London accent from a Merseyside one. For American audiences trained to hear English accents in films about Jesus as authoritative and uniform, the rich diversity of British speech might come across as a sort of Tower of Babel, and surely it is for this reason that the BBC has never released a Region-1 DVD version of *The Passion* for the US market.

At the end of his remarks above, Stafford-Clark specifically noted: 'And James Nesbitt's hard Northern Irish accent felt like the voice of an outsider, underlining his role as head of a Roman occupying force'. The way in which Nesbitt's Pilate speaks, his natural Ulster brogue made even more curt with exaggerated military intonation, has been singled out particularly for censure by critics. In his scholarly volume *Screen Jesus*, Peter Malone called the accent 'more than a little disconcerting and distracting', adding the rhetorical question: 'Pilate was a foreigner in Judea, but with such an accent?'[33] Nastier, but in some ways more edifying, was the assessment of the acerbic *Sunday Times* TV critic A. A. Gill who, in addition to ridiculing Nesbitt's Roman miniskirt, pointed out that the actor's Northern Irish accent 'did bring a certain hint of religious bigotry and violence to the role'.[34] What Malone seems to miss and Gill snidely insinuates in these remarks is the fact that Nesbitt had been cast as Pontius Pilate because of and not in spite of his accent. It is precisely to summon up for the UK audience the recent bloody history of

Northern Ireland and to import into their depiction of the Roman occupation of Judaea the uncomfortable legacy of British imperialism that Nesbitt was cast in the role, so that we might hear Pilate speaking with an Ulster intonation and be reminded of the Troubles.

As an actor, James Nesbitt has never attempted to cover up his native Northern Irish accent – not the way in which his fellow County Antrim native, 1950s Hollywood star Stephen Boyd (Messalla in 1959's *Ben-Hur*), had done throughout his career, opting to sound 'transatlantic' – but rather has embraced the sound of his voice as an integral part of his onscreen identity. Nesbitt's greatest role is undoubtedly that of the Protestant civil-rights activist, Ivan Cooper, in Paul Greengrass's critically acclaimed *Bloody Sunday* (2002), in which a would-be peaceful march in 1972 led by the protagonist turns into a massacre of unarmed Catholic civilians by British soldiers. Throughout the film, which is shot in the hand-held style of a documentary, Nesbitt's Cooper is talking – with military commanders, police officers, his wife, the street toughs on either side of the conflict, his civil rights colleagues on the Catholic side – at times quietly on the phone at home, at other times hoarsely through a bullhorn in the streets. In a situation that we know from the film's title and from history to be relentlessly sliding into violence and bloodshed, the only instrument that Cooper has available to try to keep the peace is his voice. Despite the urgency heard in his hard Ulster accent, however, there is nothing that can keep thirteen innocent lives from being mowed down and the chaos from erupting once again.

As *Bloody Sunday* opens, we have a pair of intersecting scenes meant to foreshadow the coming conflict: Cooper, at a press conference, is announcing the peace march that he will lead, while Major General Robert Ford (Tim Piggot-Smith) is telling a separate press conference: 'In view of the continuing adverse security situation in the Province, all parades, processions, and marches will be banned until further notice'. The general is in battle dress, and behind him is an enormous map of the vicinity, blocked off into quadrants laid over the region's natural and political topography. It is as striking an image of control as one might hope for, as it is drawn from countless military briefings from the period. In *The Passion*, filmed only a few years after *Bloody Sunday* (in between, Nesbitt had starred as a hard-bitten Northern Irish detective in five seasons of *Murphy's Law*), he is cast again as a man with authority in a region riven by religious conflict. But where events in Derry had overtaken Ivan Cooper, despite his best efforts to keep the peace, Nesbitt's Pilate is determined not to have a riot break out in Jerusalem. He plays the part with a disdain that his accent brings out brilliantly, but beneath it this Pilate is aware of just how volatile a situation he presides over. In his initial scene, he tells an aide: 'There are always troublemakers in Passover week ... Five years ago, there was a riot. We had to finish it breaking bones'. Throughout *The Passion*, as in *Bloody Sunday*, there is a sense of the military occupation being a powder keg that any false move could set off, but while the Paras spectacularly lost control in Derry, Nesbitt's Pilate feels that he has managed to maintain order when only one person has been killed, and that one under Pilate's direct orders. In his final scene in *The Passion*, Pilate tells his wife as they leave Jerusalem to return to Rome: 'I've served [the emperor] well'. In the end, this Pilate has handled his troubles better than his notorious accent might have suggested.

The Troubles played a far greater part in a production about Jesus that was broadcast at their height in 1969. *Son of Man*, by Dennis Potter, appeared as an episode of the BBC1's Wednesday Play series and featured Robert Hardy as Pilate and Colin Blakely as Jesus. Potter's teleplay was a deliberately provocative version of the Passion narrative, capturing the confrontational zeitgeist of the late 1960s. 'Tough Guy Christ Shocks Viewers', declared the *Daily Mirror*, while other critics found it to be a Gospel for the times. Even a half-century later, the impact of *Son of Man* is arresting: when he is asked whether the Jews should pay taxes to the Roman heathens, for instance, Blakely's Jesus aggressively demands a coin from his questioner. 'And whose head is that on the coin?' Caesar's, he is told. 'Now, you give to Caesar what belongs to Caesar, and give to God what belongs to God', he says quietly and predictably, before finishing in loud exasperation: 'And SHUT UP!' The Prince of Peace he may be, but this Jesus seethes with frustration about the status quo.

Staged on a rickety, improvised set and filmed with hand-held cameras (which here and there can be glimpsed in the hands of extras in some of the crowd scenes), *Son of Man* has an unrehearsed quality to it, as though the events it depicted were not thousands of years old but very much of the here and now. The sense of the old order locked in deadly combat with the forces of revolution can be felt – and heard – throughout *Son of Man*. Robert Hardy, Potter's Pilate, would go on to later fame playing Winston Churchill in several productions, and as the Roman prefect brings a strong sense of the British colonial administrator to the role. And, as John R. Cook notes in his assessment of Potter, 'the request for the Northern Irish, "barrel-chested" Blakely to play Christ was the playwright's own'. Having seen Blakely in a televised version of Shaw's *Saint Joan*, Potter felt his Jesus needed to draw on the actor's quality of pent-up emotion.[35] Although it had been originally scheduled to air during Holy Week, BBC executives had feared that *Son of Man* might be too controversial for its audience and held off broadcast until Wednesday, 16 April 1969. As it happened, the next day, a twenty-one-year-old woman named Bernadette Devlin was elected as the MP for Mid-Ulster, the youngest woman ever to go to Parliament and one of the fieriest advocates for civil rights ever to grace its halls. As Devlin would say in her maiden speech on behalf of her constituents, '[t]here is no place in society for us, the ordinary peasants of Northern Ireland. There is no place for us in the society of landlords because we are the have-nots and they are the haves'. Devlin was present when those have-nots took up arms at the Battle of the Bogside in August of the same year; when Bloody Sunday took place a scant three years later, she was so offended by Home Secretary Reginald Maulding's claims in the House of Commons that the Army had fired in self-defence that she marched across the chamber and slapped him. Calling her action 'a simple proletarian protest', she lamented later: 'I'm just sorry I didn't get him by the throat'.

As angry as Blakely's have-not Northern Irish Jesus might be, he refrains from delivering any such proletarian protests, advocating instead a message of non-violence every bit as maddening as a slap across the face might have been to the British Pilate he confronts. Early in *Son of Man*, we see how a tricky religious and political situation needs more than a military solution: a Roman commander (Godfrey Quigley) in breastplate and helmet is pointing out on a map the potential insurrections of the Jews and Samaritans and other 'smelly tribesmen'. He promises: 'There is no trouble we can't put down'. We might well be watching the self-confident military briefing with which *Bloody Sunday* begins, and Pilate is convinced that a ruthless first strike will be effective. 'Put them down', he says. 'Put them down hard'. The scene now cuts to Roman soldiers brutally rounding up unarmed peasants, one of whom is hacked to death in the crush and, as we watch him die, Jesus' voice is heard offstage, saying: 'An eye for an eye and a tooth for a tooth'. The crowd of listeners cheers this, as he comes into view, as well as his command to love their kinsmen, although they are more sceptical about his insistence on loving their enemies. 'If a Roman soldier was to [hit you on the cheek], turn the other cheek'. The crowd loudly demurs. 'Pray for your persecutor', Jesus continues, with growing irritation. 'He is a man as you are a man. It is easy to love only those who love you. Would I come to tell you easy things? Do you want me to tell you easy things?' Some of the crowd have clearly taken his words to heart, however. Later we see Pilate slap a household servant named Ruth (Wendy Allnutt) who tells him to do it again. 'I've seen the Messiah', she informs him gently. 'I am following his way, his truth. You cannot and will not hurt me'.

Her fearlessness unnerves Pilate. Earlier, when he had met with his military advisers, who dismissed Jesus of Nazareth as a nobody, the prefect had castigated them as damned fools. He goes on to say: 'We do not have to fear the force of arms, sir, we Romans. Ideas are what we fear, sir. Ideas. Do you know what an idea is, sir? No. Well, I'll tell you. An idea is stronger than an army. It's sharper than a lance. It's more enduring than an empire. And it's more slippery than an eel. Ideas are what we fear, soldier. Now do you understand?' The matter comes to a head when Jesus is at last apprehended and brought before him, blindfolded. Pilate orders the covering removed, and Jesus bids him a good afternoon, but the prefect bears down on him with all the arrogance he can muster from his position of unquestioned authority. He tries the old tactic of conjuring up for the prisoner the pain he is about to feel. 'Aren't you afraid of the nails?' he asks with a condescending smile, to which Jesus replies with a smile of his own, 'Yes'.

> PILATE:
> I find no fault in him, except stupidity. Tell me, do you love your enemies?
>
> JESUS: (Still smiling)
> Yes.
>
> PILATE:
> Do you? Well, what about me? Do you love me?
>
> JESUS:
> Yes, Pontius.

Pilate then slaps him hard across the face. Jesus falls but slowly stands up again, at which the look on Pilate's face changes radically. Rattled by his own cruelty, Pilate apologises, twice saying: 'That was not necessary'. Jesus agrees with him and then fixes him in the eye, this time saying without a smile: 'Don't be afraid'. Over the course of just a few minutes, the tables have somehow turned – who is giving the orders here? – as the British Pilate falls back before an Irish Jesus with a steady voice.

NOTES

1 Telford (2015).
2 Sellers (2003).

3 Landy (2005: 15–19).
4 Parker (1950: 237).
5 Barthes (1977: 179–89).
6 Cicero, *On Duties* 1.132, translated by Miller (1921: 135).
7 Brown and Moloney (2017: 283).
8 Balsdon (1979: 138 with 281 n 6).
9 Nietzsche (1920: 134–35).
10 MacPherson (1926: 221).
11 Quintilian, *Institutio Oratoria*, 11.16, 19, 30, and 42, translated by Butler (1922: 251, 253, 259 and 265).
12 Dennen, interview (25 July 2016).
13 Heston (1995: 196).
14 Wood (1975: 183–84).
15 Wyke (1997: 71).
16 On the complexities of the transition to sound, see Crafton (1997: 1–18).
17 Crafton (1997: 422).
18 Both reviews quoted by Druxman (2011: 157).
19 *Voices From the Hollywood Past* (1975), 'Band 2 – Basil Rathbone'.
20 Cooper (1935: 2).
21 'Good man, v.' *OED Online.* Oxford University Press, Third Edition, June 2011 (accessed 1 December 2020).
22 Quoted in Suit (2018: 152).
23 Butterfield (2015: 106), who observes: 'In practice, this use of an unsupported *better* is much more common in North America, Australia, and NZ than in Britain'.
24 Travers (1988).
25 Richards (2008: 165).
26 As quoted by Hitchens (2004: 23).
27 Palin, as cited in Idle (1979: n. p.), See also http://www.montypython.com/book_The%20Life%20of%20Brian:%20Monty%20Python's%20Scrapbook/28#q9pBbBfMxxJmoVFg.99 (accessed 1 December 2020).
28 Larsen (2018: 288–89). My great thanks to Dale Larsen for sharing the manuscript of this book before it appeared in print, and for the inspired conversation in his office at BYU.
29 Larsen (2008: 111).
30 Hajdu (2009: 252).
31 Palin (2011).
32 BBC (n. d.).
33 Malone (2012: 175).
34 Quoted by Donaghy (2008).
35 Cook (1995: 57).

9 Grand and Not-So-Grand Inquisitors of the Reagan Age

In the deep darkness, the iron door of the prison suddenly opens, and the old Grand Inquisitor himself slowly enters carrying a lamp. He is alone, the door is immediately locked behind him. He stands in the entrance and for a long time, for a minute or two, gazes into [the prisoner's] face. At last he quietly approaches, sets the lamp on the table, and says to him: 'Is it you? You?' But receiving no answer, he quickly adds: 'Do not answer, be silent. After all, what could you say? I know too well what you would say. And you have no right to add anything to what you already said once. Why, then, have you come to interfere with us?'

– Fyodor Dostoyevsky, 'The Grand Inquisitor',
from *The Brothers Karamazov*[1]

'Jesus is "in" these days', Richard Cardinal tells Daniel in *Jesus of Montreal* (*Jésus de Montréal*), a critically acclaimed drama from 1989 by Quebec filmmaker Denys Arcand. 'But you'll have to do the weekend talk shows'.[2] Daniel (Lothaire Bluteau) plays an actor in the film who is starring in a radically innovative Passion play of his own composition that *tout le monde* is buzzing about, while Richard (Yves Jacques), with a distractingly attractive young woman of seventeen on his arm, is talking to him about career opportunities. A commanding view of the city unfurls in the distance behind them as they stroll along the floor of the lawyer's skyscraper office. Although it is set in a Canadian city, as the title makes clear, it is the culture of 1980s materialism spreading from south of the border that is the movie's principal topic. Arcand's previous film, titled *The Decline of the American Empire*, had starred some of the same actors and dealt with some of the same moral issues, but *Jesus of Montreal* is a far more allegorical movie. In this scene, Richard exemplifies everything the director is striving against, in a way that is simultaneously heavy-handed and light-hearted. If Daniel is Jesus in Arcand's telling, Richard is certainly 'the devil who took him to a very high mountain and showed him all the kingdoms of the world and their splendour', as we read in the Gospels of Matthew (4:8) and Luke (4:5). Just as certainly, Richard's surname points to the Cardinal who, as the Grand Inquisitor in Dostoevsky's *Brothers Karamazov*, has been an enduring symbol of the church's entrenched power, not about to let even Jesus himself interfere with it. And, of course, with his expensive tailored suit and slicked-back hair, Richard is also a Gordon Gekko *à la Quebec*, a character borrowed by Arcand from Oliver Stone's *Wall Street*, the 1987 indictment of the gospel of greed, to give particular cinematic point to his Canadian morality play. 'I don't have much to say', Daniel demurs when the idea of a talk show is floated, but Richard is dismissive. 'We could draft up something. Some ways of saying nothing go over so well. Think of Ronald Reagan'.

Throughout *Jesus of Montreal*, as well as Martin Scorsese's *Last Temptation of Christ* (the controversial film that came out about the same time), it is difficult *not* to think of Ronald Reagan, the former actor who had become President of the US with the support of televangelist Jerry Falwell's Moral Majority. Formerly head of the Screen Actors Guild, Reagan had been instrumental in the McCarthyist effort to blacklist Hollywood 'leftists', including Jules Dassin, whose *He Who Must Die* (*Celui Qui Doit Mourir*) is also discussed in this chapter. Elected president based on the slogan 'Morning in America', the telegenic Reagan presented a sunny optimism that was rooted in a made-for-the-movies nostalgia and a conservative form of institutional Christianity. His administration's blanket dedication to supply-side economics led to rampant consumerism and a drastically increased and decidedly un-Christian wealth gap between rich and poor, a paradox not without cultural expression. While homelessness surged under Reagan, *Dallas* and *Dynasty* were the nation's most popular TV shows, with *Lifestyles of the Rich and Famous* a perennial favourite as well. The tension in the period between God and Mammon perhaps found no better symbol than the 1987 indictment for fraud of another televangelist, Jim Bakker. Together with his wife Tammy Faye, Bakker had run the *PTL* (*Praise The Lord*) *Club* media franchise, whose 'version of the prosperity gospel could be seen as the cargo cult of junk-bond capitalism', in Frances FitzGerald's considered opinion.[3] Writing for *People* magazine, Dave Barry said of the couple:

Their message seemed to be, Hey, if you're doing the Lord's work, the Lord wants you to be comfortable. He wants you to have nice clothes and antique cars and luxury residences with gold-plated bathroom fixtures and an air-conditioned doghouse. And yes, if you are a faithful laborer in His vineyards, the Lord frankly sees nothing wrong with getting a couple of giraffes. The Lord wants you to have fun! That was how Jim and Tammy felt, and they gave their followers a way to feel righteous and be entertained. Watching the PTL Club was like watching a mutant version of Wheel of Fortune, where Pat Sajak and Vanna White won all the prizes.[4]

Amid such blatantly hypocritical onscreen orthodoxies, it is unsurprising that the film narratives of the Gospels arising at this time featured a selfless saviour whom church leaders hated as a heretic.[5]

Given the nature of the windmills they were tilting at, we can hardly fault Scorsese and Arcand for the quixotic nature of their late-1980s films about Jesus. Perhaps because the Catholic establishment he is taking on is less outrageous, Arcand's is the gentler movie, albeit not an especially subtle one. In his review for *New York* magazine, David Denby complained that 'there are only two kinds of characters, the completely honorable ones and the complete rotters. [...] In other words, the conception of the movie is smug from the beginning'. It may be that the critic has overestimated the amount of sophistication one should expect from a morality play, even an updated one. As the film opens, Daniel is gathering around himself a number of disciples from among his underground theatre friends who correspond faithfully to their New Testament counterparts. Perhaps the most precise parallel is the Magdalene character, the beautiful Mireille (Catherine Wilkening), whom we first see in the shooting of a perfume commercial appearing as a Botticelli Venus figure. Her boyfriend, the Svengali-like Jerzy (Boris Bergman), discourages her from taking part in Daniel's Passion Play, telling her: 'Sweetheart, your talent is all in your ass'. Later, Daniel accompanies her to an audition for another commercial, where she is ordered to strip for the casting agent. The product being marketed is a new brand of beer called Appalache, with a dance number that even Arcand must know is over-the-top: 'Nothing's sacred to you, but a good glass of brew! ... The young crowd's here, we worship beer!' The blasphemy here is amplified to a ludicrous level with an upbeat tempo, of course, but it is all too much for Daniel who, taking Mireille away from the crass spectacle, overturns the caterer's tables, smashes the cameras and slaps a director across the face, in an explicit allusion to Christ's cleansing of the Temple (Matthew 21:12–13). Updated Biblical analogies such as this scene or the meeting with Richard described above and others scattered at various points throughout the film are imaginatively conceived – and fun to spot – although they do little to undercut Denby's critique about Arcand's lack of nuance.

Throughout the movie, Arcand lays on the absurdity liberally, but *Jesus of Montreal* should not be considered a farce. This Passion-play-within-a-Passion-play format is earnest in the extreme, and even academic, in its pursuit of truth. In revising the play for performance at Saint Joseph's Oratory, Daniel consults with a New Testament scholar who directs him to new excavations on Israel's West Bank and computer analyses of the text, the sorts of things a dramatist can make use of but that he, as a church-funded theologian, is not allowed to incorporate into his work. The result is a play that is far less canonical than the Catholic authorities are expecting (although a viewer might end up thinking, 'Hmmm, sounds like *somebody*'s been introduced to postmodern hermeneutics in their Intro to the New Testament course'). But the earnestness of *Jesus of Montreal* is never greater than when it is dealing with religion as a genuine balm for spiritual anxiety. 'You must find your own path to salvation', the audience is told in the play's final choral remarks: 'Life is really very simple. It just seems overwhelming when you think only of yourself. If you forget yourself and ask how to help others, life becomes perfectly simple'. This message is not lost upon Father Leclerc (Gilles Pelletier), who had commissioned Daniel to 'freshen up' the old play that the church had been producing, but he is furious with the final result which he understands to be, at its heart, anti-clerical. Father Leclerc – his name, like Richard Cardinal, unsubtly points to his position of authority – is one among numerous Grand Inquisitor figures in the film. Yet even the priest (who is not above sleeping with one of the actresses) is a sympathetic character and genuinely worries about the inner lives of the refugees from Guatemala and Haiti who pack his church on Sundays. 'They don't care about the latest archaeological findings in the Middle East!' he yells at Daniel and the acting troupe when he orders the play to be cancelled. 'They want to hear that Jesus loves them'.

Within the Passion play itself, René (Robert Lepage) plays the role of Pontius Pilate, before whom Daniel's Jesus is brought in chains. René's Pilate is framed in this night-time scene by a large statue of Jesus (here blindfolded), beneath which is inscribed *Condamné à Mort*, 'Condemned to Death'. The setting is the first station of the cross, and the composition of the scene tells it all – even before Pilate has pronounced his sentence in the play, before he has even had Jesus brought before him, it has all been determined ahead of time what he will do. But we are reminded, too, that René is trying to bring to life a story that is already, quite literally, set in stone before him. Later in the film, when Father Leclerc will tell the actors that the play will not be allowed to continue, it is at this very same spot where the confrontation will take place, and where another sort of condemnation will occur. The actors will ridicule the priest, asking if it would be possible for them to perform the play in the style of the *Comédie-Française*, of New York method acting, in street slang, or in Japanese kabuki, each time coming out from behind the statue of Jesus with a renewed energy. The only one without any sense of connection to the statue in this later scene is Father Leclerc himself. During the Passion Play, René is framed still further in the distance by the illuminated windows of the church, covered with a curtain on which is written SPQR. In this setting, and in his not exactly Roman robes, René looks like both a priest and a prefect, a true representative of both the Roman Empire and of the Roman Catholic Church. As with his appearance, René's manner betrays ambivalence, his tone lodged somewhere between wry and uninviting. 'You speak of founding a kingdom, a kingdom not of this earth', he asks, without evident sincerity. 'A sort of Elysium? After we die?' Daniel's Jesus denies this, and then is asked what he teaches. 'Greater love hath no man than to offer his life for friends', he says, to which Pilate replies with slight amusement: 'Isn't that a bit optimistic? You wouldn't last a week in Rome'. It is the Rome of the Emperors that he is referring to, we presume, although the Rome of the Church might be inferred.

René's Pilate turns away from this exchange, walking behind the statue of Jesus to tell the high priest that Jesus is harmless. When Caiaphas complains that he rails against the priests, Pilate responds, with a superciliousness equal to what he's shown Jesus just a moment ago: 'I've always held priests to be either idiots or profiteers'. When reminded that the priests support Rome, and that Tiberius might be told of his inaction, René's Pilate yields, not so much convinced by the argument but tired of hearing it. He comes back out from behind the enormous statue of Jesus to face Daniel's Jesus, who tells him, when asked, that the priest hates him 'for telling the truth'. René's Pilate begins a long response: 'What is truth? My soldiers will take you. They're brutes, of course. We don't get the elite. You'll be whipped, then crucified. It won't be pleasant. You're not Roman, but try to be brave. Who knows, I may be doing you a favor'. It is unclear what his purpose is in saying these things – does he hope to frighten Jesus, to intimidate him, or simply to inform him of what is coming next? René is sitting on the stairs looking at Daniel as he offers these comments, with the foot of the statue of Jesus visible behind him. Now, however, he goes on to make a series of more agnostic philosophical observations about suicide and the uncertainty of the afterlife, going off script from Pilate's predetermined Biblical remarks. René's Pilate begins to walk around and, subtly but significantly, the statue of Jesus no longer appears in the scene as he concludes his thoughts:

> A philosopher said, 'the freedom to kill oneself during hardship is the greatest gift man has'. In a few hours you'll cross the Styx, the River of Death, whence no one has returned, except Orpheus, it is said. Perhaps your kingdom lies on the far shore. Or maybe Jupiter Capitolinus awaits you, or Athena, or the god of the Germans, or the Franks. There are so many gods. Perhaps the river has no other shore and vanishes into darkness. You at least will know. Courage. Take him away.

There is a shrugging sort of irony about this speech here, and we sense that Arcand, in having Daniel compose this speech for his Pilate, is trying to have it both ways – to give voice on the stage to an aloofness about religion, but also to condemn such aloofness.

When Daniel, in gathering his disciples at the beginning of the film, had first come to find him, René had been recording a French voice-over to a Carl Sagan-style documentary at a Montreal planetarium. As planets and galaxies colourfully swirl across the screen, René is reciting from a script, which reads: 'But we will be long gone. The world began without man and will end the same way. When the last soul vanishes from Earth the universe will bear no trace of man's passing'. As he finishes up the dubbing session, he tells the director that it 'leaves a lot unanswered'. 'Yeah, and though it's valid today, in five years it may change', is all the reply that he gets. These cosmic questions trouble René. At first, he rejects the opportunity to work on the play, but later comes back to Daniel, agreeing to participate if he can be allowed to recite Hamlet's soliloquy. Toward the end of the play, he does so:

> Who would fardels bear,
> To grunt and sweat under a weary life,
> But that the dread of something after death,
> The undiscovered country from whose bourn
> No traveler returns.

As the weary Pilate, he is one from whom we hear a tinge of envy in his voice as he condemns Christ at the first Station of the Cross. Jesus will encounter the infinite nature of the cosmos; he will visit the undiscovered country. As he tells him, '[y]ou, at least, will know'.

Outside of the play, there is yet one more Pilate that Daniel's Jesus has to face. Summoned to court to answer for his destruction of the Appalache set, he is called before a judge played by Denys Arcand himself. Rebuffing the legal help of Richard, Daniel states that he will make no defence. 'I plead guilty', he says, to which Arcand's judge replies: 'I'll ask the psychologist to see you' – an updated version of Pilate's sending Christ off to Herod. But it is a fine observation on the director's part, delivered with an understatement that perhaps David Denby did not notice, that if Jesus were to come into a courtroom today, the judge would likely send him off for professional help. When Daniel returns from meeting the doctor, the judge is a little put off by her assessment. 'I don't know what you did to her', he says, 'but she claims you're "better adjusted than most of the judges in this court". Hardly flattering to us'. Sensing, as had René's Pilate, that Daniel is harmless, he postpones his sentencing. 'But we'll set a date now for you to return, without fail', he insists. 'Without fail, got it?' Daniel does promise to return without fail – and he will keep this promise, although not without complications, and not precisely in the way in which he or the judge have understood their agreement. Father Leclerc will cancel the play, the actors will put it on over his objections, the police will intercede, and a mêlée will ensue in which Daniel will be grievously wounded. There will be two trips to the emergency room, interrupted by a descent into a subway station, but Daniel in the end will die on the operating table. As he breathes his last, the doctor asks for his body: 'He's young, he's healthy, and he's got Type O blood. That's a godsend', he says, and we watch as Daniel's organs are transported to hospitals all over the world, bringing new life and hope to those who were sure they were at the end of their line. In a final Biblical analogy at the movie's conclusion, Daniel's disciples are gathered to carry on this work. There is some disagreement among them about what exactly the best way is to go about this might be – an avant-garde theatre perhaps? – but Richard is at hand to guide them along, or, like the devil he is, to tempt them off the straight and narrow path. As the song of two young women busking in the subway fades into the 1980s guitar soundtrack over the final credits, it is anybody's guess what might be next for these actors – considering their futures, perhaps one of them will go on to run for high public office, and there will be reason to think of Ronald Reagan once again.

In a review generally praising Arcand's film, critic Jonathan Rosenbaum had noted in his *Chicago Reader* column that he was initially averse to seeing *Jesus of Montreal* for reasons having to do with an entirely different film that he had seen thirty years before – the film was Jules Dassin's *He Who Must Die* (*Celui Qui Doit Mourir*), a French art-house movie based on Nikos Kazantzakis's novel *The Greek Passion* about the restaging of a Passion Play in 1920s Turkey. As Rosenbaum writes, . . .

> I was a teenager at the time, and being none too versed in what was considered sophisticated in film in 1959, I was moved to tears. This was at a time when the French New Wave had barely made a ripple in the American consciousness, and shortly before Dassin's film was ridiculed by critics I admired, like Pauline Kael and Dwight MacDonald, as the acme of arty pretension. [. . .] Whether or not MacDonald's terse verdict ('a pretentious pastiche of Eisenstein-cum-socialist realism') was just, I must confess that the weight of his and Kael's and Andrew Sarris's scorn has stayed with me more than most of the film has. So much so that whenever I hear about a similar film–anything that involves Jesus reappearing in the 20th century and being recrucified – I automatically cringe.[6]

Although the intelligentsia sniffed at it, reviewers in the mainstream press universally gushed over *He Who Must Die*. 'It abounds in a daring sort of candor and relentless driving toward its points of allegorical contact in a succession of searching and searing episodes', wrote Bosley Crowther for the *New York Times*, while in the *New Yorker* John McCarten called *He Who Must Die* 'one of the best pictures of recent years'.[7] Like the teenaged Rosenbaum, however, young viewers in particular found the film compelling. 'It is one of the few recent movies that can qualify as art', wrote a reviewer for the *Harvard Crimson* (13 October 1959). Recalling his own youthful days as a Catholic activist in the 1950s, Maurice Berube writes that he wielded Dassin's depiction of Christ as 'my shock weapon', and 'with great sophomoric delight [. . .] I would challenge Sunday-only Catholics in parlor discussions'. Shot in grainy black-and-white with priests in dark cassocks against the sun-bleached background of Crete, Dassin's film conveyed a strong sense of moral absolutes, while the Passion Play that it re-enacted in French concerning rural Greek peasants under Turkish control offered a radically new set of contexts through which to think about the traditional Christian story.

For all the splash it made at the time, however, *He Who Must Die* is known now more in oral tradition than by any actual viewing, as it is not available currently for purchase in DVD format or on any streaming platform. If it is remarkable that a film hailed as one of the best of recent years by no less than the *New Yorker* itself should fall so utterly and completely out of the canon, the reason has less to do with the avant-garde aesthetics of highbrow critics than the reactionary politics of McCarthyism. In the 1940s, Jules Dassin had been a well-regarded Hollywood director, specialising in the film noir genre, with works such as *The Naked City*, *Brute Force* and *Thieves' Highway* receiving critical and popular acclaim. Although some assume that he was French, Dassin (who pronounced his name DASS-in) was born in Connecticut and raised in Harlem – he was an American citizen, in other words, until it was insinuated otherwise by the US House Un-American Committee (HUAC). Like many other artists during the Depression, Dassin had been a member of the Communist Party of the US, a fact about which he was fairly open and unembarrassed, feeling that it had been an expression of his commitment to social justice rather than a betrayal of his country. Insiders in Hollywood, however, including Ronald Reagan as the president of the Screen Actors Guild, gave up the names of Dassin and others to the committee and allowed their reputations to be smeared as unpatriotic. 'The Party tried very hard to present Communist or Socialist ideas as an advance in America's development that was in fact rooted in American traditions. Well, they failed in this. The American people couldn't buy it. The association with the Soviet Union was too powerful', Dassin told an interviewer decades later. 'I don't see that the ideas we tried to present were wrong. And the intentions were, as far as I'm concerned, always pure'.[8]

Although Dassin had been subpoenaed and was prepared to defend himself, HUAC was disbanded before he was called to testify. The director was never formally blacklisted, but he left the US in semi-voluntary exile and was unable to find employment as a filmmaker for the next several years. By 1960, the redbaiting fever had broken in America, and Dassin's love-letter to Greece, the scandalous *Never on a Sunday* (in which he starred together with Melina Mercouri, whom he would marry), was nominated by the Academy for Best Picture. Political grudges still remained, however. 'Ronald Reagan Blasts Hollywood Reds' was the name of a 1961 editorial singling out Dassin's affiliations with the Communist Party – a senator from New Hampshire later had Reagan's piece entered into the US Congressional Record.[9] It is difficult to prove, of course, but the years of ignominy caused by the McCarthyist witch-hunt seem to have had an unjustly adverse effect on Dassin's subsequent reputation. In the late 1970s, when old movies were being released on VHS for home entertainment, only a handful of Dassin's movies were converted, and in subsequent transitions to DVD and streaming formats, much of his work has continued to remain unavailable. My own copy of *He Who Must Die*, which I found only after much online searching, is a bootleg version recorded from a TV broadcast which I bought from a dubious seller on eBay – my rather full summary of the plot below is predicated on the assumption that most readers, having refrained from such shady purchases, may not know the film very well.

As noted, Dassin's *Celui Qui Doit Mourir*, released with the English title *He Who Must Die*, was based on Nikos Kazantzakis's 1948 novel Ο Χριστός Ξανασταυρώνεται, translated in 1954 by Jonathan Griffin into English as *Christ Recrucified* in the UK and *The Greek Passion* in the US. The story is set on the Anatolian coast shortly after the First World War, in a Greek village called Lycovrissi ('Wolf's Spring') under the control of a Turkish overlord only called the Agha, whom Kazantzakis describes as 'fattening in Oriental splendor on gifts from his Greek subjects, cruel, demanding, sensuous and fuddled, living for the pleasures of raki and pretty boys'.[10] In the film, the Agha is a less threatening figure, played by character actor Grégoire Aslan, who had a penchant for portraying risible authority figures. Shortly after *He Who Must Die*, for instance, he would play the elder Herod, literally kicked off his throne by Frank Thring in 1962's *King of Kings*, and in 1963's *Cleopatra*, he was the unsavoury regent of the young Ptolemy, Pothinus, at whom Rex Harrison's Julius Caesar would sneer. Although the story is not without its comic elements, *The Greek Passion* is ultimately a tragic tale. Many readers would have been aware that the novel takes place in the time shortly before the Treaty of Lausanne of 1923 and the consequent population exchange between Greece and the new Turkish republic, the wide-scale and involuntary deportation of Muslims from Greece and Christians from Turkey that left hundreds of thousands dead. The events of Kazantzakis's novel, tragic in themselves, take on an added dimension of frustration and pointlessness in light of the looming resettlement plans of which none of the characters is aware. To his credit, Dassin does not dwell on these larger geopolitical considerations in his production, although, as an exile himself, they were undoubtedly somewhere in the back of his mind as he made the movie.

He Who Must Die opens not in Lycovrissi (unnamed in the film) but with another Greek village being destroyed by the Turks as the opening credits unfurl. The distraught survivors, having gathered up their few meagre belongings, draw together around their priest, Father Fotis (Jean Servais, the debonair star of *Rififi*, here equally charismatic although far sterner), who leads them out of the ruins to what he promises will be a new home. We cut then to Lycovrissi, where the villagers are enjoying relative prosperity and give little trouble to the corrupt and effete Agha who, never coming out of his apartment, flirts with his bouzouki-playing houseboy and sips raki beneath his handlebar moustache. Slightly comical yet nonetheless in absolute control, he enjoys making the villagers and their chief priest, Father Grigoris (Fernand Ledoux), wait before giving his approval to put on the traditional Passion Play. Once he approves, the politics of the town kick into high gear, as various characters jockey for the leading role in the Passion: the part of Saint Peter is ultimately given to the postman Yannakos (René Lefèvre), Saint John to Michelis Patriarchaeas (Maurice Ronet), son of the village's archon and wealthiest man, and Jesus to Manolios (Pierre Vaneck), a sweet shepherd with a stutter. The part of Mary Magdalene is given to Katerina (Melina Mercouri), a beautiful widow and prostitute, with whom the brutal leather worker Panayataros (Roger Hanin), cast as Judas, is madly in love. The petty jealousies of the town, magnified by the Passion Play, are amplified to a still greater degree by the sudden arrival of Father Fotis and the haggard band of refugees looking for asylum from their desperate plight. Dassin follows Kazantzakis's novel closely at this point in the film to demonstrate the hypocrisy of the church leadership, as Grigoris himself speaks against accepting the refugees and then, without any evidence, declares them to be bringing cholera to the town. Denied any assistance from the clearly thriving town, Fotis leads his group of disheartened exiles onto the nearby mountain of Sarakina. The Agha, in the meantime, pays no attention to any of these proceedings, convinced as he is that it is the nature of Greeks to clash with each other. 'Christians are Allah's mistakes', he later tells his houseboy, Youssafaki. 'He realized it as soon as he created the first one, then he created a second one. And they pounced on each other. Since then, Christians have been killing each other'.[11]

It is only a matter of time before various members of the town furtively visit the mountainside, where Fotis has declared that the refugees will build a new town and see for themselves that they are not suffering from any illness. Manolios, the shepherd cast as Jesus, in particular is eager to inform Father Grigorios, who also acts as chief intermediary with the Turks, that there is no cholera among the refugees on the Sarakina. It is a shock to the young man when his tidings of good news are met with fury – told to shut up, he is then slapped across the face and made to apologise for disputing the priest's word. Bewildered, the shepherd pauses, does as he is bid and leaves in humiliation. Manolios may have trouble expressing himself at this moment but, having come face to face with the hypocrisy of the village's leadership, he realises that he cannot unsee what he has seen or unknow what he has known. As the film proceeds, the pressure of being the village's Jesus will come to influence Manolios's actions more and more, as it will for many of the others around him.

The campfires on the Sarakina seen at night increasingly trouble the consciences of those in the village below, who begin to supply the refugees with food and provisions. None of it is enough to curtail the widening misery, however, typified in the death of one little girl in her mother's arms. Father Fotis enjoins Manolios to go to the villagers for help, and when the shepherd demurs on account of his speech impediment, he is told that God will give him the words, as he had done for Moses in the Bible. It is now the day of the Passion Play in Lycovrissi, and all the villagers are gathered in the town square for the holiday feast. When they see Manolios attempting to get their attention to speak, they make fun of their stammering Jesus and are joined by the unsmiling Grigoris and other elders. As the shepherd begins to address them, however, his speech becomes clearer and surer – 'It's a miracle!' the villagers gasp – and his revelation that there is no plague on the mountain is likewise taken as divine. Father Grigoris tries to silence him, to no avail, and the people amid much cheering begin to fill a tablecloth with food and clothing for the poor people of the Sarakina. Unbeknownst to Manolios, however, Yannakos and the others have been pilfering a wealthy family's storehouse all this while, certain that they possess a moral justification to do so, and when the crowd is informed of the robbery, a hush falls over the holiday gathering. Pressed by the priest to respond to the burglary of his friends, the shepherd replies simply: 'God bless the thieves'. Grigoris seizes the moment to shame Manolios by calling him an anti-Christ: 'I told you you'd get cholera. Well, you got it! The cholera of heresy, the cholera of rebellion. Go away! I excommunicate you!' His efforts undermined by the illegal activities of his friends, Manolios leaves the village, his motives deliberately misconstrued. In this moment of humiliation, we have a sense of what the young viewers who had identified with the protagonists of *Rebel without a Cause* or *Blackboard Jungle* just a few years earlier found appealing about *He Who Must Die*. Although it takes place in Asia Minor in the early 1920s, the politics of 1950s America hang heavily over the film, from the manifest tensions of the generation gap to the unshakeable sense that traditional institutions are interested solely in protecting their own privilege.

Those forces of entrenched self-interest are felt keenly in the scenes that follow which, with swift but inexorable motion, bring the film to its climactic final moments. When a rich landowner dies and his son grants the property to the Sarakini, Father Grigoris refuses to certify the deed, angrily maintaining that such a thing would destabilise the internal social order of Lycovrissi and upset its carefully maintained coexistence with the Turks. Hearing of this decision, the people of the Sarakina are enraged, and one of them passionately says to Father Fotis: 'If we let children starve to death, I think we sin against God'. Manolios shouts his assent, and after a long stare into the middle distance, the priest gives his as well, quoting the Gospel of Matthew: 'I did not come to bring peace but a sword' (10:34). Taking up sticks, stones and rifles, they descend upon the town and meet with armed resistance led by Grigoris. Although one of the villagers attempts to prevent the inevitable conflict by running between the lines and shouting 'Stop! We are all Greek!', gunfire breaks out and casualties ensue. Dassin's film was produced in the mid-1950s, but it was based on a novel originally published in 1948, and it is hard not to see in this pitched street battle an allegory of the Greek Civil War (1946–49) and the larger struggle between NATO and the Soviet Union for which it was a proxy. In *The Greek Passion*, Kazantzakis had not been especially understated about drawing overt parallels between the events of his novel and contemporary post-war Greek politics. At one point, the roughneck chosen to play Judas in the Passion Play spreads the rumour that Manolios and Fotis are Communist agents attempting to dupe the villagers – it is a rumour that eventually reaches Grigoris, who confronts the landowner's son. 'I know your secret!' he declares, and he continues his accusation: 'Bolsheviks! You receive orders from Moscow to overthrow religion, country, the family and property, the four great pillars of the world!' Although this is vigorously denied – 'That's as much as to say that Christ is a Bolshevik!' – for the remainder of the book, the priest will not be shy about referring to Manolios as 'the Bolshevik' and claim that 'the Muscovite' is standing close behind him to direct his every action.[12] Although Kazantzakis had drawn close correspondences between the events of his story and those taking place on contemporary political scenes, Dassin resists the urge in *He Who Must Die* to render his Father Grigoris as an Old World Joe McCarthy.

In moments such as the shepherd's excommunication and his forced submission before the priest, it is easy to see the rejection of both Kazantzakis and Dassin by figures of cultural authority as source material, but it is understandable why the filmmaker has not followed the novelist's lead here in giving explicit anti-Bolshevik motives to the villagers. As *He Who Must Die* comes to its close, the allegorical model of the film begins to play down the overtly political elements from the novel and adhere more closely to the Biblical material with which it began.

After the street battle and the retreat on both sides from initial fighting, Manolios and the landowner's son lead the Sarakini into his well-fortified family compound, and Father Grigoris feels it is time to involve the Turkish overlord in the conflict. How the story resolves from this moment on in *He Who Must Die* presents a useful contrast to its depiction in *The Greek Passion*. Although in Kazantzakis's novel an elder had been selected to play the part in the village Passion Play, it is clear that the true Pontius Pilate of *The Greek Passion* is the disinterested imperial figure of the Agha. 'Wolves don't eat one another; Greeks do', he says to himself, as he looks out with bemused detachment from his balcony onto the conflict below. 'There he is, take him, you blessed *romnoi*, and enjoy your meals! I wash my hands of it; I drink my raki, I savor these succulent camel sausages'.[13] When the priest comes to him with two other village leaders demanding that the shepherd be handed over, the overlord agrees to act. As the crowd outside cries 'Death to Manolios!', the overlord carries on a quiet interrogation of the young shepherd, who finally tells the Agha that he will surrender so long as the Sarakini will not be touched. When the Agha exclaims that they are Bolsheviks, Manolios tells him that that they are just 'poor people who want to live in peace and have roots in the earth; that's all'. The overlord is annoyed by this, as it seems to make sense to him; the situation is far from clear, and the decision far from simple. Manolios demands once again that he be given up to the crowd, but the Agha stops him. 'Come, admit that you're a Bolshevik, so I can get in a rage and give you up without it breaking my heart', he demands. Manolios, in what is a perverse but sincere act of mercy, then begins to admit to being a Communist, to hoping to destroy the Ottoman Empire, to wanting to spread revolution and to desiring to set fire to the mosques of Constantinople. The more enthusiastic his pretence, the more the Agha encourages him until, genuinely angered by the things that Manolios is saying, he leaps from his chair and kicks the young man into the street where the angry crowd throws itself upon him.

In *He Who Must Die*, the Agha is a more hapless character and, although he is equally unconcerned about the troubles between the Christians, far less given to rage. 'Don't be coming bothering me', he tells Grigoris in the film, when the priest comes to him after the street battle. 'Leave me alone. It's none of my business'. But Grigoris sees it differently. 'It's more your business than mine', he says. 'Those men were killed more by poison than by bullet – the poison of rebellion. If you don't stop it in this village, the poison will spread. It will contaminate everything. What will you say when it gets to Constantinople, and you're blamed for it?'

Understanding the threat, the Turk agrees to the priest's demand that Manolios be turned over. In the following scene, one drawn not at all from the novel, the Agha in full military outfit rides up on horseback to the compound with a large contingent of armed Turkish troops. Dassin has very much lightened the interaction between Manolios and the Agha, and all references to Moscow and Bolshevism have been removed. He calls for Manolios to come out and talk with him and adds, pointing to a Gatling gun: 'Or this machine will speak for me'. Manolios jumps the fence and approaches the Turkish commander. The Agha laughs and, dismounting, invites Manolios to sit beside him. Taking off his fez, the symbol of his office, but fanning himself with it now and again as a reminder of his military authority, he encourages the young man to renounce his radical position. 'I'm just an old Turk and politician. But I can see things. If you do what I tell you, you're safe'. He pats the young man's arm and gives him a patronising smile. Returning the fez to his head, he walks back to his horse and once again laughs. From here, the story runs to its depressing conclusion: Manolios will turn away and then, suddenly grabbing a shovel, attack the soldier at the Gatling gun. When he is captured, he will be brought back to the village and tossed into the church where, after a hasty tribunal, he is stabbed to death. The priest then leads the villagers on an assault against the Sarakini who, in the final scene of the film, defiantly point their rifles out from the compound at the invaders.

There was a genuine storyteller's wisdom on Dassin's part in playing down the Cold War themes when bringing Kazantzakis's novel to the screen. The determination of authority figures to put the worst possible construction on his motives was something Dassin knew about all too well, however, and he refracted much of his own troubles as a member of the blacklist into the treatment of his Manolios. What reviewers took away from *He Who Must Die* was not a condemnation of controversial foreign policy objectives – as they might have, had words such as 'Bolshevik' and 'Muscovite' been cavalierly tossed around – but rather an indictment of authorities too easily swayed to look after their own interests at the expense of justice. There was no need to draw parallels between groundless accusations of anti-Communism too pointedly, given that the tale of the village Passion Play disintegrating into hypocrisy was sufficient enough for mainstream audiences: young viewers in movie houses across Middle America, after all, had made a hero out of James Dean as a rebel *without* a cause. 'If Christ returned to Earth today', Crowther had written in his review of Dassin's film for the *Times*, 'these selfish people would still crucify Him for His social teachings, this drama says'. Whether he was aware of it or not, Crowther was reacting strongly not just to Dassin's allegory about McCarthyism, but also to the suspicion of powerful institutions latent in the literary text upon which the film was based. Kazantzakis's own troubles with church authorities formed the basis of much of his work, of course, and he would return with increased boldness to the themes of *The Greek Passion* a few years later in a controversial novel that would itself be turned into a controversial film by Martin Scorsese, *The Last Temptation of Christ.*

'In Kazantzakis's jaundiced opinion', scholar Thomas Lindlof wrote in *Hollywood Under Siege: Martin Scorsese, the Religious Right, and the Culture Wars*, 'the Church has kept a grip on its earthly protectorate of power and privilege by holding out the promise of eternal life to its flock'.[14] In *The Greek Passion*, Father Grigorios is depicted as a priest heavily invested in maintaining the status quo, although the novelist has softened the picture by reminding us of the delicate relationship that the village he presides over has with the Turkish authorities. In both the book and Dassin's film, the Agha is a passive figure in the background, who nevertheless might become quite dangerous if provoked. Grigorios sees it as his duty to the Christian villagers to keep the peace with the imperial overlords but, in doing so, he ultimately fails those most in need of his protection, during the Easter season no less. It is for this betrayal of his pastoral duty that both Kazantzakis and Dassin condemn the priest, offering him as a version of Dostoevsky's Grand Inquisitor for mid-century Europe and America. A similar theme is developed in *The Last Temptation of Christ*, where Kazantzakis explores the concept of Jesus' fully human nature: in this story, the devil offers Jesus an alternative life in which he is spared the crucifixion and instead becomes a happily married man with children. Toward the end of the novel, living under the guise of 'Master Lazarus', he now encounters a former persecutor named Saul, himself going by the name Paul, testifying to the death and resurrection of Jesus. In Scorsese's film, it is Jesus (Willem Dafoe) himself we see confronting Paul (Harry Dean Stanton, cast intentionally to 'lend a televangelist fervor' to the role).[15] 'Why are you telling these lies?' Jesus angrily asks Paul, revealing that it is he who is the son of Mary and Joseph, but that God saved him from death on the cross. Paul's initial reply reminds us more of Father Leclerc's defence in *Jesus of Montreal* than of that of Father Grigoris in *He Who Must Die*:

> Wait just a minute. What's the matter with you? Look around you. Look at all these people. Look at their faces. Do you see how unhappy they are? Do you see how they're suffering? Their only hope is the resurrected Jesus. I don't care whether you're Jesus or not. The resurrected Jesus will save the world and that's what matters.

'You can't save the world by lying!' Jesus furiously responds, but Paul has a ready answer for him. 'I created the truth out of what people needed and what they believed. If I have to crucify you to save the world, then I'll crucify you. And if I have to resurrect you, then I'll do that, too'. Telling Jesus that he is glad to have met him 'because now I can forget all about you', Paul walks away, his version of the truth justified, at least to himself, by the ultimate good be believes it can do, and of course by the fame he expects to win in offering it.

The question about truth, which in the Gospels derives from Pilate, however, does not arise when Dafoe's Jesus is brought earlier in the film before the Roman prefect played by David Bowie. Here we feel a version of the Grand Inquisitor being presented, although the defence of power he presents is not at all couched in Paul's rationalising language of spiritual comfort. In Kazantzakis's novel, the Roman official is little interested in comforting anybody – hating the people over whom he rules, he carries a perfumed handkerchief before his nose lest he breathe in the 'Jewish air', while around his neck he nihilistically wears a razor blade (called grimly 'my Messiah') with which to cut open his veins at a moment's notice.[16] It is a less sneering Pilate we see in the film – according to the director's commentary on the DVD, Scorsese had wanted the Roman prefect to be 'young and imperious' and endowed with a certain amount of charisma. The lead singer of The Police, Sting, had originally been cast in the role, but given the delays in production, was unavailable for filming when Scorsese was finally able to begin. Consequently, another, perhaps even more charismatic musician was chosen for the part. As a cross-over superstar whose videos had featured in heavy rotation on MTV throughout the 1980s, Bowie occupied a unique position in the world of celebrity. Over a long and varied career, he had taken on numerous roles on screen and in song: of the latter, his prefect resembles less the genderfluid glam-rock persona of Ziggy Stardust than it does the

Edward VIII manqué guise he adopted for the album *Station to Station*, the Thin White Duke. Many viewers will remember Bowie as Thomas Jerome Newton in the mid-1970s sci-fi hit *The Man Who Fell to Earth*, or his turn as Jareth the Goblin King in the cult favourite fantasy musical *Labyrinth* from 1986. But perhaps the role most connected to this Pilate is that of Major Jack 'Strafer' Celliers in 1983's *Merry Christmas, Mister Lawrence*, set in a Japanese POW camp. Cast as an almost Byronic rebel, Bowie's Celliers exerts a powerful hold over his men as well as the commandant played by Ryuichi Sakamoto. The name of the film, and Bowie's appearance in it, point to a connection with Peter O'Toole in *Lawrence of Arabia*, and that sense of the stylish and alluring British official clad in Eastern robes can certainly be felt in *Last Temptation*'s Pilate as well (Figure 9.1).

Although he is onscreen for a little over three minutes, Bowie inhabits the role of Pilate memorably and convincingly. He looks the part, due in no small part to the way in which he wears his toga, made of 'small squares of natural deerskin [. . .] so supple it might look like silk', according to the noted Lebanese couturier Jean-Pierre Delifer who designed the costumes for the film.[17] Upon seeing Bowie in it, director Martin Scorsese said:

I'm sitting in my director's chair and there are some chairs behind me and suddenly I feel a tap on my shoulder and I turn around and there I was face-to-face with the ancient world, a being from the ancient world. I suddenly looked into the face of history. His face was right up close to mine and he was

Figure 9.1 In his deerskin toga, David Bowie's Pilate radiates authority and condescension in *The Last Temptation of Christ* (1989).

smiling and his hair was done as Pontius Pilate, he was in his toga ... It was the most shocking, beautiful thing I had seen. This was the ancient world and it has come alive! He was an alien in the best sense of the word! That's my fondest memory of him. I was stunned; I couldn't speak ... David? Yes! Let me see the toga. It was fantastic. That's why I wanted him to stay a little still during the shoot because he became that world. He didn't have to show his authority by moving, he could just glare and speak, you see.[18]

As ancient commentators noted, the toga was a garment inhibiting movement that, if properly arrayed, enforced a palpable gravitas upon its wearer. The art historian Richard Brilliant coined the term 'appendage aesthetic' to describe the manner in which the conservative toga focused attention on the wearer's right arm, barely able to move, the right hand and above all the face – it is an insight borne out well in Scorsese's enthusiastic description of Bowie's Pilate 'just glaring and speaking'. Beyond taking a seat alongside Willem Dafoe's Jesus at one point, Bowie barely moves in this scene, and, in that relative lack of locomotion, he communicates his graceful command of the situation. In addition, the filming location in the imperial Moroccan city of Meknes itself lends a menace to Bowie's presence in the scene. In Kazantzakis's novel, Pilate had sat 'on a raised throne which was decorated with grossly carved eagles' during his interview with Jesus. This setting was replicated in the original screenplay written by Paul Schrader but altered in a revised version to 'an open theatre', where the prefect is watching a play in rehearsal. The suggestive interpretations that this theatrical setting might have offered are tantalising to ponder – an allusion to the play-within-a-play of *The Greek Passion* comes to mind, of course – but ultimately Scorsese opted to place the scene in the official's private stables, complete with whinnying horses. The prefect is, we sense, a busy man, and the matter of Jesus is not so significant that it cannot be handled while he inspects his mount. The scene was filmed in the substructure of the Villa Imperiale, the palace of Sultan Moulay Ismail, whose long rule over Morocco from 1672 to 1727 was characterised by both grandeur and brutality. The sultan's reputation for hostility toward Christianity, reflected in the title of a book published during his lifetime – *Barbarian Cruelty: Being A True History of the Distressed Condition of the Christian Captives under the Tyranny of Mully Ishmael Emperor of Morocco* came out in London in 1693 – perhaps informs Pilate's contempt toward Jesus here as well?[19]

The short scene that constitutes the entirety of the discussion with the prefect gives the impression of a colonial master speaking down to a subordinate.

PILATE:
So, you are the King of the Jews?

JESUS:
'King' is your word.

PILATE:
Well, you are Jesus of Nazareth, aren't you?

JESUS:
Yes, I am.

PILATE:
That's what they're saying you are. The King, the Messiah. It's also said that you do miracles. Is this good magic or bad magic? Could we have some kind of a demonstration? I mean, can you do a trick for me, now?

JESUS:
No, I'm not a trained animal. I'm not a magician.

'That's disappointing', replies Bowie's disdainful Pilate, his momentary hopes for amusement dashed. Evidently, Jesus is nothing more than another Jewish politician, perhaps one more dangerous than the Zealots. When Jesus refuses to answer his questions, Pilate drops his tongue-in-cheek stance. 'Say something', he demands and then, after a long pause, insists: 'You *had* better say something'.

Moving away from commands, Pilate sighs in exasperation and changes tactics: 'All right. Tell me what you tell people on the streets'. Having failed to persuade Jesus to speak *up* to him in the language of the empire, Pilate instead coaxes Jesus to speak *down* to him, as he would to the crowds and not to an imperial official. Dafoe's Jesus tells him about the Prophet Daniel's vision of a statue smashed by a stone. 'God threw the stone. The stone is me. And Rome', he says, although it is Pilate who finishes the sentence: 'And Rome is the statue, yes'. At this moment, with cool pragmatism, Bowie's Pilate sits beside Jesus, to speak with him as an equal in a less formal tone.

PILATE:
It's one thing to want to change the way that people live. But you want to change how they think, how they feel.

JESUS:
All I'm saying is that change will happen with love, not with killing.

PILATE:
Either way, it's dangerous. It's against Rome. It's against the way the world is. And killing or loving, it's all the same. It simply doesn't matter how you want to change things. We don't want them changed.

This part of the conversation is filmed from behind, so that we see the actors' backs – it is a tête-à-tête, on which we seem to be eavesdropping; as in Dostoevsky's Grand Inquisitor chapter, it is a private discussion. Bowie's Pilate speaks frankly with Jesus about Rome – here, the empire, but perhaps also the Catholic Church – and its relationship to power. In this worldview there is little room for change (a very surprising thing to hear from Bowie, one of whose best-loved hits was called 'Changes'), and no room at all for pardon. He stands again and begins to walk out of the frame, quietly informing the prisoner: 'You do understand what has to happen? We have a space for you up on Golgotha. Three thousand skulls there by now. Probably more. Guard! I do wish you people would go out and count them some time. Maybe you'd learn a lesson'. He turns to leave. 'No, probably not'. Exit Bowie's Pilate, with a superior shake of the head and hands unwashed – even the horses who are neighing so insistently at the start of the scene have fallen silent as he walks off, and we cut quickly to a scene with the Roman soldiers kicking Dafoe's Jesus in the groin. In the novel, Kazantzakis has Paul inform Jesus, as Master Lazarus, that Pilate ended up filled with regret for his actions toward Jesus: 'They found him yesterday, at dawn – crucified. It seems his mind began to totter. He couldn't sleep. He would get out of bed, find a basin and wash his hands all night long, shouting, "I wash and rinse my hands; I am innocent!" But the blood remained on his hands, and he would get more water and wash them again. Then he would go out and roam Golgotha. He could find no rest'.[20] Bowie himself had conceived Pilate's end, and indeed his entire life leading up to it, in quite another way.

In a handwritten page of notes titled 'P. P. reflects' that was on display at the Victoria and Albert Museum's traveling exhibit *David Bowie Is* (2013–18) and that can now be seen on the app associated with the exhibit, the singer listed a number of character elements that he felt helped to explain the personal history of the Pilate he portrays in *The Last Temptation of Christ*.[21] None of these notes especially originate with Kazantzakis's novel. Some can be traced to scholarly research about Pilate, as, for instance, the remarks below, evidently deriving from a reading of Josephus (or a history based on Josephus):

> He misread the Hebrew situation time and time again
> At one time he brought pagan statues and [plays?] into Jerusalem and started a riot. He backed off.
> A second time he syphoned [sic] off church funds to build which caused another huge protest. This time he used Roman force to beat it down.

Other observations, however, are the products of Bowie's own imagination and perhaps drawn from the star's own personal experience. For instance, his ruminations on Pilate's childhood and marriage suggest some intriguing parallels with his own life:

> his father caroused [and] partied a lot.
> loose women, successful but party loving friends
> so P. had to listen to an awful lot of reveling as a child in his bedroom
> His father was a divorce/corruption attorney who paid little attention to him.
>   Father was very [smart?]
> His mother disappeared from the marriage very young
> His need to impress thru' his work was essential.
> He always had a bad relationship with his wife. He had no sense of warmth
>   or love. She was very sensitive, given to prophetic dreams.
> They drifted apart early in their marriage. It was a marriage of convenience.

Bowie himself had had a fairly middle-class boyhood, and although his mother was evidently a cold individual with some schizophrenia in her background, she did not leave his father, who was not a lawyer but a publicity agent for a children's charity and could hardly have been called a carouser.[22] The sketch offered here seems more suited to Bowie himself, frankly: the insistence on Pilate's own broken marriage and that of his parents seem to relate somehow to the star's difficult divorce a few years before writing these notes, while the partying and revelling that he had 'to listen to [. . .] as a child in his bedroom' would appear to echo his worries about what his son Joe was experiencing as the child of a 1970s rockstar.[23] It is unfair to psychologise on the basis of a series of hastily-compiled private comments, of course, but the page does carry the title 'P. P. reflects' (the underlining emphatically Bowie's own), suggesting that Bowie is looking at Pilate as a mirror figure. His impression of the prefect's death, in any event, offers some suggestive grounds for comparison:

> He was eventually recalled to Rome and charged with misrule and mistreatment of the Hebrews for which he was punished by drowning in a lake in Roman Switzerland in the shadow of a mountain which is known today as Mount Pilate.

There is, in fact, a medieval tradition about Pilate that records his exile to Lausanne and death in Lake Geneva, a legend that undoubtedly had some significance for the singer. For decades Bowie made his residence in the fourteen-room Château du Signal, a grand manor once owned by Coco Chanel; located in the Sauvabelin woods high above the very same city, it had a commanding view of the very same body of water.

It is worth considering, as well, the time of life when Bowie was playing the role of Pilate. The 1980s, a time of relative artistic disappointment for Scorsese, had brought Bowie extraordinary commercial accomplishment – his *Let's Dance* album topped the charts early in the decade, and the worldwide *Glass Spider* tour (which had concluded just before filming his scenes as Pilate) was an extravagant spectacle representing the very height of Reagan-era 'Coffee Achievers' excess – but it all left him feeling empty. 'I saw myself as a character in his early fifties running around doing his old hits for the rest of his life, because he had programmed his audience and himself into that expectation', the rock star told *Interview* magazine some years later, saying that the success 'meant absolutely nothing to me. It didn't make me feel good. I felt dissatisfied with everything I was doing'.[24] To rejuvenate himself, Bowie joined a four-person band called Tin Machine whose style was more authentic garage-rock than arena extravaganza. In 'Bus Stop', a short song from this obscure chapter of the superstar's career, he dealt in a blasé style with the loss of faith: Bowie wonders whether a young man's vision of Jesus is real or just a matter of indigestion, as he prays at a bus stop. In concerts in the early 1990s, Tin Machine would perform this song several times in a campy country style, and one can sense Bowie's desire to distance himself from its sentiments by singing them in a funny voice – but still he sings them. Not long after, at Wembley Stadium in 1992, Bowie closed out his set for the Freddie Mercury memorial concert before a sold-out crowd by dropping to his knees and reciting the Lord's Prayer. He did so, as he told an interviewer afterwards, because it was a time when 'I felt totally, absolutely alone. And I probably was alone because I pretty much had abandoned God'.[25]

In 1989, when *The Last Temptation* was drawing worldwide protest and he was singing 'Bus Stop' with Tin Machine, Bowie was in his early forties – not an old man, by any measure, but hardly a youth. It is not too much to think of his young man praying at the bus stop as being very much like the young actor Daniel, or the shepherd Manolios, or perhaps even Martin Scorsese in his twenties first reading Kazantzakis's novel – all earnestness, passion and intensity. Who does not cheer for Daniel as he destroys the set of Appalache beer, or admire the stuttering shepherd as he gathers provisions for the sick and dying on Mount Sarakina? But, in fact, Denys Arcand was also in his forties when he made *Jesus of Montreal*, as was Jules Dassin when he made *He Who Must Die*, and Scorsese held on to his dream of bringing *The Last Temptation* to the screen well into middle age, when perhaps the themes of the novel were no longer entirely relevant. The types of Christ we see in *Jesus of Montreal, He Who Must Die* and *The Last Temptation* are filled with youthful zeal as they confront authority figures of varying sorts. Arcand's Father Leclerc, Dassin's Father Grigorios and Scorsese's Saint Paul are all represented as frauds, true heirs to Dostoyevsky's Grand Inquisitor, willing to peddle falsehoods in the name of some greater good and clever enough to be able to explain away whatever trouble this may bring to their consciences. The Pilate figures of these films are less hypocritical and perhaps more sympathetic as a result. In *Jesus of Montreal*, for instance, we see not one but two forms of Pilate: there is René, playing the prefect in Daniel's revised Passion Play, in whom we sense in a true seeker, one who has watched Carl Sagan documentaries and read *Hamlet* in pursuit of higher wisdom. More at peace with the imperfections of the world is the judge before whom Daniel is brought, although not understanding why the young man would refuse counsel; he is played by Denys Arcand himself. For Jules Dassin, the hedonistic Agha is likewise content with the way things are, even though he occupies a greater position of privilege: so long as one can live unbothered by the powers in far-off Istanbul, is the world so bad a place, are its injustices so hard to bear, that one cannot simply make peace with it all with a glass of raki in hand and a sweetly singing boy at one's side? Bowie's Pilate is perhaps the most comfortable in his position of power and even willing to argue that power is all that really matters, all that has ever mattered, all that will ever matter – the singer himself felt trapped in his worldly success, however. The questions that all these Pilate figures ask about faith in general and about Jesus in particular are of the sort that arise *nel mezzo del cammin di nostra vita*, as Dante starts off the *Inferno*: 'in the middle of our life's journey'. None of these films is really by or about young men; they are, rather, works of ventriloquism about young men by men in middle age who have achieved material success, perhaps, but still have unanswered questions.

As a coda to considerations of Pontius Pilate in the age of Reagan and the end of the Cold War, let us look to a British production. 'A writer burns his book because he knows it can never be published', so the narrative voice-over states at the beginning of 1991's *Incident in Judea*, an adaptation for Channel 4 TV of part of Mikhail Bulgakov's classic Soviet satire *The Master and Margarita*. Originally written in the 1930s, Bulgakov's novel is a biting critique of Stalinism as well as a rollicking work of creativity that, for political reasons, would not come out in print for another three decades. Its eventual publication in English in the mid-1960s fired the imaginations of many readers, including Mick Jagger who, as is noted in Chapter 7, based the lyrics to 'Sympathy for the Devil' on its plot. A daring, humane and deeply comic work of literature, *The Master and Margarita* is composed of two artfully combined storylines. The first of these, set in the Moscow of the author's own time, concerns some Russian intellectuals who are visited by Satan and includes a number of fantastic elements, among which an enormous talking cat might be the most memorable. The second and more realistic storyline, set in ancient Jerusalem, treats Pontius Pilate and his confrontation with Yeshua Ha-Notsri (Jesus of Nazareth), whom the prefect reluctantly has put to death. *Incident in Judea*, adapted for television by director and co-screenwriter Paul Bryers, deals only with the second storyline and centres on the relationship of Pilate to Yeshua and, more significantly, to his own abiding sense of shame.

According to the Internet Movie Database, there have been numerous adaptations for the screen of *The Master and Margarita* since the novel was first published – several have been released in Russian, two in Polish, two in Hungarian and two in Italian – but Channel Four's *Incident in Judea* is the only English-language version to appear to date (although, as noted in the Epilogue, a production to be directed by Baz Luhrmann is evidently in current development). Featuring in Bryers's production as Yeshua is the young Mark Rylance, just at the beginning of his extraordinary career, with the veteran John Woodvine starring in the part of Pontius Pilate. A classically trained actor, Woodvine had been a mainstay of the Shakespearean stage in Britain and had been cast in dozens of television productions over the course of his long career. As a director, Bryers had worked with Woodvine before, on *A Vote for Hitler*, another Channel Four production, and knew the sense of physical toughness that the actor would bring to the role. Also considered for the part had been Anton Lesser who, as can be seen from his later playing of Thomas More in BBC2's *Wolf Hall* (2015) and Qyburn in HBO's *Game of Thrones* (2013–19), without doubt would have made for a 'more cunning' Pilate, as Bryers put it. However, he remarked: 'I was casting for the Bulgakov version of Pilate – the ex-cavalry officer who fought for the Roman legions in Germany and found himself out of his depth as a colonial administrator in Judea. John seemed right for that role'.[26]

As *Incident* opens, Afranius (John Carter) addresses the audience directly about the story they are about to watch and its authorship by Bulgakov. As the head of Pilate's secret police, he then walks off into the streets of Jerusalem, and we cut to see Woodvine's Pilate making his way along the colonnade of the palace. He is attended by his beloved dog Banga and holding his head, for he suffers from migraines which the rigours of his job and the heat of Jerusalem only exacerbate. He sits and is told about Yeshua, a preacher from Galilee, whom Herod has refused to judge, and orders that the prisoner be brought before him for questioning. 'Good man', Rylance's sweet-faced Yeshua begins to reply, when he is cut off by Pilate. 'I believe in Jerusalem, everyone calls me a savage beast. That is entirely correct', he says. He orders a soldier to take Yeshua away for a moment and pound some respect for the prefect's position into him. Returned before Pilate after his beating, Yeshua denies that he wants to destroy the Temple or any other thing. 'It's all because he follows me around the whole time writing down everything I say', Yeshua tells him, referring to Matthew the Levite, who fails to record anything that is actually true. Pilate has a splitting headache, and in an interior monologue we hear him wrestling with the desire simply to send Yeshua off to be hung, so that he can lie down, or perhaps be with Banga, or perhaps commit suicide. But hearing of Matthew's misrepresentations, Pilate is stirred to ask: 'What is truth?' 'The truth', Yeshua replies, 'in this instance, is that your head aches'. It aches so badly, he continues, that Pilate was having cowardly thoughts of death and that speaking to Yeshua himself is a form or torture to him, and that all he really wants to do is to be with his dog. 'But your agony will soon be over', he then says; miraculously, Pilate's migraine clears away. Yeshua offers to take a stroll now with Pilate and to share his thoughts with him. 'You've lost all faith in people. You can't give all your love to a dog'. Pilate warms to Yeshua, whom he has up to now called 'a tramp' but now calls 'my philosopher', although he retains his jaded demeanour. Are the people who have perjured against him, or the soldiers who beat him – are these all 'good men', as Yeshua insists on calling everyone? But it is hard even for Pilate to have a hard heart against the pleasant smile of Rylance's Yeshua, and the prefect indicates to his scribe that he will let the young man go and hire him to work in his library at Caesarea.

When the scribe offers him a scroll with another charge to which Yeshua must answer, Pilate's eyes grow wide. 'Have you at any time said anything about the great Caesar?' Woodvine's Pilate asks, mixing intimidation with genuine concern. The charge has been brought by a certain Judas of Karioth, and Yeshua recalls for the prefect a conversation that they had had a few days before. Judas had wanted to know his opinions on the power of the state, and he had replied: 'I said to him, among other things, that any kind of power was a form of violence against the people, and the time will come when there will be no earthly power, either of the Caesars or any other kind. The state as we know it will wither away, and men will enter a condition of truth and justice. And there will be no need for any kind of power'. At this, Pilate explodes. 'What business have you, a tramp, a filthy vagabond, a criminal lunatic, to talk about the power of Caesar?' He speaks privately but angrily to Yeshua, who has a foreboding that something terrible is about to happen. 'You should release me, hegemon', he says, but Pilate cuts him off – there is no way he can let the young man go after he has expressed such opinions, and the prefect has no intention of taking his place in the punishment that must follow as a result. In the hearing of all, he tells the scribe to record a sentence of death for Yeshua, who is taken away. A tense scene follows with Caiaphas (Lee Montague), who cannot be convinced to release Barabbas instead of Yeshua and reminds Pilate of the young man's remarks about Caesar. Chastened by this encounter, Pilate exits the chamber and proceeds before the people to pronounce the death sentence. We see the crucifixion of Yeshua, very briefly, as the scene concludes.

Seated in his chamber, Pilate is alone with his thoughts when Afranius enters in a dark-hooded robe, a mannered and menacing figure. He never addresses Pilate in the second person, but instead responds to his questions with affected replies such as: 'What is it that the prefect wants to know?' (Carter, the actor who plays Afranius, will later gain fame as the courtly Mr Carson, the head butler of *Downton Abbey*.) Responding to Pilate's request about Yeshua's death, he indicates that the young man thanked those who took his life and said that he did not blame them. All he added was this, Afranius notes: 'He said that he considered cowardice to be one of the worst of the mortal sins'. Woodvine's Pilate looks away and takes a sip of wine at this moment. 'W-what was he talking about?' he asks, pretending not to know. (Of this moment, Bryers wrote me: 'I remember directing John to be very taken aback by this, by the way – he loathes cowardice in himself and others, I said, and this really hurts'.) From Woodvine's subtle uneasiness, we sense just how deeply Pilate is affected by this accusation from beyond the grave; he then tells the head of his secret police how he has heard that Judas will be assassinated this night. Taking the hint, Afranius rises to leave, bowing his head as he says pointedly: 'The command of the prefect will be executed'. In the night-time scene that follows, we see Judas ambushed and killed, with a quick cut bringing us back to Pilate sleeping in his chamber. A back-lit Yeshua appears to him in an apparition. 'You're right', Pilate tells him. 'Cowardice is a terrible sin'. 'Can you really believe, with your intelligence, that I would ruin my career for a man who's committed a crime against Caesar?' He grows more agitated. 'I would', he insists quietly. 'I would now. Not this morning, maybe . . .' Yeshua reaches out a hand to calm him and tells him that they are together now. 'When people remember me', he says, 'they will remember you in the same breath'.

'Maybe I had a British colonial official in mind, in 1940s Palestine', Bryers wrote me, in response to a question about the characterisation of the prefect in this production. 'Looking back on it I think the Pilate John Woodvine played in *Incident in Judea* was part Roman cavalry officer, part British colonial officer, and a very small part Soviet commissar'. In fact, the uncoupling of the Pilate story from the larger critique of the Communist system was a matter that the director found troubling for his conception of the programme at the time. 'I wanted to make it clearer by having Pilate as a Soviet commissar in some unnamed Soviet republic – Armenia, Kazakhstan? – with 1930s costumes and settings'. The idea of updating this already unusual Passion story, however, was not one that his producers at Channel Four wanted to pursue. The significance of Pilate's story to the critique of Soviet rule, to Bryers's mind, lay in the prefect's failure of nerve at the moment when he might have saved an innocent man's life. 'Stalin's machine was kept going by the ease with which people betrayed each other, casual betrayals in order to get a nice flat once its occupant had been arrested', he told the poet Craig Raine, in what was an acute review of *Incident* for *The Observer*.[27] The Stalinist terror would not ultimately have been possible, Bryers maintained, 'without the collusion of middle-rank officialdom – this is the political cowardice of Pilate'. He killed Judas, according to the director's line of thought, as a way of killing the Judas in himself.

This assessment of the prefect's lack of courage was a matter with which Raine took issue in his review for *The Observer*. As he remarked, '[h]ere we disagree. Indubitably, Bulgakov has sympathy for Pilate, whatever his shortcomings. This shines through the narrative. It can also be supported by events in Bulgakov's own life. He knows at first hand what it was like not only to stand courageously alone, to feel mortally afraid, but to compromise, to fall drastically short of the highest moral standards. He was too intimately acquainted with human weakness to condemn Pilate for his pathetic limitations'. With a scholarly knowledge of the Russian author's life, Raine noted that, as a doctor with the White Army, 'Bulgakov witnessed the torture and murder of a Jew – and did not interfere. Or could not interfere'. At some point later, he allowed the murderer, who had by then become his patient, to die in his care, a futile act of retribution that Raine sees as a source for Pilate's own pointless revenge against Judas. As Raine's review concludes, '[i]n Bulgakov's work, reference to the Devil, Faust, and Mephistopheles abound. Why? Because Bulgakov's life was one long terrorised pact with the Devil. In Russia, in the Thirties, it could not have been otherwise and there is real moral courage in recognizing the true facts of life – just as there is courage in making one's cowardice the subject and centre of a novel which, if it survived, Bulgakov must have known, would keep his name alive forever and also the personal shame encoded there'. In the very final scene of the film, Pilate has Matthew – the man who followed Yeshua writing down everything he said – brought before him. He wants to see the parchment, to see if Yeshua had said he forgave those who killed him, as well as his statement about the sin of cowardice. But none of it has been recorded there in Matthew's text. When he begs Matthew to take a gift from him, all the disciple asks for is a clean goatskin on which to write. What he intends to write, Pilate seems to hope, will not be so damaging to the prefect's future reputation – it will, in any event, not be thrown into the flames.

As it was Easter Sunday, the airing of *Incident in Judea* on 31 March 1991 had been well-timed – here was a radical reconsideration of the events of the Passion, after all, from a literary source that was for many a cult favourite, and its depiction of Pilate's troubled conscience offered viewers serious food for thought. International events, however, made the broadcast of Bulgakov's work even timelier still. Earlier that month, a referendum concerning the preservation of the USSR had been held across nine of the Soviet republics, an initiative bringing to fruition Premier Mikhail Gorbachev's concept of *perestroika*; on the very day when *Incident* appeared, in fact, the Republic of Georgia had voted to declare itself independent, thus marking the beginning of the end of Communist rule. Within only a few months, the Soviet Union would be completely dissolved. As we have noted, the production begins with the following words: 'A writer burns his book because he knows it can never be published'. Bulgakov had begun writing *The Master and Margarita* in the late 1920s, but he had put an early version of the manuscript into the fire out of fear of the Soviet political authorities – the manuscript that was eventually published, and which would inspire generations of readers afterward, was one that had been kept hidden for many decades by his wife, not the author himself. The cowardice and the sense of compromise that his Pilate feels were emotions not alien to Bulgakov, living as he did under a despot's reign. But the weakness of Pilate might have meant a very different thing to one writing under Stalin than it did to those producing or reviewing a film while the Soviet system was coming apart. By the time Channel Four's production aired in 1991, it was clear that the novelist's satirical critique of the system was destined to outlive the superpower he had worried would censor his work's existence. Reagan and Thatcher were no longer in power in the West, and the USSR would itself soon cease to exist.

NOTES

1 Dostoevsky (1990: 250).
2 *Jésus de Montréal* is a French-language film, but all quotations are taken from the English subtitles.
3 FitzGerald (1990: 86).
4 Barry (1989).
5 See Lindlof (2008: 127–29) for a good account of this background.
6 Rosenbaum (1990).
7 Berube (2002: 114).
8 McGilligan and Buhle (1997: 209).
9 Reagan, quoted in full and entered into the Congressional Record by Bridges (1961: A3800).
10 Kazantzakis (1954: viii).
11 *He Who Must Die* (*Celui Qui Doit Mourir*) is a French-language film, but all quotations are taken from the English subtitles.
12 Kazantzakis (1954: 311).
13 Kazantzakis (1954: 420).
14 Lindlof (2008: 16).
15 Lindlof (2008: 56).
16 Kazantzakis (1960: 379–80).
17 Lampert (1988: 69).
18 Jones (2017: 349).
19 Brooks (1693), while clearly not a dispassionate account, gives us a sense of the sultan's contemporaneous reputation in the West.
20 Kazantzakis (1960: 470).
21 David Bowie Archive (2019). My great thanks to Heather Pottle for drawing my attention to this resource.
22 Jones (2017: 7).
23 Parsons (1993); see Jones (2017: 316–17), where Joe – nicknamed Zowie and now known as Duncan Jones (the director of 2009's *Moon*) – recalls fondly his boyhood years with his father.
24 Sischy (1995).
25 Parsons (1993).
26 Paul Bryers, personal communication (29 July 2020).
27 This and all subsequent quotations are from Raine (1991: 46–48).

10 'We at War': Pilate for the New Millennium

I ain't here to argue about his facial features
Or here to convert atheists into believers.
I'm just trying to say the way school needs teachers
The way Kathie Lee needs Regis,
That's the way I need Jesus.
So here go my single, dog – radio needs this.
They say you can rap about anything, except for Jesus
That means guns, sex, lies, video tapes
But if I talk about God my record won't get played?

– Kanye West, 'Jesus Walks' (2004)

In early March of 2004, I gave a lecture at the Candler School of Theology at Emory University in Atlanta on the pricing of *eidolothuton*, 'idol meat', in which I tried to demonstrate that an important passage from First Corinthians could be illuminated by reference to evidence in a late antique source about Roman sacrificial practice.[1] The talk was received politely, even though not everyone was persuaded by it – my use of classical material did not really square with the traditional outlines of Pauline scholarship – and I got the strong sense that there were certain disciplinary boundaries one was not encouraged to cross. Whatever their justifiable reaction might have been to my argument, however, my hosts were warm and friendly. An enjoyable reception and dinner followed, but because it was a Monday, everybody was understandably eager to bring the evening to an early conclusion. There was teaching to be done the next day, and meetings and the full range of activities that keep the schedules of busy academics overstuffed with commitments. I was dropped off at the tasteful guesthouse downtown which they had set up for me and, because there was no TV in the room, I decided to take a walk around the neighbourhood to pass the time before going to bed. A used book store nearby kept me busy for an hour or so before it closed, and on the way back to the hotel, I passed by the Lefont Plaza Theatre, which was advertising on its marquee a 9:45 PM screening of *The Passion of the Christ*.

Mel Gibson's controversial film had been released less than a week before, on Ash Wednesday, and its opening weekend box office had been impressive, close to $84 million. More impressive had been the critical reaction. 'This film is the most violent I have ever seen', Roger Ebert had written in his review. 'It will probably be the most violent you have ever seen. This is not a criticism but an observation'. David Ansen, *Newsweek's* movie critic, agreed: 'Relentlessly savage, "The Passion" plays like the Gospel according to the Marquis de Sade'.[2] Not everyone had such a negative reaction to the film, of course. 'I loved it. I'll tell you why', responded Quentin Tarantino, when asked by an interviewer for his reaction.

> I think it actually is one of the most brilliant visual storytelling movies I've seen since the talkies – as far as telling a story via pictures. So much so that when I was watching this movie, I turned to a friend and said, 'This is such a Herculean leap of Mel Gibson's talent. I think divine intervention might be part of it'. [...] It has the power of a silent movie. And I was amazed by the fact that it was able to mix all these different tones. At first, this is going to be the most realistic version of the Jesus story – you have to decipher the Latin and Aramaic. Then it throws that away at a certain point and gives you this grandiose religious image. Goddamn, that's good direction! It *is* pretty violent, I must say.[3]

As a fellow filmmaker, Tarantino well understood the enormous artistic risks that Gibson had taken with *The Passion of the Christ*, but to have the director of *Kill Bill, Part 2* (which would come out a few months later) call the film out for being 'pretty violent' was no negligible matter. Was this *really* a movie I wanted to see, I debated with myself. But here I was, standing in front of the Plaza, with nothing to do otherwise – there was no TV back in the room, as I noted, and everything else was shutting down – so I bought a ticket, found a spot near the rear of the theatre and settled into my seat.

In the weeks and the months to come, I would have many discussions about *The Passion of the Christ*. Bloody and brutal, most people said. Repulsive and anti-Semitic. Most of these were opinions I shared, to be sure – I had found the film hard to watch that night and really struggled not to walk out of the theatre at various points. But it was almost universally the case, in these subsequent conversations I would have, that the person with whom I was speaking had not, in fact, watched the movie, and they looked askance at me because, in fact, I had. But I am glad that I chose to go see *The Passion of the Christ* that night. I did not enjoy the movie, as I have indicated, nor did I feel morally uplifted by it – quite the opposite. I felt that I had indulged myself in a form of morbid curiosity by entering the theatre. What had made this event so worthwhile for me that evening, however, was getting to observe the reaction of my fellow moviegoers, a reaction the likes of which I had never encountered before and have not seen again since. The sobbing of the audience throughout the film was loud and sincere, and at times the crowd's emotions were barely controlled. During the thirty-nine lashes, for instance, one woman kept yelling 'Stop!', as though she were witnessing an actual beating before her very eyes. She was hardly the only one to have this sort of reaction, which reached its fever pitch with the crucifixion. As I watched, I became engrossed not just in the film itself – and it must be said that, if nothing else, Mel Gibson knows how to make an engrossing film – but also in the experience of the film that other viewers were having. The theologians whom I had addressed earlier in the day were back in their suburban homes getting a good night's sleep, but here in downtown Atlanta close to midnight on a Monday was a theatre full of people suffering deeply along with their Saviour.

Perhaps because I had just been making the case that very afternoon for a Roman perspective embedded within the Christian material, I was especially attuned to the activities of Pontius Pilate as I watched *The Passion of the Christ*. While the ordeal of Jesus was having a deep impact upon the rest of the audience, as the director had explicitly intended, I found myself instead considering the prefect's situation, as he navigated the difficult circumstances in which he found himself. I watched his face and listened to him – this is such a rarity! – as he spoke Latin. As Tarentino had noted, Gibson had taken pains to give his film a palpable authenticity in terms of its sound, with actors speaking only in ancient languages. 'It is as it was', Pope John Paul II was reported to have said (falsely, as it turned out) after a private screening of the movie, although if it were as it had been, we might surely have expected a prefect in first-century Judaea to have spoken with his subjects chiefly in Greek, if in fact he spoke to them without a translator. As to the visual components of the mise-en-scène, there was certainly much to recommend about Gibson's film, and although one might be forgiven for viewing much of it with eyes tightly closed, the attention to period details conveys a real and tactile sense of antiquity. Much of *The Passion* had been filmed in the southern Italian city of Matera, where Pasolini had shot *The Gospel According to Saint Matthew*, but the scenes of the praetorium and Pilate's residence were shot at Rome's Cinecittà Studios, where *Quo Vadis*, *Ben-Hur*, *Barabbas* and *Cleopatra* had all been filmed in the 1950s, and where the HBO-BBC miniseries *Rome* would be filmed only a few years later. While I watched *The Passion*, I will not say that I felt transported by it, but certainly I found myself in a space recognizable in terms of its general appearance and feel. The demonstrative identification of my fellow moviegoers with the story of Jesus strangely encouraged in me a similar engagement with the story of the Roman prefect.

The Pilate of *The Passion* is played by Hristo Shopov, a gruff Bulgarian actor who the year before had played the warden of a gulag in Paul Feig's *I Am David* (a film also featuring *The Passion*'s Jesus, Jim Caviezel). The sternness of the Communist commandant's manner can be felt in Shopov's performance as Pilate, which is likewise heightened by the actor's striking resemblance to the scowling emperor Vespasian, conqueror of Judaea. When first we see the prefect, he is wearing a breastplate and moving briskly through one of the hallways of his residence while his wife Claudia (played by the Italian actress Claudia Gerini) follows on his heels, earnestly imploring him to spare Jesus' life. 'He's holy. You'll only bring trouble on yourself', she tells him in Latin, but he is unimpressed. 'Do you want to know my idea of trouble, Claudia?' he replies curtly, before he exits the shot. 'This stinking outpost, that filthy rabble out there'. As an introduction to Pilate and his wife, only fifteen seconds long, it is a brief but efficient scene. Filmed in the walk-and-talk technique of a 1990s TV show, we sense that, like one of the staffers hastening through a corridor of *The West Wing*, Pilate is a man with a demanding schedule. But, in addition, there is a friction that we can feel immediately between the couple. Her concerns are private, while his are public; she is compassionate, but he is hard of heart. This tension, although strongly marked, is not overdone, and as A. O. Scott noted in what was otherwise an unadulterated pan of the film in the *New York Times*, 'the only psychological complexity in this tableau of goodness and villainy belongs to Pontius Pilate and his wife, Claudia'.[4]

That sense of Pilate as a busy man continues in the next scene, as we watch him stride purposely along the colonnade of the praetorium, looking down into the courtyard where the high priests have brought Jesus in chains. Between the columns we see armed soldiers, standing rigidly at attention with shields and spears, from behind whom Pilate now appears, framed from below at an extreme angle, coming to a stop at the marble throne on which he rests his arm. We have a quick shot of Jesus, who has clearly been beaten before his arrival here, and then back to Pilate, giving a brief look of exasperation before he shoots a knowing glance at his lieutenant, Abenander (Fabio Sator). 'Do you always punish your prisoners before they're judged?' he barks at the priest. As we know from his remarks to Claudia, Pilate is not a gentle individual, but the evident mistreatment of the prisoner is an affront to his sense of procedure. At the foot of the staircase, a closely packed Jewish crowd is shouting catcalls and growing increasingly unruly – before them stands Caiaphas, played by Mattia Sbragia, in a performance that elicited, just as Rudolph Schildkraut's had in DeMille's *King of Kings* in 1927, strong responses among many critics.[5] Throughout the scene, Shopov's Pilate manages to appear wary though not panicked, as the priest and the prefect face off in a game of brinkmanship that the Roman is not confident of winning. He reacts with genuine surprise to the demand that the prisoner be put to death, but when Caiaphas tells him that Jesus has 'forbidden his followers to pay tribute to the emperor', Pilate's sense of alarm grows. Looking to alter the dynamic of the situation, he orders Jesus to be brought into the privacy of the praetorium itself, to be questioned in broken Aramaic. When Jesus replies in Latin, Abenader reacts with surprise, but Pilate keeps his wits about him. Significantly, the low-angle by which the prefect has been framed up to now is replaced with an eye-level shot, putting the prefect and prisoner on an equal footing. They are face-to-face when Pilate asks him: *Veritas? Quid est veritas?* – his examination now reduced to a rhetorical question.

Emerging from the praetorium, the prefect announces that, because he is a Galilaen, Jesus will be sent off to Herod for judgment. It is a clever move, as the sharp reaction of the priests demonstrates, but a quick glance over to the window reveals that not everyone is impressed by the decision. Pilate sees his wife, who shows by the look on her face that she knows he has dodged his responsibility rather than face up to it. Soon, she finds him sitting alone inside, the man too busy to stop for a conversation before now hunched forward in a chair in their private quarters. Claudia approaches her husband gently to comfort him. 'What is truth, Claudia?' he asks her, the question clearly gnawing at him. 'Do you hear it, recognize it when it is spoken?' She replies that, if he will not hear the truth, no one can tell it to him. 'Do you want to know what *my* truth is, Claudia?' he continues. 'I've been putting down rebellions in this rotten outpost for eleven years. If I don't condemn this man, I know Caiaphas will start a rebellion. If I do condemn him, his followers may. Either way, there will be bloodshed. Caesar has warned me, Claudia. Warned me twice. He swore that the next time the blood would be mine. That is my truth!' Caiaphas' mention of Caesar has been roiling Pilate as much as Jesus' mention of truth, evidently, and his worries about keeping the peace seem to be tied up with those about keeping his position. The source for this conversation is not Biblical, but perhaps reflects the economic conditions of the early 2000s: the recession with which the Bush administration began was nowhere near as serious as that with which it ended, but the bursting of the dot-com bubble and the subsequent downturn in the market had left many white-collar workers fearing for their jobs. But for the breastplate, Pilate might be any executive worried about global finances and consumed with concern about downsizing (Figure 10.1).[6]

The remainder of the scenes in *The Passion of the Christ* involving Pilate follows the Gospels closely, although they are presented in far bloodier detail. The prefect is outplayed by Caiaphas as he offers the crowd the choice of releasing Barabbas or Jesus. When they demand that Barabbas be released and Jesus be crucified, Pilate looks forlornly up at Claudia who is watching again from the window. 'No!' he shouts. 'I will chastise him, but then I will set him free'. The crowd jeers loudly as Pilate tells Abenader to make sure that the punishment is severe, though not fatal. The sixteen minutes or so that follow, in which Jesus is whipped by the jeering Roman soldiers, are easily the most violent in this excessively violent film, and they

Figure 10.1 Pilate (Hristo Shopov) comforted by Claudia (Claudia Gerini) in Mel Gibson's *The Passion of the Christ* (2004).

were rightly called out by critics for their repellent, brutal intensity. When I watched this scene for the first time, I can assure you I felt utterly nauseous, while many of my fellow moviegoers wept and cried out, their willing suspension of disbelief dissolving in the face of their religious faith. When he is brought back to the praetorium, Pilate reacts visibly to the horrific sight of Jesus' beaten body – he looks over at a panting Abenader, who has carried out the prefect's command at some personal cost, we sense. Pilate does not look up at Claudia in the window, although we are given a brief glimpse of her, overcome with horror. We then see Pilate and Jesus from behind, shot in silhouette, as the implacable crowd fills the screen. *Ecce Homo*, the prefect intones, presenting Jesus to the crowd with a wide sweep of his hand, as if to say: 'Is this not enough?' 'Crucify him', Caiaphas demands, as the crowd takes up the cry. The low-angle shot once again gives way to a framing at eye-level between the bloodied face of Jesus and Pilate, conversing once again in quiet Latin. 'Speak to me. I have the power to crucify you, or else to set you free', the prefect says and is told in reply: 'You have no power over me except what is given you from above. Therefore, it is he who has delivered me to you who has the greater sin'. With all the crowd at his command, Caiaphas reminds the prefect that freeing Jesus would mean he is 'no friend of Caesar's'. There is a quick exchange of helpless glances between the prefect and his wife, before Pilate turns his gaze back to the courtyard, which is now devolving into a mêlée between the soldiers and the crowd. A brass basin is brought out and Pilate looks at Caiaphas as he lifts his hands to wash them. 'I am innocent of this man's blood', he says. 'His blood be upon us' – the infamous line from Matthew (27:25) – is then said in Aramaic by Caiaphas, although (in a half-hearted attempt by the director to avoid the accusation of anti-Semitism) not captioned in the subtitles. Claudia is seen one last time, her head lowered as she turns away from the sight of her husband's disgrace. 'Do what they wish', Pilate commands, his final line in the film, even though he will be seen one last time, as the earthquake following the crucifixion shakes the foundation of his residence where he is seated alone.

The tension that Gibson portrays between Claudia and Pilate reflects the pull of the personal and the push of the public – the demands of conscience measured against those of duty – and in our final glimpse of him, the prefect is a lonely man, abandoned by his wife even as he has abandoned his principles. In the scene immediately following Pilate's question to Christ – *Quid est veritas?* – there had been a quick shot of Claudia scanning the people below and seeing

Mary, followed by a shot of Pilate returning to face the crowd. It is a brief but meaningful moment, a pause in the action that encourages reflection. In the space of a few seconds, Gibson has pointedly captured Pilate's dilemma: where his wife has observed a mother about to lose a son, for him it seems increasingly a mob about to explode. Each sight is true, of course, but which truth can Pilate permit himself to see? Whether he likes it or not, Caesar's proxy must likewise render to Caesar: the empire, above all, demands order, and Shopov's Pilate realises that it is his job to provide it. The Pax Romana came at a price, of course, as the Romans themselves were aware. 'There was peace in the end, no doubt', Tacitus had written of Emperor Augustus' reign in the *Annals* (1.10), 'but it was a bloody one'. It is in the context of this bloody peace that the Pilate of Gibson's 'Gospel according to the Marquis de Sade' might also be evaluated. The savagery of the thirty-nine lashes and the crucifixion itself in *The Passion* may serve a salvific function in Gibson's Catholic theology, but the use of such punishments was a component of the imperial strategy for maintaining order.[7] The dealings of Shopov's Pilate with Jesus are vividly rendered as part and parcel of the Pax Romana, and his evident inner conflict – intensified for us by the presence of Claudia – is the spiritual price he pays for keeping that peace.

As the new millennium dawned, the Pax Romana seemed to offer to many an instructive way of thinking about the Pax Americana. The associations were not simply historical in nature. The Commander-in-Chief of the US Central Command at the time, General Anthony Zinni, was explicit about the comparison, according to Pulitzer Prize-winning reporter Dana Priest: 'Zinni chuckled that he had become a modern-day proconsul, descendant of the warrior-statesmen who ruled the Roman Empire's outlying territory, bringing order and ideals from a legalistic Rome. Julius Caesar, Caesar Augustus – they would have understood'.[8] Zinni, who would go on to be the special envoy to Israel and the Palestinian Authority, undoubtedly might have found a sympathetic listener in Pontius Pilate as well. As the post-9/11 wars commenced, filmmakers also found ancient empires 'good to think with', as Claude Levi-Strauss might have put it, and various productions of the period made pointed reference to contemporary events in their depiction of antiquity. Wolfgang Petersen, for instance, the director of 2004's *Troy*, acknowledged 'a direct connection between Bush's power politics and that of Agamemnon in the *Iliad*, this desire to rule the world, to trample everything underfoot that gets in your way'.[9] A few years later, the Persian warriors of *300*, Zack Snyder's film version of the Battle of Thermopylae, appear to have been patterned after mujahideen, although the allegory of imperial invasion was open to interpretation (as a reporter's question to the director revealed: 'Is George Bush Leonidas or Xerxes?').[10]

While it was still even in theatres, critics were reading *The Passion of the Christ* through a similar political lens, equating the Roman military presence in ancient Judaea with the American involvement in the contemporary Middle East. 'For many who have viewed the movie, Jesus could stand in for all the Americans and indeed all citizens of the globe who have been violated, even distantly, by savage acts of terrorism', wrote Mark Juergensmeyer, for instance. He went on to observe:

> It is paradoxical in this regard that the perpetrators of terrorism in the Gibson film are Jewish rather than Muslim – the shadowy, bearded and robed figures lurking in the background in the movie are, of course, members of the Jewish Sanhedrin and not the Muslim al-Quaeda. But is it such a stretch to imagine that in Middle America, any bearded, robed enemy of Christendom might be viewed as a part of a generic 'Other' capable of the most hideous anti-American terrorist acts?[11]

Although overstated, the perspective that Juergensmeyer offers here, freed from a traditional Christian interpretation, makes space for alternative readings of the ancient story. Gibson was not in favour of the war, in fact, but not long after the *Passion* opened, the photos of the atrocities in Abu Ghraib surfaced. Commentators in the press were quick to juxtapose them with Gibson's film: a partisan piece in *Salon*, for instance, was titled 'American Torture, American Porn: Abu Ghraib and "The Passion of the Christ" are Connected in the Dark Basement of the American Psyche'.[12] The vitriol of this and other essays may have seemed unwarranted, but the association was not unjustified. Sabrina Harman, a National Guard soldier who participated in the brutal mistreatment of the prisoners at Abu Ghraib and took the infamous photograph of the hooded man, was at the time wracked with a guilt that seems familiar from Hristo Shopov's Pilate. As she texted her girlfriend, 'I can't handle whats going on. I cant get it out of my head. I walk down stairs [...] to find "the taxicab driver" handcuffed backwards to his window naked with his underwear over his head and face. He looked like Jesus Christ'.[13] That she had, in the name of a noble call for securing peace, participated in torturing a member of a hated religious group was too much for this soldier to bear.

Just as Cecil B. DeMille's *King of Kings* had done seventy-five years before, so did Gibson's movie dominate the landscape of religious cinema at the beginning of the twenty-first century. One exception to this general rule was the limited release in 2006 of *La Inchiesta* (*The Final Inquiry*), an Italian film about an investigation into the disappearance of Jesus' body. A re-make of an obscure Italian film with the same name from 1987 featuring David Carradine and Harvey Keitel, *Final Inquiry* has a cast made up of numerous celebrities not precisely in their prime: Dolph Lundgren (who in 1986 had starred as the boxer Ivan Drago, the Russian antagonist of *Rocky IV*) plays a German bodyguard named Brixos, Mónica Cruz (the younger sister of Penélope, for whom she is a dead ringer) appears as a young Jewish woman named Tabitha, F. Murray Abraham (who had won an Oscar for Best Actor for *Amadeus* twenty-plus years before) is Tabitha's father, and Max Von Sydow phones in a perfectly adequate performance as Emperor Tiberius. And featured as Pontius Pilate is none other than Hristo Shopov, looking much as he had in *The Passion of the Christ*, although perhaps statelier in a cream-coloured toga while holding court in his tastefully appointed chamber of polychromatic marble. His hair is once again closely cropped, and there is the same arrogant look upon his face, but as soon as Shopov begins to speak, the entire impression is ruined. In *The Passion*, famously, all of the actors had spoken ancient languages, with Shopov's Pilate brusquely addressing Jesus in broken Aramaic and his subordinates in a more commanding Latin. The natural timbre of the Bulgarian actor's voice is hoarse and raspy, but in *Final Inquiry* he has been overdubbed with a smooth-as-silk British accent. The effect is jarring, for, although the actor is carefully enunciating each English word, it is obviously not his own voice coming out of his mouth.

With a cast composed of actors hailing from so many various countries – as noted, Shopov is from Bulgaria, while Cruz is from Spain, Lundgren and Von Sydow both from Sweden, and the rest of the cast from Italy – the desire to even out the 'vocal palette' of the production may be understandable. Yet, having managed to secure Mel Gibson's own Pontius Pilate from the biggest-selling Bible film ever, altering the sound of Shopov's voice seems like a cardinal error. Overdubbing Pilate is not the only problem with the film, however. While *Final Inquiry* has 'The Passion of the Christ knock-off' written all over it, the production is more flawed in its presentation than in its conception. The star of the production is the little-known Daniele Liotti in the role of Titus Valerius Taurus, an investigator sent by the emperor to learn more about the mystery of Jesus' death, which he pursues doggedly. Originally a miniseries, *Final Inquiry* had been recut for theatrical release, and as such various storylines are discernible although not entirely comprehensible: there is a mostly preserved testament to the faith of the Apostles, a coherent love story, elements of a buddy movie and hints of palace intrigue involving Von Sydow's Tiberius and Caligula. It is a pity that lost in the shuffle is the full version of the detective story pitting Taurus the investigator against Pilate the powerful official with a dreadful secret to hide.

Dramatic territory very similar in nature to *The Final Inquiry* was to be explored with far greater success in *Risen*, a film released to select theatres in 2016, in which the resurrection is treated as a detective story, and which features Pilate not as a corrupt official but rather as a symbol of worldly despair. Of particular note about *Risen* is its production company and intended viewership: *Risen* was made specifically for a Christian market by Affirm, a subsidiary of Sony Pictures founded with the intention, according to its online mission statement, of 'producing, acquiring, marketing and distributing films which inspire, uplift, and entertain audiences [. . . and of meeting] the increasing demands from audiences looking for quality, mainstream films that reflect their spiritual beliefs and values'.[14] Affirm came into being in the mid-2000s, as did a few other production companies geared toward this demo, a development almost entirely owing to the phenomenal success of *The Passion of the Christ*. Hollywood insiders had been initially doubtful about Gibson's project, but when *Passion* made over $600 million in box-office receipts (versus the $30 million it had cost to produce), executives at all the major studios concluded that perhaps they *could* find a way to serve both God and Mammon.[15] Consequently, companies such as Affirm, Pure Flix and others came into being, geared toward an American evangelical niche in the market, looking for entertainment products that those in the industry call the 'faith-and-family' category.

There is nothing especially new about films being made from a Christian perspective, of course, but a principal difference between movies such as *The Robe* and *Quo Vadis* and faith-based features such as *Heaven Is For Real*, *God's Not Dead*, *The War Room* and *God's Not Dead 2* made by Affirm and other companies is the matter of scale. Indeed, in the twenty-first century, big budgets tend to work *against* such films, at least for the US market. 'Christian movies are one of the very few genres of film that people go to with the intention of enjoying them whether they objectively suck or not', journalist Tim Stanley reported for the *Telegraph*. 'And their flaws actually affirm that they're not slick Hollywood products from the liberal stable. Just like Donald Trump's gaffes prove he's no PC shill, so bad acting in Christian movies proves that they're not being cranked out by godless socialists'.[16] In other words, the poor production values and artificial dialogue of these features somehow signal to the core viewership the bona fides of the film's religious commitments and lead to commercial success. In a prime example of the first shall be last and the last shall be first, low-budget fare from Affirm and other like-minded companies has often generated substantial returns on investment, while better-financed films made for the mainstream market on religious themes have just as often been unsuccessful: Ridley Scott's Moses movie *Exodus: Gods and Kings* (2014), Darren Aronofsky's *Noah* (2014) and Timur Bekmambetov's *Ben-Hur* (2016) all lost money at the box office, while in virtually the same time frame *Heaven Is For Real* (2014), dismissed as a piece of Sunday School propaganda, made an 850-percent profit and the ham-fisted *God's Not Dead* (2014), despite being 'about as subtle as a stack of Bibles falling on your head' (in *Variety*'s words), generated a return of over 3,000 percent. Among evangelically focused production companies, such profit is not without honour, of course, and the companies making cheaply produced faith-based ventures have been largely unconcerned about getting the approval on aesthetic or any other grounds of the non-Christian critic or moviegoer. But while the payoff is often very high for such productions, originality and imagination are just as often very low. 'The faith-film category has come to mean agenda-driven, fear-driven, low-quality, low-budget, on-the-nose, teaching, industrial films that willingly overlook excellence and story because they know they can', a former executive in the Christian film industry told *The Atlantic*. 'They have trained an audience to expect trite, theologically thin, bumper-sticker movies, designed for church outings'.[17]

Studio heads all over the entertainment world are seeking to make money, while those on the creative side are interested in making art, and this tension is felt in the faith-film industry just as it is everywhere else in Hollywood. It is within this context – the desire of the Christian filmmakers to display their artistic integrity by doing more than preaching to the choir – that *Risen* must be situated. To begin with, the substantial sum of $20 million was spent to make this film, and while its box office doubled its production costs (nowhere near the fivefold return that *God's Not Dead 2* made the same year), it was produced in the hopes of being taken and treated more seriously among mainstream viewers and media. With *Risen*, it is easy to see how the budget was spent. First of all, a well-known and reasonably talented director was hired (Kevin Reynolds, whose previous work included 1991's *Robin Hood: Prince of Thieves* and 1995's *Waterworld*), most of the film was shot on location in Malta and

Spain, a more expensive PR campaign was rolled out and, not least of all, bigger-name actors were cast, including Joseph Fiennes (the star of 1998's Oscar-winning *Shakespeare in Love*) as Clavius the Roman military tribune, Tom Felton (Draco Malfoy in the *Harry Potter* series) as his lieutenant Lucius and the Oscar-nominated Peter Firth in the role of Pilate. The most significant element of *Risen*'s production was the development by screenwriter Paul Aiello of a more complicated and nuanced screenplay, in which the certainty of faith that we see in the more pious Affirm vehicles has been subjected to questioning.

The open engagement with doubt in *Risen* represents an important development of the faith-based film and perhaps demonstrates how this particular genre is maturing beyond its own tendency toward profitable banality. As the film's detective – with all tenacity and detachment required of the genre – Clavius displays a thoroughgoing scepticism that he is bewildered to have to abandon ultimately. This is not to imply that the story is a dull dramatisation of a philosophical debate, by any means: there are numerous tried-and-true components of the police procedural throughout, including examination of witnesses in film noir lighting and a traditional chase scene. But while the inquiry that Clavius pursues ultimately will return to the bedrock faith that Affirm filmgoers expect, Aiello has framed the story as a police drama in which a forensic procedure leads to an unpredetermined and hence 'objective' outcome, the sort that fans of the television show *CSI* have come to expect on a weekly basis. The tension inherent between certainty and doubt is made clear from the film's very beginning. We see Clavius walking through a desert landscape and coming to an inn, where he will relate to the innkeeper what has happened to him. As a tribune, Clavius has been involved in putting down a Zealot revolt. When he returns to Jerusalem, he is summoned by Firth's Pilate to oversee the crucifixion of Yeshua (Cliff Curtis), as Jesus is regularly called in the film, although he is still bloody from battle. After his death, Yeshua's body is placed in the tomb, but, fearful that his followers will steal it, a Roman seal is put on the tomb and two hapless soldiers are put on watch. As it happens, the body disappears, and again Pilate turns to Clavius, ordering him to find the body before it decomposes. What unfolds next, the longest part of the film and its real heart, has been called 'the greatest manhunt in history' by the film's publicists (and *CSI: Ancient Jerusalem* by online wags), as Clavius digs through burial pits and cross-examines a host of suspects, including the negligent guards, Mary Magdalene and the Apostle Bartholomew.

A dogged investigator, Clavius leaves no stone unturned, but none of the details are adding up – a few days later, he has tracked the Apostles to their abode outside the city and bursts in on them, using his sword to force open their door, only to find – *Ecce homo!* – Yeshua. At this point in the film, the Roman soldier backs up from the doorway into the sunlight; Fiennes is shot from below, with the sun overwhelming his appearance, a powerful if traditional image of enlightenment. Quite literally blindsided, Clavius hesitantly calls off the case, although Tom Felton's Lucius presses him to continue. If ever viewers were unsure about the integrity of Clavius' moral character, all uncertainty is erased at this moment, when we see the censorious look on the face of the actor best known to us as the smarmy Draco Malfoy. When Yeshua disappears, again, Clavius follows the Apostles as they depart, eventually joining them as they make their way to Galilee. In one memorable moment, he demands an explanation about the resurrection from the Apostle Peter, who expresses his own surprised puzzlement about the situation, blurting out: 'I don't know, I don't know, I don't know! I wish I did, but I don't!' If an honest encounter with doubt is where *Risen* begins, however, it is not (as the title would suggest) where the movie ends. After his encounter with Peter, Clavius meets the risen Yeshua and, ever the detective, continues his questioning. As critics noted, however, the film at this point becomes more traditional and tedious, as the messaging becomes more explicit and *Risen* starts resembling the rest of the offerings in the Affirm catalogue. 'Tribune, do you really believe this?' Clavius is asked in the desert inn at the film's end, after he has left the Apostles behind to pursue his own journey. He looks out into the distance in response, saying: 'I believe . . . I can never be the same'.

If Clavius' story in *Risen* is one of spiritual progress, with the pursuit of truth almost always represented by the tribune's motion and haste, Pilate's story by contrast is one of stasis, a spiritual ennui that is figured in terms of lassitude and lethargy. 'In most films, Pilate is usually represented as so rigid', producer Patrick Aiello told me, when I spoke with him and his brother Paul, *Risen*'s screenwriter, in July 2016. 'We wanted to see him more worn-down. You note that he's always reaching for a glass of wine'.[18] It is true – throughout the film, Firth's Pilate constantly seems to be drinking, not in a hoist-your-glass but in a drown-your-sorrows fashion. There is a moment early in the film, when Pilate offers Clavius a drink as the tribune steps into the bath, where the prefect seems to be trying to wash not just his hands but his entire body. Each is disheartened about the day's events, which have included the crucifixion and the sealing of the tomb, and as they try to soak away their troubles, they talk:

PILATE:
Your ambition is noticed. Where do you hope it will lead?

CLAVIUS:
Rome.

PILATE:
And?

CLAVIUS:
Position. Power.

PILATE:
Which brings?

CLAVIUS:
Wealth. A good family. Someday place in the country.

PILATE:
Where you'll find?

CLAVIUS:
An end to travail. A day without death. (Pause) Peace.

PILATE:
All that for peace? Is there no other way?

Pilate, who has had a goblet in hand the entire time, then exits the bath for bed, saying: 'Tomorrow promises further punishment'. It is uncertain whether he means that which he will inflict or that which he will suffer: he is the chief military and political officer in this part of the world, but the imperial job seems to demand more of the prefect than it gives. Weighed down with responsibility, Peter Firth's Pilate is a warrior for whom peace is an unlikely prospect, because his war-weariness is in fact a disenchantment with the things of this world, and his battle is ultimately with himself (Figure 10.2).

As a dramatic matter, so Patrick Aiello told me, the jokes about *CSI: Ancient Jerusalem* all had a sound basis because *Risen* is very much patterned after a TV detective show. 'The film really follows the template of *Chinatown*', he said. 'And yeah, the Netflix mandate is at work here. Procedural dramas have a great shelf life. This is a template that is in the zeitgeist, a very easy formula to work with and for viewers to handle'. Twenty-first-century Americans love such shows – *CSI* has been on since before the George W. Bush presidency – and so *Risen* gives them the story of Jesus as a dramatised police case. Indeed, we see a sundial and an anachronistic hourglass on Clavius'

Figure 10.2 Peter Firth's Pilate is unable to wash his hands quite enough, as Joseph Fiennes's Clavius looks on in *Risen* (2016).

desk, as we might see a clock on a detective's, iconographic emblems of the detective's race against time. In a deleted scene, Clavius handles the physical evidence of the crown of thorns and the Shroud of Turin-like blanket that covered Yeshua's corpse. What we are to understand is that Clavius is a dispassionate investigator working on a case, following to their logical conclusions the results of his inquiries. But there comes a moment when the logical conclusion is thus: a man whom he has seen die and whom he himself has buried is, as he has seen, decidedly not dead. This cannot be true, he thinks, and yet it must be. In an ordinary mystery, we might expect the detective to walk away from the case in frustration at such a turn of events, as happens at the end of *Chinatown*. In *Risen*, however, Clavius walks away from his world and into the surrounding desert.

Another question I had for the Aiello brothers was the name of Fiennes's character, Clavius, a Latinate-sounding name but not really a classical one. 'Do you know who Christopher Clavius was?' Paul asked in response. For those who may not be familiar with the history of science, Clavius (1537–1612) was a significant figure, a German-born Jesuit who was a leading mathematician and astronomer.

A highly respected figure in his day, Clavius was an admirer of Galileo, with whom he corresponded, even though on religious grounds he could not bring himself to accept the Copernican system for which Galileo would eventually be condemned. Nonetheless, toward the end of his own life, intellectual honesty compelled Clavius to ponder what impact Galileo's insights would have on the church's geocentric understanding of the universe. As one scholar remarks, '[t]he failure of the Ptolemaic cosmology to measure up to the scientific demands of early seventeenth-century astronomy must have bewildered Clavius'.[19] Having peered through Galileo's telescope, Clavius became uncertain about what was really true in the system of which he was a principal part; as for the Clavius of *Risen*, the evidence of his own eyes required a massive paradigm shift. Artfully and indeed learnedly, Aiello's screenplay employs the name of a principal figure in the Scientific Revolution as a way of pointing to the transformative experience of the epiphany for his Roman tribune. While sceptical viewers may not necessarily come to the same conclusion that the film's sceptical protagonist has, nonetheless they recognize that in what is ordinarily an unchallenging sort of movie, *Risen* is hunting after bigger intellectual game – even critics who panned the film offered grudging admiration for the ambitious script. 'For a film that could have easily become bogged down in Sunday School reverence, or culture-war opportunism, *Risen* presents an intriguing, oblique approach to a Bible movie', wrote one critic,[20] an opinion shared by many reviewers.

The ambition of the Aiello brothers' film becomes more evident still when compared with productions treating the same material made by Mark Burnett and Roma Downey, presidents of Lightworkers Media production company. Downey (the famous Northern Irish actor who starred in CBS's long-running fantasy series *Touched by an Angel*) had married Burnett (producer of *Survivor*, also on CBS, and NBC's *The Apprentice*, the programme responsible for turning the failed real-estate developer Donald Trump into a reality TV star) in 2004, and the pair went on to become, in their own words, 'the noisiest Christians in Hollywood'.[21] Of the numerous works made for the faith-based demographic by the evangelical power couple, two productions in particular – *A. D. The Bible Continues* and *Ben-Hur* – stand out for discussion concerning the role of Pontius Pilate. Running for a single season in 2015, *A. D. The Bible Continues* was a televised miniseries produced for NBC that covered events following the Passion and starred Vincent Regan as the prefect. The Danish actor Pilou Asbaek, meanwhile, played Pilate in Lightworkers' 2016 version of *Ben-Hur*, a big-budget theatrical remake directed by Timur Bekmambetov and released by Paramount pictures in August 2016. Both *A. D.* and *Ben-Hur* bear the all the hallmark features of Downey and Burnett's style – sumptuous production values, elaborate sets, well-known cast members and faster-paced editing – but embedded within its avowed family-friendly content is a marked penchant for ancient analogies that map easily onto contemporary politics. By and large, Judeo-Christian figures of the productions appear sympathetic and 'relatable', while others are depicted as more dismissive stereotypes. This tendency is particularly pronounced in the portrayal of Pilate in both *A. D.* and *Ben-Hur* – not since Hurd Hatfield's performance in Nicholas Ray's 1961 *King of Kings* have we seen representations of the prefect quite so cartoonishly villainous.

A. D. The Bible Continues, which premiered on Easter Sunday 2015, was a sequel to Downey and Burnett's *The Bible*, a series that, appearing on the History Channel two years earlier, had been seen by 100 million viewers worldwide, according to the producers. Impressed by the success of this unlikely hit, the couple had been approached by NBC with an open invitation to go and do likewise for their network and given a generous financial package with which to do so. Where *The Bible* had covered the events of the Old and New Testament up to and including the Passion, *A. D.* was intended to dramatise the lives of the Apostles and other early Christians struggling to make sense of their lives in the wake of Jesus' resurrection. Watching the series, it is clear to see how much money went to casting, locations and other matters of production. That the show suffered from numerous internal conflicts over the series' ultimate purpose is equally clear. As Simon Block, the screenwriter for the first two episodes of *A. D.*, told me when we exchanged emails in 2017, the programme was originally imagined as 'the story of how faith develops among a small group of devoted followers of an individual, not as a religious tract, with supernatural elements ago-go'.[22] When the show was first pitched, Block remarked, there had been broad agreement among all parties with this initial approach, the focus of which would be on the psychological dimensions of belief in the face of extraordinary challenge:

A drama about the intense nature of 'faith'. What a brilliant idea. No angels or bolts of lightning. Just men and women of faith enduring unbelievable persecution and hardship to establish a human-oriented movement that said all men are equal (before God). [. . .] I grew up in the 70s, and loved the *Jesus of Nazareth* series starring Robert Powell as the man himself. After that, nothing else came close in terms of a close reading of the Bible. So why not try something different?

To emphasise the nature of the struggle, the creative team had wanted to strip away anything having to do with the otherworldly, and as a figure very much of this world, Pontius Pilate plays a key role in its expression. Producer Mark Burnett had emphasised this particular point in various interviews he gave to promote the series. 'You could rename *A. D.* the *House of Cards, AD 33* because there were so much politics going on', the producer told the Christian Broadcasting Network. 'Nothing's changed unfortunately. If you look at it 2,000 years later, governments are still behaving in a way where they don't recognize truth, and that's why the first words you hear in *A. D.* are, "Truth. What is truth?" when Pilate speaks to Jesus'.[23] But the desire to counterbalance Pilate's steely-eyed view of realpolitik with something showily miraculous was a critical failure, in Block's eyes, not because it was rooted in a spiritual outlook but for precisely the opposite reason. NBC had staked a lot of money on *A. D.* and expected a significant return on its investment, a profit which Burnett as executive producer was determined to make. 'But it was a terribly missed opportunity to make something much more interesting, even for Christians', Block concluded ruefully of the series' failure, opining that a unique concept about human nature had been monetised instead as a low if profitable pleasure. 'It's really no surprise that Mark's greatest creation on television is Donald Trump'.[24]

The part of Pilate was played by Vincent Regan, a veteran Welsh actor with a square jaw and bright blue eyes, whose credentials include several memorable roles in the ancient epic genre. In *300* (2003), he was the captain fighting alongside Leonidas to hold the pass at Thermopylae, roaring to the Spartans just before the Persian forces descend upon them: 'Earn these shields, boys!' As Eudorus, one of the Myrmidon warriors, Regan felt the rage of Brad Pitt's Achilles after informing him of the death of Patroclus in *Troy* (2004), while the next year he took a lead role as Marc Antony in *Empire*, ABC's 2005 miniseries which suffered from negative comparison with HBO's *Rome*. In *The Nativity*, a more highly praised miniseries from BBC One, Regan would play King Herod before once again donning a cuirass for the part of the Roman prefect in *A. D.* Pilate's wife, Claudia, in the series is played by Joanna Whalley, a sharp English actress whose career has tended more to the femme fatale than the woman of faith ever since her breakout role as the exotic dancer Christine Keeler in *Scandal* (1989), the fictionalised account of the Profumo affair. The tension between Pilate and Claudia throughout *A. D. The Bible Continues* can only be described as histrionic. Unlike the tender wife played by Claudia Gerini in Mel Gibson's *The Passion of the Christ*, Whalley's

Claudia is a purse-lipped scold, whose palpable disapproval of her husband's actions is matched only by Pilate's own violent defensiveness. When we first see her in the opening episode of *A. D.*, she is entering the chambers of her husband, who directs her attention to the scene unfolding on Calvary through the window. 'Are you enjoying the spectacle?' he asks her, with barely contained malice, at which she spits back: 'Spectacle? Is that how you regard the crucifixion of the Nazarene?' She has had a dream about Jesus, as she notes, but it seems to have inspired her to do little more than vent resentment against her husband. When later in the same scene, she tells Pilate that 'Killing him won't be the end of him', he, enunciating every word of his reply, responds: 'It usually is, my darling'. This is not the end of the melodrama, however, and their bickering reaches fever pitch (at least for this episode) when Pilate – in lines singled out by the *New York Times* TV critic as 'almost laughably visceral' – bellows: 'Enough of your dreams and nonsense, Claudia. The Nazarene was only ever flesh and blood, and we have butchered the former, and spilt the latter all over the city. But if you should dream of him again, be sure he proves his true identity by his real incarnation – not as a handsome prophet with charisma, but as a rotting pile of meat on the floor!'[25]

The relationship of Pilate and Claudia has a so-bad-it's-good quality, campily overacted for dramatic effect, that exists in deliberately pointed contrast to the portrait of the marriage of Caiaphas, played by Richard Coyle, another blue-eyed actor (there are a lot of blue eyes in *A. D.*, as a matter of fact – Peter, Judas and the Virgin Mother have them as well). The high priest's otherwise unattested wife, Leah (Jodhi May), offers unequivocal support to her husband, emphatically telling him within the hearing of those sceptical of this treatment of Jesus: 'You did the right thing'. Later, after he has kissed his laughing children goodnight, Caiaphas confesses in private to Leah that his heart is broken over the whole affair with the Nazarene, to her gentle reassurance. As the series proceeds, the distinction is heightened between the Roman prefect, a man so cruel even his own wife does not like him, and the Jewish high priest, whose partner stands by him like an ancient Near Eastern version of Tammy Wynette. The juxtaposition between the home life of Mr and Mrs Pilate and that of Mr and Mrs Caiaphas serves more than a simple dramatic function. The evident purpose in depicting the high priest as a good-hearted family man only carrying out his duty, as opposed to the unqualified Roman villain of the piece, is an attempt to undercut the inherent anti-Semitism of the traditional Passion narrative for a twenty-first-century television audience.

Throughout much of *A. D.*, there is astute attention paid to the interactions between the various groups of people who have been left behind to process the meaning of the Passion. Beyond the tense homelives of the prefect and the high priest, there is the wariness felt by Peter (Adam Levy), as he deals with the Zealots who would appropriate Jesus' movement for their own ends, as well as a diverse set of anxieties experienced by many of the other disciples. Thus, it is an unexpected development when, as the Roman guards are keeping watch over it, the sealed tomb begins to glow in the final moments of the first episode. Dumbfounded, the soldiers stare at the light, although one of them looks away to see, coming through the parting clouds, something like a fiery meteor emerging from the sky. The music dramatically rises as the celestial object speeds with laser-like precision for the tomb, on top of which an armed figure bathed in light then appears – it is an angel (Lonyo Engele), who draws out his sword and rolls away the stone, as the guards stand stock-still in wide-eyed wonder. It may be that the sudden occurrence of the meteor was intentionally designed to represent the nature of a miracle – the unforeseen intrusion of the divine into everyday human life – but the jarring sense of two different plotlines being tossed unceremoniously together at this final moment seems instead to have come from disagreements arising during production. As noted, two different visions of what *A. D. The Bible Continues* ought to be about and how the story ought to be told, can distinctly be felt throughout the series' run, as the network executives and the writers whom they had hired in Britain failed to come to any mutually satisfying agreement. It is worth noting that this final miraculous scene proceeds without dialogue, the writing team having refused to supply any. The tension felt in many faith-based productions between the creative team and the producers, whose eye is on the bottom line, is very much in evidence with *A. D.* As Block noted, '[o]nce you add a special effect that breaks the rule of the show that nothing is supernatural, all hell breaks loose and it basically becomes a Jesus-based version of every supernatural film you've ever seen, from *Poltergeist* to *The Exorcist*. In effect, it just becomes silly'.

A year after *A. D.* was rolled out onto television screens, a reboot of *Ben-Hur*, the cinematic classic from 1959, was opening in theatres around the world. As was the case with *A. D.*, *Ben-Hur* was produced by Downey and Burnett and featured a slick and extensive advertising campaign aimed at faith-based as well as mainstream markets. As was the case with *A. D.*, *Ben-Hur* had been bankrolled at enormous expense by a major production company (this time Paramount), its budget of $100 million going to costly sets, costumes and complicated on-site cinematography. And as was the case with *A. D.*, *Ben-Hur* ended up an enormous flop, losing a great deal of money as it failed to find a viewership – a 'very expensive movie for a very small audience', as one executive at a rival studio put it.[26] The producers were aware that the story they were bringing to the screen was one with limited name recognition. For older viewers, the 1959 spectacle was a touch-stone of cinematic achievement, its climactic chariot race a treas-ured memory of the crowded-theatre big-screen experience or, more likely, a late-night re-run guilty pleasure. Younger viewers had no such familiarity, however. 'There is a *Ben-Hur* generation and a 'Ben-Who' generation', Burnett told the morning talk show hosts of ABC's *Good Morning America*, itself a programme beloved by geriatric viewers.[27] The strategy of tying megachurch attendance to megaplex audience that had worked for *The Passion of the Christ*, however, was simply no longer viable in the mid-2010s. If, as Marshall McLuhan said, the medium is the message, then the message that *A. D.* and *Ben-Hur* were sending via their respective media was very much an out-of-date one: the younger members of the faith-based community were, like everyone else in their generation, too busy looking at their iPhones to tune into network TV or shell out money at a retail movie chain.

When Pontius Pilate (Pilou Asbaek) first is seen in this version of *Ben-Hur*, it is in a military and indeed imperialistic context – the Roman soldier Messala (Tony Kebbell) is telling Judah, his step-brother and a member of the royal family (played by Jack Huston, himself a member of Hollywood royalty and of actual British nobil-ity), how Pontius Pilate gave him a battlefield commission during combat in Persia, a scene we see in flashback. 'He reminded me of what we were fighting for', Messala tells his old friend. 'Things you and I believe in, Judah. A civilised world, progress, prosperity, sta-bility'. If those are qualities that Messala associates with Pilate, they are little in evidence when the prefect arrives on the scene himself shortly thereafter at the head of his army. As the Romans march into Jerusalem, they sing a rousing war-chant – 'Legio Aeterna Victrix', composed by Giorgio Antonini and Danilo 'Leo' Lazzarini, which has been uploaded onto numerous online sites by hundreds, nay legions, of dedicated fanboys – while Asbaek's Pilate rides arrogantly along-side them, outfitted in crimson armour and draped in an enormous fur pelt. The security for this magnificent entrance, intended to intim-idate the Zealots and the Jewish people who accept the idea of politi-cal liberation from Rome, has been put into Messala's hands. 'Pontius Pilate has to ride through Jerusalem with no trouble', he tells Judah, demanding to know the names of any possible troublemakers, but his efforts are in vain. As the Romans file through the city streets, an arrow is shot at the prefect, only narrowly missing, by a young Zealot named Dismas (Moises Arias) from the roof of the Hurs' manor where he has been in hiding. The Roman soldiers break into the palatial residence by force, and Judah's subsequent arrest and dispatch, as well as that of his whole family, set the rest of the film's plot in motion.

This guerrilla attack upon Pilate as he parades through Jerusalem represents a critical departure – one with no little significance – from the same scene as depicted in the 1880 novel by Lew Wallace, and the motion pictures based on it from 1925 (directed by Fred Niblo) and 1959 (directed by William Wyler). For Wallace and the twentieth-century film tradition, the Roman commander entering the city was not Pontius Pilate but Valerius Gratus, and the incident that nearly takes his life is not an arrow that has been fired with hostile intent but instead a rooftile that has fallen by chance. In the novel, Judah is a boy who has leaned very far out over the parapet of his house to look upon the Romans below and, as Wallace writes, . . .

> . . . in the act rested a hand upon a tile which had been a long time cracked and allowed to go unnoticed. The pressure was strong enough to displace the outer piece, which started to fall. A thrill of horror shot through the youth. He reached out to catch the missile. In appearance the motion was exactly that of one pitching something from him. The effort failed – nay, it served to push the descending fragment farther out over the wall. He shouted with all his might. The soldiers of the guard looked up; so did the great man, and thatmoment the missile struck him, and he fell from his seat as dead.[28]

Varus is *not* killed – he is only 'as dead' – but this outcome is of little consequence, since nobody believes Judah when he insists that the tile was dislodged by mistake. In Fred Niblo's 1925 *Ben-Hur*, the scene from the novel is faithfully represented, although Ramon Navarro's Judah plays a young man rather than a boy, as does Charlton Heston who, in Wyler's award-winning film from 1959, takes the blame for his sister Tirzah (Cathy O'Donnell), pleading truthfully: 'It was an accident!' The plea is without avail for Heston, however, even though Stephen Boyd's Messala examines the parapet himself later and unintentionally loosens a random tile.

The alteration of this critical event in the 2016 *Ben-Hur*, the screenplay for which was written by Keith Clarke and John Ridley (the Oscar-winning writer for *12 Years a Slave*), can hardly be over-estimated. To substitute Gratus at this important moment with Pilate, who will succeed him later as prefect in the novel, is a sensible enough decision: to appeal to the attention spans of contemporary audiences, this version of *Ben-Hur* clocks in at a full hour and a half shorter than Wyler's classic, and hence it was necessary to make cuts. The replacement of the rooftile's fall with a deliberate attack, however, goes to the very heart of the story. Following the incident, after all, the Hurs are apprehended, and their fates sealed. The fall of the tile is a powerful literary symbol: dropping from the rampart of their wealthy manor, it signifies the fall of the House of Hur. It serves as a revelation of life's unpredictability, the sort of small event the ramifications of which are neither intended nor understood at the time. A certain ripped-from-the-headlines feel is gained by the alteration, of course, although the purpose of it does not seem entirely clear. As the reviewer for the *Daily Beast* noted, '[t]he episode clearly evokes modern insurgent tactics – the sniper fire and IED's to which Western troop convoys are exposed, as they pass through the streets of Fallujah and Ramadi – leaving an American moviegoer puzzled as to which side in this ancient struggle he or she is on'.[29] At this point, Judah lyingly confesses in the 2016 film, an act which is meant to be noble but is, in fact, the very essence of phoniness. The tile that had fallen on Gratus' head in the novel is ultimately an act of Providence, an occurrence representing the intrusion of the divine into the characters' lives, leading them onto the path of wisdom and ultimately salvation. To change this moment instead into a terrorist attack is to remove from the scene, and from the story as a whole, all sense of purpose and grace. Where there had been mystery, now there is only malice.

When next we see Pilate, as he is presiding over the famous chariot race (it is much to the director's credit that, in this version of *Ben-Hur*, the event we all have come to see is depicted at the very beginning of the film and then given again to us in full at the very end). Frank Thring's prefect in the Charlton Heston vehicle from 1959 had looked upon the spectacle with a sort of wry detachment and his opening remarks had concluded with an understated 'To the best of these, a crown of victory. The race begins. Hail, Caesar!' Asbaek's Pilate, by contrast, is flamboyant in his blood-red cuirass (Figure 10.3): holding his hands out wide in the manner of a Satanic circus-master, he bellows: 'You will see them race for glory! You will see them fight for honor! You will see them die for you!' The prefect's promise of slaughter and gore at what might otherwise be assumed to be a contest of strength and skill at first may seem gratuitous, but the allusion by the prefect to gladiatorial games seems blatant, and by the filmmakers to the movie *Gladiator* more blatant even still. But

Figure 10.3 Pilou Asbaek's Pilate as evil showman, wearing blood-red armour in *Ben-Hur* (2016).

as the race in *Ben-Hur* comes to its conclusion, a struggle in which Messala has lost a leg and nearly his life, the reference to blood sport takes on deeper meaning. The night before the race, Sheik Ilherdim (a dreadlock-sporting Morgan Freeman, the film's biggest star) had approached the prefect to offer him six-to-one odds on Judah's victory, a wager the prefect is only too happy to take. When Messala eventually loses, Pilate slams his hand in anger but cheerfully pays off his debt. 'Condolences on your loss', says Freeman's Sheik, smiling slightly at winning his bet. As the crowd runs around them, whooping in a savage frenzy, Pilate asks: 'Loss?' He gestures broadly to the crowd once again. 'Look at them. They want blood. They're all Romans now'. He turns on his heel and walks away with what is probably the movie's best line. The film continues for another fifteen minutes, during which time Jesus is crucified and Judah is reconciled with Messala, but it is hard not to feel that the ending beyond Pilate's cynical appraisal is anything other than tacked on.

The story of *Ben-Hur* might be set in antiquity, but the aesthetic of the movie is decidedly contemporary. For the chariot race, for instance, Bekmambetov employed GoPro cameras mounted in the sand to capture not just extreme close-up images but even the frantic sound of the thundering horses and squealing wheels. 'A lot of the action scenes were inspired not by classical paintings but by YouTube videos', the director told an interviewer for the Motion

Picture Association website, indicating that his version of the famous set-piece naval battle was patterned after online security footage of a bus crash. The arrest of Judah and his family by Roman soldiers likewise was meant to have a distinct present-day feel. 'You see them face down on the ground with bags on their heads – that's based on YouTube videos from Iraq and Afghanistan', he went on. More than a dozen years before the release of Bekmambetov's *Ben-Hur*, critics of US foreign policy had drawn controversial comparisons between the shocking photographs of tortured prisoners from Abu Ghraib and scenes from Mel Gibson's *The Passion of the Christ*. The depiction of ancient Roman imperialism in terms of modern urban warfare now, however, seems a natural point of reference for a movie aimed at mainstream audiences in the mid-2010s. 'I feel like *Ben-Hur* really is about us, today', Bekmambetov observed, as he explained the choices for how he had reimagined the 1959 classic. 'It's about terrorism, power, ego. People will either learn how to live together and forgive each other, or else we will all kill each other'.[30]

'We at war'. Thus begins Kanye West's single 'Jesus Walks', released in late May 2004, three months after the premiere of Gibson's controversial film and a few weeks after the publication of the Abu Ghraib photographs. As Lola Ogunnaike wrote in the *New York Times*, 'Mel Gibson, it turns out, is not the only entertainer with a passion for Christ'.[31] (The *Times* would not to be the only media outlet to juxtapose West and Gibson in this explicit fashion, and a year and a half later the rapper would grace the cover of *Rolling Stone* magazine wearing a bloody crown of thorns under a headline proclaiming 'The Passion of Kanye West'.) As both West's song and Gibson's movie attest, the culture was ready and even eager in the first decade of the new millennium for a sincere reconsideration of Jesus, even in the face of industry resistance. This embrace of Jesus, open and evidently sincere, in works intended for mainstream consumption, had been unthinkable in the decades immediately before. A hard-hitting, gospel-inspired number destined to win that year's Grammy and reaching double-platinum status in sales, 'Jesus Walks' remains to this day one of the rapper's biggest hits and is often played with guest performers in concert to uproarious response. When director Sam Mendes opted to have the song, with its heavy tramp of marching soldiers, play over the opening credits for *Jarhead*, the 2005 film rendition of Anthony Swofford's memoir about serving in Operation Desert Storm, a connection between 'Jesus Walks' and the American wars in the Middle East was cemented. But that is only part of what West's song is about. As the rapper continues in his opening, '[w]e at war. We at war with terrorism, racism. But most of all, we at war with ourselves'. He builds on references to global and racial conflict, issues very much in the news in the Bush era and continuing depressingly into the present day. The final battlefield that West sees, however, is 'with ourselves', although it is not entirely clear what the singer means by this. Is this reference a recognition that the political climate of the contemporary US and the West generally, already riven in 2004 when *The Passion of the Christ* was first released and having grown still more fragmented in the decade and a half since then, is the place of ultimate warfare? Or does the superstar instead call us to don the armour of Christ, as St Paul had urged in the Letter to the Ephesians, so as to do battle with and for our own souls?

From the images of Pontius Pilate in the opening decades of the new millennium, is it possible to say into which war it is that Kanye's Jesus has walked? If *A. D. The Bible Continues* and *Ben-Hur* failed to make much headway as entertainment vehicles, there is nevertheless a way in which each production partook in the us-versus-them political culture of the period in which they were made. Both *A. D.* and *Ben-Hur* featured a villainous Pontius Pilate who was – as Dwight MacDonald had said of Hurd Hatfield's performance in 1961's *King of Kings* – 'right out of the Grand Guignol'. Vince Regan's Pilate in *A. D.* was a familiar enough face from the ancient epic film genre, playing a heavy with exaggerated grimness, and the Pilate of *Ben-Hur* was an even more instantly recognizable presence, performed by the Danish actor Pilou Asbaek, featuring at the time as the roguish pirate king Euron Greyjoy in HBO's *Game of Thrones*. Regan presented his prefect as a thin-skinned disciplinarian, prone to outbursts of private rage, while Asbaek was instead an ostentatious egotist, eager to have every eye focused on himself alone. However different in temperament, each of these prefects is meant to draw attention away from the high priests and thus from the traditional anti-Semitism of the Passion narrative, an admirable dramatic goal no doubt. But, in addition, these versions of Pilate give us a version of a polarising political type that became increasingly familiar as the 2010s wore on. As the executive producer of *The Apprentice*, it is worth noting, Burnett had been an instrumental figure in the rise of Donald Trump and would go on to stage-manage several events of the Presidential Inauguration in January 2017. Is it too much to suggest a prototype for the hectoring bullies of Burnett's Biblical productions in the reality-TV work with which he was simultaneously involved? With the images of the prefect as presented by Burnett, we might contrast Peter Firth's Pilate in *Risen*, whose power and privilege have not made him hard and mean. He wonders, instead, what it is all about, but seems to lack the moral courage to confront his despair in any real way. In like fashion, Hristo Shopov had played the prefect in *The Passion of the Christ* as a figure struggling with difficult choices and unable to thread a narrow path of decency between them. It is intriguing that, by the mid-2010s, we do not see a Pilate drawn with the subtlety and sympathy that had been shown by Mel Gibson, a sentiment that critics of the film would surely have taken exception to at the time – I am certain it is not a notion that would have occurred to me, as I sat in the back row of the Plaza LeFont Theatre in Atlanta, watching the film with my hands over my eyes.

NOTES

1 The talk has now appeared as a contribution to a festschrift for Jerzy Linderski, cf. McDonough (2004).
2 Ansen (2004).
3 Powers (2004).
4 Scott (2004).
5 Cf. Bartov (2005: xi–xiv).
6 See Mahler (2003) on this topic: 'By the numbers, women have been hit as hard as men, but white-collar men tend to experience unemployment differently, organizational psychologists say. [...] For men, grappling with joblessness inevitably entails surrendering an idea of who they are – or who others thought they were'.
7 Cf. Hengel (1977: 33–38, 61–63).
8 Priest (2003: 70).
9 As cited by Winkler (2009: 206).
10 Cieply (2007).
11 Juergensmeyer (2004: 281).
12 Camon (2004).
13 Harman's text message, dated 20 October 2003, is quoted by Gourevitch and Morris (2008: 52). The inconsistent use of apostrophes, typical of texting, is Harman's own.
14 http://www.affirmfilms.com/about/ (accessed 30 July 2021).
15 This and all subsequent financial figures cited in this article are derived from the online source *Box Office Mojo*, http://www.boxofficemojo.com/ (accessed 1 December 2020).
16 Stanley (2016).
17 Quoted by Wilkinson (2015).
18 Conference call with Paul and Patrick Aiello (28 July 2016), with all quotations verified by e-mail (10 August 2016).
19 Lattis (1994: 219).
20 Ebiri (2016).

21 Keefe (2019).

22 Block, personal communication (18 and 23 April 2017).

23 Goodwyn (2015).

24 Cf. Keefe (2019), who notes that, at the 2016 Emmys, host Jimmy Kimmel pointed to Burnett, sitting in the audience, and said: 'Thanks to Mark Burnett, we don't have to watch reality shows anymore, because we're living in one'.

25 Genzlinger (2015).

26 Lang (2016).

27 *Good Morning America* (2016).

28 Wallace (1998: 113).

29 Romm (2017).

30 Hart (2016).

31 Ogunnaike (2004).

Epilogue: A Time of Handwashing

'Pilate needed to scrub his hands with soap and warm water for at least 20 seconds to avoid taking any responsibility for the crucifixion', said one researcher. 'He should have sung "Happy Birthday" twice or the "Full House" theme song. Then, a good thorough drying with a paper towel or Dyson Airblade would have sealed the deal. As it stands, just running a little water over his hands wasn't near enough to help him avoid judgment from God'.

Pontius Pilate responded to whether or not the allegations are true from the afterlife, saying, 'What is truth?'
    – 'Scholars Now Agree Pontius Pilate Didn't Wash His Hands Long Enough To Avoid Responsibility For Crucifixion',
Babylon Bee (30 March 2020)[1]

The prefect of Judaea, Pontius Pilate, was looking out at an angry mob below, and I have been watching him again and again now for several years, as he assesses the situation in the streets and is deciding how he must respond. In the end, Pilate will talk to those to whom he is predetermined to talk (to the crowd, to the high priests, to his wife, to Jesus) and do that which he is predetermined to do (to display the beaten Jesus, to release Barabbas, to dispatch Jesus to the cross, to wash his hands). It has been a chore, at times, to watch Jesus condemned to the cross again and again, and to watch prefect after prefect come to terms with the decision he has made, from tortured indecision to malicious self-justification to casual dismissal of another person's life. There are times I have suffered under Pontius Pilate, to be sure. Each time he speaks and acts, however, although I have known how it would all turn out, I have been fascinated to see how it would unfold. What expression would there be in his face, what catch in his voice, what unexpected glance or gesture? There is a constancy from production to production in the portrayal of Jesus that verges on monotony – there he is, as always, in his robe and sandals, with beard and hair of a certain length and a steadfast look in his eye. Pilate, however, has always been allowed a far wider range of appearances on stage and screen. Sometimes he wears a toga, at other times a breastplate, at still other times he wears some notional outfit conveying antiquity and authority. At times, he is blond, at other times dark-haired, and, in some instances, he is – like Telly Savalas – bald. Pilate's motivations run the same gamut as his attire. He can be an older man, with an air of resignation about him, he can be an arrogant youth, or as seems to be often the case, he is a man in middle age just hoping to make it through a holiday weekend.

Jesus is rightly treated with the utmost reverence on the screen, and his unchanging appearance is an indication of the unchanging nature of his mission. By contrast, as I have tried to demonstrate over the course of this book, Pontius Pilate changes from film to film and show to show, reflecting the time in which the production was made in ways that often show close correspondence to the period's social and political circumstances. Victor Varconi had said, for instance, many years later to be sure, that he had played the part of Pilate 'as a Nazi' in Cecil B. DeMille's 1927 *King of Kings*. Figures suggested by the culture of televangelism and the telegenic Ronald Reagan run through the films of the late 1980s, even as a decade earlier we feel the moral uncertainty of the Watergate era suffusing representations of the Passion. The rebellious youth culture of the 1960s lies just beneath the surface of the films of the period, in a way that was not perceptible even a few years earlier. Cold War imagery informed many of the films and television programmes of the 1950s, especially on the small screen, even as the wars in Iraq and Afghanistan can be felt in movies since the dawn of the new millennium. 'Must then a *Christ* perish in torment in every age to save those that have no imagination?' asks one of the characters in George Bernard Shaw's *Saint Joan*. The answer to the question is clearly in the affirmative, and, just as clearly, there needed to be a Pilate to speak for and act on the authority of each of those ages.

There is a story told about Oscar Wilde that, when taking the oral examination required for graduation from Oxford, he was given a passage from the story of the Passion to render from ancient Greek into English. As it is told, Wilde began to translate, easily and accurately. The examiners were satisfied and told him that this was enough. Wilde ignored them and continued to translate. After another attempt the examiners at last succeeded in stopping him and told him that they were satisfied with his translation. 'Oh, do let me go on', said Wilde, 'I want to see how it ends'.[2] He had been joking, of course. Wilde was an exceptionally well-read individual, whose knowledge of the Bible was equal to anybody's of his elite background. As self-avowed aesthete, furthermore, he found the story of Jesus – Christ, the Man of Sorrows – a deeply moving one, particularly the representation of his final days. There is nothing, Wilde wrote in *De Profundis*, 'that, for sheer simplicity of pathos wedded to sublimity of tragic effect, can be said to equal or even approach the last act in the tragedy of Christ's passion'. Beyond the homeliness of his final meal, the anguish in the moonlit garden and the falseness of his friends, Wilde singled out for comment 'the magistrate of civil justice calling for water in the vain hope of cleansing himself of that stain of innocent blood that makes him the scarlet figure of history'.[3] That Wilde wrote these words when he was himself unjustly imprisoned gives particular weight to this poetic characterisation of Pilate. Before his Oxford examiners, Wilde might have laughed at the details of the Passion narrative with an undergraduate's youthful impertinence, but in his forties he knew from personal experience how great an atrocity it is when those to whom the sword of authority has been given are more concerned with maintaining their position than with carrying out the demands of justice. Although he joked, perhaps, that 'either those curtains go or I do' on his deathbed, Wilde ended his life as convert to Catholicism. There is much to ponder in the phrase 'scarlet figure of history', I will admit, and I have often thought of it as I assessed the performances surveyed in this study, but I would be lying if I did not say that there is something in the flippancy of 'I want to see how it ends' that moves me even more as I come to the conclusion of this book about Pontius Pilate.

Throughout the writing of this book, I have sought to highlight how the social and political circumstances surrounding productions about Jesus have influenced the representation of the Roman prefect, but, as we end, is it possible to prophesy what future portraits of Pontius Pilate might be like? In fact, several projects currently in some state of consideration can be discussed, although – given the tightly controlled mechanics of publicity in the entertainment industry – little can be said with certainty. Earlier in the decade, a screenplay for a film about Pontius Pilate by Vera Blasi (author of the well-received films *Women on Top* and *Tortilla Soup*) was optioned by Warner Brothers and generated a good deal of Hollywood buzz when Brad Pitt was mentioned as a possibility for the main role.

The story 'reads almost like a Bible-era *Twilight Zone* episode in which a proud, capable Roman soldier gets in way over his head', wrote one reporter, who was given exclusive access to the project.[4] Warner Brothers ended up passing the script on to another studio, perhaps aware that Paramount was investing heavily in (and would lose a lot of money on) the remake of *Ben-Hur*. But Pitt was still mulling the project a few years later, as an interviewer for the *New York Times* reported:

> On the topic of exotic worlds, he mentions a film he'd like to make about Pontius Pilate, mostly because the script, which focuses on a mediocre Roman official stuck in the middle of nowhere with difficult people he doesn't like, makes him smile. Jesus doesn't get much screen time. 'It certainly won't be for the "Passion" crowd', he says, which reminds me that Mel Gibson's torture-porn epic is one of the things that drove me out of the church. Pitt bursts into laughter. 'I felt like I was just watching an L. Ron Hubbard propaganda film'.[5]

Pitt's dismissal notwithstanding, Mel Gibson has recently revealed his plans for releasing a sequel to *The Passion of the Christ*, with the provisional title *The Passion of the Christ: Resurrection*, although online wags have offered less pious suggestions ('Beyond Martyrdome' gives a good idea of the flavour). Randall Wallace, the Oscar-nominated screenwriter of *Braveheart* and director of *Heaven Is for Real*, was hired to write the script which inside sources indicate will include the harrowing of Hell and various battles with demons. Several members of the original cast have been signed, including Jim Caviezel as Jesus, although Hristo Shopov's name does not appear among them, indicating that there will not likely be a representation of Pilate in the new film as currently planned.[6] Another project that is evidently in the early stages of development is a film adaptation of Bulgakov's *The Master and Margarita*, which Baz Luhrmann is set to direct – few details are currently available on the project, but if his *Moulin Rouge* (2001) and *The Great Gatsby* (2013) are any guide, we might expect even the Pilate and Yeshua part of the story to be a cinematic extravaganza.[7]

While numerous screen versions of the Passion story are in the process of being made for niche Christian markets, a film on the topic intended for a mainstream audience is *The Last Planet*, written and directed by Terrence Malick, which is in post-production at the time of this writing. When he was at the Vatican promoting his film *A Hidden Life* in December 2019, Malick told reporters that filming had just been completed for *The Last Planet*. As he is reported to have said, '[w]e have just finished shooting, I am very happy. A few days ago we finished shooting in the desert of Jordan, a multicultural film with a cast that brings together Middle Eastern actors, a German troupe, and even Italian artists in the costumes department and set design. [...] Now I go back to Texas to edit the film'.[8] In addition to Jordan, other on-site locations included Morocco, Israel, Malta, Turkey and Iceland, as well as the nature preserve of Tor Caldara outside Anzio in Italy. According to other sources, the entirety of the movie was filmed using only natural daylight. The cast features a number of well-known actors, including Matthias Schoenaerts as Peter, Aidan Turner as Andrew, Joseph Mawle as Saul and the Hungarian actor and poet Geza Rohrig as Jesus. Perhaps the most notable role will be played by the renowned Shakespearean actor Mark Rylance, who told *The Guardian*: 'Terry wrote four versions of the character of Satan and I thought I would play only one. But I heard I was going to play all four. One of them must have been a woman at some point, but it was when he asked me to grow a beard that I realised I wasn't going to do it that way'.[9] Who may be playing Pilate is still unclear, although both Ben Kingsley and Joseph Fiennes are reported as having been cast in the film. Fiennes, who had recently played the Roman soldier Clavius in 2016's *Risen*, may be the likely choice, although Kingsley would undoubtedly bring his customary gravitas to the role. One of the producers told *Variety* that it will be 'a highly spiritual film about the Bible with a dark genre twist', although what precisely *The Last Planet* will entail is difficult to discern. When I wrote to Malick's agent, I was told: 'Terrence is shy of speaking about a picture he hasn't yet finished, but thanks you for wishing to talk. He looks forward to reading your book. Terry also said that his wife was born in Sewanee and, from what he hears, you live in paradise'.[10] It is true – the part of Tennessee in which I live is quite beautiful – and I offered to show the director and his wife around if ever they should find themselves back in this part of the world. I also hope, when *The Last Planet* or any of the films currently under production do appear, to be able to write a review that perhaps Edinburgh University Press will let me post on their site in connection with this book. But, given the way in which I have abused their saintly patience with the lateness of this manuscript, they would be within their rights to cast a sceptical Scottish eye on my request.

To be honest, the times have not been the most auspicious in which to write, as many a reader will know. The polarised politics, the protests, the destruction of monuments, the existential anxiety of the Covid-19 pandemic – all have conspired to make for an environment that is not particularly conducive to academic productivity. For much of the year, I have been following the Center for Disease Control's mandate to wear a facemask when I leave the house and to wash my hands for at least twenty seconds numerous times a day (to make this easier to remember, the CDC advised singing 'Happy Birthday', but I have taken to singing the final stanza of 'Trial Before Pilate' from *Jesus Christ Superstar* instead). In addition, I have been teaching many of my courses entirely on Zoom, with students beaming in from disparate locations to appear as postage-stamp-sized images on my computer. We live in a time now when much of what we consume as education or entertainment is done on personal laptops or phones. Our relationship to screens, like our relationship to one another, has grown increasingly atomised. I will admit that I have found myself wondering, during the long dismal months of lockdown, just what sort of Passion might be produced in the wake of this cultural upheaval of 2020. I am no screenwriter, but insofar as I have thought about the matter, it is difficult to imagine that the Pontius Pilate to emerge in the years to come will not reflect the leadership that we have witnessed over the last few years. In Britain, there is widespread sense among many that Prime Minister Boris Johnson is a fundamentally dishonest man, and he was called out on the floor of European Parliament for 'lying to the people of the UK' about Brexit, while his plan to handle the Coronavirus has been laughably insufficient. In the US, the consensus is far greater still that the president is a dangerous and reckless liar. When asked about his response to the pandemic at a Rose Garden press conference early on in the course of the pandemic, Trump told a reporter from NBC: 'No. I don't take responsibility at all'. He later suggested that the lockdown should end and that the churches be packed on Easter Day, although he had not consulted with any medical authorities on the matter before he proclaimed it. When asked later why he had chosen Easter, the president replied: 'I just thought it was a beautiful time. It would be a beautiful time, a beautiful timeline. It's a great day'. (The country did not reopen on Easter, in fact, and by the year's end over 200,000 more people had died from the virus.) In response to wide-scale demonstrations during the summer over the death of George Floyd, armed law-enforcement officials would use tear gas to clear the streets in front of the White House so that Trump could march out to an Episcopal church and pose for a photo op in front of it. Over his head he held a Bible upside-down as though it were a blunt instrument and not a book containing the Golden Rule.

Over the past several years, as I have been watching film after film and programme after programme about the signal failure of a powerful leader, the corrosion of our politics has grown increasingly rank, and our sense of despair has grown increasingly great. A miasma of depression has settled over the Western democracies, and I have to imagine that, when all is said and done, we will want artists to help us process the anxieties of the period, to help us sort through the maelstrom of emotions. 'Fear doesn't travel well', the playwright Arthur Miller once wrote, in an essay titled 'Why I Wrote "The Crucible"' for the *New Yorker*. With consummate skill, I am sure most will agree, Miller captured in his play about the Salem Witch Trials the pervasive sense of dread that Senator Joe McCarthy had provoked in the hearts of many Americans living through the 1950s. And yet, as the playwright observed, '[w]hat terrifies one generation is likely to bring only a puzzled smile to the next'.[11] In what may be a testament to the resilience of the human spirit, I suspect we will look back at the era of BoJo and Trump and wonder why these leaders with their flimsy scruples and fly-blown hairstyles ever had us so worried. When, as they perennially do, filmmakers turn once again to the Passion narrative, it will be worth thinking about Pontius Pilate and this period, during which, as the Coronavirus ravaged our lands, our leaders time and again acted as though there were no such thing as truth and we were all obsessively washing our hands.

NOTES

1 https://babylonbee.com/news/scholars-now-agree-pontius-pilate-didnt-wash-his-hands-for-20-seconds-bears-some-responsibility-for-jesus-cru cifixion (accessed 1 December 2020).
2 Sutherland (1977: 383).
3 Wilde (1999: 71).
4 Fleming (2014).
5 James (2016).
6 Ashton (2020).
7 Ellen (2020).
8 Chattaway (2019).
9 Shoard (2019).
10 Megan Lynch, personal communication (3 August 2020).
11 Miller (1996).

Works Cited

FILM

A Fish Called Wanda (1988). Directed by Charles Crichton. Metro-Goldwyn-Mayer.

Barabbas (1961). Directed by Richard Fleischer. Dino De Laurentiis Company/Columbia Pictures.

Ben-Hur (1959). Directed by William Wyler. Metro-Goldwyn-Mayer.

Ben-Hur (2016). Directed by Timur Bekmambetov. Lightworkers Media, Paramount, MGM.

Day of Triumph (1954). Directed by John T. Coyle and Irving Pichel. Century Films.

From the Manger to the Cross (1912). Directed by Sidney Olcott. Kalem Company.

Gospel Road: A Story of Jesus (1973). Directed by Robert Elfstrom. Twentieth Century-Fox.

He Who Must Die (*Celui Qui Doit Mourir*) (1957). Directed by Jules Dasssin. Indusfilms/Prima Film/Cinétel/Filmsonor.

In the Heat of the Night (1967). Directed by Norman Jewison. United Artists.

Jesus Christ Superstar (1973). Directed by Norman Jewison. Universal Pictures.

Jesus of Montreal (*Jésus de Montréal*) (1989). Directed by Denys Arcand. Cineplex Odeon Films/Orion Classics.

King of Kings (1927). Directed by Cecil B. DeMille. DeMille Pictures Corporation.

King of Kings (1961). Directed by Nicholas Ray. Samuel Bronston Productions, MGM

Last Days of Pompeii (1935). Directed by Ernest B. Schoedsack and Merian C. Cooper. RKO Radio Pictures.

Monty Python's Life of Brian (1979). Directed by Terry Jones. HandMade Films.

Pontius Pilate (*Ponzio Pilato*) (1962). Directed by Gian Paolo Callegari and Irving Rapper. Glomer Film, Lux Compagnie Cinématographique de France.

Risen (2016). Directed by Kevin Reynolds. Written by Paul Aiello. Produced by Patrick Aiello. Sony/Affirm.

Salome (1953). Directed by William Dieterle. Columbia Pictures.

Sopralluoghi in Palestina per il Vangelo secondo Matteo (*Location Hunting in Palestine for The Gospel According to Matthew*) (1965). Directed by Pier Paolo Pasolini. Arco Film.

The Final Inquiry (*La Inchiesta*) (2006). Directed by Giulio Base. Millennium Films.

The Greatest Story Ever Told (1965). Directed by George Stevens. George Stevens Productions, United Artists.

The Last Temptation of Christ (1988). Directed by Martin Scorsese. Universal Pictures.

The Passion of the Christ (2003). Directed by Mel Gibson. Icon Productions.

The Passover Plot (1976). Directed by Michael Campus. Atlas Film.

The Robe (1953). Directed by Henry Koster. Twentieth Century-Fox.

TELEVISION

A. D. The Bible Continues (2015). Created by Mark Burnett and Roma Downey. Lightworkers Media/United Artists, NBC.

'Archie in the Lock-up' (1971). *All in the Family*, Season 2, Episode 3. 2 October. Created by Norman Lear. Directed by John Rich. CBS.

Ben-Hur (2010). Created by Steven Shill. ABC (in the US)/CBC (in Canada).

Crossfire Hurricane (2012). Directed by Brett Morgan. Milkwood Films, HBO.

Friday Night, Saturday Morning (1979). Series One, Episode Seven. 9 November. BBC2.

'Give Us Barabbas!' (1961). *Hallmark Hall of Fame*. 24 March. Directed by George Schaeffer. NBC.

Hill Number One (1951). Created by Father Patrick Peyton. Family Theatre.

I Beheld His Glory (1953). Directed by John T. Coyle. Cathedral Films.

Incident in Judea (1991). Directed by Paul Bryers. Channel 4.

Jesus of Nazareth (1977). Directed by Franco Zeffirelli. RAI/ITV.

Pontius Pilate (1952). *Studio One*, Season 4, Episode 30. Produced by Worthington Miner. Directed by Franklin Schaffner. CBS.

Son of Man (1969). *Wednesday Play*. 16 April. Written by Dennis Potter. BBC1.

The Living Christ (1951). Directed by John T. Coyle. Cathedral Films.

The Passion (2008). Produced by Nigel Stafford-Clark. BBC.

'Tricky Dick & the Man in Black' (2018). *ReMastered*, Season 1, Episode 2. 2 November. Created by Jeff and Michael Zimbalist. Directed by Sara Dosa and Barbara Kopple. Netflix.

APPS

David Bowie Archive (2019). *David Bowie Is* app. Sony Music Entertainment and Planeta.

SOUND RECORDINGS

Beggar's Banquet (1968). Rolling Stones. London: Decca.
Claudia's Letter (1962). Narrated by Marjorie Lord. Orchestra and Choir Music by Earl Hagen. Vinyl. Anaheim, CA: Fan Record Co.
Jesus Christ Superstar (1970). New York: Decca/MCA.
Voices From the Hollywood Past (1975). Produced by Tony Thomas. Vinyl. Pacific Palisades, CA: Delos Records, Inc.

SONGS

'Jesus Walks.' Words and music by Kanye West, Curtis Lundy, Che Smith and Miri Ben Ari. © 2004 EMI Blackwood Music Inc., Please Gimme My Publishing, Inc., Curwan Music, Songs Of Universal, Inc., Mirimode Music, Universal Music – MGB Songs and Solomon Ink. All rights on behalf of EMI Blackwood Music Inc. and Please Gimme My Publishing, Inc. administered by Sony Music Publishing (US) LLC, 424 Church Street, Suite 1200, Nashville, TN 37219. All rights on behalf of Solomon Ink administered by Universal Music – MGB Songs. All rights on behalf of Mirimode Music controlled and administered by Songs Of Universal, Inc. International copyright secured. All rights reserved. Reprinted by permission of Hal Leonard LLC.

STREAMING VIDEOS

Boggs, Bill (1976). 'Bill Boggs interviews Kojak's Telly Savalas in London'. https://www.youtube.com/watch?v=a1xwufbeRIs (accessed 1 December 2020).
Good Morning America (2016). 'Mark Burnett and Roma Downey Talk New "Ben-Hur"'. 19 August. ABC. https://www.goodmorningamerica. com/news/video/mark-burnett-roma-downey-talk-ben-hur-41504306 (accessed 30 July 2021).
Watergate Hearings (1973). Part 5 of 6. 30 July. Boston, MA: Library of Congress, American Archive of Public Broadcasting (GBH and the Library of Congress), Boston, MA, and Washington, DC. http://america-narchive.org/catalog/cpb-aacip-512-4f1mg7gg9h (accessed 30 July 2021).
Your Bet Your Life (1949). 'You Bet Your Life #49-13 Unaired test film (Secret word 'Name', never aired on TV)', *You Bet Your Life*. 28 December. CBS. https://www.youtube.com/watch?v=5oZaXJst18k (accessed on 1 December 2020).

BIBLIOGRAPHY

Abele, Robert (2011). 'The Slap Heard Round the World'. *DGA Quarterly* (Spring 2011), https://www.dga.org/Craft/DGAQ/All-Artic les/1101-Spring-2011/Shot-to-Remember-Norman-Jewison.aspx (accessed 1 December 2020).

Adams, Marjory (1961). 'So Many Films Being Made in Rome, Studio Space is a Problem'. *Boston Sunday Globe.* September 10: 28-A.

Alexander, Doris M. (1959). 'The Passion Play in America', *American Quarterly* 11.3: 350–71.

Allen, John L. Jr (2004). 'Week of Prayer for Christian Unity; Update on 'The Passion'; Caritas work in Bam, Iran; The Concert of Reconciliation; Anticipating a visit from Dick Cheney'. *National Catholic Reporter.* 23 January. http://nationalcatholicreporter.org/word/word012304.htm (accessed 1 December 2020).

Alonso, Harriet Hyman (2007). *Robert E. Sherwood: The Playwright in Peace and War.* Amherst: University of Massachusetts Press.

Altman, Rick (2004). *Silent Film Sound.* New York: Columbia University Press.

Amorai-Stark, Shua, et al. (2018). 'An Inscribed Copper-Alloy Finger Ring from Herodium Depicting a Krater'. *Israel Exploration Journal* 68:2, 208–20.

Ansen, David (2004). 'So What's the Good News?' *Newsweek.* 29 February. https://www.newsweek.com/so-whats-good-news-131485 (accessed 1 December 2020).

Arendt, Hannah (1964). *Eichmann in Jerusalem: A Report on the Banality of Evil.* New York: The Viking Press.

Ashton, Will (2020). 'The Passion of The Christ 2: What's Going On With Mel Gibson's Planned Sequel', *Cinema Blend.* 13 October. https://www. cinemablend.com/news/2556543/the-passion-of-the-christ-2-whats-go ing-on-with-mel-gibsons-planned-sequel (accessed 23 October 2020).

Atkinson, Brooks (1940). 'Robert E. Sherwood's "There Shall Be No Night" Brings Alfred Lunt and Lynn Fontanne Back to Town in a Drama about Finland's Resistance'. *New York Times.* 30 April: 25, https:// www.nytimes.com/1940/04/30/archives/the-play-in-review-robert-e-sher woods-there-shall-be-no-night.html (accessed 7 July 2020).

Balsdon, J. P. V. D. (1979). *Romans and Aliens.* Chapel Hill: University of North Carolina Press.

Banister, C. Eric (2014). *Johnny Cash FAQ: All That's Left to Know About the Man in Black.* Milwaukee: Backbeat Books.

Barry, Dave (1989). 'Jim and Tammy Faye Bakker'. *People.* 4 October. https://people.com/archive/jim-tammy-faye-bakker/ (accessed 28 July 2020).

Barthes, Roland (1972). *Mythologies*, trans. Annette Lavers. New York: Farrar, Straus & Giroux/The Noonday Press.

Barthes, Roland (1977). *Image Music Text*, trans. Stephen Heath. London: Fontana Press.

Bartov, Omer (2005). *The 'Jew' in Cinema: From* The Golem *to* Don't Touch My Holocaust. Bloomington and Indianapolis: Indiana University Press.

Bawden, James (2017). 'Interview with Hurd Hatfield', in James Bawden and Ron Miller (eds), *You Ain't Heard Nothin' Yet: Interviews with Stars from Hollywood's Golden Era*. Lexington: University Press of Kentucky, 350–55.

BBC (n. d.). '*The Passion*. Articles: Questions and Answers'. http://www.bbc.co.uk/thepassion/articles/q_and_a_1.shtml (accessed on 1 December 2020).

Bellow, Saul (1963/2016). 'Adrift on a Sea of Gore'. *Horizon* 5.4 (March 1963), republished in Benjamin Taylor (ed.), *There Is Simply Too Much to Think About: Collected Nonfiction* New York: Penguin, 2016: 145–49.

Berg, Sandra (2006). 'When Noir Turned Black (Interview with Jules Dassin)'. *Written By: The Magazine of the Writer's Guild of America, West*. November. https://web.archive.org/web/20130518192152/http://www.wga.org/writtenby/writtenbysub.aspx?id=2247 (accessed 22 May 2020).

Berube, Maurice R. (2002). *Beyond Modernism and Postmodernism: Essays on the Politics of Culture*. Westport, CT-London: Bergin & Garvey.

Bial, Henry (2015). *Playing God: The Bible of the Broadway Stage*. Ann Arbor: University of Michigan Press.

Birchard, Robert S. (2004). *Cecil B. DeMille's Hollywood*. Lexington: University Press of Kentucky.

Bloom, Allan (1987). *The Closing of the American Mind*. New York-Toronto-London-Sydney: Simon & Schuster.

Bond, Helen K. (1998). *Pontius Pilate in History and Interpretation*. Cambridge: Cambridge University Press.

Borgnine, Ernest (1989/2012). 'Guideposts Classics: Ernest Borgnine's Inspiring Good Friday Vision', *Guideposts*. 9 July 2012, reposted from March 1989. https://www.guideposts.org/better-living/entertainment/movies-and-tv/guideposts-classics-ernest-borgnines-inspiring-good-friday (accessed 1 December 2020).

Boxall, Ian (2018). 'From the Magi to Pilate's Wife: David Brown, Tradition and the Reception of Matthew's Text', in Christopher R. Brewer, et al. (eds), *The Moving Text: The Interdisciplinary Perspectives on David Brown and the Bible*. London: SCM Press, 17–36.

Boyd-Pates, Tyree, and Taylor Bythewood-Porter (2018–19). 'Los Angeles Freedom Rally, 1963' Exhibit, California African American Museum. 26 September 2018 – 3 March 2019. https://caamuseum.org/exhibitions/2018/los-angeles-freedom-rally-1963 (accessed 1 December 2020).

Bradbury, Ray (2003). *Fahrenheit 451*. New York-London-Toronto-Sydney: Simon & Schuster.

Braun, Michael, et al. (eds) (1970). *Jesus Christ Superstar: The Authorized Version*. London: Pan Books Ltd.

Bridges, Styles, The Honorable (1961). 'Extension of Remarks: "Ronald Reagan Blasts Hollywood Reds"'. *United States Congressional Record* 107.22: A3800.

Brooks, Francis (1693). *Barbarian Cruelty: Being A True History of the Distressed Condition of the Christian Captives under the Tyranny of Mully Ishmael Emperor of Morocco*. London: J. Salusbury at the Rising-Sun in Cornhil and H. Markman at the King's Arms in the Poultry. https://penelope.uchicago.edu/morocco/index.xhtml (accessed on 1 December 2020).

Brown, Sherri, and Francis J. Moloney, S. D. B. (2017). *Interpreting the Gospel and Letters of John*. Grand Rapids, Michigan: William B. Eerdmans Publishing.

Buchanan, Judith (2007). 'Gospel Narratives on Silent Film', in Deborah Cartmell and Imelda Whelehan (eds), *The Cambridge Companion to Literature on Screen*. Cambridge, UK-New York: Cambridge University Press, 47–60.

Butler, H. E. (trans.) (1922). *Quintilian: Institutio Oratoria*. Cambridge, MA: Harvard University Press/London: William Heinemann Ltd.

Butterfield, Jeremy (ed.) (2015). *Fowler's Dictionary of Modern English Usage*, 4th edition. Oxford: Oxford University Press.

Camon, Alessandro (2004). 'American Torture, American Porn: Abu Ghraib and "The Passion of the Christ" are Connected in a Dark Basement of the American Psyche'. *Salon*. 7 June. https://www.salon.com/2004/06/07/torture_37/ (accessed 1 December 2020).

Carson, Clayborne, et al. (eds.) (2005). *The Papers of Martin Luther King, Jr. Volume V: Threshold of a New Decade, January 1959 – December 1960*. Berkeley, Los Angeles, London: University of California Press.

Carter, Warren (2003). *Pontius Pilate: Portraits of a Roman Governor*. Collegeville, MN: Liturgical Press.

Cash, Johnny, and Patrick Carr (1997). *Cash: The Autobiography*. San Francisco: HarperSan Francisco.

Chattaway, Peter (2019). 'Terrence Malick Has Finished Shooting his Jesus Movie'. *Patheos*. 7 December. https://www.patheos.com/blogs/filmchat/2019/12/terrence-malick-has-finished-shooting-his-jesus (accessed 1 December 2020).

Chrissochoidis, Ilias (ed.) (2013). *CinemaScope: Selected Documents from the Spyros P. Skouras Archive*. Stanford: Brave World.

Cieply, Michael (2007). 'That Film's Real Message? It Could Be: "Buy a Ticket".' *New York Times*. 5 March. https://www.nytimes.com/2007/03/05/movies/05spartans.html (accessed 1 December 2020).

Connor, Michael (2018). 'The Presence of Frank Thring'. *Quadrant Online*. 11 August. https://quadrant.org.au/magazine/2018/07/presence-frank-thring/ (accessed 1 December 2020).

Cook, John R. (1995). *Dennis Potter: A Life on Screen*. Manchester and New York: Manchester University Press.

Cooper, Merian C. (1935). *Handbook of Publicity Data (29 May 1935)*. Merian C. Cooper correspondence on *The Last Days of Pompeii*; MSS 2008; Merian C. Cooper papers; L. Tom Perry Special Collections; Arts & Communications Archives; 1130 Harold B. Lee Library; Brigham Young University. Series V, Subseries I, Box 11, Folder 9.

Cousins, Norman (1963). 'An Editorial: Pope John and His Open Window'. *Saturday Review*. 19 January: 20–22. https://www.unz.com/print/SaturdayRev-1963jan19-00020/ (accessed 1 December 2020).

Crafton, Donald (1997). *The Talkies: American Cinema's Transition to Sound, 1926–1931*. History of American Cinema 4. Berkeley, Los Angeles, London: University of California Press.

Crowther, Bosley (1965). 'Screen: The Greatest Story Ever Told'. *New York Times*. 16 February: 40.

Davis, Walter (2004). 'Passion of the Christ in Abu Ghraib'. *Counterpunch*. 19 June. https://www.counterpunch.org/2004/06/19/passion-of-the-christ-in-abu-ghraib/ (accessed 1 December 2020).

DeMille, Cecil B., and Donald Hayne (1959). *The Autobiography of Cecil B. DeMille*. Englewood Cliffs, NJ: Prentice-Hall.

Detroit Free Press (1967). 'Premiere for "Pilate" Scheduled at Palms'. 21 November: 8.

Donaghy, James (2008). 'Your Review: The Passion'. *The Guardian*. 25 March. https://www.theguardian.com/culture/tvandradioblog/2008/mar/25/youreviewthepassion (accessed 30 July 2020).

Dostoevsky, Fyodor (1990). *The Brothers Karamazov,* trans. Richard Pevear and Larissa Volokhonsky. New York: Farrar, Straus and Giroux.

Douglas, Lloyd C. (1942). *The Robe*. Boston: Houghton Mifflin.

Druxman, Michael B. (2011). *Basil Rathbone: His Life and His Films*. Duncan, OK: Bear Manor Media.

Dyer, Richard (1998). *Stars*. Revised edition. London: British Film Institute Publishing.

Ebert, Roger (1968). Review of Romeo and Juliet. 15 October. https://www.rogerebert.com/reviews/romeo-and-juliet-1968 (accessed 1 December 2020).

Ebert, Roger (1973). Review of Jesus Christ Superstar. 15 August. https://www.rogerebert.com/reviews/jesus-christ-superstar-1973 (accessed 1 December 2020).

Ebiri, Bilge (2016). 'Risen Takes a Novel but Grim Approach to the Familiar Crucifixion Tale'. *Vulture.com*. 20 February. http://www.vulture.com/2016/02/risen-takes-a-grim-approach-to-the-crucifixion.html?mid=full-rss-vulture (accessed 1 December 2020).

Eckhardt, Joseph P. (1997). *The King of the Movies: Film Pioneer Siegmund Lubin*. Madison-Teaneck: Fairleigh Dickinson University Press/London: Associated University Press.

Eisenhower, Dwight D. (1953). 'Address to the American Society of Newspaper Editors', 16 April. https://americanrhetoric.com/speeches/dwighteisenhowercrossofiron.htm (accessed 1 December 2020).

Eisenschitz, Bernard (1993). *Nicholas Ray: An American Journey*, trans. Tom Milne. London-Boston: Faber and Faber.

Ellen, Rosa (2020). 'The Master and Margarita's Enduring Literary Legacy inside Russia and Beyond'. *ABC Radio National*. 31 July. https://www.abc.net.au/news/2020-08-01/master-and-margarita-mikhail-bulgakov-legacy-russia-and-beyond/12465490 (accessed 1 December 2020).

FitzGerald, Frances (1990). 'Reflections: Jim and Tammy'. *The New Yorker*. 23 April: 45–87.

Fitzpatrick, Peter (2012). *The Two Frank Thrings*. Clayton, Victoria: Monash University Publishing.

Fleming, Jr., Mike (2014). '"Pontius Pilate" – Sans Brad Pitt – Headed for Jeff Robinov's Studio 8?' *Deadline.com*. 16 December. https://deadline.com/2014/12/pontius-pilate-brad-pitt-jeff-robinovs-studio-8-1201327396/ (accessed 1 December 2020).

Foer, Franklin (2011). 'The Browbeater. Review of Dwight Macdonald, *Masscult and Midcult: Essays Against the American Grain*', *The New Republic*. 22 November. https://newrepublic.com/article/97782/dwight-macdonald-midcult-masscult (accessed 19 July 2020).

Fox, Margalit (2011). 'Bruce Gordon, TV Mobster, Dies at 94'. *New York Times*. 25 January: 23. https://www.nytimes.com/2011/01/26/arts/television/26gordon.html (accessed 7 July 2020).

France, Anatole (1908). 'The Procurator of Judaea', in Frederic Chapman (ed. and trans.), *Mother of Pearl*. London: John Lane, The Bodley Head/New York: Dodd, Mead, and Company, 3–26.

Fraser, C. Gerald (1982). 'Worthington Miner, Producer in the Early Days of TV, Dies', *New York Times*. 13 December: D18.

Friedan, Betty (2001). *The Feminine Mystique*, with an introduction by Anna Quindlen. New York, London: W.W. Norton & Company.

Galinsky, Karl (2007). 'Film', in Craig W. Kallendorf (ed.), *Blackwell Companion to the Classical Tradition*. Malden, MA-Oxford: Wiley-Blackwell, 393–407.

Gauntier, Gene (1929a). 'Blazing the Trail: When the Movies Were Young, New and Silent'. *Woman's Home Companion*. February: 20–21, 92, 94, 97–98.

Gauntier, Gene (1929b). 'Blazing the Trail: Conclusion'. *Woman's Home Companion*. March: 18–19, 142, 146.

Genzlinger, Neil (2015). 'Review: 'A.D.: The Bible Continues', an NBC Mini-Series'. *New York Times*. 3 April. https://www.nytimes.com/2015/04/04/arts/television/review-ad-the-bible-continues-an-nbc-mini-series.html (accessed 1 December 2020).

Gill, Brendan (1960). 'Switchover'. *New Yorker*. 22 October: 38.

Goodwyn, Hannah (2015). 'Mark Burnett and Roma Downey's The Bible Continues with A.D.', *CBN.com*. 5 April. https://www1.cbn.com/televi

sion/mark-burnett-roma-downey-the-bible-continues-with-a.d. (accessed 1 December 2020).

Gourevitch, Philip, and Errol Morris (2008). 'Exposure: The Woman behind the Camera at Abu Ghraib'. *The New Yorker*. March 24: 44–57.

Graham, Sheilah (1961). 'Hollywood by Sheilah Graham'. *Scranton Times*. 12 October: 21.

H. D. [Hilda Doolittle] (1928). 'The King of Kings Again'. *Close Up* 2.2. February: 21–32.

Hajdu, David (2009). 'Elmer Fudd', reprinted in *Heroes and Villains: Essays on Music, Movies, Comics, and Culture*. Cambridge, MA: Da Capo Press, 250–54.

Hardeman, Simon (2018). 'Satanism and The Rolling Stones: 50 Years of "Sympathy for the Devil".' *The Independent*. 5 December. https://www. independent.co.uk/arts-entertainment/music/features/rolling-stones-sym pathy-devil-mick-jagger-anniversary-satanism-a8668551.html (accessed 1 December 2020).

Harriman, Margaret Case (1941). 'Profiles: The Candor Kid – Part 1'. *The New Yorker*. 4 January: 21–29.

Harris, Mark (2014). *Five Came Back: A Story of Hollywood and the Second World War*. New York: Penguin Publishing Group.

Hart, Hugh (2016). "YouTube-Inspired Director Used GoPro Cameras to Capture *Ben-Hur* Chariot Action." *The Credits*. 18 August. https://www. motionpictures.org/2016/08/youtube-inspired-director-used-gopro-cam eras-capture-ben-hur-chariot-action/ (accessed 3 March 2022).

Hay, Peter (1990). *Movie Anecdotes*. New York, Oxford: Oxford University Press.

Hengel, Martin (1977). *Crucifixion in the Ancient World and The Folly Of The Message Of The Cross*, trans. John Bowden. Philadelphia: Fortress Press.

Heston, Charlton (1995). *In the Arena: An Autobiography*. New York: Simon & Schuster.

Hitchens, Christopher (2004). *Blood, Class, and Empire: The Enduring Anglo-American Relationship*. Nation Books: New York.

Hofstadter, Richard (1964). 'The Paranoid Style in American Politics'. *Harper's Magazine*. November. https://harpers.org/archive/1964/11/ the-paranoid-style-in-american-politics/ (accessed 1 December 2020).

Houck, Davis W., and David E. Dixon (eds) (2006). *Rhetoric, Religion and the Civil Rights Movement, 1954–1965*. Waco: Baylor University Press.

Hourihane, Colum (2009a). *Pontius Pilate, Anti-Semitism, and the Passion in Medieval Art*. Princeton, NJ, and Oxford: Princeton University Press.

Hourihane, Colum (2009b). 'She Who Is Not Named: Pilates' Wife in Medieval Art', in Katrin Kogman-Appel and Mati Meyer (eds), *Between Judaism and Christianity: Art Historical Essays in Honor of Elisheva (Elisabeth) Revel-Neher*. Leiden: Brill, 215–39.

Idle, Eric (ed.) (1979). *Monty Python's The Life of Brian: MONTY-PYTHONSCRAPBOOK*. London: Eyre Methuen.

James, Marlon (2016). 'Five or Six Things I Didn't Know About Brad Pitt'. *T: The New York Times Style Magazine*. 7 September. https://www. nytimes.com/2016/09/07/t-magazine/brad-pitt-marlon-james-interview. html?_r=0 (accessed 1 December 2020).

Jewison, Norman (2005). *This Terrible Business Has Been Good to Me: An Autobiography*. New York: St. Martin's Press/Thomas Dunne Books.

Jones, Dylan (2017). *David Bowie: A Life*. New York: Crown Archetype.

Juergensmeyer, Mark (2004). 'Afterword: The Passion of War', in Shawn Landres and Michael Berenbaum (eds), *After the Passion is Gone: American Religious Consequences*. Walnut Creek, Lanham, New York, Toronto, Oxford: Altamira Press, 279–88.

Jump, Herbert A., Rev. (1910). *The Religious Possibilities of the Motion Picture*. Printed for Private Distribution. https://archive.org/details/reli giouspossibioojumpiala/mode/2up (accessed 1 December 2020).

Kazantzakis, Nikos (1954). *The Greek Passion*, trans. Jonathan Griffin. New York: Simon and Schuster.

Kazantzakis, Nikos (1960). *The Last Temptation of Christ*, trans. Peter Bien. New York, London, Toronto, Sydney, Tokyo: Simon & Schuster.

Keefe, Patrick Radden (2019). 'How Mark Burnett Resurrected Donald Trump as an Icon of American Success'. *The New Yorker*. 7 January. https://www.newyorker.com/mag azine/2019/01/07/how-mark-burnett-resurrected-donald-trump-as-an-icon-of-american-success (accessed 1 December 2020).

Keil, Charles (1992). '*From the Manger to the Cross*: The New Testament Narrative and the Question of Stylistic Retardation', in Roland Cosandey, et al. (eds), *Une Invention du Diable? Cinéma des premiers temps et religion/An Invention of the Devil? Religion and Early Cinema*. Sainte Foy/Les Presses de L'Université Laval/Lausanne: Éditions Payot, 112–20.

Kilpatrick, George Dunbar (1953). *The Trial of Jesus*. London: Oxford University Press.

Kinsey, Alfred C., et al. (1953). *Sexual Behavior in the Human Female*. Philadelphia and London: W. B. Saunders Company.

Klemesrud, Judy (1971). 'In a Country Setting, the Women Talked About "The Women".' *New York Times*. 18 October: 42.

Lampert, Ellen (1988). 'Last Temptation of Christ'. *Theatre Crafts* 22.9. October: 66–69, 79–81.

Landy, Marcia (2005). *Monty Python's Flying Circus*. TV Milestones Series. Detroit: Wayne State University Press.

Lang, Brent (2016). '"Ben-Hur": 5 Reasons the Biblical Epic is Summer's Biggest Flop', *Variety*. 21 August. https://variety.com/2016/film/ box-office/Ben-Hur-box-office-bomb-1201841796/ (accessed 1 December 2020).

Larsen, Dale (2008). *Monty Python's Flying Circus: An Utterly Complete, Thoroughly Unillustrated, Absolutely Unauthorized Guide to Possibly All the References.* Lanham, MD, and Plymouth, UK: Scarecrow Press.

Larsen, Dale (2018). *A Book about the Film* Monty Python's Life of Brian: *All the References from Assyrians to Zeffirelli.* Lanham, Boulder, New York, London: Rowman & Littlefield.

Lattis, James (1994). *Between Copernicus and Galileo: Christoph Clavius and the Collapse of Ptolemaic Cosmology.* Chicago and London: University of Chicago Press.

Levitt, Shelley (1994). 'A Thirst for Life'. *People.* 7 February: 41.5 https://people.com/archive/a-thirst-for-life-vol-41-no-5/ (accessed 1 December 2020).

Lindlof, Thomas R. (2008). *Hollywood Under Siege: Martin Scorsese, the Religious Right, and the Culture Wars.* Lexington, KY: University Press of Kentucky.

Llewellyn-Jones, Lloyd (2017). 'Salome, Nice Girl: Rita Hayworth and the Problem of the Hollywood Biblical Vamp', in Eran Almagor and Lisa Maurice (eds), *The Reception of Ancient Virtues and Vices in Modern Popular Culture: Beauty, Bravery, Blood and Glory.* Leiden-Boston: Brill, 206–30.

Lloyd Webber, Andrew (2018). *Unmasked.* New York: HarperCollins.

Lord, Daniel A., S. J. (1956). *Played by Ear: The Autobiography of Daniel A. Lord, S. J.* Chicago: Loyola University Press.

Los Angeles Times (1998). 'Jean Marais: Longtime French Movie Star'. 11 November. https://www.latimes.com/archives/la-xpm-1998-nov-11-mn-41606-story.html (accessed 18 October 2020).

Luce, Clare Boothe (1951). *Pilate's Wife. Treatment for the Screen.* Unpublished typescript, Margaret Herrick Library.

Luce, Clare Boothe (ed.) (1952). *Saints for Now.* New York: Sheed & Ward.

Macdonald, Dwight (1969). *Dwight Macdonald on Movies.* Englewood Cliffs, NJ: Prentice-Hall, Inc.

MacPherson, Jeanie (1926). *Screenplay for King of Kings.* Cecil B. DeMille papers; L. Tom Perry Special Collections; Arts & Communications Archives; 1130 Harold B. Lee Library; Brigham Young University. MSS 1400. Box 280. Folder 7.

Mahler, Jonathan (2003). 'Commute to Nowhere'. *New York Times.* 13 April. https://www.nytimes.com/2003/04/13/magazine/commute-to-nowhere.html (accessed 1 December 2020).

Malone, Peter (2012). *Screen Jesus: Portrayals of Christ in Television and Film.* Lanham, MD, Toronto, Plymouth, UK: Scarecrow Press.

Martin, Ralph G. (1991). *Henry and Clare: An Intimate Portrait of the Luces.* New York: G. P. Putnam's Sons.

Mayer, David (1994). *Playing Out the Empire: Ben-Hur and Other Toga Plays and Film, 1883–1908.* New York, Oxford: Clarendon Press.

McClintock, Pamela, and Lesley Goldberg (2016). '"Ben-Hur" Fallout: Film, TV Biblical Epics in Need of Redemption'. *Hollywood Reporter.* 23 August. https://www.hollywoodreporter.com/news/Ben-Hur-fallout-film-tv-921704 (accessed 1 December 2020).

McDonough, Christopher M. (2004). 'The Pricing of Sacrificial Meat: Eidolothuton, the Ara Maxima, and Useful Misinformation from Servius', in Christoph Konrad (ed.), *Augusto Augurio: Festschrift for Jerzy Linderski.* Stuttgart: Franz Steiner Verlag, 69–76.

McGilligan, Patrick (2011). *Nicholas Ray: The Glorious Failure of an American Director.* New York: It Books.

McGilligan, Patrick, and Paul Buhle (1997). *Tender Comrades: A Backstory of the Hollywood Blacklist.* Minneapolis, London: University of Minnesota Press.

McKahan, Jason (2014). '*King of Kings* and the Politics of Masculinity in the Cold War Biblical Epic', in Steven Rybin and Will Scheibel (eds), *Lonely Places, Dangerous Ground: Nicholas Ray in American Cinema.* Albany: State University of New York Press, 219–30.

McKinnon, Scott (2011). '". . . And the Theatre was Full of Poofs and I Thought it was Fantastic": Researching the History of Gay Men and the Movies', in Yorick Smaal and Graham Willett (eds), *Out Here: Gay and Lesbian Perspectives VI,* Clayton: Monash University Publishing, 201–16.

McLuhan, Marshall (1964). *Understanding Media: The Extensions of Man.* Second edition. New York: New American Library.

Miller, Arthur (1996). 'Why I Wrote "The Crucible".' *The New Yorker.* 13 October. https://www.newyorker.com/magazine/1996/10/21/why-i-wrote-the-crucible (accessed 1 December 2020).

Miller, Scott (2011). *Sex, Drugs, Rock & Roll, and Musicals.* Boston: Northeastern University Press.

Miller, Walter (trans.) (1921). *Cicero: On Duties.* London: William Heinemann Ltd./New York: The Macmillan Co.

Moon, Spencer (1997). *Reel Black Talk: A Sourcebook of 50 American Filmmakers.* Westport, CT, and London: Greenwood Press.

Morris, Sylvia Jukes (2014). *Price of Fame: The Honorable Clare Boothe Luce.* New York: Random House.

Moss, Marilyn Ann (2004). *Giant: George Stevens, a Life on Film.* Madison: University of Wisconsin Press.

Nassour, Ellis, and Richard Broderick (1973). *Rock Opera: The Creation of* Jesus Christ Superstar *from Record Album to Broadway Show and Motion Picture.* New York: Hawthorn Books, Inc.

Neubauer, Adolph (1885). 'On the Dialects Spoken in Palestine in the Time of Christ', in S. R. Driver, et al. (eds), *Studia Biblica et Ecclesiastica: Essays in Biblical Archaeology and Criticism and Kindred Subjects.* Oxford: Clarendon Press, 39–75.

Nietzsche, Friedrich W. (1920). *The Antichrist,* trans. H. L. Mencken. Alfred A. Knopf: New York.

Odom, Robert L. (1945). 'Spurious "Dream of Pilate's Wife"', *The Ministry* 18.10: 7–8.

Ogunnaike, Lola (2004). 'A Trinity of Videos for One Religious Rap'. *New York Times*. 23 June. https://www.nytimes.com/2004/06/23/ar ts/a-trinity-of-videos-for-one-religious-rap.html (accessed 1 December 2020).

Ohad-Karny, Yael (2005). 'Anticipating Gibson's *The Passion of the Christ*: The Controversy over Cecil B. De Mille's *The King of Kings*'. *Jewish History* 19.2: 189–210.

Palin, Michael (2011). '"The King's Speech" is My Family's Story, Too'. *Daily Telegraph*. 11 January. https://www.telegraph.co.uk/ news/health/8250798/The-Kings-Speech-is-my-familys-story-too.html (accessed 1 December 2020).

Parker, Roscoe S. (1950). 'Pilates Voys'. *Speculum* 25.2: 237–44.

Parsons, Tony (1993). 'David Bowie Interview'. *Arena*. Spring/Summer. https://welcomebackbowie.wordpress.com/articles/david-bowie-inter view-in-arena-springsummer-1993/ (accessed 1 December 2020).

Paul VI (1965). 'Nostra Aetate: Declaration on the Relation of the Church to Non-Christian Religions'. 28 October. https://www.vatican.va/archive/ hist_councils/ii_vatican_council/documents/vat-ii_decl_19651028_nos tra-aetate_en.html (accessed 1 December 2020).

Peyton, Patrick (2018). *All for Her: The Autobiography of Father Patrick Peyton, C. S. C.* Notre Dame, IN: Ave Maria Press.

Portuges, Catherine (2012). 'Hollywood on the Danube: Hungarian Filmmakers in a Transnational Context'. *AHEA: E-journal of the American Hungarian Educators* Association 5. https://ahea.pitt.edu/ojs/ index.php/ahea/article/view/83/72 (accessed 1 December 2020).

Powers, Jonathan (2004). 'Kill Bill . . . Or Else!' *LA Weekly*. 15 April. https://www.laweekly.com/kill-bill-or-else/ (accessed 1 December 2020).

Priest, Dana (2004). *The Mission: Waging War and Keeping Peace with America's Military*. New York and London: W. W. Norton.

Raine, Craig (1991). 'A Devil to Deal With'. *The Observer Magazine*. 31 March: 46–48.

Ramsaye, Terry (1926). 'The Motion Picture', *Annals of the American Academy of Political and Social Science* 128: 1–19.

Reinhartz, Adele (2013). *Bible and Cinema: An Introduction*. London and New York: Routledge.

Rice, Tim (1999). *Oh, What A Circus: The Autobiography, 1944–1978*. London: Hodder & Stoughton.

Richards, Jeffrey (2008). *Hollywood's Ancient Worlds*. London and New York: Continuum.

Robertson, Nan (1970). 'Cash and Country Music Take White House Stage', *New York Times*. 18 April: 33. https://www.nytimes.com/1970/04/18/ archives/cash-and-country-music-take-white-house-stage.html (accessed 1 December 2020).

Rogers, Katie (2020). 'Protesters Dispersed with Tear Gas So Trump Could Pose at Church'. *New York Times*. 1 June. https://www.nytimes.com/2020/06/01/us/politics/trump-st-johns-church-bible.html (accessed 1 December 2020).

Romm, James (2017). 'The New "Ben-Hur" Is an Ancient and Modern Mess'. *The Daily Beast*. 12 July. https://www.thedailybeast.com/the-new-Ben-Hur-is-an-ancient-and-modern-mess (accessed 1 December 2020).

Rosenbaum, Jonathan (1990). 'Modern Messiah' (Review of Denys Arcand's Jesus of Montreal). *Chicago Reader*. 19 July. https://www.chicagoreader.com/chicago/modern-messiah/Content?oid=876020 (accessed 1 December 2020).

Ross, Helen, and Lillian Ross (1962). *The Player: A Profile of an Art*. New York: Simon and Schuster.

Rubin, Carl B. (1973). *Opinion and Order, Leeds Music Limited v. Robin, US District Court for the Southern District of Ohio - 358 F. Supp. 650 (S.D. Ohio 1973)*. 3 May. https://law.justia.com/cases/federal/district-courts/FSupp/358/650/1412348/ (accessed 1 December 2020).

Said, Edward W. (2004). *Orientalism*. New York: Vintage Books.

Salinger, J. D. (1961). *Franny and Zooey*. Boston-Toronto: Little, Brown, and Co.

Salzer, Anselm (1911). 'Passion Plays'. *The Catholic Encyclopedia*. New York: Robert Appleton Company. https://www.newadvent.org/cathen/11531a.htm (accessed 1 December 2020).

Schaefer, George (1996). *From Live to Tape to Film: 60 Years of Inconspicuous Directing*. Los Angeles: Director's Guild of America.

Schaffner, Franklin (1985). *Worthington Miner: A Directors Guild of America Oral History*. Metuchen, NJ, and London: Directors Guild of America/The Scarecrow Press, Inc.

Schonfield, Hugh J. (2005). *The Passover Plot*. 40th Anniversary Edition. New York: The Disinformation Company.

Scott, A. O. (2004). 'Film Review: Good and Evil Locked in a Violent Showdown'. *New York Times*. 25 February. https://www.nytimes.com/2004/02/25/movies/film-review-good-and-evil-locked-in-violent-showdown.html (accessed 1 December 2020).

Sellers, Robert (2003). 'Welease Bwian', *The Guardian*. 27 March. https://www.theguardian.com/culture/2003/mar/28/artsfeatures1 (accessed 1 December 2020).

Shanley, John P. (1961). 'Give Us Barabbas!' *New York Times*. 27 March: 53.

Sheen, Msgr. Fulton J. (1946). 'Claudia and Herodias', in *Love on Pilgrimage: Twelve Addresses Delivered in the Nationwide Catholic Hour*. Washington, DC: National Council of Catholic Men, 63–70.

Sherwood, Robert (1950). *Roosevelt and Hopkins: An Intimate History*. Revised edition. New York: Harper & Brothers.

Sherwood, Robert E. (1945). *There Shall Be No Night*. New York: Charles Scribner's Sons.

Sherwood, Robert E. (1953). *The Trial of Pontius Pilate*. 3rd Revised Script. Unpublished Manuscript. NBC Archives, Wisconsin Historical Society.

Shoard, Catherine (2019). 'Mark Rylance to Play Four Versions of Satan for Terrence Malick'. *The Guardian*. 9 September. https://www.theguardian.com/film/2019/sep/09/mark-rylance-satan-terrence-malick-geza-rohrig-matthias-schoenaerts-the-last-planet (accessed 1 December 2020).

Sischy, Ingrid (1995). 'David Bowie'. *Interview*. September. http://www.moredarkthanshark.org/eno_int_interview-sep95.html (accessed 1 December 2020).

Smith, J. Carington (1984). 'Pilate's Wife?' *Antichthon* 18:102–7.

Solomon, Jon (2001). *The Ancient World in Cinema*. Revised and expanded edition. New Haven and London: Yale University Press.

Sontag, Susan (1966). 'Notes on "Camp",' in *Against Interpretation and Other Essays*. New York: Picador.

Stanley, Tim (2016). 'Has Hollywood Finally Found God?' *The Telegraph*. 25 April. http://www.telegraph.co.uk/films/2016/04/25/has-hollywood-finally-found-god/ (accessed 1 December 2020).

Stevens, Mrs. Lorenzo (1927). 'Oh, Rapture! Oh, Bliss!' *Picture-Play* 25.6. February: 114.

Streete, Gail P. (2018). *The Salome Project: Salome and Her Afterlives*. Eugene: Cascade Books.

Streissguth, Michael (2007). *Johnny Cash: The Biography*. Philadelphia: DaCapo Press.

Suit, Kenneth (2018). *James Friederich and Cathedral Films: The Independent Religious Cinema of the Evangelist of Hollywood, 1939–1966*. Lanham, MD: Lexington Books.

Sutherland, James (ed.) (1977). *The Oxford Book of Literary Anecdotes*. London: Futura Publications.

Telford, William R. (2015). '*Monty Python's Life of Brian* and the Jesus Film', in Joan E. Taylor (ed.), *Jesus and Brian: Exploring the Historical Jesus and his Times via Monty Python's Life of Brian*. London, Delhi, New York and Sydney: Bloomsbury, 3–18.

Thomas, Gordon (2014). 'Easter 2014, Part Un. A Tale of Two Kings: DeMille's Silent Classic on DVD – in Both Versions'. *Bright Lights Film Journal*. 20 April. https://brightlightsfilm.com/easter-part-un-demilles-king-of-kings-silent-1927/#.X85g5hNKjNI (accessed 1 December 2020).

Tillich, Paul (1952). *The Courage to Be*. New Haven: Yale University Press.

Time (1963). 'Gospel According to Claudia'. 12 April: 52.

Travers, Peter (1988). 'Picks and Pans Review: The Last Temptation of Christ', *People*. 22 August. https://people.com/archive/picks-and-pans-review-the-last-temptation-of-christ-vol-30-no-8/ (accessed 1 December 2020).

Tunberg, Karl (1958). *Ben-Hur. MGM Screenplay.* https://www.scribd. com/document/478332218/BEN-HUR-1959-Karl-Tunberg-1959-07-01-Draft-pdf (accessed 1 December 2020).

Van Dyke, Catherine (1929). 'A Letter from Pontius Pilate's Wife'. *Pictorial Review* April: 9, 74, 76–78.

Varconi, Victor, and Ed Honeck (1976). *It's Not Enough to Be Hungarian.* Denver: Graphic Impressions, Inc.

Wagy, Tom (1985). *Governor LeRoy Collins of Florida: Spokesman of the New South.* Tuscaloosa: University of Alabama Press.

Wallace, Lew (1998). *Ben-Hur,* with an introduction and notes by David Mayer. Oxford-New York: Oxford University Press.

Weinstein, David (2007). 'Why Sarnoff Slept: NBC and the Holocaust', in Michele Hilmes (ed.), *NBC: America's Network.* Berkeley, Los Angeles and London: University of California Press, 98–116.

Weintraub, Rodelle, and Clare Boothe Luce (1974). 'The Gift of Imagination. An Interview with Clare Boothe Luce'. *The Shaw Review* 17. 1: 53–59.

Wilde, Oscar (1999). *De Profundis, The Ballad of Reading Gaol, and Other Writings.* Introduction by Anne Varty. Ware: Wordsworth Editions.

Wilford, Hugh (2008). *The Mighty Wurlitzer: How the CIA Played America.* Cambridge, MA: Harvard University Press.

Wilkinson, Alissa (2015). 'Can Indie Filmmakers Save Religious Cinema?' *The Atlantic.* 18 March. https://www.theatlantic.com/enter tainment/archive/2015/03/not-your-typical-god-movie/385315/ (accessed 1 December 2020).

Winkler, Martin M. (2009). *Cinema and Classical Texts: Apollo's New Light.* Cambridge and New York: Cambridge University Press.

Wood, Michael (1975). *America in the Movies, or, 'Santa Maria, It had Slipped My Mind'.* New York: Columbia University Press.

Wroe, Anne (1999). *Pontius Pilate.* New York: Random House.

Wyke, Maria (1997). *Projecting the Past: Ancient Rome, Cinema and History.* New York and London: Routledge.

Zeffirelli, Franco (1984). *Franco Zeffirelli's Jesus: A Spiritual Diary,* trans. Willis J. Egan, S. J. San Francisco: Harper & Row, Publishers.

Zeffirelli, Franco (1986). *The Autobiography of Franco Zeffirelli.* New York: Weidenfeld & Nicolson.

Index

Page references in *italic* text indicate an image. Pontius Pilate is abbreviated to PP.